THE·ENCYCLOPEDIA·OF
MIND, MAGIC
&MYSTERIES

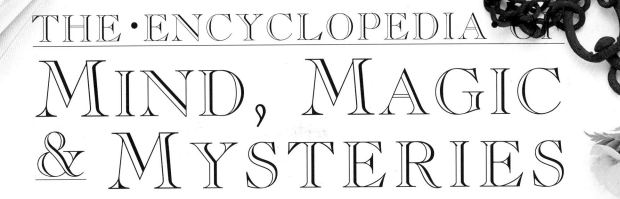

THE·ENCYCLOPEDIA OF
MIND, MAGIC
& MYSTERIES

FRANCIS X. KING

A DORLING KINDERSLEY BOOK

First published in Great Britain in 1991
by Dorling Kindersley Ltd,
9 Henrietta Street, London WC2E 8PS

Copyright © 1991 Dorling Kindersley Limited, London
Text Copyright © 1991 Francis X King

Reprinted 1992, 1993, 1995

This edition published in 1999 for Greenwich Editions,
10 Blenheim Court, Brewery Road, London N7 9NT

Art Editor
NIGEL PARTRIDGE
Senior Editor
SEAN MOORE
Editor
SUSIE BEHAR
Assistant Editor
DAMIEN MOORE

Production Manager
MICHEL BLAKE

Picture Research
CLIVE WEBSTER
Studio Photography
PHILIP GATWARD

All rights reserved. No part of this publication may be
reproduced, stored in a retrieval system, or
transmitted in any form or by any other means,
electronic, mechanical, photocopying, recording or
otherwise, without the prior written
permission of the copyright owner.

A CIP catalogue record for this book is
available from the British Library.

ISBN 0 86288 248 6

Computer Page make-up by
The Cooling Brown Partnership
London, Great Britain.

Reproduced by
GRB Grafica Fotoreproduztion, Verona, Italy.

Printed and bound by
Neografia, Slovakia

Text film output by
Creative Input, London, Great Britain.

CONTENTS

INTRODUCTION

> "*We always find something, eh, Didi, to give us the impression that we exist?*"
>
> Samuel Beckett

A CENTURY OR SO AGO it was believed by the majority of educated Europeans and North Americans that the scientists, mathematicians, theoreticians, and technologists had come to understand the nature of the physical world, and that they were in the process of mastering it. Today, the foundations of that confident belief have been shaken to the very roots.

↠ IGNORANCE TO TRUTH ↞

Classical physics, formulated by Isaac Newton some two centuries earlier, seemed to explain every type of dynamic physical system, from those involving atoms and molecules, to those concerned with planets and comets. Mysticism, magic, and belief in the supernatural were beginning to be looked upon as odd relics of a pre-scientific age, destined to be intellectually rejected as quaint hangovers from the past by all sensible people.

The history of humanity, it was claimed, was as an evolutionary progression from ignorance to truth, from darkness to light, from the superstitious barbarism that had inspired the building of Stonehenge and the pyramids of Egypt, to the new technology that had created the steam engine and the armoured warship.

↠ ABSURD RELIGIONS ↞

There were, so it was thought, many regrettable hangovers from the past. Primitive peoples like, for example, the North- and South-American Indians and the Australian aborigines, each with their shamans and witchdoctors; or the ossified culture of the great Chinese Empire, with its "completely absurd" mystical religions such as Buddhism, and its "ridiculous" traditional therapies, like acupuncture and moxibustion.

Such relics, however, were generally held to be doomed to eventual extinction – the Chinese, Indians, and aborigines, would soon recognize the superiority of western technology and philosophy, and would abandon their ancestors' futile superstitions.

↠ GOD PLAYING DICE ↞

By 1940, the confidence of the late-nineteenth century had turned to disillusion. Newtonian physics had, save for certain purposes, completely broken down. All of its supposed certainties had vanished amidst a welter of argument and confusion.

The infinite, three-dimensional space of Euclidean geometry had given place to Albert Einstein's concept of space-time as a single continuum; Newton's concept of absolute motion had been abandoned in favour of the theory of relativity and its many paradoxes; and at the level of sub-atomic particles, the hand of chance was shown to operate in a way that has since been described as "God playing dice".

↠ SHATTERED UNIVERSE ↞

The ordered universe of Newton's theories of mechanics fell apart – it was seen to be, at the very best, true only on a partial, local level. No longer did any reputable physicist or theorist assert that if a person could ascertain the precise position and state of motion of every particle of matter in the universe, then he or she could, in theory, accurately predict the future of the universe. This so-called "crisis in physics" that had suddenly become apparent, did not, as one might imagine, cause an incredible furore; it was, in fact, only of any interest to a small minority of people.

To every westerner, however, it was obvious that technological progress did not always result in an increase in human happiness. Certainly it had failed to prevent the slaughter of 1914–18, and the sinking of Russia and Germany into totalitarian barbarisms served by a perverted science.

→ THE RIGHT QUESTIONS ←

Some people, only a small minority, but a significant one, began to feel that modern technology might not have all the answers. Could it be, they asked themselves, that what some termed traditional wisdom represented more than outmoded superstitions? That the mystical philosophies of ancient India and China were more in conformity with reality than western empiricism and materialism? That shamans who purported to visit "the world of spirit" were genuinely in touch with superhuman forces? That those who built Stonehenge and the other great megalithic structures were possessed of some hidden wisdom, some lost knowledge that could be rediscovered?

→ THE WRONG ANSWER ←

Could it be that the devotees of the new technology were on the wrong path, that modern man and woman had long since strayed from the path of wisdom?

Fifty years or so ago, only a very small number of people were asking such questions, and fewer still were asking them in public. Today, however, there are many hundreds of thousands of people who are concerning themselves with these and other similar questions, and an astonishingly large number of them are answering in the affirmative – we *have* been following a wrong path.

As a consequence of this, today there are students and devotees of interrelated subjects such as the oriental martial arts and eastern alternative medicine, the mystical polarity-philosophies of India and China, yoga and meditation, and the Buddhist and Hindu forms of tantrism, to be found in almost every country and city throughout the western world. And, just as eastern philosophy has affected the West, so, in this exchange of wisdom, western occultists have adapted eastern techniques to suit their own particular needs.

It is not only the supposed wisdom of the Far East that has its followers. There are individuals and groups in the West who have sought their own secret traditional wisdom, studying the techniques of American Indian shamanism; the mystical philosophies of alchemy and white magic; the wisdom to be found in ancient western legend, myth, and folklore; and the teachings that are supposedly conveyed through the mysterious designs and symbols of, for example, astrology and the tarot.

→ INCREASED RESEARCH ←

The ever-increasing interest in, and adherence to, the mystical philosophies of East and West has coincided with a dramatic growth in psychic research. That is: the investigation of claims of clairvoyance, remembering past incarnations, telepathy, psychokinesis, and premonitions, and other subjects concerned with supernormal powers and inexplicable, perhaps miraculous, phenomena. The aspects both of psychic research, and of the search for the hidden wisdom of those cultures that are so distant in space and time from our own, have been dealt with in the pages of this, hopefully, comprehensive book.

It would be reasonable to loosely describe both of the above themes as concerned with "the supernatural" – an unsatisfactory phrase, but, unfortunately, the best available. It is important to remember, however, that there is a darker side to the supernatural – one that is concerned with those fears and terrors that are as old as humanity itself.

On December 9, 1990 the London *Sunday Telegraph* – one of the more serious British national newspapers, nearer in tone to the *Wall Street Journal* than, say, to America's *National Enquirer* or to Britain's infamous *News of the World* – reported a highly improbable sequence of events that, so it would seem, took place on the previous day – December 8.

A distraught father had contacted the Essex Police Force to report that, after hearing his two-year-old son screaming from his bedroom he had rushed upstairs and found the child floating some five feet (150 cm) in the air, as though suspended by invisible ropes. When the police reached the house, they encountered a scene that was reminiscent of Stephen Spielberg's film, *Poltergeist*. Furniture had been thrown about, the family dog was cowering underneath the stairs, and the little boy's father seemed to be in a state of shock.

⇢ TROUBLED HOUSE ⇠

Once they had satisfied themselves that no crime had been committed, that the father who had called them was not drunk, under the influence of drugs, or suffering from some obvious mental illness, the police came to the conclusion that the case was one for a priest, and sent for the chaplain of a local hospital. It is *this* fact that is the most astonishing about the story, even more so than any events that occured after the priest's arrival. The police are not known as confirmed believers in the supernatural, and one would have expected a sceptical reaction at least. Instead, they called for a priest.

The priest came to the house, but, on arriving, refused to enter it. He felt that to do so might stir up what the *Sunday Telegraph* referred to as "evil spirits" – the priest suggested that an exorcist should be called in.

The priest's attitude was probably not a surprise to the officers, who had, after all, called him, and it may be significant that some neighbouring families told the police that they too were of the opinion that evil forces were at work in the troubled house. This strange incident provides a bizarre illustration of present day attitudes towards the uncanny and the supernatural.

The word that is most often conjured up as the "reason" for any phenomena that scientists and sceptics cannot otherwise explain, is "coincidence". It may well be a coincidence that twins, who have been separated since birth, have grown up and each married a woman with the same name, each given their children the same names and so on; it may be coincidence that someone dreams the names of the winning horses in advance of a series of races; it may even be a coincidence that an image appears, on the photograph of an air squadron, that seems to be of a soldier from that squadron who had died only days before. By the time the reader has read this book, though, I hope that he or she will realize that there are simply too many such amazing stories for them all to be explained away so glibly.

⇢ REASONABLE DOUBT ⇠

The undeniable success of homeopathy defies such an explanation; as do the remarkable lines and designs scored across the Nazca desert in South America; and as do the thousands of inexplicable experiences of hitherto sceptical, reasonable people, who are thereafter labled as cranks. *There*, it seems, lies the crux of the matter: it is hard to believe until you have seen. Consider, for example, a man who happily walks under ladders until, one day, he trips up after doing so; the next day he braves fate by walking under another ladder – straight into a lamp-post. Afterwards, although he *knows* that both accidents were coincidences, he is less likely to walk under a ladder again. As the *Sunday Telegraph* story shows, the attitude of the public towards the supernatural is ambivalent, to say the least. It is perhaps best summed up by the seemingly paradoxical statement that has been attributed to a number of different people: "I don't believe in ghosts, but I'm terrified of them".

→ RATIONAL MOMENTS ←

In other words, when we endeavour to be rational, most of us can bring ourselves to assert that we believe that there is not a grain of truth in either legends of supernatural horrors – vampires, werewolves, monsters, and so on – or in the countless tales of hauntings, ghosts, goblins, and vengeful demons.

At certain times, however, perhaps when we are alone in the darkness of the night in eerie surroundings, or encounter some utterly mysterious event in our own lives, we sense that prickle at the back of the neck that is associated with danger, with a feeling of general uneasiness, or even with real fear.

Some depth psychologists, writing forty or fifty years ago, endeavoured to explain such fears in Freudian terms involving unconscious feelings of guilt. It was asserted, for instance, that many vivid dreams of attack by vampire-like creatures were symbolic expressions of guilt concerning adolescent masturbation, and that stories of men receiving messages from deceased parents were an expression of the guilt felt by all males because of their suppressed desires to murder their fathers and marry their mothers.

→ SIMPLE THEORIES ←

Very few would argue the truth of such simplistic theories today. For there are people who clearly have no feelings of guilt whatsoever concerning their adolescent sexual activities, who display the same fear of certain aspects of the supernatural as did the sexually repressed and emotionally disturbed patients of Sigmund Freud and the other European psychoanalysts of eighty years ago. It has also been recorded that men who never knew either of their parents have seen, or believed that they have seen, the ghosts of their parents.

It would seem that there is an inherent tendency in some human beings, even those who regard themselves as materialists without any belief in the supernatural, to sense and sometimes fear the uncanny – even to "see ghosts". In this book, besides an examination of mysticism, East and West, and a consideration of laboratory research on such inter-related enigmas as mediumship, telepathy, and seemingly supernormal abilities, an attempt is made to analyse the darker side of the supernatural, from poltergeists to possession.

→ SENSATIONAL PHENOMENA ←

This attempt is made without any intention to sensationalize, for the alleged phenomena are quite sensational enough in themselves.

All that I have endeavoured to do is to outline some of the evidence in a way that will enable the readers to decide for themselves, firstly, whether the subject is worth further investigation and, secondly, whether it is of such a nature that there is some likelihood that objective, rather than subjective factors are involved – in other words, whether those who believe that they "see" ghosts are, in fact, reacting to some reality that lies outside their own minds.

The brain and, more particularly, the mind of man and woman, is one of the great regions that is largely uncharted by science. Human beings are quite astonishing creatures, capable, individually, of unbelievable feats: mathematic, philosophic, poetic, scientific, the list is endless – who knows what else the mind is capable of. Who knows what ancient powers lie buried, or what fledgling abilities have yet to be developed? Who can deny that there is much about the workings and capabilities of the human brain and mind that we do not yet understand? It is the mind of man and woman that is the main subject of this work: the mind, its magic, and, of course, its mysteries.

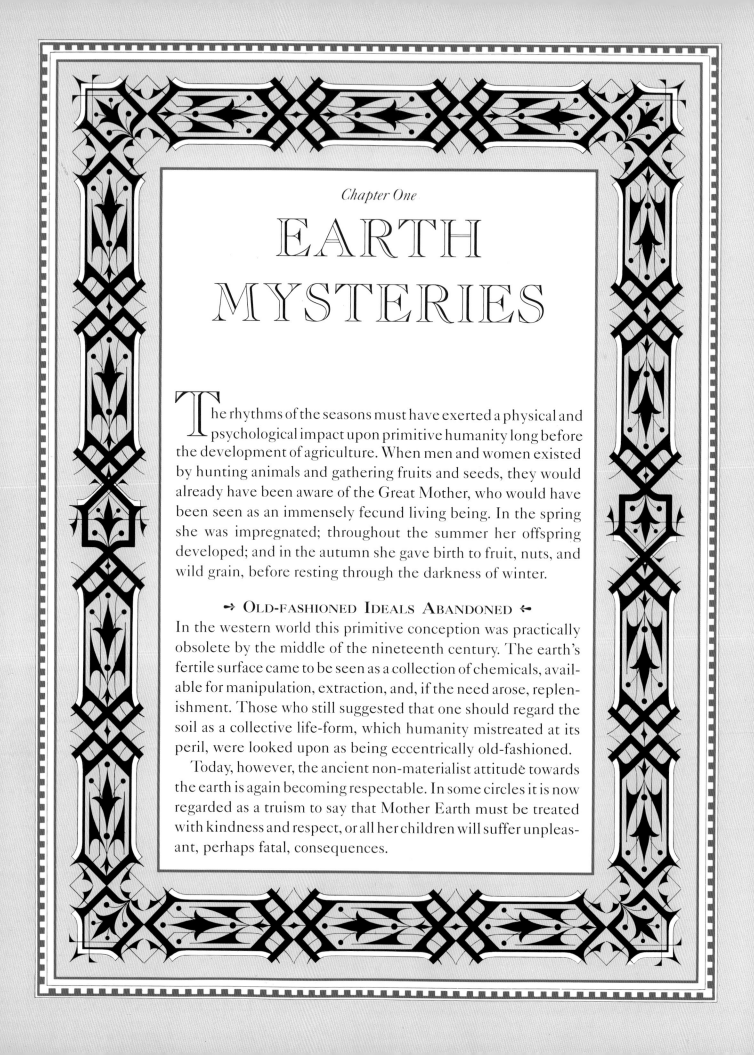

Chapter One

EARTH MYSTERIES

The rhythms of the seasons must have exerted a physical and psychological impact upon primitive humanity long before the development of agriculture. When men and women existed by hunting animals and gathering fruits and seeds, they would already have been aware of the Great Mother, who would have been seen as an immensely fecund living being. In the spring she was impregnated; throughout the summer her offspring developed; and in the autumn she gave birth to fruit, nuts, and wild grain, before resting through the darkness of winter.

➳ OLD-FASHIONED IDEALS ABANDONED ↢

In the western world this primitive conception was practically obsolete by the middle of the nineteenth century. The earth's fertile surface came to be seen as a collection of chemicals, available for manipulation, extraction, and, if the need arose, replenishment. Those who still suggested that one should regard the soil as a collective life-form, which humanity mistreated at its peril, were looked upon as being eccentrically old-fashioned.

Today, however, the ancient non-materialist attitude towards the earth is again becoming respectable. In some circles it is now regarded as a truism to say that Mother Earth must be treated with kindness and respect, or all her children will suffer unpleasant, perhaps fatal, consequences.

Organic farming is gaining more and more acceptance, and even supermarkets are stocking wholefood and organic produce. The mystical idea of Mother Earth as a living being has been revived. The "primitive" concepts associated with such occult teachings as those underlying much organic farming, notably the biodynamic agriculture developed by the followers of Rudolf Steiner, are now looked upon as worthy of serious consideration.

↬ IDEAS ABOUT THE EARTH ↫

Many of Steiner's ideas about the earth are still considered to be eccentric. Yet his strange teachings work very well indeed – most people who have eaten biodynamically grown fruit, vegetables, and grain-derived foods, feel that they taste better than similar products grown by orthodox methods.

One fact inclines some to see truth in Steiner's teachings about the links between all living things and non-material energies. This is, that these teachings provide a linked rationale for the problems connected with what are collectively known as "Earth Mysteries": for dowsing, for instance, which can be explained by Steiner's theories on "etheric formative forces"; or for the possible existence of "leys", linking up ancient sacred sites; or for the giant designs traced out in the Peruvian desert.

↬ COINCIDENTAL ALIGNMENTS ↫

On the other hand it has to be admitted that there are many people who are totally sceptical about the existence of Earth Mysteries. They assert, for example, that ley lines are non-existent; some sceptics have even gone to the length of saying that megalithic sun/moon alignments are purely coincidental.

In this chapter no attempt is made to argue the objective reality of Earth Mysteries. Instead, enough information is given to enable readers to consider the probability of such mysteries being real or imaginary and, where such enigmas as dowsing are concerned, to experiment for themselves.

THE GIANT'S PICTURE BOOK

"What is wrong with the idea that the lines were laid out to say to the gods: Land here!"

Eric Von Däniken

AGAINST THE BLEAK BACKDROP of the Peruvian desert near Nazca there exists an astonishing menagerie of gigantic birds, animals, and insects, accurately delineated in yellowish-white earth. The origins and meaning of these extraordinary phenomena are, as yet, unknown.

Observed from the air, the lines clearly take the form of beautiful figures. Seen from the ground, however, these complex patterns are apparently no more than impressive abstractions, and some of the formations cannot be made out at all. Indeed, when the Pan-American Highway was built, the roadmakers cut straight through some of the designs without realizing they were there.

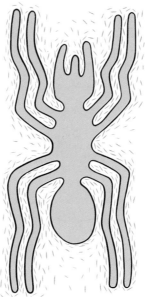

SPIDER (ABOVE)

→ HOT-AIR BALLOONS ←

It has been suggested that the Nazca designers directed their labourers from the air, by utilizing a form of hot-air balloon. The Nazca workers created the lines by removing all the stones scattered on the surface and digging out any stones just beneath the surface. If this theory is true, it means that hot-air balloons were already in existence by AD 600 if not much earlier, and were not, as is generally believed, invented in France in the 1780s. Experts believe that the figures were begun in 400 BC and were completed 1000 years later.

The idea that the principle of the hot-air balloon was known to the inhabitants of Peru in 400 BC is not as unlikely as it may appear. The basic concept is simple – that combustion gases confined in some sort of containing envelope will lift that envelope high into the air. Primitive man could possibly have thought: "When I light a fire, the smoke rises high in the air. If I

BIRD (BELOW)

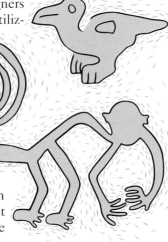

MONKEY (ABOVE)

Spaceman's Landing Strip
One school of thought holds that this strange figure (above) is a depiction of a spaceman.

Spouting Whale (right) *These lines on the Pampa de San José, Peru, form the accurate outline of a whale.*

could put the smoke in some sort of bag, it would probably make the bag rise into the air."

The idea of ancient hot-air balloons may seem fantastic, but in fact an ancient pot exhibits a design showing a sphere from which hangs what could be a stylized passenger gondola.

So did the Peruvians of 400 BC really have the technology and materials necessary to make a balloon capable not only of flight but also of carrying passengers? An experiment conducted in 1975 would appear to show that they did. This experiment was instigated by an American, Jim Woodman, the founder of Air Florida. He was assisted by Julian Nott, an expert British balloonist, and several members of the International Explorers' Society.

Because of the dry climate of Peru, some textiles interred with the dead some 1500 years ago have been preserved. A

Animals and Insects
(From top to bottom) The spider, bird, and monkey designs at Nazca: the monkey, in particular, is a mystery, as these animals are not found in the desert.

HUMMING BIRD (ABOVE)

piece of such cloth was subjected to a searching examination by Jim Woodman and his team of experts. They reported that the weave of the textile was exceptionally loose, and that its weight was heavy for the area of its surface – it was obviously not ideal material for the fabric of a hot-air balloon. Despite this, Jim Woodman arranged for the manufacture of a modern imitation of the graveyard relic. Amazingly, when shaped into a crude balloon and inflated by hot air from a smoky wood fire, the loosely woven fabric functioned satisfactorily – carbon particles from the smoke became trapped in the interstices of the weave and made it sufficiently impervious to retain hot air.

➼ MODERN RECONSTRUCTION ↢

In November 1975, perched astride a primitive gondola made from reeds, Jim Woodman and Julian Nott endeavoured to fly the curious construction, to which they were prepared to entrust their lives – a contraption based solely on a "blueprint" decorating an ancient Peruvian pot. All of the technologies and materials they used were available to the early Nazca "inventors". Triumphantly, although a little unsteadily, they rose into the air in their balloon

Snake Art
The Great Serpent Mound (above) is found in Ohio, USA. It is thought to have been created by an ancient tribe of American Indians, and represents a snake – an animal that was deified and worshipped by many of the Indian tribes.

Medicine Man
Shamanism dominated American-Indian culture. The shaman, often known as the "medicine man", would perform sacred, magical, and ceremonial rites, such as swearing in a new chief (right).

and looked down upon the Nazca figures, perhaps seeing them as their original designers had some 2500 years earlier. In this way, Woodman and his co-workers had established the possibility that the lines, which were described by the writer, Richard Cavendish, as a "giant's picture book", were drawn with the aid of aerial observation.

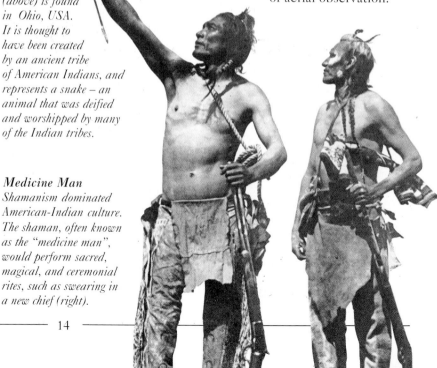

It is not just the Nazca figures that can be fully appreciated only from the air. The same is true of a number of ancient man-made features of the European landscape. For example, while the almost certainly prehistoric White Horse of Uffington (p.22) looks splendid from ground level, the contours of the English hillside on which it is carved slightly distort its appearance. So its full magnificence is only revealed when it is viewed from above. But what purpose were the patterns intended to serve?

↠ Flying Figures ↞

Certain occultists have their own ideas as to the construction of hill figures. They say that there were once various legendary figures who had the ability to fly, or to "physically levitate"; or had the power to separate their body from their soul and, in spirit form, direct the construction of hill figures and other ancient constructs from the air. For example, King Bladud of Bath, a monarch from the Dark Ages, was reputed to have flown from the west of England to an ancient holy site (where London's St. Paul's Cathedral was later built). Most people, myself included, find this extraordinary explanation very difficult – if not impossible – to accept.

As far as the Nazca designs are concerned, the author, Eric von Däniken, proposed a theory

Ancient Land Art
The extraordinary semi-abstract patterns (below) were created by Californian Indians, probably thousands of years ago. Much ingenuity and effort went into the patterns. An aerial view reveals the various forms of animals lying within complex concentric spirals. Like the Nazca patterns, no one is sure of their meaning or purpose. However, it is possible that the curves and spirals were a symbol of the widespread serpent cult. Among the many nature spirits of the American Indians were numerous snake gods of varying importance. There were many rituals concerned with these gods, such as the "snake dance" – the dancers would imitate the snake god by forming a winding human chain.

Spiral Mazes

Spiral mazes would seem to be an archetype. Almost exactly the same pattern of enclosed spirals can be seen worldwide on, for instance, ancient Cretan coins, or in the sacred symbols of the North-American Hopi Indians. The design of the maze is symbolic of death and spiritual renewal.

English Maze
The maze above is carved on a rock in Tintagel, a place often associated with Arthurian legend.

that gained great popularity in the 1960s in his bestselling book, *Chariots of the Gods*. He had no doubt as to the real nature of the area on which the Nazca designs are drawn.

↠ Visitors from Outer Space ↞

It was, he said, the remains of a landing area used by travellers from outer space, and the patterns outlined on it were part of an elaborate directional system that was used to guide pilots.

This curious theory seems highly improbable to me. For one thing, the Nazca terrain is quite unsuitable for the safe landing of anything heavier than a very light aircraft. And why should spacemen go to the bother of inducing the local inhabitants to mark out the figures of American humming birds, and monkeys?

Many other explanations have been proposed – unfortunately none are satisfactory. To add to the mystery, computer analysis of the Nazca figures has shown no evidence of any astronomical alignments similar to those associated with other megaliths. As Professor Hawkins, of the Smithsonian Institute, Washington, has suggested, we must continue our search for an explanation of the Nazca lines "beyond the computer".

THE SCIENCE OF DOWSING

"They would as soon as doubted the power of gunpowder in blasting rock as the influence of the magical wand in pointing out the invisible course of mineral veins"

Hazel Twig
A Y-shaped twig is a popular dowsing tool (below).

So WROTE the Reverend Richard Warner in 1808, describing the use of the divining rod by the miners of the Mendip Hills in Somerset, England. A century and a half later, during the Vietnam War, American engineers often found that they could detect cleverly constructed enemy booby traps by using two pieces of thick wire, bent at 90° to form an L-shape. One wire was held outstretched in each hand, pointing straight ahead like a pair of revolvers. As a trap was approached the wires would swing together and cross,

Dowsing
These 16th-century dowsers hope to find precious metal (below).

Virgula divina
Glück rür
Haspler
Instrumentum Tractorium
zerfetzer
Grübener
Hakwer
Butman

seemingly independently of the will of the soldier who held them. Despite the fact that in scientific terms this made no sense at all, for some soldiers it worked in the most practical way possible – it saved their lives.

→ AN ANCIENT CRAFT ←

What the soldiers were doing was essentially the same as what English tin and lead miners had been doing 150 years earlier: employing the mysterious craft of dowsing for practical purposes. Early nineteenth-century English beliefs about dowsing were recorded by the Reverend Richard Warner in his *Tour Through Cornwall in the Autumn of 1808*. Warner noted, sceptically, that the superstitious Cornish miners abstained from whistling when underground as it brought them bad luck, and that they also firmly believed "in the efficacy of Divanatoria or Divining [dowsing rod] Rod".

Virgula

No one really knows how dowsing works; and even after many scientific tests, which have often surprised sceptics with their rate of success, many people still look on successful dowsing as mere coincidence or luck. In recent years, however, dowsing has gained some credibility, and dowsers have occasionally been employed by the police, for instance, to help find the bodies of people who have drowned.

Modern diviners, who may belong to one of the many American or European societies of

Archaeological Discovery
Dowsers have assisted archaeologists in their work, especially in the search for metal objects (right).

dowsers, use the dowsing rod for many different purposes – for finding water, locating pipes, and to aid the investigation of archaeological sites.

The origins of dowsing are veiled in obscurity. Some historians think that it was first practised in the late Middle Ages. On the other hand there are descriptions in classical literature of a divinatory process that is obviously similar to dowsing. The earliest mention of dowsing in the modern sense, however, can be found in a German manuscript that dates from about 1430.

➤ MAKING A DOWSING ROD ➤

It is easy to make your own dowsing tools: find a small object that is heavy in relation to its size, such as a wedding ring or a glass lustre from a chandelier. Suspend it from a thread about 70 cm (2 ft 6 in) in length. You now have a pendulum that can be used either out in the open or for map dowsing (p.20). If you want a more traditional dowsing implement you can use a Y-shaped twig – hazel is the customary wood to use. The twig should be fairly stout, but springy enough for you to bend its arms apart slightly, holding one arm in each hand. In practice, however, while a twig may look and feel authentic, it is rather difficult to use. It may be better to make and use a set of

"booby trap locators", such as the ones used by American soldiers in Vietnam (p.16). A pair of wire coat hangers can be transformed into dowsing tools of this type. Use pliers or metal shears to make two cuts in each coat hanger. Take the two smallest pieces of coat hanger and pull the shorter length of each back, making a rough right angle to the longer one (see below). You can use these just as they are, holding the short lengths in your hands, but you will probably find them more satisfactory if you make handles for them by sleeving the

First Description
The oldest surviving mention of divining is by Agricola (above). He describes how German miners used the divining rod to find iron ore in the 15th century. American soldiers used a similar principle in order to detect booby-traps hidden by the enemy in the Vietnamese jungles.

Homemade Tools
A pendulum (below left), such as an ordinary crystal from a chandelier, makes a very delicate dowsing tool, particularly useful for map dowsing.

Simple Tool
An object such as this medal (below) makes an adequate pendulum.

Do it Yourself
To make your own dowsing rod (right), take a coat hanger and make two cuts in it. Pull the two shorter lengths back, at a right angle to the longer lengths.

short ends in cotton reels previously glued together; or, bind the handles with surgical tape. These "booby trap locators", which you can make for yourself (p.17), are designed to be used over the ground. The dowser holds them while walking over the area of land beneath which something of interest may be concealed – perhaps a water supply, or even those subtle energy flows that are believed to be marked by ley lines (pp.26-29).

⇥ BEGINNER'S LUCK ⇤

If you try dowsing in a frequented place, it is inevitable that you will attract curious onlookers. Such people are an irritation even to an experienced dowser; to a beginner they may not only be an embarrassment, but a positive hindrance, preventing the dowser achieving the feeling of calm detachment that is essential for success. It is best to begin experimenting in a

secluded place, such as a private garden, rather than on a site open to the public.

Hold one locator in each hand; keep your elbows bent and tucked into your ribs, and point the longer arms of the locators straight in front of you, bent slightly towards the ground – rather as though you were holding a pair of pistols, expecting trouble without being sure where it might come from: think of yourself as being a psychic gunfighter.

Walk over your chosen ground without grasping your two locators either too

Subtle Divining Rod
The Y-rod (directly below) is the traditional form of divining rod. To use, you hold the two handles slightly apart, allowing the tip to register very subtle dowsing reactions. The Y-rod is highly sensitive, and therefore the novice may find it difficult to use.

L-Rods
These are popular dowsing tools (above), which are easy to use and to make – you can improvize with two adapted wire coat hangers (p.17). To use, you hold each shorter length loosely, allowing the longer parts to register a reaction.

Pendulums
Any small object hung on a piece of string can be used as a pendulum (left). Although a crystal pendant is a frequent choice, a small brass or wooden object is just as suitable. The ideal length of the string is between 10 cm (4 in) and 25 cm (10 in). Pendulums are excellent tools for map dowsing and radiesthesia (p.21). Some people use pendulums for fortune telling (see below).

Tapper Stick and Bowl
The wise man or "witch doctor" of the Yoruba peoples of Nigeria, West Africa, used a tapper stick and bowl (right) to make predictions. The bowl was filled with sand, and then tapped – the resulting sand patterns were a form of divination used, for example, to locate water, or to indicate where and when the tribe could expect rain. The tapper stick and bowl's other and more common use, is as a begging bowl held by blind people, who would tap the side to attract the attention of people passing by.

tightly or too loosely. Keeping the locators in place should involve only slight muscular effort. You should try to exercise enough control to prevent a gust of wind, or jerky steps over uneven ground or such like, from causing locator movement that could be misinterpreted as a dowsing-rod reaction.

⇢ IN THE SWING ⇠

You may get no reaction at all on your first walk. Do not despair; repeat your walk, varying the route slightly, and go on repeating it. Unless you belong to the tiny minority of people in whom the dowsing faculty is completely absent or dormant, you will sooner or later get a dowsing reaction. That is to say the locator wires will either: swing in towards each other; both swing in the same direction; both swing outwards; or one might stay still while the other swings right or left. These movements are not supernatural; they are caused by involuntary and unconscious muscular movements made by the experimenter when his or her dowsing faculty is in action.

Nevertheless, they are sometimes accompanied by phenomena that, on first experience, can be alarming. The first dowsing experiment that I undertook began disastrously; I spent almost two hours tramping across Wareham Heath in Dorset, England, without getting any reaction whatsoever. Suddenly the rods swung together and at the same moment I experienced

Varied Reactions
There are several different types of dowsing reaction (right): the locator wires may swing together, swing apart, or both swing in the same direction. It could take some time to get a reaction, but only a very few people will experience no reaction at all.

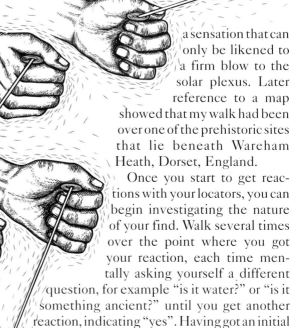

a sensation that can only be likened to a firm blow to the solar plexus. Later reference to a map showed that my walk had been over one of the prehistoric sites that lie beneath Wareham Heath, Dorset, England.

Once you start to get reactions with your locators, you can begin investigating the nature of your find. Walk several times over the point where you got your reaction, each time mentally asking yourself a different question, for example "is it water?" or "is it something ancient?" until you get another reaction, indicating "yes". Having got an initial response, you then ask supplementary questions, each more specific than the last, until you have all the information you need.

⇢ SENSITIVE INDICATOR ⇠

You can use a pendulum instead of locators, although, if you are in the open air, the slightest breeze may cause it to give misleading answers. For this reason, radiesthesia, or pendulum dowsing, is usually done with maps. It has been suggested that in radiesthesia, a form of extra-sensory perception comes into play. When a pendulum is held over a map, such phenomena as slight changes in ground temperature that may affect a dowsing rod, are not present, so the movement of the pendulum must be due to something less tangible – a sixth sense on the part of the dowser, perhaps.

If you wish to try this technique, hold the pendulum at whichever point on its thread is most comfortable for you. Within a very short time you will get some movement. This is caused by unconscious muscular reactions. Whatever the nature of the movement – circular, side to side, or backwards and forwards – consider this

Dowsing Genius
The late T.C. Lethbridge (left) was an academic archaeologist who found dowsing of incalculable value in his field work. Lethbridge did an enormous amount to popularize pendulum dowsing and radiesthesia, writing several books on the subject, and giving a demonstration on television. He has been called the "Einstein of radiesthesia".

to be the "neutral" or "normal" movement for you. Move the pendulum over a large scale map and take any change in the pendulum's direction as a dowsing reaction. Then go over the same point on the map again and again, asking mental questions in the same way as with locator dowsing. Eventually you may find that you have dowsed, for example, the site of an ancient temple, perhaps, or a burial ground.

⇝ UNORTHODOX TREATMENT ⇜

Radiesthesia is used in alternative medicine as an unorthodox method of both diagnosis and treatment, known as radionics. This method originally involved suspending a pendulum over a chart listing various ailments. Today's practitioners use a box-like instrument with a number of dials that register different numerical values.

Radionics, to a very large extent, depends on the sensitivity and extra-sensory perception of the therapist – in fact, the patient does not even have to be present in person. Instead, a strand of hair or a blood sample will be enough to make a diagnosis.

The basic premise of radionics is that everything consists of energy, and that the energy fields surrounding the body have great significance. It is possible, practitioners believe, to tune in to the energy levels of the patient, and to manipulate that energy to improve the health of the patient.

⇝ THE ETHERIC BODY ⇜

Both eastern and western philosophical traditions have defined what is known as an "etheric body" – the subtle energy from which our physical body arises. Ill-health, say radionics therapists, arises from disturbances in this body of energy, rather than in the physical body. Radionic treatment seeks to redress a disturbed energy balance by a transfusion of energy from the therapist to the patient.

Radionics experts stress that this type of therapy will work only if the patient truly believes in it. These claims, however, are viewed sceptically by many orthodox doctors.

Shocking Success
This radionics machine (below) is the type frequently used by some radiesthesists to dowse accurately without walking over the ground. The first radionics machine was developed in the 1920s, by the distinguished Amercian physician, Abrams. This original machine was tested by the British Medical Association and King George V's physician, Lord Horder. To his astonishment he found that it worked.

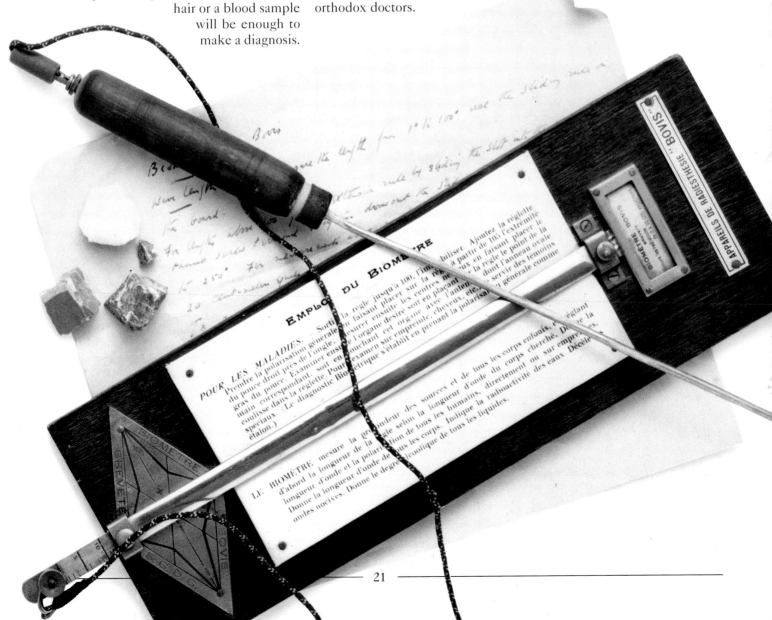

TEMPLES OF THE STARS?

"There were giants in the earth in those days ... when the sons of God came in unto the daughters of men and they bare children to them"

Genesis 6:4

THE FIGURE OF THE Cerne giant looms, outlined in chalk against a background of green English turf, over the Dorset village of Cerne Abbas. He is naked and holds aloft an enormous club, but his most notable feature is his exaggerated ithyphallicism – the tip of his erect penis reaches upwards above his navel.

A Neolithic god of fertility, kept free of weeds by simple country folk for more than 3000 years? Or a coarse practical joke dating from after 1660? It was the latter theory that Edward Waring tried to establish in his book *Ghosts and Legends of the Dorset Countryside.* Mr. Waring could, of course, have been wrong.

→ FERTILITY SYMBOL ←

The Cerne giant looks more like a primitive fertility symbol than a seventeenth-century forerunner of the "follies" that were built a century later. Even during the Victorian age there were reports of barren women sleeping on the giant's member in the hope that they would be made fertile.

However, it is hard to believe that the giant's most notable attribute would not have been mutilated by some of the more fanatical English Puritans – men who smashed stained-glass windows, and sawed up maypoles because their phallicism made them "stinking idols".

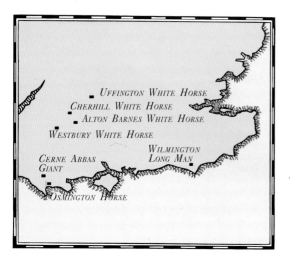

Hill Figures
The giant figures that mark the English landscape (below) are shrouded in mystery. Cut into chalk hills, their meaning and the date of their origin is uncertain. One popular theory holds that they were centres of prehistoric religions.

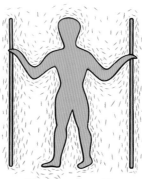

WILMINGTON LONG MAN

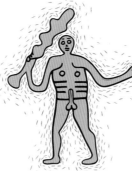

UFFINGTON HORSE

CERNE ABBAS GIANT

Hill Triangles
This map (left) shows the position of hill figures in the south of England. If the dots are joined by lines, the various groups of figures form distinct isosceles triangles.

Whatever the truth about the Cerne giant, the uncertainty that surrounds both its origins and any purpose it was intended to serve, provides a good illustration of a major problem encountered with all hill figures that are not of recent origin. It is impossible to date them with any real accuracy – they may be prehistoric, Roman, or even Saxon. Archaeologists have yet to come to some consensus opinion as to the figures' ages. All that can be said with any certainty is that some of them are much older than others, and some may be very old indeed.

Carved on English hillsides are three well-known figures of white horses – at Uffington, Cherhill, and Pewsey. The Uffington horse certainly predates the other two, and is possibly of prehistoric origin, in which case it was outlined in the chalk thousands, rather than hundreds, of years before the others. Yet while the origins of the three horses were far apart in time, there is a curious link between them; if they are joined up by lines drawn on a map, they mark the angles of an isosceles triangle. This could, of course, be mere coincidence, but other similar triangles have been discerned in the landscape. For example, there is one with its apex at Arbor Low, a Derbyshire stone circle, and its other two angles at Othery Church, in Somerset, and the prehistoric site on Mersea Island off the coast of Essex.

→ GREAT ZODIACS ←

It is possible that the connecting "lines" that can be construed as linking the white horses and other ancient monuments have no real significance – that the alignments are coincidental. The same applies to the vast zodiacs, some of them 16 km (10 miles) in diameter, which have been detected in various parts of England. These are outlined by roads, rivers, ancient monuments, and other features. Such zodiacs are said to exist at Kingston-upon-Thames in Surrey, at Nuthampstead in Hertfordshire, at Holderness in Yorkshire, at Lampeter in Wales, and – the best known of all of them – at Glastonbury in Somerset.

According to the biographer, Richard Deacon, it was John Dee, the astrologer, and his medium Edward Kelley, who first discovered the Glastonbury Zodiac. Together, Dee and Kelley were responsible for the extraordinary body of

The map labels:
UFFINGTON WHITE HORSE
CHERHILL WHITE HORSE
ALTON BARNES WHITE HORSE
WESTBURY WHITE HORSE
CERNE ABBAS GIANT
WILMINGTON LONG MAN
OSMINGTON HORSE

esoteric techniques known as Enochian Magic (pp.74-75). Mr. Deacon quotes Dee as asserting that the Glastonbury Zodiac showed:

"astrologie and astronomie carefullie and exactly married and measured in a scientific reconstruction of the heavens which shows that the ancients understode all which today the learned know to be factes."

Unfortunately Mr. Deacon gives no exact source for his text – a great pity, as Dee's use of the word "scientific" could have been its first recorded appearance in English.

Whatever the extent of Dee's knowledge of the Glastonbury Zodiac, its existence was first revealed to the general public in 1929 by an Englishwoman, Katharine Maltwood. She discerned it, outlined by roads and natural features, on an Ordnance Survey map and wrote of it in her book, *Glastonbury's Temple of the Stars*.

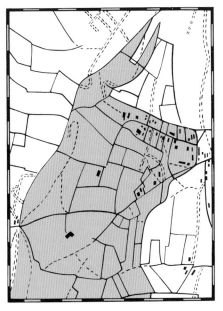

Westbury White Horse
This white horse (above) is found on Salisbury Plain, England. It is believed by archaeologists to have been carved in AD *878, to celebrate King Arthur's victory over the Danes.*

Glastonbury Zodiac
In 1929, Elizabeth Maltwood put forward a theory that Glastonbury, a town already associated with many legends, was a centre of scientific and technological knowledge. Using an Ordnance Survey map, she perceived that certain man-made and natural features would form a zodiac if connected by imaginary lines (left). Such a configuration may have been used by prehistoric man to foretell natural disasters.

SACRED STONES

"The ancients were as wise as we are, perhaps wiser. Could we have done as much with as little?"

Isaac Asimov

ACCORDING TO the twelfth-century chronicler, Geoffrey of Monmouth, the magician Merlin miraculously levitated enormous Irish rocks, made them fly hundreds of miles through the air to Salisbury Plain in England, and there used them to build the stone circle known as Stonehenge. A more rational suggestion about the origin of Stonehenge was made in the seventeenth century by the architect, Inigo Jones; it was, he said, a monument erected by the Romans. To prove his point he prepared a plan of Stonehenge to show that its proportions were in keeping with the laws of classical architecture.

↠ DRUID TEMPLES ↞

Jones's plan was extremely inaccurate. A later survey by John Aubrey was altogether more thorough than that of his predecessor and from it he concluded that the monuments were pagan temples. Aubrey was correct in this conclusion, although he was mistaken in his belief that Stonehenge, Avebury, and similar constructions were probably Druid temples. Although it is possible that the Druids made use of these monuments, there is no doubt that Stonehenge, like other megalithic structures, was built long before the Druids arrived in Britain.

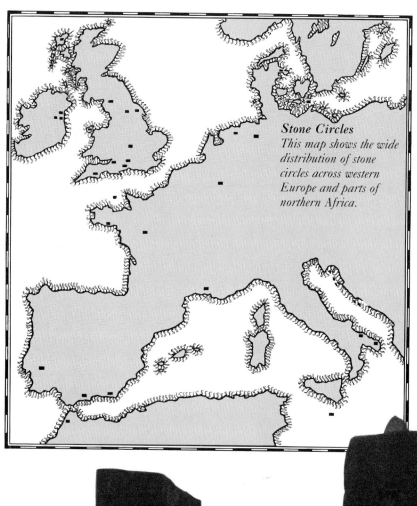

Stone Circles
This map shows the wide distribution of stone circles across western Europe and parts of northern Africa.

Stonehenge took a long time to build. The original earthworks were probably begun as early as 2600 BC. The smaller stones, the "bluestones", were erected some centuries later, while the "sarsens", the huge blocks that make up the familiar uprights and lintels, may not have have been in place until 1500 BC. These sarsens were quarried about 8 km (5 miles) away from where they now stand. The bluestones, on the other hand, came from several sites as much as 32 km (20 miles) apart, in the Preseli Hills of South Wales, some 320 km (200 miles) from Stonehenge. It is not known for certain whether they were first brought to Salisbury Plain by Neolithic people or, some 200,000 years earlier, by a vast glacier.

→ ANCIENT OBSERVATORIES ←

In the last hundred years, a theory has gained credence that the stones were used, amongst other things, as sacred observatories for the study of the sun, moon, and planets. It was argued that not only the world-famous monuments at Stonehenge and Avebury, but all the thousands of megaliths, great and small, scattered across Europe and northern Africa, were used for this purpose. At first the idea was treated with some derision. It seemed unthinkable that the supposed "savages" would have had the knowledge

Stukeley's Theory
An 18th-century clergyman, Stukeley, (below) found notoriety when he claimed that Stonehenge was built by the Druids.

Stonehenge
The vast megalithic stones that form Stonehenge (below) have for centuries been the subject of speculation. No one can tell for sure what their purpose was. It is known, however, that they are prehistoric; the first stones were probably laid in 2600 BC.

or inclination to concern themselves with such complicated activities as, for example, forecasting the date of the next lunar eclipse with extreme accuracy.

Over the decades, however, evidence grew that the Neolithic "savages" may have been the custodians of an astonishingly advanced culture, probably one dominated by a caste of priestly magician-astronomers who possessed considerable knowledge of mathematics. In the 1960s, Professor Thom demonstrated very persuasively, that this had, in fact, been the case.

→ CONCLUSIVE ARGUMENT ←

Generally speaking, archaeologists have resented academics from the more rigidly mathematical disciplines who have ventured into their territory. Yet the arguments and conclusions of Professor Thom, who held the Chair of Engineering at Oxford University, have been largely accepted by a substantial number of archaeologists.

These archaeologists have accepted Professor Thom's arguments because of his method. The painstaking observations and measurements of megalithic sites were made over decades and were considerably more accurate than any previous measurements. Professor Thom showed, for example, that a standard unit of length, the "megalithic yard", was current throughout Neolithic Britain. His conclusions, based on years of observation, precise mathematical work, and brilliant reasoning are summarized on the following page.

Professor Thom's conclusions on the stone circles can be summarized as follows:

a) The geometry of the ground plans of British stone circles is extremely complex, proving that those who built them were far from being savages. The designers seem, for example, to have had at least a working knowledge of what, centuries later, came to be known as the "theorem of Pythagoras" – that the area of a square constructed on the longest side of a right-angled triangle is equal to the combined areas of squares on the other two sides.

b) While the majority of stone circles are not true circles (many of them are, for example, flattened ellipses), all of them were constructed according to preconceived plans employing the megalithic yard as a basic unit of measurement – equivalent to 82 cm (2 ft 9 in).

c) As well as the stone circles, it is likely that a substantial number of menhirs (isolated single standing stones) were employed in making extremely accurate astronomical observations – the menhirs being used as backsights against features on the horizon, such as trees, for example, or mountain peaks.

d) The data gathered in this way would have been unnecessarily complex for the simple calculations needed by Neolithic farmers to ascertain, for example, the right time of year to plant crops or provide shelter for animals.

⇢ PRIESTLY MAGICIANS ⇠

If Professor Thom's theories are correct then Neolithic Britain, and probably the whole of western Europe, was not, as was previously thought, dominated by bands of unsophisticated barbarians. On the contrary, it was the home of a sophisticated culture, probably managed by an élite of priestly magicians. This élite had acquired an astronomical and mathematical knowledge unequalled until classical times. In addition they had sufficient political power to ensure that vast gangs of labourers would toil at such places as Avebury and Stonehenge to execute their architectural designs.

Some students of prehistory, most of them sympathetic to concepts associated with modern occultism, have gone so far as to assert that the supposed priestly élite was possessed of knowledge and skills that are largely forgotten

Mystery Hill
Pagan groups still celebrate rites (above) amid the constructions on Mystery Hill, USA.

Hagar Qim
This temple of megaliths in Malta was used by believers in the Neolithic Cult of the Dead (below).

today. They were, so it is suggested, not just astronomers, geometricians, and architects, but masters of "Earth Mysteries". They had at their command a superscience concerned with subtle tellurian (earthly) energy flows and their relationship to equally mysterious cosmic energies associated with the sun, moon, and planets.

If this was so, it would certainly explain why the caste of Neolithic priest-magicians wanted to make astronomical observations of an accuracy far greater than that required for calendrical purposes. It would also explain some of the puzzling alignments that would have been observed in relation to a number of megalithic structures – the curious phenomenon, for example, which takes place once every nineteen years at Knowth in Ireland.

↠ COSMIC ENERGIES ↞
During the daylight hours of the date in question, the sun shines down one of the two passages in a stone-chambered mound, while the moon shines down the other passage during the night. Pure coincidence? Or a planned control of subtle cosmic energies, a mingling of the forces of Apollo and Artemis, the Greek deities who personify the sun and the moon?

An interesting but perhaps far-fetched theory concerning Knowth and similar structures has been developed by some modern occultists who have been influenced by the ideas of

Wilhelm Reich (1897–1957). Reich asserted that it was possible to make what he called "orgone energy accumulators" – batteries that would concentrate and store a mysterious force that would manifest itself in matter and energy. Perhaps, he suggested, chambered mounds were accumulators of this type, and the great stone circles were control centres at which the stored energies were directed to practical use by the magicians who fully understood their potential.

Stone Zodiac
According to Prof. Thom, the Carnac stones (above) in France were erected for astronomical reasons.

APOLLO AND ARTEMIS
An ancient Greek geographer wrote of an island at the far north of Britain in which there was a great circular temple, dedicated to the god Apollo. Every eighteen years, said the geographer, the god physically descended to earth at this temple, and danced before worshippers.

A charming folk-story or an unlikely tale told by a traveller? Either is possible, but some scholars believe that the account gave a muddled description of Stonehenge and its astronomical use in relation to an eighteen- or nineteen-year sun and moon cycle.

↠ SUN AND MOON ↞
Apollo was the sun god, and one of the most revered gods of ancient Greece, although his origins go back into pre-history.

According to the Greeks, however, he and his twin sister, Artemis, goddess of the moon, were the children of Zeus, king of the gods, and the goddess Leto.

Artemis had three separate forms. She was the chaste huntress, a goddess of fertility, and an old crone who ruled over witchcraft and childbirth. The changing forms of the moon were equated with these three aspects of Artemis – a crescent symbolized the huntress; a disc, symbolized the goddess of fertility; and the dark of the moon equated with the witchcrone.

Apollo and Artemis appear in many different guises and under other names. Their association with the sun and moon respectively have made them archetypal astronomical symbols, as well as embodiments of the principles of masculinity and femininity. As such they were revered by those who built the great megalithic and astronomical structures of western Europe.

God of Gods
Apollo, one of the most revered and terrifying of the Greek gods, is represented here (right) in one of his gentler roles, as the patron of music.

SHADOWS OF THE PAST

"Patrick, Bishop of the Hebrides, desired Orlygus to build a church wherever he found upright stones ..."

W. Johnson

THE ENGLISH ANTIQUARIAN John Aubrey (1626–1697) noticed a curious pheno-menon associated with some walled fields near the English village of Silchester. In hot, dry weather, towards the evening, when the sun was low in the sky, curious shadows and markings, linear and rectangular, would appear amidst the crops. Aubrey surmised that these markings showed where the soil was thin and unusually dry because it covered the foundations of long-vanished roads, paths, and buildings.

➻ HISTORY REVEALED ↩

Aubrey was absolutely right. Excavations carried out in the eighteenth century and since have revealed that beneath the fields of Silchester lie the remains of a complete Roman town. Complete, that is, save for any sign of a major temple to the gods and goddesses of classical antiquity. The probable reason that no temple was found at Silchester either by enthusiastic excavators of more than two centuries ago or by

John Aubrey
The seventeenth-century antiquarian, John Aubrey (above), studied the stone circles of Avebury and Stonehenge.

Ancient Sites
There is evidence that Winchester Cathedral (right), like other places of Christian worship, was built on the site of an ancient stone circle.

modern archaeologists, is to be found in the text of a letter. The letter was written in AD 601 by Pope Gregory the Great to Abbot Mellitus, who was about to leave for England in order to assist Augustine, who was to become the first Archbishop of Canterbury, in his task of converting the heathen and warlike Anglo-Saxons to Christianity.

The Pope informed Abbot Mellitus that he had been "earnestly pondering over the affairs of the English" and had come to the conclusion that:

"the temples of the idols in England should not on any account be destroyed. Augustine must smash the idols, but the temples them-selves should be sprinkled with holy water and altars set up in them in which relics are to be enclosed ... I hope the people (on seeing their temples are not destroyed) will leave their

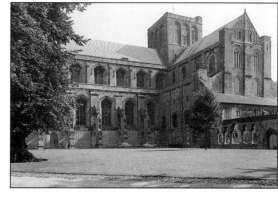

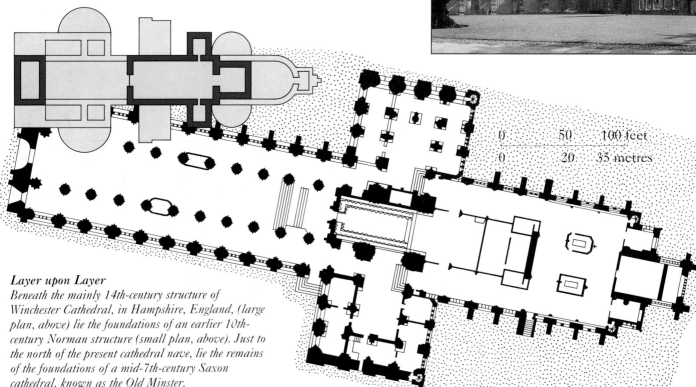

Layer upon Layer
Beneath the mainly 14th-century structure of Winchester Cathedral, in Hampshire, England, (large plan, above) lie the foundations of an earlier 10th-century Norman structure (small plan, above). Just to the north of the present cathedral nave, lie the remains of the foundations of a mid-7th-century Saxon cathedral, known as the Old Minster.

| 0 | 50 | 100 feet |
| 0 | 20 | 35 metres |

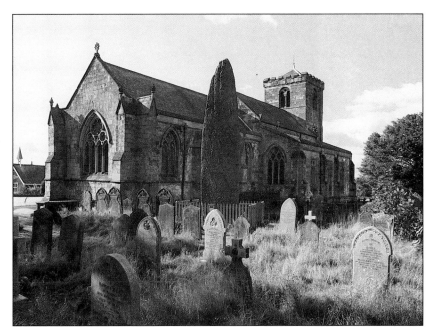

The patterns of the past still survive and influence us today – should the medieval church at Silchester be destroyed by lightning and its rebuilding be paid for by some benefactor, it is likely that the architect would roughly follow the ground plans of the present building. This building probably followed the outlines of an earlier Christian structure, built upon the foundations of a Roman temple that itself replaced a Celtic holy place – and so the chain reaches back, perhaps for 4000 years.

It is for this reason that Silchester and other medieval Christian places of worship seem to be orientated in ways reminiscent of the alignments associated with megalithic structures; and why ley hunters (pp. 30–31) feel justified in asserting that cathedrals built in the thirteenth century stand on the same lines of force as stone circles erected some 2000 years before by prehistoric man.

idolatory and yet continue to frequent the places as formerly, so coming to know and revere the true God .... And since the sacrifice of many oxen to devils is their custom, some other rite ought to be solemnized in its place .... On such high days the people might well ... celebrate the occasion with pious feasting."

⇢ NEW FAITH FOR OLD ⇠

There was nothing particularly new in the Pope's advice, save that it was to be applied to England. For centuries the Church had been following a policy of converting pagan holy places to Christian usage. There is a Gaelic phrase, *"Am bheil thu dol don clachan?"* that means "Are you going to church?" The word *"clachan"* has two meanings: it signifies both a stone circle and a place of worship. In churches built on sites where the gods of Egypt had been worshipped, Coptic theologians debated whether Christ had one or two natures; in shrines where Aphrodite, goddess of love, had received flowers from her devotees, Greek Christians burned candles before icons of the Blessed Virgin Mary.

Pope Gregory's advice was followed in England and in other parts of Europe. The Cathedrals of Canterbury and York, and St. Paul's Cathedral in London, were built on what were almost certainly the sites of pagan holy places. The foundations of the Roman temple at Silchester probably lie below the medieval church and graveyard, which were likely to have been constructed upon the ground plan of earlier constructs dating from the dark ages. It is possible that Silchester's Roman temple was itself built upon the site of a Celtic sanctuary.

Church and Monolith
The ancient monolith in close proximity to the Church at Rudstone, England (above), clearly illustrates the decision made by the early-Christian Church to erect their places of worship on ancient pagan sacred sites. The Church leaders saw that it would be easier to convert the pagans to Christianity if they were allowed to pray in their own temples. This system spread Christianity around the world, but had the other long-term effect of combining pagan and Christian rituals. It was also easier to coincide Christian holy days with pagan feasts: Christmas, for example, coincides with the pagan festival of the Winter Solstice.

TEMPLE OF SECRETS
According to the unorthodox Egyptologist R.A. Schawaller de Lubicz, author of the *Temple of Man*, the religious structures of ancient Egypt, such as the nineteenth-century buildings at Karnac, were erected according to the philosophy of a secret society called the "Temple". He maintained the Temple was the custodian of the secret keys of universal knowledge.

Egyptian Temple
According to de Lubicz, the temples at Karnac in Egypt (below) expressed a secret wisdom.

LINES OF POWER

"*I was to discover that in a great many spheres of learning, the effects of the earth force were accepted*"

G. Underwood

ON JUNE 30, 1921, Alfred Watkins had a vision. Sitting in his car outside the Herefordshire village of Blackwardine, idly glancing at a map, he saw, in his mind's eye, a web of straight lines criss-crossing the countryside. They connected hill-tops and other natural features, old churches, ponds, and ancient monuments such as the tumuli (mounds) built by Neolithic man. Watkins decided to name them "ley lines" after the Saxon word "ley" meaning a "cleared glade". Watkins wrote of his discovery:

"I followed up the clue of sighting from hill-top, unhampered by other theories, found it

European Phenomenon
In the 1920s, Alfred Watkins (right) announced his discovery of ley lines on the English landscape. Independently of Watkins, an account was published of similar lines found in Germany.

Ley Line Alignment
The staves that are held by the ancient figure of the Long Man of Wilmington (below) have long puzzled students of pre-history. Alfred Watkins believed they were used as guides in the planning of ley lines.

yielding astounding results in all districts, the straight lines to my amazement passing over and over again, through the same class of objects."

Although Watkins had occult interests and connections, he did not attach any occult or spiritual significance to the invisible linear alignments he believed he had discerned. What he had discovered, so he asserted in his *Old Straight Track* (1924), were the sighting points used by prehistoric people in laying out an elaborate system of trading routes. These he thought of as no more than the shortest connections between one centre of human population and another – in a sense no more than a by-product of a trade in salt and other commodities.

↦ FAIRY CHAINS ↤

Nevertheless, there was a poetic quality in the way in which he later described his discovery:

"Imagine a fairy chain, stretched from mountain peak to mountain peak ... great standing stones brought to mark the way at intervals, and on a bank leading up to a mountain ridge ... the track cut deep so as to form a guiding notch on the skyline ...."

The occultist, Dion Fortune, is often credited as being the first to suggest that the lines crossing the landscape and connecting prehistoric monuments had some spiritual significance. There is no doubt that in her novel, *Goatfoot God*, published in 1936, Dion Fortune expressed, through the mouth of one of her characters, her belief that stone circles and other ancient monuments were spiritual power centres. They were connected by lines of force that traced invisible geometrical figures across the landscape. She had been anticipated, however, by Wilhelm Teudt, a German pastor who had discovered, independently of Alfred Watkins, a linear network covering his own country and linking together ancient sacred sites.

→ THE ORIGIN OF ASTRONOMY ←

Teudt announced his discovery in 1929 in his book *German Holy Places*. There were, he said, invisible lines of force on which Teutonic sacred sites were strung like pearls on a necklace. The "pearls" were astronomically orientated to a considerable degree of accuracy. So much so, indeed, that one of Teudt's admirers wondered "whether astronomy arose in Babylon or ... as is far more likely, the ... science originated ... from the genius of the Germanic nomadic people who were also responsible for the astronomical features of the pyramids".

Anyone can share Watkins's excitement on first discovering his "fairy chains". One of the most famous ley lines is easy to draw on a large-scale map of the south of England. It passes through Stonehenge and Old Sarum – the latter a man-made hill. The ley line begins at a prehistoric burial mound situated at just over 1.6 km (1 mile) north-north-east of Stonehenge.

It can be traced for over 29 km (18 miles) in a south-south-easterly direction until it ends at Frankenbury Camp, a prehistoric earthwork probably raised for defensive purposes. In the course of its length the ley passes through the centres of Stonehenge, Old Sarum, Salisbury Cathedral, and another prehistoric construction, Clearbury Ring.

On a map the ley line is fairly convincing – but, if its existence is accepted, it can hardly have been one of Watkins's "old straight tracks".

Feng-shui Compass
This compass (below) is used in the ancient Chinese art of geomancy. In the hands of a geomancer, the compass will show the most auspicious position for a building, ensuring that it lies in harmony with earth energies, and keeping such things as bad luck and the work of evil demons away from the building's inhabitants.

Geomancy
Such is the belief in Feng-shui that even sophisticated Chinese, such as Hong Kong businessmen, will use a geomancer, and even today offices are designed according to its rules.

used for trade purposes. There seems to be no good reason why anyone who was trading in flints, metals, or salt should have thought fit to transport them from the fortified encampment of Frankenbury to a grave mound more than 29 km (18 miles) away.

⇢ TRACING LEY LINES ⇠

With a little ingenuity the novice can discern ley lines on a fairly large-scale map of an area that includes tumuli and other ancient monuments: old churches, cathedrals, and outstanding natural features, such as isolated hills, caves, lakes, and river crossings. Anyone can rule a line on a map that runs through or very close to four or more such features over a reasonably short distance.

Readers who want to try it for themselves can do so very easily. Get a large scale map – the old 1 inch to the mile or the more recent 1:50,000 scales are excellent – and a transparent ruler. Find an ancient monument, or some other point that may be of significance in ley hunting on the map. Place the centre of the edge of your ruler on the point you have selected and slowly rotate it through a circle until, if you are lucky on your first attempt, you have four or more significant points in a straight line. Rule the line on the map with a sharp pencil. You may have detected a ley line. The shorter the line on the map the more likely it is to be a genuine ley – four points on a line representing a distance of 50 km (31 miles) is more likely to be the result of coincidence than the same number of points representing, say, 13 km (8 miles).

The line you have drawn on the map will not be a line in the geometrical sense of the word, that is to say, a one-dimensional figure having length but no breadth. However fine the pencil you have used, your line will have some breadth – on a 1:50,000 scale map this breadth is unlikely to represent a distance of less than 8–12 metres (20–40 ft) on the ground. So the ley you may have traced is not so much a line as a corridor.

⇢ THICK OR THIN ⇠

The smaller the scale of the map you have used (and you have to start with a fairly small scale map if you want to draw really long ley lines, such as those that form the great isosceles triangle on p.19) the wider the corridor will be. Even if a so-called line is really a corridor this does not mean that it does not exist. If the lines drawn on the map really do show the flow of

INVISIBLE PATHWAYS

The aborigines of Australia believe in a network of invisible pathways made up of ancient tribal songs. These songs tell of the history of the tribes and the land. The aborigines believe that it is their religious duty to walk these tracks singing the songs, and so pay homage to the land and their ancestors.

Aborigines
The indigenous people of Australia (above) have a rich spirit-culture.

Bruce Chatwin
The writer Bruce Chatwin (right) brought the song-lines to world attention.

subtle energies, it does not greatly matter whether those energies flow through tiny channels or along great invisible rivers.

Having traced the ley line on a map, the next step, unless your line is extraordinarily long, is to survey it from ground level, walking its length with the aid of a map and a compass.

→ A VARIETY OF STRUCTURES ←

As you walk you might find significant points on the line which were not marked on your map. You may find a well that was once regarded as sacred, or an ancient burial mound, which could date from Neolithic times, the Bronze Age, Saxon times, or even from the days of the Roman Empire. The oldest type, the Neolithic long barrow, is unchambered, although there is usually some evidence that it has been used for burials. These barrows appear as mounds of earth of up to 30 m (100 ft) in length and width. You may find a *"cursus"*, which is a Neolithic structure of parallel banks delineating a path. Some of these are aligned with long barrows. The longest known *"cursus"* can be found in Dorset – it is almost 10 km (6 miles) long.

On the other hand you could find that some of the markers you pinpointed as significant on your map are not really significant at all – that, for instance, what you had thought was an ancient church is in reality a Pentecostal chapel, erected only ten years ago.

→ ENTERTAINING DIVERSIONS ←

If you have experimented with the dowsing techniques described on pages 16 to 21, it could be well worth supplementing your visual observation of the ley line by attempting to trace its course with the aid of a dowsing rod or a set of wire "booby trap locators" (p.17). If you do so, you may be able to trace extensions to, or branches from, the ley that were not visually apparent either on the map or on the ground.

You may even find diversions from the line that are strange and, in a sense, amusing. Two well-known and highly competent British dowsers traced a ley that, as it were, made a brief diversion to see an old friend – an ancient stone. The ley in question followed more or less the line of the present A5 highway – but, at a crossroads close to a St. Alban's church, it bent to a stone in the churchyard, then bent back upon itself to resume its original course.

Although it may be stating the obvious, in the course of following a ley line you may have to cross private property. It is always advisable to check with the landowners before you do so – they are usually sympathetic.

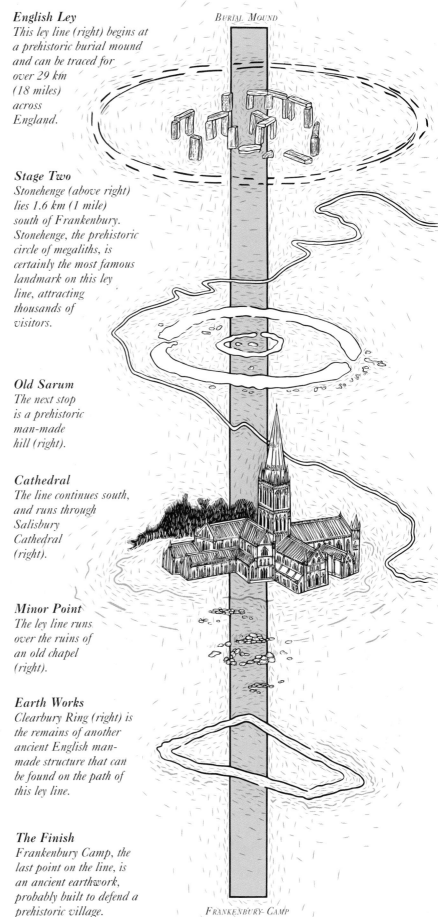

English Ley
This ley line (right) begins at a prehistoric burial mound and can be traced for over 29 km (18 miles) across England.

Stage Two
Stonehenge (above right) lies 1.6 km (1 mile) south of Frankenbury. Stonehenge, the prehistoric circle of megaliths, is certainly the most famous landmark on this ley line, attracting thousands of visitors.

Old Sarum
The next stop is a prehistoric man-made hill (right).

Cathedral
The line continues south, and runs through Salisbury Cathedral (right).

Minor Point
The ley line runs over the ruins of an old chapel (right).

Earth Works
Clearbury Ring (right) is the remains of another ancient English man-made structure that can be found on the path of this ley line.

The Finish
Frankenbury Camp, the last point on the line, is an ancient earthwork, probably built to defend a prehistoric village.

BURIAL MOUND

FRANKENBURY CAMP

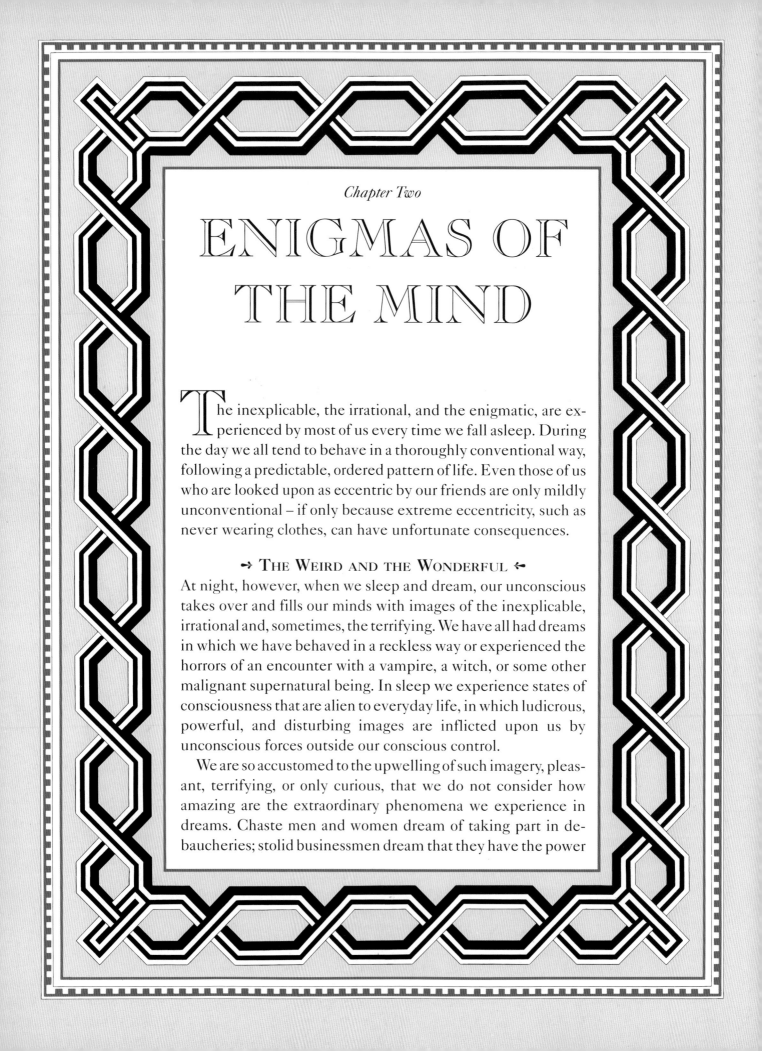

Chapter Two

ENIGMAS OF THE MIND

The inexplicable, the irrational, and the enigmatic, are experienced by most of us every time we fall asleep. During the day we all tend to behave in a thoroughly conventional way, following a predictable, ordered pattern of life. Even those of us who are looked upon as eccentric by our friends are only mildly unconventional – if only because extreme eccentricity, such as never wearing clothes, can have unfortunate consequences.

→ THE WEIRD AND THE WONDERFUL ←

At night, however, when we sleep and dream, our unconscious takes over and fills our minds with images of the inexplicable, irrational and, sometimes, the terrifying. We have all had dreams in which we have behaved in a reckless way or experienced the horrors of an encounter with a vampire, a witch, or some other malignant supernatural being. In sleep we experience states of consciousness that are alien to everyday life, in which ludicrous, powerful, and disturbing images are inflicted upon us by unconscious forces outside our conscious control.

We are so accustomed to the upwelling of such imagery, pleasant, terrifying, or only curious, that we do not consider how amazing are the extraordinary phenomena we experience in dreams. Chaste men and women dream of taking part in debaucheries; stolid businessmen dream that they have the power

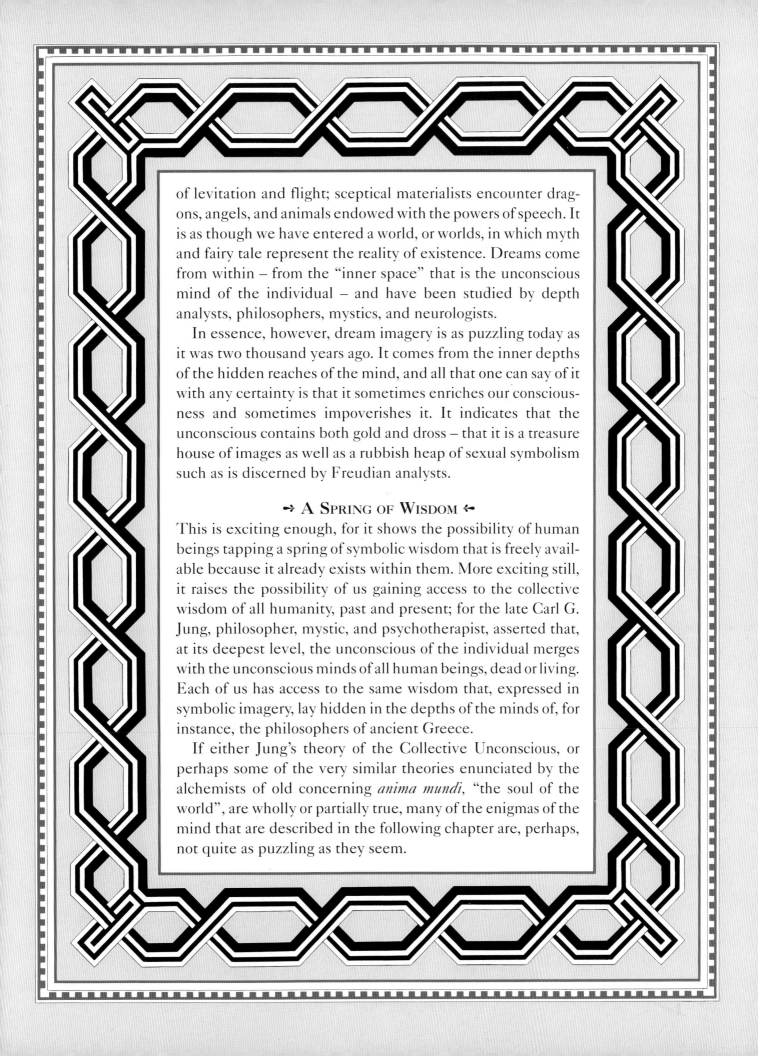

of levitation and flight; sceptical materialists encounter dragons, angels, and animals endowed with the powers of speech. It is as though we have entered a world, or worlds, in which myth and fairy tale represent the reality of existence. Dreams come from within – from the "inner space" that is the unconscious mind of the individual – and have been studied by depth analysts, philosophers, mystics, and neurologists.

In essence, however, dream imagery is as puzzling today as it was two thousand years ago. It comes from the inner depths of the hidden reaches of the mind, and all that one can say of it with any certainty is that it sometimes enriches our consciousness and sometimes impoverishes it. It indicates that the unconscious contains both gold and dross – that it is a treasure house of images as well as a rubbish heap of sexual symbolism such as is discerned by Freudian analysts.

↦ A Spring of Wisdom ↤

This is exciting enough, for it shows the possibility of human beings tapping a spring of symbolic wisdom that is freely available because it already exists within them. More exciting still, it raises the possibility of us gaining access to the collective wisdom of all humanity, past and present; for the late Carl G. Jung, philosopher, mystic, and psychotherapist, asserted that, at its deepest level, the unconscious of the individual merges with the unconscious minds of all human beings, dead or living. Each of us has access to the same wisdom that, expressed in symbolic imagery, lay hidden in the depths of the minds of, for instance, the philosophers of ancient Greece.

If either Jung's theory of the Collective Unconscious, or perhaps some of the very similar theories enunciated by the alchemists of old concerning *anima mundi*, "the soul of the world", are wholly or partially true, many of the enigmas of the mind that are described in the following chapter are, perhaps, not quite as puzzling as they seem.

WILD TALENTS

"*We are living in an energy field not only of our own thoughts and emotions, but of everyone else's*"

Professor N. Khokhlov

THE EARLY RESEARCHERS who attempted to apply scientific methods to the investigation of "wild talents" – the supernormal faculties apparent in certain people – began by trying to classify those talents. This was a perfectly sensible approach, one that had been the basis of the development of the sciences of zoology and botany out of the amateur field of natural history.

At first, classification seemed to be almost as effective a tool for the psychical researcher as it had been for the biologist, and towards the end of the nineteenth century it was beginning to be felt that the work of classifying psychic phenomena was well on the way to completion.

Psychic phenomena had been sorted into a number of categories, such as "telepathy" – the

Disaster Preview
In 1912 the White Star Line's SS Titanic *(below), struck an iceberg on its maiden voyage and sank with great loss of life. Amongst the victims was W.T. Stead, the leading advocate of spiritualism of his time. Stead seems to have received a "psychic message" urging him not to embark on the ship. This was just one of a number of psi events associated with the disaster. Stead chose to disregard his own premonition, with tragic consequences. Many other of the world's great disasters have been foreseen by psychics.*

direct transmission of thought from one mind to another; "clairvoyance" – seeing, in the mind's eye, events occurring somewhere else; and "precognition" – knowing what is going to happen before it takes place. Before long, however, it became apparent that it was impossible to confine a particular phenomenon to its own category – separate psychic events could be explained in several different ways.

➤ PSYCHIC CONFUSION ←

Take, for example, a simple experiment involving two human subjects, one of whom was endeavouring to transmit thoughts to the other – perhaps the suits of a randomly selected series of playing cards. If the success rate was significantly better than might have been expected from coincidence or chance (one "hit" in four), the obvious explanation was either fraud or telepathy. There were, however, other possible explanations that were difficult to exclude altogether. In the case of telepathy, for

instance, it is possible that the supposed recipient of telepathic messages could, by some unconscious use of *clairvoyance*, have been "seeing" the cards that the would-be telepathic transmitter was looking at.

The situation became even more confused when the results of a number of such tests were submitted to detailed analysis. It appeared that a time-displacement factor was sometimes involved. A number of telepathic recipients were scoring well above chance – but with the card selected *after* the one that they had tried to receive telepathically at each individual stage of the series, suggesting powers of precognition.

It seemed that the results of such experiments could be explained, or partially explained, on the basis of telepathy, clairvoyance, or precognition. Eventually the situation became so confused that a number of researchers decided to use an all-embracing term for the phenomena. They therefore adopted the abbreviation ESP ("extra-sensory perception") and the Greek letter "psi" to indicate all modes of perception inexplicable in terms of conventional psychology.

→ WIDE-AWAKE DREAMING ←

Psi faculties are not confined, so it would seem, to a tiny élite of gifted psychics and mediums. There is evidence that many ordinary people possess psi abilities that only occasionally manifest themselves, and so are often attributed to hallucination or coincidence.

Hallucinations have a dream-like quality – in a sense they are dreams, but experienced in a wide-awake state – although they appear real enough at the time. The American psychologist, William James, wrote that the sensation experienced by someone having a hallucination was "as good and true ... as if there was a real object there". However, maybe these "hallucinations" are really the result of ordinary men and women trying to interpret unusual perceptions – ones that they may have received through channels other than the five senses.

The answer may well be yes. Some years ago the Society for Psychical Research conducted a survey of 17,000 people, which revealed that over ten per cent of them had experienced a supposed hallucination – generally "seeing" or "hearing" something that had no basis in the

immediate physical environment. Of the more than 1700 hallucinations, about one tenth related to real events and could well have involved psi. Therefore, something over one in a hundred people possibly had an ESP experience strong enough to induce them to "see visions" or "hear voices".

→ COINCIDENCE? ←

Less dramatic varieties of psi may be very common indeed – so much so that we take them for granted and attribute them, almost automatically, to coincidence. Most all of us have had the experience of being on the point of making a remark to someone we know well and being forestalled by our companion, who says almost exactly what we were intending to say. Telepathy, or precognition – our unconscious minds travelling a second or two forwards in time and hearing what our companions have not yet said – or just coincidence?

Psychic Sisters
In 1848 in New York, there was a string of supposedly psychic events, such as mysterious bangs and crashes, which took place around three sisters, Margareta, Leah, and Kate Fox (above). All three worked at one time or another as professional mediums. However there is evidence that, at times, when their powers were waning, they resorted to fraud.

Psychic Investigator
Hereward Carrington (right), a shrewd and experienced American psychic investigator, exposed many fraudulent mediums during the first two decades of the 20th century. Nevertheless, he became convinced that some mediums do produce authentic psychic phenomena, ultimately arguing that many mediums possess "wild psychic talents".

If psi phenomena are not all to be attributed to fraud, statistical freak, or delusion, then they must be associated with a human faculty, or faculties, unknown to conventional science. In other words, if psi phenomena are genuine, then the individual human being is a far more complex and mysterious organism than has been generally thought; a being potentially capable of thought transmission, travelling through time, and perceiving reality through modes of perception beyond the five senses of touch, hearing, taste, smell, and sight.

So is the psi faculty largely passive? Is it basically a psychic apparatus for receiving messages, or does it have an "active mode" in which it can manipulate and change the outside world, for good or ill? If so, a good many of the phenomena classified as "hauntings", "poltergeist activity", "possession", "physical mediumship" and so on, can be accounted for without reference to ghosts, demons, or other conventional supernatural entities.

⇢ MOVING TABLES ⇠

Take, for example, the physical phenomena that are frequently associated with seances – moving tables; trumpets, and accordians, allegedly manipulated by discarnate spirits playing tunes; the sudden movement or the appearance from nowhere of material objects, and so on. Many reports of such events having taken place can be dismissed as fraudulent. But if any of them did happen, the conventional spiritualist explanation – that there was direct intervention by a spirit or spirits – is difficult to accept.

For the sake of argument, let us leave aside fraud as a possible explanation. The difficulty here in accepting that the physical phenomena of the seance room are caused by direct spirit manipulation of the world of physical matter and energy, is a philosophical one. If the world of spirit exists at all, it is by definition totally separate from the world of physical matter and energy that we live in.

As an analogy consider the relationship between steam (water in a gaseous state) and energy (for example, electrical current). Steam by itself does not create the energy to drive, say, a video recorder. Equally, spirit forces by themselves do not create the means to "drive", say, an accordion. What is missing from the equation? In the case of spirit forces, we find the

The Ancient of Days
William Blake portrayed God (above) as the creator of an ordered universe – a view challenged by spiritualists.

Trumpet Call
There are several instances of instruments being played "by spirits" at seances. For some unknown reason, one of the most popular instruments in the spirit world would seem to be the trumpet (left).

Magical Music
Musical instruments that were allegedly played by spirit hands featured in many 19th-century seances. While there were many frauds perpetrated, it would seem that some of the phenomena were not so easily explained. There is, for example, one very well authenticated account of an accordian in a sealed case starting to play of its own volition. Of course, another explanation for such occurrences would be that a form of psychokinesis (pp.42-43) was taking place – someone was causing the accordion to play by the power to move matter of his or her mind.

human psi faculty. The spirit contacts the soul of an entranced medium and prompts the soul to instruct the brain that it controls to get the psi faculty to cause the accordion to play.

→ STRANGE HAPPENINGS ←

A number of reported cases of physical phenomena associated with mediumship support the hypothesis that spirits can and do influence the physical world through the human psi faculty. Take, for example, the strange and remarkable physical effects witnessed at many of the seances conducted by the Italian medium, Eusapia Palladino, around the turn of the century. Eusapia seems to have happily resorted to

fraud when she felt that her powers were not at full strength but, nevertheless, was sometimes the centre of events that it is difficult to explain in terms of either deception or conventional physics.

On one occasion, for example, observers were sitting in on one of Eusapia's seances when blows were heard on a door that connected the room with a verandah. The key of the door shot out of the lock and landed on the table at which the observers were sitting; it vanished from sight and then reappeared.

In 1965, the San Francisco rock group "Mother McCree's Uptown Jug Champions" changed its name to the "Grateful Dead". Under this name it became one of the most successful rock groups of the 1970s and still flourishes today. We can assume from the name that one or more of the original members of the group had an interest in the supernatural – the Grateful Dead are ghosts who return to the world of the living in order to reward those who have done them some favour. In 1971 the group took part in one of the most interesting psi experiments of modern times.

↦ THE DREAM LABORATORY ↤
The inspiration for this experiment was a visit paid by the band to the "dream laboratory" at the Moses Maimonides Medical Center, State University of New York. Here a team led by the psychiatrist, Dr. Montague Ullman, was investigating the possibility of precognitive and telepathic elements being present in the dreams of experimental subjects.

The large-scale psi experiment, in which the Grateful Dead participated, involved the entire audience at six successive concerts given by the group almost 80 km (50 miles) away from the dream laboratory. On the evening of each

The Grateful Dead
The successful rock group, the Grateful Dead (above) took part in one of the largest ESP experiments ever held. In 1971, the group gave a series of concerts in the State of New York. The audience at each of the concerts was shown an image for a full fifteen minutes while the group played. They were asked to mentally transmit this picture to an English psychic, Malcolm Bessent, who was asleep, 80 km (50 miles) away. When Bessent awoke he was asked to give detailed descriptions of his dreams. Four out of six of his dreams contained images similar to those projected to each audience. Such experiments have convinced many interested in the occult of the existence of telepathy.

concert, Malcolm Bessent, an English psychic, went to sleep in the laboratory under the observation of members of Dr. Ullman's team. After he had gone to sleep, an enlarged photograph of him was briefly shown to the audience at the concert.

↦ RANDOM SELECTION ↤
Immediately afterwards a picture, selected by a random process, was projected to the audience for a quarter of an hour while the group played. The audience was instructed to concentrate on the projected picture and endeavour to transmit it mentally to the sleeping Bessent.

When Bessent awoke he gave detailed descriptions of his dreams – and on four of the six evenings these dreams bore significant resemblances to the themes associated with the projected picture. For example, at one concert the picture shown to the audience was a highly coloured delineation of the seven spinal chakras (p.194), the subtle energy centres which many occultists believe to be present in every human being. Bessent's dream descriptions on the relevant evening included references to "nature's energies", someone levitating, an "energy box", sunlight, and the spinal column.

Card Tricks?

Zener cards, like the ones below, are frequently used to test a psychic's powers of telepathy. The cards were designed by a Harvard biologist, J.B. Rhine, in the 1920s. Each pack consists of twenty-five cards of five different symbols: a star, a circle, a square, a cross, and three wavy lines. Each symbol appears on five cards. In a typical experiment the cards would be shuffled and the "sender" would turn them over one by one, concentrating on the image on the card for a minute or so, while the "percipient" tries to identify each card by drawing whichever image comes into his or her head. This test would be repeated again and again, with the deck shuffled each time, to reduce the possibility of a chance good result. Sometimes the sender and the percipient would be in separate buildings. Time and time again zener card experiments have been successful, with correct guesses well above the level of chance.

This sounds fairly vague, but the actual picture of the chakras shown to the concert audience featured a yogi seemingly suspended without support, his spinal column outlined by the glowing chakras and a stream of energy entering his head, with a halo, resembling a conventional portrayal of a radiating sun, shining forth from the topmost of the chakras.

→ TIME TRAVEL ←

There was an odd spin-off from the Grateful Dead experiment, that seems to suggest that some psychics have the ability to journey through time. The research team decided to see whether there was any possibility that the pictures that the concert audiences were trying to transmit to the sleeping Malcolm Bessent could be "picked up" – intercepted, as it were – by another psychic. The second psychic that they involved in the experiment was a woman named Felicia Parise.

At first sight the comparison between Felicia Parise's descriptions of her dreams and the nature of the pictures shown to the concert audiences is disappointing to those keen to see a positive result to the tests – of the six experiments only one was "successful" enough to be considered, without any doubt, a "hit". When, however, all six of her dream descriptions were compared with *all* of the projected pictures – those projected before, during, and after Parise's tests – a remarkable phenomenon became apparent. Felicia Parise's unconscious mind was seemingly travelling through time while she was sleeping. For the pictures that she produced bore a remarkable similarity to the pictures that were projected to the concert audiences *a day or two later*, and the similarity was too close to be easily argued away as coincidence. In other words, some of her dreams were not in the least telepathic – but they were prophetic. Was Felicia Parise looking through a gap that separates the present from the future?

There is some evidence that many of us, quite unaware that we possess any psychic faculties, are doing the same. There is a method outlined on page 53 by which the interested reader can test himself or herself and can decide whether he or she is an unconscious time traveller or prophet.

MIND OVER MATTER?

"There's no trickery, no chemicals .... I don't know myself how I do it; the mind is very powerful"

Uri Geller

IN 1973, URI GELLER appeared on BBC television and gave a demonstration of his psychic powers, or rather, as others asserted, his expertise as a conjuror of tricks. He appeared to be able to bend spoons and other metal objects; to sense telepathically what was in the minds of others; and to induce wrist-watches to stop or start. After the programme was over, the BBC switchboard was swamped by hundreds of telephone calls from viewers whose working watches had stopped or whose out-of-order watches had restarted while they had been watching Uri Geller in action.

↠ STOPPED WATCH ↞

Recently I was watching, in the company of a small child, a television programme featuring Kermit the Frog. Suddenly I observed that the hour hand had fallen off my watch. There is

Psychokinesis
Metal bending is a favoured way of a psychic proving his or her power of psychokinesis – the ability of the mind to cause movement in inanimate objects.

Metal Bender
Uri Geller (below) found instant fame when he appeared on television, and seemed to be able to bend metal objects using only the power of his mind. His abilities have been tested by scientists with a great degree of success.

little doubt that during the same programme hundreds of watches had inexplicably stopped or started – not at all an uncommon phenomenon.

Neither I nor, as far as I know, anyone else thought fit to telephone the television company to inform them of the behaviour of his or her watch – for the simple reason that we do not associate Kermit with the supernatural.

↠ REASONABLE DOUBT ↞

This may seem a rather trivial point, but in fact it is very important in relation to psychical research. We all have a tendency to attribute perfectly ordinary events to supernormal influences, if we experience them in the sort of context we associate with the supernatural. In a commonplace context, however, like watching Kermit, we do not give a second thought to such events. Metal bending is one of the most dubious areas of psychical research, with deliberate fraud and deceit abounding. For this reason it is essential that all claims be scientifically investigated.

Uri Geller is the best known of supposed psychic metal benders, and he has been subjected to a great many tests in reputable laboratories. Some of these have produced results that have convinced scientists of distinction that he has mental powers over inanimate objects that are

SCIENTIFIC ENQUIRY

Professor John Hasted, the professor of experimental physics at the University of London, has conducted many experiments into the phenomena of metal bending. After Uri Geller's performance in 1973, on BBC television, Professor Hasted invited him to repeat his metal-bending "performance" under strict laboratory conditions.

Several experiments were conducted. In one, Geller managed to bend a key without actually holding it: he simply stroked one end, and the key, as observed by Professor Hasted, curled up. He could see no trickery whatsoever in this or other successful experiments, and was forced to conclude that: "the Geller method of breaking steel is unlike anything described in the (metallurgical) literature."

Professor Hasted has since conducted many experiments to test the supernormal abilities of other supposed psychic metal benders. In particular he has studied those who claim to be able to bend metal at a distance without physical contact. Special equipment, which would register any slight changes in an object's shape, was developed to test these claims. In a substantial number of experiments, Professor Hasted could discern no trickery whatsoever in the metal bending.

Tested by Technology
Professor John Hasted tests psychokinetic powers using specially developed equipment (left).

inexplicable in terms of conventional physics. For instance, Eldon Byrd, of the US Navy's Maryland research laboratory, has affirmed that Geller, under full observation, has bent metal objects "in a way that cannot be duplicated". Similarly, Dr. George Owen, of Canada's New Horizons Research Foundation, has said that

Hasted's Theory
John Hasted's experiments (left) with supposed metal benders all seem to have been based on the supposition that some hitherto unknown force akin to electro-magnetism might be at work. This materialistic approach was criticized by other psychic investigators on the grounds that the power to bend metals, such as that demonstrated by Uri Geller, was, if it existed at all, a "wild talent" operating outside space, time, and, by definition, beyond the realm of physics.

Uri Geller has abilities that are "paranormal and totally genuine". Apart from his metal-bending feats, Uri Geller has performed other quite astounding feats using his supernormal powers. Under controlled conditions he has caused measurable weight loss and gain in a one-gram weight. He has caused a Geiger counter to register 500 times its normal count. In Tokyo, in 1984, he was able to stop and erase an image from a computer graphics system.

Despite his successes, there are still sceptics. The stage illusionist, James Randi, has repeatedly declared that he can duplicate all of Geller's effects by trickery. Yet despite this claim, James Randi had never satisfactorily duplicated all of Geller's effects. As occult writer, Colin Wilson, has stated: "Many scientists who have tested him have concluded that his powers are genuine – or to put this controversial topic at its lowest: no sceptical opponent has been able to prove that he is not genuine".

SOUL SEARCHING

"The mental telescope is now discovered which may pierce the depths of the past"

Professor J. Rhodes Buchanan

PSYCHOMETRY, WHICH LITERALLY means "soul measurement", involves a "sensitive" holding some physical object, anything from an ancient piece of pottery to a sealed letter, and endeavouring to "pick up" something of its history, and the emotions of those who have handled it, by psychic means.

For example, I was told by a former Reuters correspondent in China of a strange encounter with a London psychometrist in the early 1940s. The psychometrist in question was handed a sealed parcel by the journalist. The former had no way of knowing its contents – two small pieces of Chinese pottery believed to date from the latter decades of the Ming dynasty, roughly the first half of the seventeenth century.

After holding the parcel to his forehead for a minute or two the psychometrist made several observations. He announced that the man who

A Mysterious Case
In 1917, a suitcase was washed up on an isolated Irish beach. It was discovered by an amateur psychometrist, an acquaintance of the poet, W.B. Yeats. It was battered, but still intact, and locked. On picking it up, the psychometrist felt sensations of confusion, panic, and suffocation. The psychometrist followed up his find and his investigations showed that the suitcase, containing mainly clothing that had been destroyed by the salt water, had belonged to a passenger on the Lusitania, *the liner that had been sunk with devastating loss of life some two years earlier.*

had handed him the parcel had a highly developed sense of humour, was extremely intelligent, was not appreciated as he should be by his friends, and was interested in the occult.

↪ A FAKE REVEALED ↩

These statements were unimpressive in the extreme, for they are the standard fodder served by bogus psychics to their clients in order to impress them. We almost all think we are highly intelligent, that our talents are insufficiently recognized by others, and even the most stolid of us are apt to believe that we have a good sense of humour. The person who visits a psychic has, by definition, an interest in the occult.

The psychometrist's next statement was more interesting; he said that the parcel contained two bowls, which was correct. He then described the man who had supposedly glazed them as Chinese which, again, was correct. However, he added that the glazer had been working in a studio lit by two kerosene lamps which, of course, seemed impossible as they were not invented until the second half of the nineteenth century, two centuries after the Ming

dynasty had fallen. The journalist paid the psychometrist his modest fee, sarcastically congratulated him on his psychic abilities, and left.

Two years later, the supposed Ming bowls were submitted to an expert examination. They were forgeries, probably made in either Shanghai or Canton at some time between 1900 and 1920. The psychometrist's description of the studio in which they were glazed was almost certainly accurate. It could not be that he had obtained this information by clues unconsciously provided by the journalist who had genuinely believed the bowls were about 300 years old.

➜ TANGIBLE EVIDENCE ➜

Eileen Garrett (1893–1970), probably the most impressive psychic of the twentieth century, scored some remarkable psychometric successes. For example, she is reported to have traced the whereabouts of a missing man by giving her impressions as she held a piece of one of his shirts.

Some experiments, carried out by the New York psychologist Lawrence LeShan, in the 1950s, provided some tangible evidence for the

Powerful Money
An old coin, such as this Austrian "Maria Therasa Thaler" (below) could be highly "charged" through its contact with various souls over the centuries.

Confederate Bill
Emotions felt during the the American Civil War (1861–1865) could be stored on this bill (below).

objective existence of a psychometric faculty that, in turn, gives more credibility to the "anecdotal evidence" such as that provided by the Reuters correspondent mentioned earlier.

For example, a Babylonian clay tablet was wrapped in paper and put in a box that was sealed in a large envelope. The sealed envelope was despatched to Mrs. Garrett, who was some 1500 miles away. She not only scored a hit by identifying the object as a clay tablet but said that it was "associated with a woman" of whom she gave a detailed description.

According to Mr. LeShan, the description tallied so exactly with that of his secretary that she could have been picked "out of a line of ten thousand women". The secretary had indeed handled the tablet "out of curiosity" immediately prior to its packaging.

Is it possible then that the life energy, visible to "sensitives" as the "aura" (pp.58-59) that surrounds a body, can be transferred to inanimate objects? And, more amazing still, could it be that this energy contains and stores information relating to an individual's life?

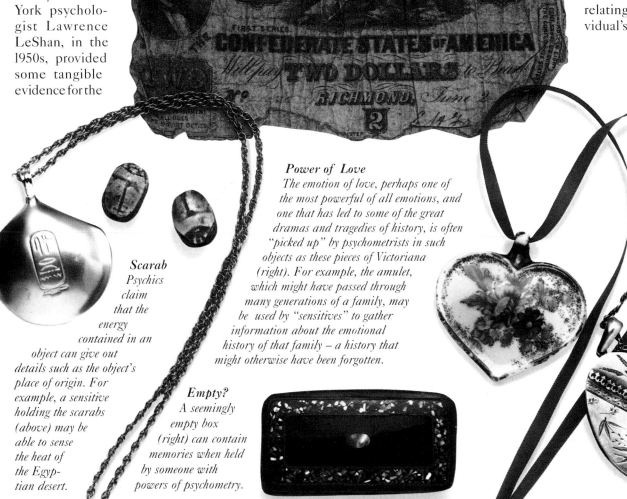

Scarab
Psychics claim that the energy contained in an object can give out details such as the object's place of origin. For example, a sensitive holding the scarabs (above) may be able to sense the heat of the Egyptian desert.

Power of Love
The emotion of love, perhaps one of the most powerful of all emotions, and one that has led to some of the great dramas and tragedies of history, is often "picked up" by psychometrists in such objects as these pieces of Victoriana (right). For example, the amulet, which might have passed through many generations of a family, may be used by "sensitives" to gather information about the emotional history of that family – a history that might otherwise have been forgotten.

Empty?
A seemingly empty box (right) can contain memories when held by someone with powers of psychometry.

TWO OF A KIND

"Chance coincidences happen more often than the laws of chance would lead one to believe" A psychiatrist

THERE IS A WIDESPREAD BELIEF that twins, particularly identical twins, are linked by some mysterious, extra-sensory bond. Even if identical twins are separated from one another at a very early age and brought up in totally different surroundings, they will not only continue to look alike but, so it is said, will also feel alike. They will develop the same tastes and inclinations: from listening with pleasure to the same music and reading the same books, to adopting identical political attitudes.

If this really is the case, and there is a great deal of supporting evidence, is there some

Thinking Alike
The McWhirter identical twins (below) are probably the best known of such pairs. In spite of the many physical, emotional, and mental similarities they shared, it could be argued that some of these were the products of environment rather than hereditary or psychic linkage. However, there have been cases of twins who share the same tastes, but who have been separated at birth, and who have not shared the same environment.

telepathic bond between twins with an identical genetic makeup? Or, an alarming prospect, are all our tastes genetically determined, so that we are predestined, for example, to like the singing of Pavarotti or the novels of D.H. Lawrence?

↠ IDENTICAL TWINS ↞

There is, as it happens, some evidence that separated monozygotic, or identical, twins can display marked resemblances in taste, way of life, and even the way they make seemingly random choices. Take, for example, the cases of Bridget Harrison and Dorothy Lowe, British twins born in 1945, separated a few weeks later, and not re-united until 1979.

Bridget and Dorothy were two of the many sets of separated identical twins whose lives were investigated by Professor Bouchard, of the

between the two separated twins. Coincidence is a possible explanation, but stretches credibility. Could the similarities be the products of genetic factors, or was telepathy involved?

→ DEATHLY COMMUNICATION ←

Consider the case of the Eller twins, two 32-year-old women who died in the State Mental Hospital in North Carolina. Both had been diagnosed as suffering from schizophrenia. In the hospital they had been separated and placed in different wards. They died at nearly the same time, of no known cause, in similar foetal positions. It was generally known that there had been some telepathic awareness between them, and the coincidences surrounding their deaths suggested to many interested in parapsychology that they had exercised some form of supernormal ability. It would seem that when one twin died, the other was aware of her death, even though she was out of sight and earshot, and that the bond between the two women was so strong that using a form of "mind over matter" – supernormal powers similar to those used by Uri Geller (p.42) – she "willed" herself to die only moments later. It is hard to believe in this instance that coincidence is the key. While it may be difficult to believe that we can be genetically programmed to die at a particular time, it is hard to accept that explanation for keeping a diary in a particular year, or for wearing specific jewelry. Surely the sum of all these resemblances constitutes quite overwhelming evidence of some kind of strong psychic bond existing between identical twins ?

University of Minneapolis. During his researches he had encountered many curious twin "coincidences" but these two women surprised even him, from the moment he met them and noticed that each of them wore seven rings and two bracelets. Subsequent enquiries revealed the following:

a) Both women had kept diaries in the year 1960; neither had kept a diary in any other year. Furthermore, these diaries were of the same make and colour, and the days for which no entries were made were the same in both diaries.

b) Both loved reading historical novels. Bridget's favourite author was Caroline Marchant; Dorothy's was Catherine Cookson – but "Caroline Marchant" is one of Catherine Cookson's pseudonyms.

c) Bridget's son is called "Andrew Richard"; Dorothy's is called "Richard Andrew".

d) They share the same favourite scent. And there were many other resemblances

Hidden Twin

In some primitive societies twins have been regarded as uncanny – two people sharing the same soul. Consequently, one or both of them have been killed at birth. If legend is to be believed, a slightly less brutal process was applied to the person known only as the "man in the iron mask" (right). This person, imprisoned for life on the orders of Louis IX (above) is thought by some historians to have been the King's identical twin. He was, some argue, imprisoned for life, lest he should be a threat to the throne.

THE REALM OF DREAMS

"The interpretation of dreams is the royal road to a knowledge of the unconscious activities of the mind"

Sigmund Freud

ACCORDING TO ONE HYPOTHESIS, dreams are our jumbled, imperfect, and distorted memories of what we have encountered in the astral kingdoms in which we have wandered, somehow outside time, while our physical bodies were sleeping. The concept of astral bodies in western occultism has largely come from the sixteenth-century alchemist, magician, and healer, Paracelsus. He was a firm believer in the influence of the sun, moon, planets, and stars

Collective Unconscious Carl Jung (below) was a devoted disciple of Freud, but later came to develop his own theory of the psyche that, like Freud, believed could be unlocked through the interpretation of dreams. However, his method varied greatly from that of Freud. Jung believed in the Collective Unconscious – that all people share the same subconscious mind. This "mind" is revealed through dreams.

upon the physical and mental well-being of men and women. But how, he asked himself, was that influence exerted? It seemed to him that stellar influences could not directly affect humanity, and he came to the conclusion that they were transmitted to human bodies through what he called "astral bodies" – "astral" simply means "starry". Astral bodies, said Paracelsus, are subtle "energy bodies" that underlie the physical bodies of human beings and animals alike. This concept captured the imagination of western occultists, who not only adopted it, but developed it in directions which would have probably surprised Paracelsus.

→ ASTRAL PLANES ←

Most contemporary western occultists believe not only in the existence of astral bodies, but also of astral planes – curious non-physical worlds. These are supposedly beyond time and space as we know them, and yet they are in no sense imaginary. On the contrary, say many occultists, the "real world" of the physicist is no more than an illusion – a reflection in our own minds of the super-reality of the astral plane.

There is a popular misconception that only those born with some innate psychic ability are capable of projecting their consciousness into the astral worlds. However, a large number of western esoteric teachers, amongst them Rudolf Steiner (p.97), have averred that we enter the strange realms of astral consciousness every time we fall asleep. If so, our dreams are memories of our travels and, as astral travel takes us beyond time and space, this theory would explain a number of well-authenticated cases of precognitive dreams.

→ DREAM SYMBOLISM ←

The idea that dreams are meaningful, rather than a mere jumble of irrelevant images, and are capable of interpretation, is a very old one. Examples of this are the systems of dream interpretation employed by Freudian and Jungian analysts (Freudians, for instance, tend to interpret any dream object longer than its width as a phallic symbol). Many people, however, while not denying the possible validity of this kind of dream interpretation, believe that the use of traditional interpretations can enable us to glimpse the future – to obtain some idea of what fate has in store for us. The idea behind this seemingly naïve belief is that in dreams we

roam through time and bring back "memories of the future" under the guise of symbols. For instance, to dream of an accident is supposed to indicate coming good fortune or, if the dreamer has been ill, a recovery in health; and to dream of a hanging is, it is said, a sure sign of future success. The idea behind this, and other examples of dreams meaning more or less their exact opposite, seems to be that in dreams we often see events reversed, just as in a mirror we see our own reflections reversed.

⇢ PROPHETIC DREAMS ⇠

Tales of prophetic dreams are probably as old as humanity itself. Stories concerning them are to be found in ancient Egyptian papyri, in the Old Testament, and in folklore. Such stories cannot be dismissed as legend and fairytale, for there are remarkable and well-authenticated accounts of precognitive dreams of very recent date.

One of the most curious of such instances involved the 1933 Derby and an 80-year-old Quaker, a lifelong opponent of betting, drinking, and smoking, named John Williams. On the morning of Derby Day, John Williams awoke from a most unlikely dream. In the dream he had been listening to a radio commentary of the big race, a thing he would not normally do, and had heard the commentator give the names of the first four horses. Of these four names he only remembered Hyperion and King Salmon.

The dream was of a sufficient intensity for John Williams first to tell two friends about it well in advance of the race and, secondly, to listen to the race commentary. To his astonishment, Hyperion came in first, and King Salmon came in second. The incident made such an impact on John Williams that he told his story to several people. Eventually it reached the ears of H. F. Saltmarsh, a distinguished member of the Society for Psychical Research. Saltmarsh investigated the matter very thoroughly and came to the conclusion that John Williams had had a precognitive dream.

⇢ NATURAL EXPLANATION ⇠

Nevertheless, there is a possible, if somewhat unlikely, natural explanation for John Williams' supposedly precognitive dream. He could have seen the list of Derby runners in a newspaper and, by sheer coincidence, dreamed the names of two placed horses. The "prophetic" nature of such a dream could only be properly accepted if he had dreamed a whole series of the names of winning racehorses. A man named John Godley – later Lord Kilbracken – did just that in the years 1946 and 1947 (p.52).

Psyche Revealed
Sigmund Freud (above) is considered to be the Father of Psychoanalysis, and one of the greatest creative thinkers of the twentieth century. Freud understood the unconscious mind as revealed through dreams as the result of sublimated sex drives. Freud believed that through the interpretation of dreams, the primal sexual urges and desires of mankind could be revealed and understood. Today, Freud's approach to the unconscious, and his rigidly sexual interpretation of dreams, is considered by many to be too narrow.

There are many different ways of interpreting dreams. Those listed here and on the following pages are traditional dream interpretations, some of which have been in existence for centuries.

BATHING: in deep water, a pleasant surprise; in shallow water, an unpleasant one.

BEDS: to buy a bed is to herald a change in residence, career, or way of life.

BLOOD: someone is going to ask for help; it would be unwise to refuse.

CAT: black cats indicate good fortune; other cats predict deception.

CUP: a full cup predicts good fortune; an empty one, disappointments.

CLIMBING: always a sign of good fortune. The higher the object being climbed, the better the coming stroke of luck.

CLOUDS: white, silver, or gold clouds are a sign of impending good fortune; grey or black clouds herald the opposite; blue clouds are prophetic of material good fortune; yellow ones of difficulties; while red clouds warn of danger.

Both primitive and sophisticated races take their dreaming seriously. Indeed the aborigines of Australia base a large part of their extraordinarily rich culture around a complex concept known as the Dream Time.

To understand the Dream Time it is necessary to know a little about aboriginal history. Some 20,000 years ago the aborigines came to the northern shores of Australia from Asia. Here they split into various group and constantly moved around in search of water holes. It is these first aborigines and the land that they created that are remembered by modern-day aborigines when they enter the Dream Time.

On one level, the Dream Time represents this time – the creation of the land and aboriginal people, and also an idyllic past that ceased to exist when, or perhaps before, Europeans reached Australia. On another level, it is here and now. Aborigines can enter it, either through symbolically meaningful dreams, or by attaining to a curious state of

DANCING: an improving relationship with someone known to the dreamer.

FLYING: a warning not to be over-ambitious.

KEYS: finding keys augurs well for your emotional life; losing keys signifies the opposite.

MARRIAGE: the marriage of other people means good fortune is on its way; the marriage of the dreamer is to be interpreted in reverse.

MOON: the moon has always been connected with human sexuality; to dream of the moon is supposed to indicate an improvement in the dreamer's emotional or sexual life.

The Reckless Sleeper
This painting (above), by the surrealist painter René Magritte shows his preoccupation with the world of dreams and dream symbolism.

Dream Sunset
Dreaming of a sunset (right) is a common dream for many people, which can be interpreted in several ways. It can signify infertility; warn of violence; or foretell of death and rebirth.

consciousness, the nature of which is difficult to convey in words. In this state the dreamer becomes detached from everyday existence and embarks upon a long mental journey. Along the way he or she communes with ancestral and other spirits and the "dream elements" in the landscape of the Australian outback – the rocks, birds, animals, creeks, insects, and waterholes. These natural features are as important to the aborigine as the spirits of their ancestors, and during Dream Time the aborigine will identify totally with them. Those who undertake such journeys seem to come into contact with the worlds of the Dream Time.

➛ VOLCANOES OF THE UNCONSCIOUS ←

Among outsiders who have tried to grasp the complex concept of the Dream Time, the most successful have not been anthropologists or psychologists, but surrealist painters and poets. The surrealist belief that while dreams and dream states are immaterial, they are in no sense unreal, has enabled followers of surrealism to sympathize with the

***Joseph and Pharaoh**
The Bible is full of prophetic dreams and their interpretations. One of the most well known is the story of the dream of Pharaoh and its interpretation by Joseph. In this painting (below) Joseph expounds to Pharaoh his interpretation of the monarch's dream of seven fat cows devouring seven lean ones, as seven years of good harvests succeeded by seven years of famine. Like many prophetic dreamers, Pharaoh was unable to interpret his own dream; very few have an interpreter to hand.*

aboriginal concept. They regard dreams as volcanoes of the unconscious, shooting forth enormously powerful and significant symbols, or archetypal forces, into everyday consciousness – they are "super-realists", known, for short, as "surrealists".

➛ SURREALIST BELIEF ←

The dream state takes the dreamer beyond the world of what is generally accepted as reality into a dimension of consciousness that is more real. Surrealist belief here coincides with ancient esoteric teachings of both East and West and with the more traditional concepts of aboriginal culture.

The idea of the dream time, as primitive as nomadic aboriginal culture, as modern as surrealism, is fully compatible with the Jungian concept of the Collective Unconscious. According to Jung, we all share the same sub-conscious mind, which contains all of the collective experience and wisdom of every human being who has ever lived on the planet Earth.

RACE: to take part in a race means that you will be faced with a great temptation that must be resisted.

RAT: to dream of a rat signifies powerful enemies. If the rat is killed in the dream, then the enemies will be defeated. If not ....

RAVEN: a bad omen; disappointment, rivalry, and loss of money are indicated.

SHARK: this is another evil dream, which means that you have an enemy who is planning your downfall.

SNOW OR HAIL: means that some important news will be received very shortly.

STRANGERS: to dream of meeting strangers is thought to indicate major changes ahead in the dreamer's way of life.

SWORD: wearing a sword indicates that you have been acting very haughtily, and if you persist in your behaviour you will experience a serious set-back.

TABLE: a good omen, prophesying domestic comfort and a contented marriage.

TEETH: tooth extraction means losing a friend.

TOAD: a warning of evil or harm; but it is evil that can be avoided.

TRAVELLING: good news is likely, probably of a financial nature.

UNCLE: you will receive a visit from a stranger and will hear surprising news.

UNICORN: you will receive a business or official letter.

VOICES: to hear voices without being able to see the speaker means sorrow and a worried mind.

WATER: looking at water warns against hasty actions; drinking it augurs good fortune to someone close to the dreamer.

YEW: to see a Yew prophecies a lucky escape from a serious accident.

ZOO: a visit to the zoo means a profitable change of employment.

On the night of March 8, 1946, an Oxford student named John Godley – later Lord Kilbracken – dreamed that he was reading the racing results in the next day's evening paper. He awoke with the names of two 7-1 winners, Bindal and Juladin, in his mind. He was not consciously aware of ever having heard of horses with these names.

↠ DREAMING THE WINNERS ↞

That morning he told a friend, Richard Freeman, of his dream; together the two friends looked at the racing pages of *The Times* and found that a horse named Bindal was running at a minor meeting that afternoon. This impressed and surprised Godley, who was even more surprised when he found that a horse named Juladin was running at another meeting.

Friends were told of John Godley's dream and placed bets. The dreamer himself backed both horses as a double. Bindal and Juladin won

their races, although neither at a price of 7-1. Almost a month later, on April 4, John Godley dreamed of a winner named Tubermore. No such horse was running at any meeting, but a Tuberose was a runner in the Grand National. This seemed near enough to take a chance and he backed it; the horse came in first.

He dreamed another slightly inaccurate name – Monumentor – on July 28. John Godley backed the nearest name he could find in the list of runners, Mentores, and won again.

He had no more prophetic dreams for a year or so, but then dreamed, not the name of a horse, but the colours it wore and the face of its jockey. The colours were those of the Gackwar (Prince) of Baroda, the face was that of the Australian rider, Edgar Britt.

John Godley discovered that the Gackwar's horse, Baroda Squadron, was running at Lingfield with Britt riding it. He wrote down the

Surrealist Sequences
In his 1941 film, Citizen Kane *(above), Orson Welles displayed surrealist influences and an interest in dream states and other types of consciousness in which archetypal dream forms manifest themselves. In his film,* Macbeth *(1948), he shows his interest in surrealism again, for Shakespeare's witches were transformed into nightmare figures – perhaps survivors of some dark pre-Christian sisterhood of evil – impinging upon the world of everyday consciousness.*

details of his dream, had it dated and witnessed by three people, and placed it in a sealed envelope, which was then date-stamped by the local postmaster and placed in his safe. Baroda Squadron won comfortably.

The future Lord Kilbracken had a number of other precognitive dreams about winning racehorses but, with the passing of the years, his gift petered out. Could it be that he was travelling through time in his dream? If so, our understanding of time would require reinterpretation.

→ VISITS TO THE FUTURE ←

As the mass telepathy experiment involving the participation of the rock group, the Grateful Dead, showed (p.40), there is some evidence that many of us are unconscious time travellers who visit the future in dreams. Some nineteenth-century psychical researchers inclined to this idea, but it first became widely known through the writings of J.W. Dunne, author of *An Experiment with Time*, and other books.

Between 1900–1902, Dunne had a series of prophetic dreams, most of them about real disasters of one sort or another. For example he dreamed, well in advance of the event, of the volcanic eruption of May 8, 1902, which destroyed St. Pierre, the main trading centre of the island of Martinique, killing 40,000 people.

Dunne began to keep a detailed record of his dreams, reading over it at regular intervals and noting dream episodes which either seemed to reflect past incidents in his own life or, more significantly, incidents which had not yet happened at the time of the dream but did take place at a later date.

Silent Dreams
In spite of the very limited special effects technology of its time, the 1920s' German silent film, The Cabinet of Dr. Caligari *(right), succeeded in giving an eerily effective interpretation of the states of consciousness associated with dreams, nightmares, and symbols from the unconscious.*

Notorious
In Alfred Hitchcock's film, Notorious, *Ingrid Bergman is slowly poisoned by arsenic administered in cups of coffee (below). Like much of Hitchcock's work, the film* Notorious *had as one of its themes, the disparity between appearance and reality. Like the surrealists, Hitchcock believed that it is intuition and dreams that accurately portray things as they really are. In his films he often presented reality under the guise of symbol, as for example here, where he repeats the image of the poisoned coffee.*

Dunne developed a curious theory of time, which he called serialism, to explain his and others' precognitive dreams. Time, he said, is not a straight line, like a stretched cord; it is more like a tangled skein of wool.

Our ordinary self, which Dunne called "Observer 1", is confined to the particular molecule of wool, "now", which it has reached in its journey from the beginning of the skein, birth, to its end, death. In sleep, however, another part of the personality, "Observer 2", takes over and roams at will through the skein of time – hence "precognitive" dreams are not precognitive to Observer 2, for whom everything has already taken place.

One does not have to believe Dunne's theory in order to test the possibility that our minds roam through time in sleep. All that is needed is to keep paper and pencil by one's bedside, to record dreams immediately on waking.

THE MIND'S EYE

"Imagination ... is but another name for absolute power and clearest insight"

William Wordsworth

IN THE 30 YEARS between 1925 and 1955, tens of thousands of Europeans and Americans began each day by standing in front of a mirror, staring at their reflections and muttering over and over again the curious slogan: "Every day, in every way, I am getting better and better."

They were following the advice of a French doctor, Dr. Coué, a famous advocate of autosuggestion – a self-induced light hypnosis in which the individual can improve his or her well-being by suggesting desired things to the unconscious mind.

While the slogan may sound faintly ludicrous, the principle underlying its use is probably sound enough. It is almost a truism to say that people usually behave as we assume they will behave. If, for example, we approach new neighbours expecting them to be friendly and

Just an Illusion
Mary Baker Eddy (above), the founder of the Christian Science movement, frequently claimed that reality is no more than a dream, and that physical matter is an illusion born of the "mortal mind". By this phrase she intended to convey the idea that the world as we perceive it is entirely a product of false consciousness.

Gaudí's Vision
The church of the Sagrada Familia (left) was designed by the Catalan architect, Antonio Gaudí. Some aspects of his strange architecture are almost risible, suggesting to those who look at them, the fairy-tale castles of Disney cartoons. However, some of the details – such as the pinnacles – possess an other-worldly quality, reminiscent of dream states and descriptions given by psychics of the astral world.

outgoing, they generally *are* friendly and outgoing. So if we believe that we are improving, it is possible that others will share that belief.

⇢ CREATIVE VISUALIZATION ⇠

While the techniques that were taught by Dr. Coué were probably effective, occultists have argued that what is called "creative visualization" is a far superior method of using light self-hypnosis to improve one's own personality. For creative visualization deals in images, not words, and therefore influences the unconscious mind on a much deeper level. There is no good reason to doubt the truth of this assertion; psychologists are agreed that visual portrayals of violence in a movie, for example, make far more impact on the viewer than a verbal or written description of the same violent actions. A strong image will inevitably lead to an emotional response. This means that behaviour, to a greater or lesser extent, will also be influenced by that image.

How images are employed in creative visualization can be appreciated by the way in which they might be used to replace the slogan "Every day, in every way, I am getting better and better", in an exercise designed to achieve the same ends as the Coué technique. The experimenter would imagine the events of the coming day in his or her mind's eye as he or she would *wish* them to happen.

⇢ PERFECT DAY ⇠

For example, if the day's planned activities included a shopping trip to the local supermarket and a visit to a library to find a particular book, those activities would be performed mentally, with everything pictured as it would ideally be. There would be a parking place for the car; all the items on the shopping list would be easily found on the supermarket shelves; the checkout staff would be helpful and so would the librarian; the book would be found with comparative ease.

Those who have experimented with creative visualization over an extended period tend to claim that, however unlikely it may seem, it works – they find that other people regard them as they want to be regarded, there is a general improvement in their quality of life, and so on.

Interestingly enough, some qualified medical practitioners have been sufficiently impressed by the value of creative visualization to teach their patients to employ it as a complement – not an alternative – to orthodox treatment. This is partly due to the acceptance by both orthodox and unorthodox medical practitioners of the belief that disease is as much a matter of the mind as of the body. Indeed techniques similar to creative visualization have been used for centuries, in particular in the East, to heal the body or to prevent disease.

↪ KNIGHTS IN ARMOUR ↩

Today, visualization can be used, for example, in addition to the chemotherapy a patient is receiving to rid the body of malignant cells. He or she is told to visualize those cells as monsters being killed and chopped into pieces by knights in shining armour. These knights are imaginative depictions of both the molecules of the drugs administered to the patient, and that patient's own defences in the body's immune system.

The Entire City
Like other surrealist artists, the painter Max Ernst, believed that art, if it is to be of any worth, had to express some inner "truth" or "reality". But truth and reality were to the surrealists the "part of nature we do not perceive", and not part of the external world. In his painting The Entire City *(above), Ernst conveys a dream-like quality – some might say almost "nightmarish". Like much surrealist art,* The Entire City *does not concern itself with a representation of the physical world; instead Ernst deploys symbols, which combine to represent a state of being.*

Creative visualization can be used in many areas of life, including business situations, personal relationships, sports, as a method of improving memory, or to overcome shyness, pain, and negative thinking. Experienced practitioners can also use it to call up their "inner selves" or "inner guides". These guides can be visualized as people; a man may call up a female "inner guide" and similarly a woman may be surprised that one of her inner guides is a man. These guides are, believe occultists, various aspects of an individual's subconscious; every individual has both male and female aspects to the psyche – Taoists term this the Yang and the Yin (pp.202-203). The guides are able to see and understand things that are usually hidden from the conscious self; some people believe that they can foretell the future.

A detailed description of such techniques is outside the scope of this book. It suffices to say that those who have used them with regularity and sincerity seem, at the very least, to have had quite remarkable changes of consciousness.

MONSTERS WITHIN

*"S*uddenly he took hold of my hand, and it seemed I no longer had a will of my own"

Multiple Personality Sufferer

WE ARE ALL OF US FAMILIAR with the theme of Robert Louis Stevenson's short novel, *Dr. Jekyll and Mr. Hyde*, the inspiration of many horror movies. Inside Dr. Jekyll, a perfectly respectable, almost saintly, human being, is a violent, cruel, and egocentric monster – Mr. Hyde. At times Dr. Jekyll is transformed into Mr. Hyde, who satisfies his lusts and then disappears, leaving the bewildered Dr. Jekyll to face the terrible consequences.

Stevenson's story has never been out of print since its first publication in 1886. Its popularity may be due to the fact that most of us sense certain Jekyll and Hyde elements in our own personalities. Curious temptations erupt into the minds of many of us and, at times, are yielded to. Afterwards we are surprised by our own behaviour – we may say, "I don't know what came over me".

In some people this tendency to behave at times in uncharacteristic ways seems to develop to a point at which a secondary personality comes into existence. On such occasions, the normally dominant, everyday personality "blacks out" and another personality takes over control of the body and the conscious mind. When the usually dominant, normal "self" returns to consciousness, it literally does not know what has taken place during its absence.

➔ THREE LEONIES ←

A well-documented example of multiple personality is seen in the case of Leonie, a poor peasant woman, downtrodden and sad, who from childhood suffered attacks of somnambulism. Leonie underwent hypnosis in an attempt to cure her attacks. Under hypnosis, her character changed dramatically; she seemed to be a completely different person – vital, sarcastic, and lively. She refused to recognize the "usual" Leonie as part of herself and considered her stupid.

As the hypnosis treatment continued, a third character emerged – a thoroughly superior Leonie who regarded the other Leonies with disdain and even some distaste.

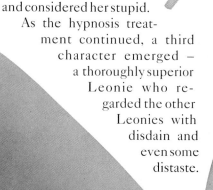

Three Faces of Eve
Multiple personality exerts a fascination over artists. The film, The Three Faces of Eve (below), explores the story of a woman with three personalities.

Jekyll and Hyde
Robert Louis Stevenson's famous novel of split personality, Dr. Jeckyll and Mr. Hyde, *has been filmed several times. Here, the evil side of Dr. Jeckyll's character, Mr. Hyde (left), is played by Spencer Tracy.*

Five in One
The renowned American psychologist and theologian, Dr. Walter F. Prince, (above) studied the strange case of Doris Fischer, a woman who seemed to have five different personalities who all argued occasionally.

An even more extraordinary case is that of Doris Fischer, whose story suggests the possibility that secondary personalities are actually spirits that have taken up residence in the body of a human being. Doris Fischer's body was a rooming-house with five tenants – all very different types of people who argued with one another occasionally. This strange case was studied by an American psychologist, Dr. Prince.

➝ THE GOOD SPIRIT ARIEL ⬅

When Dr. Prince came into contact with Doris Fischer, he found that he was dealing with five patients, rather than one. First there was Ariel, who claimed not to be part of Doris but a good spirit sent to look after her; Dr. Prince never felt able to reject this claim completely, for he sensed in Ariel a wisdom and maturity lacking in the other four personalities. These other personalities were Doris, Sick Doris, Sleeping Doris, and Margaret. Plain Doris was the "normal" Doris Fischer, an essentially placid individual who was puzzled by the ways in which she had behaved when she had lost consciousness and one of the other personalities had taken over control of her body.

Sick Doris was a stupid creature, dull to the point of abnormality, who behaved in a mechanical and unintelligent way when dominant. Sleeping Doris was little more than a computer – she seemed to have almost total recall of the actions of the other four personalities. Margaret was mischievous, doing foolish things and then vanishing, leaving one of the other personalities to face the consequences of her actions.

Under Dr. Prince's auspices, Doris recovered her mental health – three of her personalities "died". Sick Doris was the first to go. She sensed she was "dying" and left behind a letter, addressed to Margaret, giving much good advice. Sleeping Doris, the computer personality, departed next, followed by Margaret. Ariel manifested herself less and less – perhaps feeling her work was done. The remaining Doris was now an integrated personality.

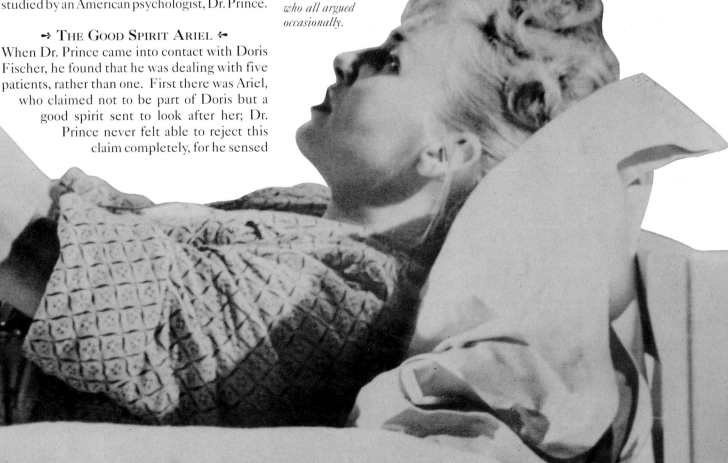

EXPLORING THE AURA

"Ever since I was a child, I have had the ability to see lights around people – and pretty colours"

Clarisa Bernhardt, psychic

SOME OCCULTISTS ASSERT that each living thing, whether it be a tree, a cat, or a human being, has an aura. By "aura" they are referring to an emanation of the subtle, non-physical energies that are held to be the invisible blueprints of the physical bodies of all living creatures. Since the early nineteenth century, it has been claimed that psychics can discern the auras of others by using a sense analogous to, but not identical with, ordinary vision.

C.W. Leadbeater and other occultists claimed that they could not only perceive the auras of

Kirlian Photography
A Russian scientist, Semyon Kirlian, believed that he had developed a method of photographing auras. The tip of the leaf (below) was removed seconds before the photograph was taken. The white "halo" surrounding the leaf is, according to Kirlian, its aura, which is present even after that part of the physical leaf has been removed. In time this "halo" will fade away from the missing leaf section, and the aura will adjust to the new shape.

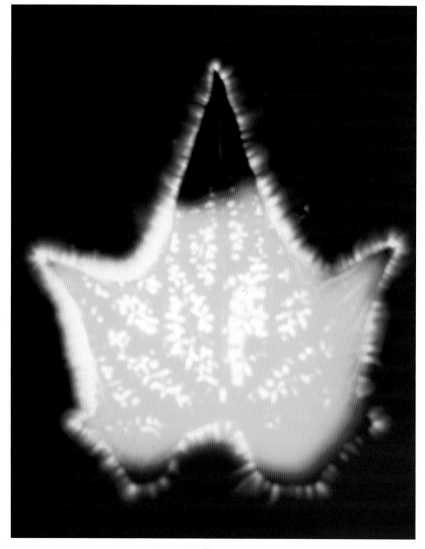

others but do so in such detail that they were able to accurately diagnose the spiritual condition of those they observed. The changing colours of the aura can, say psychics, reveal much about the personality and physical condition of an individual. Some psychics claim that they can actually see halos around young children and even certain adults.

➻ KILNER SCREENS ↢
In the early part of the twentieth century Dr. Kilner, a physician at St. Thomas's hospital in London, who claimed to have the ability to discern the human aura as a faint glow, believed that he had discovered a method by which most non-psychics could also perceive auras. Dr. Kilner believed that as auras were a form of radiant energy, the eyes could be sensitized to see this energy. He saw three distinct layers in an individual's aura; these layers extended for about a third of a metre (1 ft) from the human body. Dr. Kilner believed that the aura was an effective indicator of the state of an individual's vitality; he was determined to find some means of making such valuable information available to men and women who were not psychic.

Kilner's method involved the use of sealed glass panels, rather like present day double-glazing units, but with the space between the sheets of glass containing a solution of dicyanin, a blue dye. A number of experimenters asserted that they were able to perceive auras through the "Kilner screens". Both screen and goggles are still manufactured and sold. The general consensus of opinion, however, is that the "auras" seen with the aid of Kilner's devices are no more than optical illusions.

➻ BIOPLASMIC ENERGY ↢
No one, however, has had the temerity to claim that the extraordinary pictures of energy fields produced by the process known as Kirlian photography are illusory. Kirlian photography is the photographing of something through which a very high voltage is passed. It was accidentally discovered in 1939 by a Soviet electrical engineer, Semyon Kirlian, who found that when he placed his own hand behind a piece of film, and passed a large voltage through it, he got a photograph not just of his hand but of what seemed to be streams of energy radiating from it.

Kirlian devoted the next 40 years to refining and developing this technique of high voltage

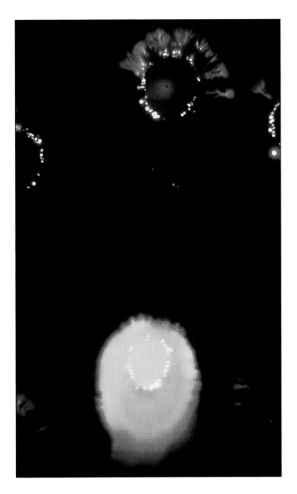

Colours of a Healer
This photograph (left) purports to show the aura emitted from the finger of a healer. The outer ring of red denotes a strong person. Within this circle is a thicker circle of orange, which indicates a healthy, vital person. The yellow inside this is indicative of someone who is helpful and kind, and also shows a developing spiritual awareness – all qualities that may be found in a healer.

Aura Goggles
While psychics claim to be able to see auras with the naked eye, Dr. Kilner, a physician at London's St. Thomas's hospital, believed that he had invented a device that enabled non-psychics to see auras. His invention consisted of goggles (below) made out of two sealed panels of glass with a solution of dicyanin (a blue dye), in between. Kilner claimed that anyone wearing these goggles would be able to see auras.

explained by more than one competent electrical engineer in terms of physical science – for example, on the hypothesis that the electrodes used have not been properly cleaned. While some of those who have made this latter suggestion have been scientists of distinction, it is only fair to add that an unorthodox English therapist, Harry Oldfield, claims to have produced the phantom leaf effect using spotlessly clean electrodes.

→ AURA OR IONIZATION ←
Perhaps the most devastating critique of occult claims that Kirlian photography makes visible the aura or "etheric body", was made by A.J. Ellison, for many years Professor of Electronic and Electrical Engineering at London's City University. For Professor Ellison had a sympathetic attitude towards occult concepts; not only was he a one-time President of the Society for Psychical Research but, as a member of the Theosophical Society, he had devoted years to the study of etheric and astral energies, and took a particular interest in Kirlian photography and the recorded "auras".

Professor Ellison's critique is too long for a full summary of it to be given here. In brief, however, he came to the conclusion that what is recorded on Kirlian photographs is in no way supernormal or inexplicable; it is simply the effect of intermittent ionization of the air around the object being photographed. These effects are known as "Lichtenburg figures" after Jiri Lichtenburg, who discovered them. Today many scientists accept this as an explanation of Kirlian photography.

photography which, so he, his assistants, and his admirers claimed, showed that all living things were surrounded by what they termed "biological plasma". Many photographs taken using Kirlian's method are both impressive and beautiful. Not only do they seem to show energy fields of a type which has led may occultists to identify them with the auras of psychic theory, but they seem to show that these fields survive after the living tissues with which they are associated have been destroyed.

→ PHANTOM LEAF ←
The supposed evidence for this is provided by what is called the "phantom leaf effect"; when a leaf, from which part has been cut away, is immediately photographed using Kirlian's method, the "bioplasmic energy" of the missing section is still recorded on the photograph.

While the phantom leaf effect is one which staggers the observer, it has been

PAST LIVES

"I am certain that I have been here as I am now a thousand times before, and I hope to return a thousand times"

J.W. von Goethe – *Memoirs of Johannes Falk*

A CENTURY AGO, belief in reincarnation – the idea that we are not condemned to eternal sorrow or bliss on the basis of only one life – was rarely found in the western world. Today, however, a surprisingly large number of those westerners who believe in the immortality of the soul are either firm believers in reincarnation or are at least prepared to consider it a possibility.

The concept of reincarnation has a long history in the West as well as in the East. There is some evidence that the Druids of ancient Gaul and Britain accepted the idea; the philosopher, Plato, taught it in ancient Greece;

Reliving The Past
One of the most famous cases of supposed reincarnation is that of a Colorado housewife (portrayed below in the film "The Search for Bridey Murphy") who, under hypnosis, was able to recall details of a past life as a 19th-century Irish woman. Although her knowledge of the period was astonishing, none of the personal details that she gave, could be verified. This has left many investigators sceptical as to the value of her claims.

and in the Middle Ages, the dualistic Cathars (pp.82-83) were convinced that all men and women returned to earth over and over again.

Certain nineteenth-century occult writers – notably Allen Kardec, the leading ideologue of the French spiritualist movement, and H.P. Blavatsky, co-founder in 1875 of the influential Theosophical Society – reintroduced the idea into the West. One of the arguments used against the theories of Kardec and Blavatsky was simple and yet seemingly devastating. If we have all lived before, why is it that most of us are unable to remember our previous lives?

Two answers were given by occultists to this question. First, the surface layers of memory are wiped away during the period between death and rebirth; it requires complex processes of psychic self-analysis for memories of previous lives to be available to the conscious

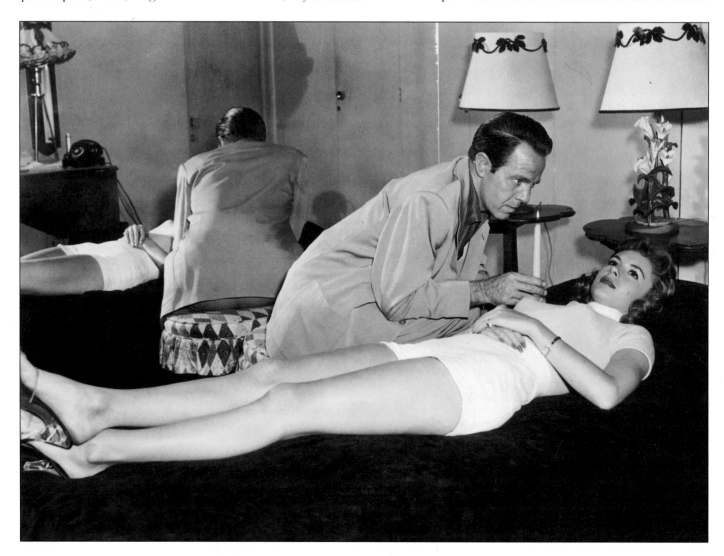

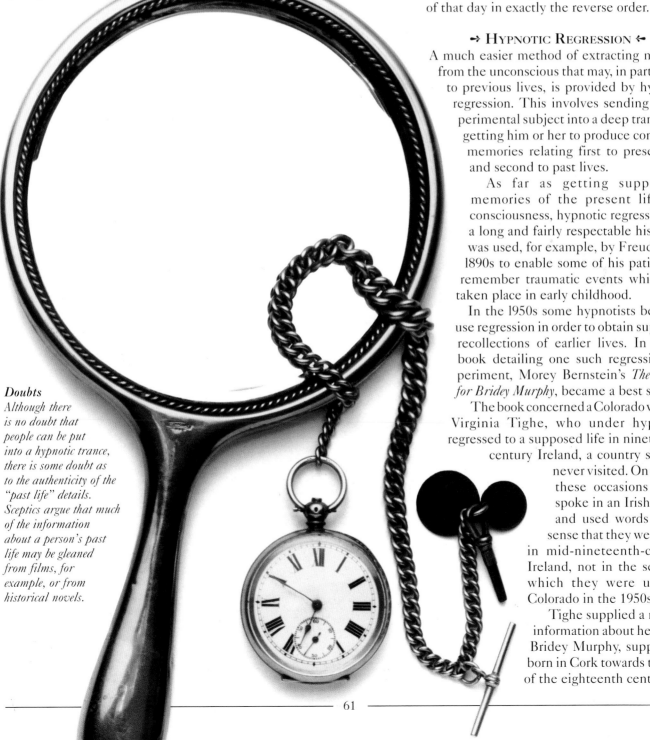

Hypnosis
Under hypnosis, some people have been able to remember past lives in great detail. A traditional way of inducing a hypnotic trance of great depth is to get the person to concentrate his or her vision upon a swinging watch, or a light reflected from a mirror (below). In fact any bright moving object can be used as a focal point.

Doubts
Although there is no doubt that people can be put into a hypnotic trance, there is some doubt as to the authenticity of the "past life" details. Sceptics argue that much of the information about a person's past life may be gleaned from films, for example, or from historical novels.

mind. Second, we all want to forget what has been unpleasant in our lives, which is why our memories of pain and illness tend to be blurred; we want even more to forget the details of the deaths that ended our past lives – and we cannot remember the details of those same past lives unless we are first prepared to bring into consciousness the painful memories of the deaths that concluded them.

Between 1900 and 1945 some western occultists devised techniques that were designed to overcome the supposed tendency of the human mind to refuse to remember past lives. Most of these methods were derived from ancient Hindu and Buddhist meditative exercises and some of those who used them claimed that they were effective. Indeed, one such occultist, the late Colin Bennett, went so far as to publish a book entitled *Practical Time Travel* in which he purported to teach his readers how to remember all the details of their previous lives.

Most of the advice given in manuals aimed at enabling the reader to recover memories of past lives is extremely hard to follow. For example, the reader might be told to spend some time at the end of each day in remembering the events of that day in exactly the reverse order.

→ HYPNOTIC REGRESSION ←

A much easier method of extracting material from the unconscious that may, in part, relate to previous lives, is provided by hypnotic regression. This involves sending an experimental subject into a deep trance and getting him or her to produce concealed memories relating first to present life and second to past lives.

As far as getting suppressed memories of the present life into consciousness, hypnotic regression has a long and fairly respectable history. It was used, for example, by Freud in the 1890s to enable some of his patients to remember traumatic events which had taken place in early childhood.

In the 1950s some hypnotists began to use regression in order to obtain supposed recollections of earlier lives. In 1965 a book detailing one such regression experiment, Morey Bernstein's *The Search for Bridey Murphy*, became a best seller.

The book concerned a Colorado woman, Virginia Tighe, who under hypnosis, regressed to a supposed life in nineteenth-century Ireland, a country she had never visited. On each of these occasions Tighe spoke in an Irish accent and used words in the sense that they were used in mid-nineteenth-century Ireland, not in the sense in which they were used in Colorado in the 1950s.

Tighe supplied a mass of information about her life as Bridey Murphy, supposedly born in Cork towards the end of the eighteenth century.

She gave, for example, the names of Belfast stores at which she had shopped, spoke of the pipes played at her funeral in 1864, and showed some knowledge of Irish folklore.

Morey Bernstein was completely convinced of the authenticity of Tighe's memories and drew the case to the attention of the editor of the magazine *Empire*, who was sufficiently impressed to despatch a researcher to Ireland in order to check historical facts. The results,

described in a lengthy report, were somewhat ambivalent. Some of Tighe's statements were verified. For example, the Belfast stores she had mentioned had actually existed. Others could not be proved – there was, for instance, no record of the baptism of Bridey Murphy, but an enormous number of such records had perished in the Irish troubles of the early 1920s. Still others seemed almost certainly incorrect; whilst Tighe was under hypnosis she used the word

Reliving History
Under hypnosis, one subject gave a detailed description of life as a sailor on board an 18th-century man o' war, the Neptune (above). There have been many similar cases – all have boosted belief in reincarnation.

have often made statements about matters of minute detail that prove to be entirely correct, and statements about major events that prove to be wildly inaccurate. One such English subject was regressed to the year 1833, and gave some very detailed information about the life of the time which proved to be entirely accurate in so far as it could be verified. However, when the same subject was asked the name of the ruling monarch, she replied "Queen Victoria" – in fact it was William IV who was on the throne in 1833, and he was not succeeded by his niece, Victoria, until four years later.

→ CASE NOT PROVEN ←

Such inaccuracies have led many sceptics to assert that all cases of supposed regression to past lives can be dismissed as fantasies. I see this as excessively simplistic. For even in relation to our present existences many of us remember the trivial events of our own lives but forget important historical events – we may remember the exact details of what we drank and ate at, say, our twenty-first birthday party in 1977, but cannot remember who was then President of the United States. In considering hypnotic regression as evidence for reincarnation, perhaps the best verdict is that peculiarly Scottish one – not proven.

Precognition?
In the early 1980s a curious experiment in hypnotic progression, which endeavoured to send hypnotized subjects forward in time, was carried out in London. Two journalists were put into a deep trance and instructed to travel ten years into the future. One saw almost nothing. The other witnessed a horrifying meteorite strike on London (below) and other catastrophic events that would culminate in the destruction of the city and most of its population. This premonition would seem to be, and hopefully is, a fantasy. But if this is the case, then a large question mark must be placed on all similar hypnotic regression experiments – for it would mean that people under hypnosis are capable of fantasizing.

"ditched" for buried, which never seems to have been in the vocabulary of the nineteenth-century Irish. On the basis of the report it was quite impossible to say whether Bridey Murphy had ever existed or whether she was a fantasy of the unconscious – an undeveloped secondary personality of Tighe (pp.58-59). The mixture of accuracy and inaccuracy in the statements made by the hypnotically regressed Virginia Tighe was not untypical. Regressed hypnotic subjects

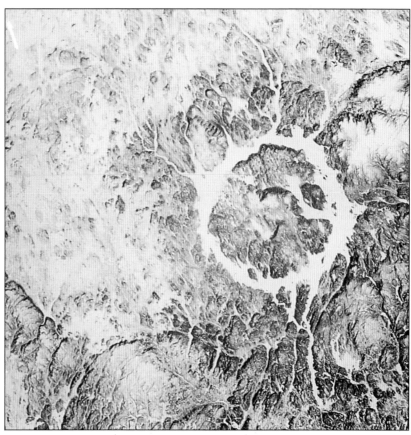

Chapter Three

SECRETS OF THE WEST

The "mystic East" is as familiar a term as the "materialist West". We have now become accustomed to associate the Orient with the spiritual and esoteric, and the West with the mundane and materialistic. If someone needed guidance in mystical traditions, they would, most probably, look to the ancient wisdom of the Orient.

However, in reality nothing could be more materialistic than the outlook of the average Tokyo or Singapore stockbroker; nothing could be less so than the attitudes of the authentic western mystic – a contemplative nun, for example, or a monk meditating on Mount Athos.

⇥ DENIAL OF EXISTENCE ⇤

In every part of the world there are many who deny the existence of any kind of reality other than that which can be scientifically proven. And in every part of the world there are those to whom the life of the spirit is of supreme importance. The mystic West is quite as existent and significant as the mystic East. For every system of psycho-spiritual training and discipline used in the Orient, there is an occidental equivalent.

It is worth giving an example of such an East-West comparison. The lamas of Tibet perform certain spiritual exercises, known as creative visualization (pp.54-55), which utilize the hidden super-energy centres of the body. The Tibetan exercises have their western equivalents in methods used by the initiates of a number of esoteric orders active in North and South America, Australasia, and Europe. There, the intention is essentially the same as it is in the eastern exercises – that is, to bring the energy centres to life. In a similar way there exist western equivalents of the tantrism of Bengal (p.200) and the ecstatic dancing associated with certain orders of Iranian Sufi mystics, "whirling dervishes".

⇸ FRAUD AND INTOLERANCE ⇷

It has to be admitted, however, that western esotericism has its faults. There are bogus "white magi" in the West, just as there are fraudulent gurus and "enlightened ones" in the East.

There is also a certain western gullibility in relation to historical matters; this has led some western occultists to make, for example, claims concerning the supposed occult wisdom of the Cathars and the Templars (pp.82-85), for which there is actually very little real evidence.

Worst of all, there is a tendency to intolerance of other aspirants' ways of working – an inclination to believe that if some other person's approach is different from one's own it must be regarded with some suspicion.

⇸ MANY WAYS IN ⇷

All of these things having been said, it is still true that the average westerner who wishes to tread the occult path towards the expansion of consciousness would usually be well advised to begin his or her spiritual journey from its western origins. This is not as difficult as it may at first appear: there are many ways in. One route is the books of Rudolph Steiner, for example, or another would be to study some of the great myths of the West, such as the legends of the Holy Grail and the Arthurian Knights of the Round Table.

THE HOLY GRAIL

"The visionary kingdom stands, unshaken by time, with the power and immortality of the imagination"

Geoffrey Ashe

THE HOLY GRAIL has been the subject of conjecture and debate since it first appeared in medieval literature. It has meant many things to many people. Christians have identified the Grail as the cup from which Jesus drank at the Last Supper. They consider the legend of Arthur and his knights and their quest for the Holy Grail as an allegorical expression of the Christian Mystic's journey from the human to the divine. Some occultists have interpreted it as neither material nor spiritual, rather as a unique link between the two. Freudians and anthropologists,

Holy Quest
One of the most famous Arthurian legends is the quest for the Holy Grail, here depicted by Edward Burne-Jones (below). The idea of a lost sacred vessel originated in the myths of the Celts; it was later incorporated in Arthurian legend, where the pagan vessel became the chalice used by Christ at the Last Supper. Its recovery by the Knights of the Round Table was synonymous with the legendary spirituality of Arthur's court.

on the other hand, have claimed that it symbolizes the female genital and reproductive organs. These various viewpoints may not be as contradictory as they seem. The closely interwoven legends of Arthur and the Grail are of central importance in western esoteric and mystic traditions, and while interpretations of the mythos are ever changing and evolving, its inner meaning is constant.

⇢ LITERARY LEGEND ⇠

Who was Arthur? A Celtic monarch and military leader who, if he existed at all, spent most of his time battling against his own family. Yet now and for centuries past King Arthur has fascinated and indeed obsessed many English writers. As a result of this obsession, much Celtic myth and legend has been incorporated into

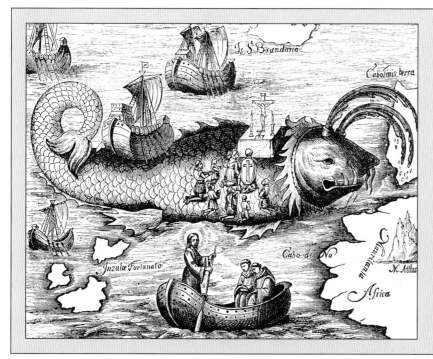

BIRDS AND SAINT BRENDAN

Not only English literature has absorbed Celtic archetypes from Arthurian mythos. Take, for example, this description of a mystic tree and the birds that sang upon it:

"... I saw so many birds ... in the pine tree ... all the birds sang in harmony yet the note of each was different ... (their song) ... filled me with such joy ... I was lost in rapture."

These lines are taken from the poem *Yvain*, an Arthurian romance written by the French twelfth-century poet, Chrétien de Troyes. The tree with its joyous birds had a number of Celtic prototypes but the poet's immediate source was probably an Anglo-Norman version of a Latin account of St. Brendan's travels, derived from lost Celtic sources.

Travelling Saint
St. Brendan is famed for his sea journeys. Here (left) he is depicted off the coast of Africa with two monks.

The Rightful King
This medieval illustration (left) shows the young Arthur miraculously withdrawing the sword, Excalibur, from a stone anvil, so proving he was rightful king of Britain.

Arthurian Ruins
Tintagel Castle (below) is, according to legend, the place where Arthur was conceived. In fact, Tintagel was a Norman castle, although excavations have revealed that it was originally the site of a Celtic monastery.

English literature; through the works of such writers as Thomas Malory in the fifteenth century, and T.H.White and Charles Williams in the twentieth century.

The Celtic/Arthurian/Grail mythos combines a number of separate myths and legends into one story, which inevitably has internal contradictions and ambiguities. Consider Merlin, for example: a key figure in the Arthurian mythos who was originally quite unconnected with it; a magician who was good, but not wholly good. Merlin started out as Myrddin, a Welsh bard who supposedly went insane after the battle of Arfderydd in AD 573. He spent years wandering in the Welsh forest of Celydonn where, as a result of his entanglement with Gwenddydd, his sister and/or mistress, he acquired the gift of prophecy. By the end of the twelfth century he

had been transformed into Merlin, the crafty son of a demon-impregnated Welsh princess and, as such, a half-man torn by moral uncertainties. Written sources for all elements of the Arthurian legend are unreliable in this way.

↦ THE STORY OF ARTHUR ↤

The cycle of romances referred to in the Middle Ages as the "Matter of Britain", and concerned with Arthurian myths and legends, concentrate largely on the quest for the Holy Grail by Arthur's knights – Lancelot, Galahad, Percival or Parsifal, and others. In most of the romances the Holy Grail represents the vessel used at the Last Supper. Earlier Arthurian legend, which mainly concerned the supernatural events surrounding Arthur himself, made no mention of the Grail. Arthur, so the legend told, was the son of Ygraine or Ygerne, the Duchess of Cornwall, by Uther Pendragon, King of the British. With the help of a magic spell cast by Merlin the Magician, Uther assumed the appearance of Ygraine's husband and thus gained access to her bed. Their offspring, Arthur, was born at Tintagel in Cornwall. After the death of Ygraine's rightful husband in battle, Uther and Ygraine were married. Arthur's birth was thus legitamized and he succeeded to the throne at the age of 15, proving his right by drawing the magic sword, Excalibur, from a stone anvil.

↦ CHIVALRY AND DECEIT ↤

Under the wise guidance of Merlin, the young king ruled well and chivalrously. His knights sat at a round table in order to avoid any disputes over precedence. Arthur and his knights travelled throughout the kingdom: killing giants; engaging in combat with enchanters; rescuing prisoners; and performing other chivalrous deeds. Merlin's considerable occult skills could not save Arthur, however, from the magical deceits of his half-sister, Morgause, who bore him a son, Mordred. As Merlin foretold, Mordred was an evil knight, destined to destroy Arthur.

Long before Arthur's downfall, according to the authors of later Grail romances, the fellowship of the Round Table had been broken up by its own knights, who left Arthur's castle of Camelot in order to seek the Grail.

The story of the Grail is also told in the French "Vulgate Cycle". After the death of Jesus, the Grail, a vessel containing drops of Christ's blood, was brought to Britain by Joseph of Arimathea. Eventually Joseph's nephew, Alain, became guardian of the Grail, preserving it in the castle of Corbenic, where there were also present "the Hallows of the Grail", the

Arthurian Romance
In this illustration to Tennyson's Idylls of the King, *the body of Elaine of Astalot (above) arrives magically, floating downstream on a barge, at King Arthur's court. Legend has it that Elaine died of unrequited love for Sir Lancelot. There are many stories in which people mysteriously appear or disappear. Their origin can be found in Celtic myths of "translations", in which people or objects are magically moved around – always for a purpose.*

most notable of them being the Bloody Lance. To this castle came, in due course, various of Arthur's knights, only one of whom, Percival, attained to the vision of the Grail, which was in essence something of incomparable purity and sanctity. The chosen knight is regarded by many contemporary occultists as the archetypal aspirant who succeeds in his or her personal quest for mystical union with the otherness that lies buried in the depths of each individual psyche – a divine spark that is part of the Absolute.

The Arthur of history – the British military leader – is of little interest to the occultist unless he or she also happens to be a historian. It is the Arthur, Merlin, Galahad, Guinevere, Lancelot, and Percival of medieval romance that are of importance. Modern esoteric groups interpret the adventures of the knights as allegorical expressions of humanity's spiritual quest.

Regal Collar
Gold torques (collars) like this one (right) were worn by high-ranking Celtic warriors, princes, and kings. It is probable that the real Arthur would have worn something similar. The interlocking gold chains are a very typical Celtic design.

Unisex Brooch
Bronze brooches (far right) were worn by both men and women. Prolonged warfare led to a thriving metal industry that in turn led to to an increase in the production of jewellery.

Iron and Bronze Spearhead
The scroll design on this spearhead (below), is found on many Celtic artefacts. It is symbolic of the serpent, a creature of spiritual significance.

The Celtic peoples had a rich culture centred around magic, superstition, and war. Their employment of symbolism in order to express their system of values and beliefs can be seen carved, painted, or wrought on their jewellery, weapons, and other artefacts. All the artefacts shown here date from the early Celtic period (800 BC – AD 43). Whether they are weapons or jewellery, they were all created with the greatest of care by skilled craftsmen.

Linchpin
This linchpin (right) came from a chariot wheel. Horse-drawn chariots were of such importance to Celtic warriors that the greatest care would be lavished on their construction.

Celtic Bronze
The spiral motif on this bronze horse-harness terret (above, right) is a common Celtic design.

A Bit of Bronze
This beautifully crafted horse's bit (above) is fashioned in bronze. It was the custom for Celtic warriors who had perished in battle to be entombed, laid out on their chariot, along with their weaponry, their ornaments, and their horse's entire harness.

Brooch
The delicate filigree on this bronze brooch (below) is a fine example of meticulous Celtic craftsmanship.

Dagger
This dagger, cast in iron and bronze (left), shows, once again, how the Celts placed enormous aesthetic value on their weapons, as well as making them as strong and effective as possible. Celtic smiths prided themselves on making their work as intricate as possible – whatever its purpose.

Swordhilt
The head on this swordhilt (right) was the motif of a popular Celtic cult. The head was considered the centre of spiritual power. The first Celts were head-hunters, who used real heads for decoration.

Knots and Curves
Curving lines, such as those which can be seen in the design of the handle of this mirror (left), and, indeed, in the pattern engraved on the back, were common design-elements in Celtic craftsmanship. Curves, knots, and geometric interlacing were used to represent shapes derived from plants, birds, and animals – even from the human form and features.

The Aston Mirror
The Celts, both male and female, were very much concerned with their appearance, so it is not surprising that archaeologists have found mirrors, like the one above, that date from the early Celtic period. The warrior mystique was as much to do with the elaborate ceremonial garb that they donned for war, as it was to do with their prowess and courage in battle. Women, who were accorded parity with men in Celtic times, also adorned themselves with fine ornaments and jewellery.

A HOLY THORN?
In the 1720s, Daniel Defoe (the author of *Robinson Crusoe*) visited Glastonbury, where he was told that "King Arthur was buried here", and informed that: "Joseph of Arimathea was here ... he fixed his staff in the ground ... on Christmas Day (January 6, by today's calendar), it ... budded ... and the next day was in full blossom ... and blows (blooms) every Christmas Day ... to this very day."

This staff is identified with a thorn tree in Glastonbury. However this is less of a miracle than it might seem – it is a whitehorn sub-species that is naturally winter-flowering .

Glastonbury Tree Off-shoot
A cutting from the Glastonbury Tree was planted at Brudnell House, England (right). Like the original staff, it flowered every January.

A curious interpretation of the myths of the Holy Grail became widely current in the twenties and thirties and still has its devotees today, some of them practising occultists. It seems to have originally derived from the obsessional concern with fertility cults of nineteenth-century anthropologists. It concerns a theory that both the Grail and the Lance with which it is associated in orthodox Christian legends, were originally the cauldron and spear of an ancient pagan Celtic cult. They supposedly symbolized the male and female sexual organs on a cosmic level, the spear being ritually plunged into the cauldron in order to confer fertility upon the land and upon those who dwelt on it.

↪ CERIDWEN'S CAULDRON ↩
There is no doubt that cauldrons featured in a number of Celtic legends, notably one concerning the Welsh bard, Taliesin; what does seem doubtful is whether these cauldrons had any connection with a fertility cult and whether one of them was the original Grail.

According to *Hanes Taliesin*, the "Story of Taliesin", a Welsh poem of which the earliest known version dates from the sixteenth century but that ultimately derives from much older sources, the bard Taliesin was originally a boy named Little Gwion who accidentally drank three drops of a potion that magically conferred universal knowledge upon him.

This magical brew had been prepared in a giant cauldron by a witch named Ceridwen. It is possible that Ceridwen was originally a goddess rather than a witch, and that her cauldron symbolized the feminine archetype: form as the

Mysterious Merlin
Perhaps the most puzzling of the characters in the legends of Arthur is Merlin the Magician (below), adviser to King Arthur. Born of the union of a demon and human, he was considered a force for good, despite the ambiguous nature he received from his parents.

complement of sexuality, fertility, and so on. But what significance other than sexual could her cauldron have had? Perhaps it represented, for example, that state of union with the divine that is said to be symbolized by the achievement of the vision of the Grail?

↪ STRANGE THEORY ↩
A number of practising occultists have made two interesting claims about Ceridwen's cauldron in conversation with me.

First, that "cauldron" was, and is, a code word indicating a physical reality – a place of initiation into a mystery cult in which the candidate is slain and reborn. In this context "slain and reborn" would seem to mean the breaking down of an individual psyche into its component parts and their restructuring so that they operate as one harmonious totality. In other words, something very similar to that interior process that Jungian depth analysts term "individuation".

Second, that the phrases "Holy Grail" and "Cauldron of Ceridwen" have always been synonymous – in one sense an object, in another sense "the womb of the great goddess" and the sexual organs of the women who worship her.

This second claim is astonishing because of its implication that a Celtic mystery cult concerned with fertility spread throughout western Europe under the guise of the quest for the Holy Grail. Furthermore the cult used the supposedly Christian symbolism of the Grail as literary propaganda, without the church ever suspecting its existence. The twentieth-century guardians of this Celtic mystery cult claim there is an ancient initiatory tradition that uses as key

Legendary Hero
This 16th-century bronze statue (left), found on the tomb of the Holy Roman Emperor, Maximilian I, shows how Arthurian legends became known throughout Europe. It is quite possible that Maximilian identified with Arthur, as the legendary king was said to have defeated the Romans, and to have been crowned Emperor.

symbols a cauldron and a spear, which are said to be the Cup and Lance of the Grail romances. Writing some 70 years ago about this tradition, the Scottish poet and occultist, Lewis Spence, remarked that its devotees try:

"to buttress the theory that the church has existed since the foundation of the world ... we are not informed as to whether it possessed hierophants in Neolithic times. This mischievous ... and absurd theory ... would identify Christianity with the grossest forms of paganism...."

→ PALESTINIAN ROOTS ←

Spence's characterization of the theory was presented in strong terms, but perhaps not too strong. Among those I have met who adhere to the theory he condemns, there have been some I regard as authentic mystics. In spite of his scepticism about claims regarding the antiquity of some supposedly Celtic traditions, Spence thought that there was "good reason to believe" an equally odd theory, namely, that the Grail tradition was originally brought into Europe from Palestine by the Knights Templar (p.84) who wove the tradition into the Celtic tales of cups and cauldrons.

It is difficult to accept that this was the case. There is not the slightest historical evidence that the Templars displayed an interest in the cycles of Grail romance; the Cistercian order was the only medieval monastic order that can be said to have even distant links with the Grail.

→ PATH WORKING ←

Those modern esoteric groups that interpret the Grail romances as an allegorical expression of humanity's spiritual quest (p.69) use a type of meditative exercise known as "Path Working" to make themselves, in a sense, part of that allegory. Path Working takes its name from a method used by western mystics to explore physically the states of spiritual consciousness symbolized by the paths on the Tree of Life. This process involves visualization, in the mind's eye, of the landscapes and symbols associated with the path being explored, and leads ultimately, it is said, to astral projection (p.247) to the realm of which the path is symbolic.

When the experimenter applies this process to the Arthurian or Grail mythos, it is said that he or she acquires a thorough knowledge of the Grail castle as it is described in the legend. He or she visualizes the castle, explores it in imagination, and perhaps makes an astral journey to it, hoping eventually to have a vision of the Grail itself.

THE ANGELS' LANGUAGE

"O thou third flame, whose wings are thorns to stir up vexation ... gird up the loins of thee and harken. Move and show yourselves"

THE ABOVE QUOTATION is a translation of the first sentence of the "Seventeenth Call", given to man by the angels in

Angel Talk
The language of angels was received through visions in a crystal ball, (below) and was coherent enough to be published.

their own language – "Enochian". In Genesis Chapter 5, Verse 24, it is said that the patriarch Enoch "walked with God: and he was not; for God took him". This has generally been understood to mean that Enoch, like the prophet Elijah and the Virgin Mary, did not suffer physical death but was carried bodily into heaven. Since then he has spent eternity talking with angels in their own tongue, which has since been termed Enochian.

→ A STRANGE FRIENDSHIP ←

The Enochian language was first revealed by angels to humans in the sixteenth century, it is said, as a consequence of the occult experiments of John Dee and Edward Kelley. The two men first encountered one another in 1582 when Kelley called upon Dee and asked to see a magic crystal reported to be in his possession. For seven years or so the two men were to spend much of their time in each other's company. Dee was a scholar with an international reputation. He was employed by Queen Elizabeth I of England as Astrologer

Royal and, some say, as a spy. Dee was deeply interested in magic. Kelley, on the other hand, was a very dubious character. His ears had been cropped for forging a deed, and he was suspected of having practised the black arts. Yet Dee took to Kelley who, unlike him, could read the crystal ball. Either Kelley *was* a natural psychic, or he was a con man of genius. As soon as he first looked into the crystal he reported angelic visions so spectacular that Dee employed him as a full time scryer or crystal gazer.

→ ANGELIC COMMANDS ←

For the next few years the two occupied themselves largely with the reception of supposedly angelic communications. Kelley did the scrying; Dee confined himself to recording the teachings received through Kelley and obeying the sometimes confusing instructions of the angels. The two men parted company not long after Kelley reported that the angels had commanded that they share everything between them, including their wives. Dee's wife, Jane, was none too pleased, and "fell aweeping and trembling for full quarter of an hour, then burst forth into a fury of anger".

The core of the material that Dee and Kelley received consisted of five lettered squares, the details of which were supposedly supplied by the angels. These are known as the tablets of Earth, Air, Fire, Water, and Spirit. Just as important were the 19 Enochian "calls" that they used to invoke the angels at the start of each scrying session. In Enochian, the first phrase of the Seventeenth Call (see opposite) reads as: "Ils d ialprt, soba upaah chis nanba zixlay dodsih".

→ LABOUR OF LOVE ←

The strange thing was that the two Elizabethan occultists made little or no use of the supposedly angelic learning that they had been given – neither man made any attempt to apply it practically. Indeed, Dee was offered, and turned down, an enormous salary to work for the Czar of Russia, so it seems financial gain was not at the forefront of his thoughts. It has been suggested that Dee used his interest in the occult as a cover for his espionage activities, and that the

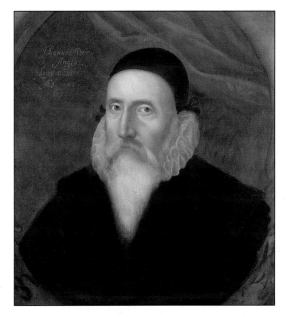

John Dee
As well as being a practitioner of angelic magic and astrologer to Queen Elizabeth I, Dee (right) is considered by scholars to be a key figure in the intellectual history of 16th-century Europe.

The Monad
A 17th-century Jesuit named Kirchar designed this version (above) of Dee's magic symbol.

Angelic Medium
Kelley (below) received the angels' language through visions.

Enochian language was an elaborate code developed by Dee or Kelley and used to pass on messages. However, there is no doubt that Dee's interest in magic was genuine, nor is there any doubt that Enochian is a translatable language, with its own alphabet and grammar.

→ ENOCHIAN MAGIC ←

Three centuries later, several British occultists, most of whom thought that they were in contact with the "Masters" – highly evolved spiritual beings – claimed that they understood the mysteries of what is often called Enochian Magic.

The first serious student of Enochian Magic since the time of Dee and Kelley was K.R.H. Mackenzie who lived in the mid-nineteenth century and claimed to be an initiated Rosicrucian (p.100). How far Mackenzie got with his studies is uncertain – but if, as has been suggested, he was the compiler of certain skeletal rituals that appeared in the 1880s, then he had apparently tried to correlate Dee's revelations with aspects of kabalism (p.104).

Contemporary admirers of Mackenzie included the occultist, Wynn Westcott, and the magician, S.L. MacGregor Mathers, who worked in co-operation to construct an elaborate system in which each of the hundreds of lettered squares that made up the tablets could be reconstructed as a pyramid. It was possible, taught the two occultists, to use astral projection techniques (p.247) to experience the mode of consciousness associated with any particular pyramid. Most of Mathers' and Westcott's instructions concerning Enochian Magic are now available in printed form (pp.248-249); they exert a strong influence on some active occult groups.

THE GOLDEN DAWN

"The mystical life is the centre of all that I do and all that I think and all that I write"
W.B.Yeats

THERE EXIST DOZENS, perhaps hundreds, of modern occult societies that derive their teachings, and the ritual techniques employed by their initiates, from the Hermetic Order of the Golden Dawn – a secret society devoted to the study and practice of ritual magic and other obscure arts. The members of the Order, in the

Constance Wilde
Oscar Wilde's wife (right) was one of the more surprising devotees of the occult wisdom of the Golden Dawn.

W.B. Yeats
The poet (below), joined the order in 1890. His interest in the occult influenced his poetry.

years between the establishment of its London "temple" in 1888 and a series of disagreements that split it apart in 1900, included some remarkable people. Amongst them were the poet W. B. Yeats, Constance Wilde, Oscar's long-suffering wife, and, the most infamous of all occultists, Aleister Crowley, many years later to be denounced in the popular press as a satanist, "the wickedest man in the world".

➜ THE SECRET CHIEFS ←

Perhaps the most remarkable of all the members of the Golden Dawn, however, was S.L. MacGregor Mathers. For it was he who was largely responsible for creating the order's magical system. He had acquired much of his esoteric knowledge from printed and manuscript material – but the most important sources of his occult learning were the teachings he claimed to have received from superhuman immortals to whom he referred as the "Secret Chiefs" or the "Masters".

There is no doubt that Mathers believed in the existence of these benevolent beings; he and his wife were convinced that they were in regular contact with them. Whether the Secret Chiefs existed or not is comparatively irrelevant, for whatever Mathers' teachers may have been, they imparted to him a system of spiritual training that remains clear, coherent, and, so it would seem, capable of effecting what can be termed "psychic liberation".

No modern occultist has believed more profoundly in the reality of the Masters than Violet Firth, who wrote under the name of Dion Fortune – an abbreviation of the Firth family motto, "Deo non Fortuna".

⇀ DION FORTUNE ↽

It has been said that all outstanding occultists are born "with the soul of a natural magician", and this was certainly true of Dion Fortune, who developed psychic abilities at a very early age. By the time she was in her mid twenties she had become the pupil of a masonic occultist named somewhat improbably Theodore Moriarty. In some

ways Moriarty was a fraud. For example, he claimed to have a doctorate from the University of Heidelberg – but research carried out by Alan Richardson, author of an excellent biography of Dion Fortune, has shown that he was not in fact possessed of this distinction. Nevertheless, his pupils admired him intensely, and he exerted a lasting influence upon Dion Fortune, who wrote of him: "He was an adept if ever there was one."

In 1919, Moriarty's system was supplemented by that which had been synthesized by Mathers – Dion was initiated into the "Rosicrucian Order of the Alpha et Omega". This was an offshoot of the Golden Dawn headed by Mathers' autocratic widow, Moina – a sister of the French philosopher, Henri Bergson.

Dion cared neither for Mrs Mathers, nor for those Alpha et Omega initiates to whom she referred as "grey bearded ancients". Her dislike

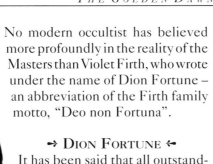

was reciprocated and Moina Mathers had her expelled from the Order and, so Fortune alleged, attempted by psychic intervention to cut her off from the contacts she had already made with the Masters.

⇀ THE INNER LIGHT ↽

The attempt was unsuccessful, and for the rest of her life Dion remained, so she believed, in contact with these advanced beings, receiving much occult teaching from them and, under their inspiration, founding her own esoteric society and writing novels in which white-magical theory was conveyed under the guise of fiction. The society she founded, the "Fraternity of the Inner Light", still flourishes today. All of her occult novels remain in print and are read by all serious students of the occult.

Magic Symbols
The censer and altar piece, above, are based on ancient Egyptian symbols, and are used in the rites of those modern societies that are influenced by the Golden Dawn.

BANNERS & WANDS

THE ITEMS SHOWN HERE were derived from "The Order of the Red Rose and the Golden Cross" *(Ordo Roseae Rubeae et Aureae Crucis)*, which influenced the teachings of such modern esoteric groups as the Golden Dawn.

Fire & Air
These badges (left) are called "lamens". They are the ritual insignia worn by the ruling officers of the O.R.R. et A.C. The colours signify the elements of fire (red/green), water (blue/orange), and air (yellow/purple).

The Banner of the West
The red cross on the above banner symbolizes the "Hidden Knowledge of the Divine Nature". The triangle signifies three of the spheres of the kabalistic Tree of Life (p.106). The red cross and white triangle are sometimes used in initiation ceremonies to symbolize spiritual cleansing.

The Banner of the East
This banner (left) is a basic feature of the temples of the Golden Dawn and the modern-day societies that are derived from it. Upon it are displayed the red and blue triangles that symbolize, respectively, the elements of fire and water.

Authority Symbol
The officer who bears the sceptre (below) is the "Cancellarius". The hexagram signifies the authority of the O.R.R. et A.C. over subsidiary esoteric orders.

Maltese Cross
The sceptre below is held by the "Praemonstrator", an officer in numerous esoteric groups.

Magic Wand
A lotus wand (left), such as was and is made and ritually consecrated by each initiate of the O.R.R. et A.C. for his or her own use in ritual magic. Men and women as diverse as W.B. Yeats, Aleister Crowley, and Constance Wilde, the wife of Oscar Wilde, would all have used a lotus wand. The 12 coloured bands symbolize the signs of the zodiac.

Officer's Badge
These lamens (right) are worn by officers of many contemporary esoteric groups. The designs are of symbolic significance. For example, the lamen of the Dadouchos depicts a right-handed swastika that is composed of 17 squares, representing the Sun, the four elements, and the 12 signs of the zodiac.

Ritual Dagger
The dagger is used in the rituals of many esoteric societies to symbolize the "air" element of the personality, as defined, for example, by the air signs of the zodiac. As with all of the items on these pages, this yellow-handled dagger (above) is derived from the Ordo Roseae Rubeae et Aureae Crucis (O.R.R. et A.C.). The order – established in Europe by 1891, and in the USA by 1900 – was originally led by S.L. MacGregor Mathers.

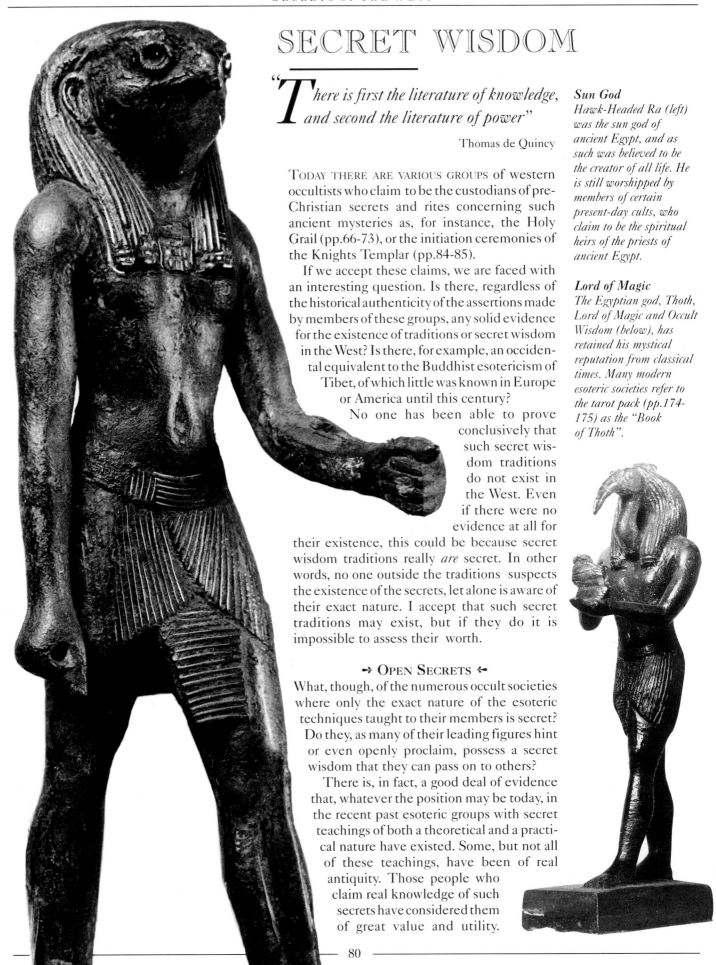

SECRET WISDOM

"*There is first the literature of knowledge, and second the literature of power*"

Thomas de Quincy

TODAY THERE ARE VARIOUS GROUPS of western occultists who claim to be the custodians of pre-Christian secrets and rites concerning such ancient mysteries as, for instance, the Holy Grail (pp.66-73), or the initiation ceremonies of the Knights Templar (pp.84-85).

If we accept these claims, we are faced with an interesting question. Is there, regardless of the historical authenticity of the assertions made by members of these groups, any solid evidence for the existence of traditions or secret wisdom in the West? Is there, for example, an occidental equivalent to the Buddhist esotericism of Tibet, of which little was known in Europe or America until this century?

No one has been able to prove conclusively that such secret wisdom traditions do not exist in the West. Even if there were no evidence at all for their existence, this could be because secret wisdom traditions really *are* secret. In other words, no one outside the traditions suspects the existence of the secrets, let alone is aware of their exact nature. I accept that such secret traditions may exist, but if they do it is impossible to assess their worth.

→ OPEN SECRETS ←

What, though, of the numerous occult societies where only the exact nature of the esoteric techniques taught to their members is secret? Do they, as many of their leading figures hint or even openly proclaim, possess a secret wisdom that they can pass on to others?

There is, in fact, a good deal of evidence that, whatever the position may be today, in the recent past esoteric groups with secret teachings of both a theoretical and a practical nature have existed. Some, but not all of these teachings, have been of real antiquity. Those people who claim real knowledge of such secrets have considered them of great value and utility.

Sun God
Hawk-Headed Ra (left) was the sun god of ancient Egypt, and as such was believed to be the creator of all life. He is still worshipped by members of certain present-day cults, who claim to be the spiritual heirs of the priests of ancient Egypt.

Lord of Magic
The Egyptian god, Thoth, Lord of Magic and Occult Wisdom (below), has retained his mystical reputation from classical times. Many modern esoteric societies refer to the tarot pack (pp.174-175) as the "Book of Thoth".

However, in the course of time, the secrets have almost invariably been leaked. What was once a secret has become public knowledge – at first just a few outsiders know the secret, eventually it finds its way into print, and wide circulation.

→ SECRET CORRESPONDENCES ←

Take, for example, an elaborate series of "secret correspondences" (p.91) that was used by the occultist, MacGregor Mathers (p.75), in the 1890s to construct rituals believed by many to have been of an extremely effective nature. At first, these correspondences remained genuinely secret, being conveyed only to trusted pupils and associates. By 1900, however, occultists at odds with Mathers not only knew of these rituals but were employing them in practical work; and in 1909 the correspondences were published in their entirety in a limited edition of 500 copies. From obscurity they made their way into

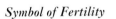

Symbol of Fertility
Diana, the moon goddess of classical antiquity (right), is shown here in her role as the many-breasted goddess of fertility. One of Diana's principal places of worship was Ephesus, where St. Paul was stoned by her devotees. Diana's association with the moon led some pagan cults to worship her as goddess of the occult, and some modern-day groups follow this tradition.

more easily available sources, and can be found today in mass-market paperbacks. Currently there are several esoteric societies in which details of Mathers' system are solemnly conveyed to initiates under curious oaths of secrecy. This is not a new practice; some 70 years ago, the infamous occultist, Aleister Crowley complained that his teachers had bound him with dreadful oaths, and then "confided the Hebrew alphabet to his safe keeping".

→ TRUE OR FALSE? ←

What should be the attitude of students of western occultism to those who claim, explicitly or implicitly, that they have access to secret teachings? Probably the wisest course to take is a cautious one of qualified scepticism: judge by the results. If a group teaches techniques that are effective in expanding the consciousness, it does not greatly matter to anyone, save the occult historian, exactly whence they came. The leaders of such a group may wrongly assert that their teachings are derived from the Knights Templar, for example, or from any other ancient religious or secret order, but if the teachings are of value to the student, then the source and the date of those teachings are of little importance.

THE MAYPOLE

Since ancient times, in both the East and West, the tree has been considered sacred or magical and, in particular, a symbol of fertility. The modern maypole dance, traditionally performed on the first day of May each year – a day associated with rebirth and renewal – was derived from ancient fertility rituals. Traditional May Day celebrations involved people collecting greenery and flowers to decorate their homes – a ritual believed to bring fertility to the community. The celebrations originally centred around a hawthorn tree, but as the tradition developed, a tall pole garlanded with flowers replaced it.

May Day Celebrations
In England, May Day celebrations (right) were a part of village life up to the end of the 18th century.

THE CATHAR TREASURE

"From all false doctrine, heresy and schism, Good Lord deliver us"

The Book of Common Prayer

THE CATHARS WERE the custodians of a secret-wisdom religion bearing a strong resemblance to modern western occultism, or so some believe. This belief has never been confined to occultists. The eminent academic historian, Sir Steven Runciman, for example, suggested that the emblematic designs of the tarot trumps (p.168) were intended to symbolize Cathar teachings – it has been suggested, for example, the tarot trump numbered XVI (pp.174-175) might have conveyed a Cathar message that the Roman Church was destined for destruction.

↦ MATTER AND SPIRIT ↤

Catharism and other medieval heresies of a similar nature, such as the Bogomilism that flourished amongst the Slav peoples who lived on the borders of the Byzantine Empire, were characterized by theological dualism. That is to say, by a belief that the universe is a battlefield on which opposites – Light and Darkness, Good and Evil, Matter and Spirit, and so on – contend for mastery. The Cathars, needless to say, saw themselves as soldiers of the Army of Light.

As far as the Cathars were concerned, there were two gods, not one or even three-in-one. One god, essentially evil in nature, ruled the world of matter; he was, they believed, to be identified with the God worshipped by orthodox Christians. The other, pure goodness, was also pure spirit and the god of the Cathars. The duty of men and women, taught the Perfecti (the full initiates of the faith), was to regulate their lives in such a way that they freed the spirit particles that were trapped within their physical bodies from the bondage of matter.

↦ VEGETARIAN CELIBATES ↤

To achieve this they believed it was essential to abstain from any sexual activity that might result in the birth of a child, and to follow a largely vegetarian diet. The process of procreation was thought to trap more spirit particles in the world of matter – to become a parent was to do the work of the Evil God. So was the eating of flesh, the product of animal sexual coupling, for the spirit particles contained within that flesh would become incorporated into the evil material body of the man or woman who ate it. Strangely enough, Cathar initiates were allowed to eat fish; Cathars believed that fish procreated without any sexual activity.

↦ THE BLOODY CRUSADES ↤

However virtuous individual Cathars may have been in their personal lives, it is apparent that by the standards of most people, past and present, their religion was profoundly anti-social; if everyone had followed its precepts, the human race would have died out – which was exactly what the Cathar leadership most desired. It is therefore virtually certain that the Church would have endeavoured to stamp out Catharism, even

Cathar Stronghold
Montségur Castle (right) has been identified as the centre of the spiritual battle between Light and Darkness that lies at the heart of the Grail legend. The castle was the last stronghold of the Cathar "Perfecti" – the initiates of the faith – from which, according to legend, they removed their spiritual treasure. The treasure, it is alleged, still survives to this very day.

Dawn Goddess
Aurora (below) is portrayed with her "horses of light". In western iconography these are contrasted with the "horses of darkness". The Cathars saw all existence as a conflict between Light and the Good God, and Darkness and the God of this World – sometimes known as the Monster of Chaos. Both powers were always active in the universe – the Good God was not all-powerful.

Church believed. But what was the treasure that was removed from Montségur, prior to the surrender of the Cathar fortress? And what were the contents of the mysterious books that accompanied that treasure?

There are those who say that the treasure was none other than the Holy Grail, that the books contained the secrets of western occultism, and that in a sense the Cathars are still amongst us – the initiates of certain present-day secret societies.

↝ THE CATHARS TODAY ↜

A remarkable book, *The Cathars and Reincarnation*, published in 1971, claims that the souls of Cathar heretics walk the earth today, reincarnated in the bodies of the men and women around us. Furthermore, destiny has ensured that the spirits of these heretics, burned at the stake or put to the sword in thirteenth-century France, have been able to meet up with each other again some 700 years after their last encounter. The author of the book, the late Dr. Arthur Guirdham, a medical practitioner with an interest in all matters psychic, produces some curious and convincing evidence to support his case that the bodies of several of his friends and patients housed the reincarnated souls of medieval heretics. Whether or not Dr. Guirdham's claims are true, his book has certainly strengthened the beliefs of those occultists who regard the Cathars as custodians of a secret-wisdom religion.

Cruel Crusade
The crusade against the wealthy Cathars was commercial in motive, and was marked by cruelty. Here (below) Cathar prisoners are abused by women and children as they lie in bondage after a battle.

if the Cathars had not been so virulent in their hatred of Rome. As it was, in 1208, the Church launched the first of a series of increasingly bloody crusades against the Cathar heartland, the territories ruled by the counts of Toulouse.

↝ THE LAST FORTRESS ↜

By 1244, the last Cathar stronghold, the great fortress of Montségur, was surrounded in such strength that further resistance was hopeless. Four Cathar intitiates left Montségur and slipped through the besieging forces by night. With them they took books and a mysterious object or objects referred to as "the Cathar treasure". The rest of the initiates, perhaps 200 in number, surrendered on the following morning; they were burned without trial. Within a century Catharism was totally dead – or so the

THE KNIGHTS TEMPLAR

*"I wont there lies a new-slain knight
And naebody knes that he lies there
But his hawk ..."*

Medieval Ballad

IN EUROPE AND THE AMERICAS a number of esoteric societies exist today that claim direct descent from the medieval Knights Templar, and assert that they are the custodians of a secret science of which the Knights Templar were the first masters.

The original Order of Knights Templar was founded in the twelfth century. Its members were soldier-monks, sworn to religious duties: first, to protect pilgrims to Jerusalem and other places associated with the life of Jesus; second, to defend the Christian kingdoms of the Holy Land from their Muslim foe. They were not particularly good at carrying out either of these tasks, and had largely turned from fighting to commerce long before 1291 – the year that saw the fall of the last fortress erected by these descendants of the first crusaders.

Trade, together with a practice among the pious of leaving legacies to the order, made the Templars rich: owners of huge estates and fleets of ships. Their wealth, and attendant pride, aroused the criticism of many of the rulers of western Europe, and the avarice of some, most notably that of Philip IV of France – the country in which the Templars had their headquarters and in which dwelt their Grand Master.

In October 1307, Philip ordered the simultaneous arrest of all Templars on French soil and the seizure of their property. There was reason to believe, said the king, that the order had become profoundly heretical; that its military monks were, in fact, black magicians.

↠ THE TALKING HEADS ↞

With the approval of Pope Clement V, a former Archbishop of Bordeaux who was under Philip's influence, a series of trials commenced. At these trials many of the accused Templars admitted, usually after torture, to witnessing or participating in both secular and ecclesiastical crimes. Such crimes included sodomy, trampling upon the crucifix, and worshipping some sort of mummified and fiercely bearded three-headed creature. The creature, swore some of the accused, was named Baphomet, was capable of speech, and taught strange and unnatural doctrines to those who listened to it.

The accused knights were all found guilty and, five years after the first arrests, the order was dissolved by papal decree. Some two years later the Grand Master of the Knights Templar was roasted to death over a slow fire.

↠ A DEGREE OF GUILT ↞

Whether the Templars were guilty of any of the crimes of which they were charged has always been an open question. The tendency amongst living historians has been to acquit them on all counts, but it is quite likely that at least a minority of Templars were guilty of some of the crimes of which they were accused. Some, for example, may well

Baphomet
The Knights Templar were accused of worshipping the three-headed deity, Baphomet (above), believing it to be a source of fertility.

Knight Templar
A traditional depiction of a Knight Templar (left), with the characteristic cloak and standard, bearing the insignia of the order – the Cross Patée.

have been practising homosexuals. Others could have acquired unorthodox religious beliefs through their trading contacts with the East; a good many of the knights must have at some time encountered adherents of dualistic cults like Catharism (p.82), and it is possible that the activities of one such cult involved the worship of a deity named Baphomet. Even so, the crime hardly merited the punishment.

Conspicuous Wealth
The wealth of the Templars was made apparent by the grandeur of their buildings, such as their church at Lutz (above). It was this wealth that excited the avarice of King Philip the Fair of France, and led to the eventual persecution of the Templars and the confiscation of most of their property.

Clement V
It was Pope Clement V (left) who, under the domination of the King of France, launched first an enquiry into the Knights Templar, and then a relentless and very cruel persecution against them. The Templars had hitherto been regarded as utterly loyal and orthodox servants of the Pope. The order was dissolved.

But was there such a god, and, if so, what were the doctrines of those who adored him? Since the eighteenth century, a number of answers have been offered to these questions – none of them very convincing. It has been said that "Baphomet" is merely a corrupt version of Mahomet – in other words, that some Templars were converts to Islam. Others have argued that the name is a Latin derivation of a Greek phrase meaning "baptism of wisdom" and that the Templars were Gnostic initiates.

➜ ROSICRUCIANS OR TANTRICS? ⬅

Amongst the members of some contemporary occult groups such assertions are still a matter for debate. Initiates of some groups claim that the Templars were the custodians of secret esoteric teachings, later associated with Rosicrucianism and esoteric masonry (pp.100-102). Members of other groups contend that the order had a particular and highly unorthodox way of interpreting St. John's Gospel. Still others affirm that the societies to which they belong were founded by Templars who escaped execution and taught and practised a magic concerned with polarity, a magic essentially similar to the tantrism of India (p.200).

THE ART OF ALCHEMY

"*Visit the interior of the earth and by purifying you will find the secret*"

The Kabalah

TOWARDS THE END of his life the psychotherapist and occultist, Israel Regardie (1907–1985), suffered some damage to his lungs in a laboratory explosion; but this laboratory was no ordinary one. For while it contained flasks, beakers, crucibles, and other equipment associated with modern chemistry, it was, in a sense, a mystical laboratory – a workshop devoted to the manipulation of those subtle forces that are held by some to underlie the worlds of matter and energy that concern modern science.

Regardie's laboratory was devoted to the study of alchemical workings – to the quest for the mysterious "Medicine of Metals" or the "Philosopher's Stone" that ancient and modern alchemists believe produces simultaneous physical and spiritual changes, termed "transmutations".

On a physical level, Israel Regardie and some other twentieth-century alchemists claimed that the mysterious medicine is capable of changing lead and any other base metal into gold and silver. On an interior psychic level, they maintain that it produces more important, although less spectacular, change – a spiritual change.

→ PSYCHIC GOLD ←

The successful completion of the laboratory processes that are involved in the manufacture of the Stone are said to start a mystic transmutation within the soul of the alchemist – the lead of everyday existence is changed into the psychic gold of authentic spirituality. Despite all his strenuous efforts, Israel Regardie was eventually forced to admit that he never accomplished a complete transmutation on either a physical or a spiritual level. However, claims of alchemical successes have been made in both the present and past by many alchemists. One person made the astounding claim: "Finally I found that which I desired, which I also soon knew by the strong scent and by the odour thereof. Having this I

Chemistry Kit
Alchemy is a much more complex branch of the magical arts than you might imagine. It is not just the search for a means of turning base metal into gold; it can involve the quest for the elixir of life, the fountain of eternal youth. The supreme goal was the Philosopher's Stone, which changed all materials to gold, and was also the elixir of life. The equipment shown here (below) is typical of that used by twentieth-century alchemists, with a large distillation jar, sand-timer, test tubes, and a mortar and pestle.

soon accomplished all of the mastery, for knowing the preparation of the first agents, and following my book to the letter, I could not have missed it. Then the first time that I made projection was upon quicksilver whereon I turned half a pound ... into pure silver. This was upon a Monday, 17th January, about noon ... the year of the restoring of mankind 1382."

facts cast considerable doubt on its authenticity. It is odd that the account specifically asserts that the date on which the first transmutation was made – January 17, 1382 – was a Monday, for it was not. Odder still, no manuscript copies of the account can be found dating from any year in the centuries that elapsed between its supposed date of composition and its first printing – during these two centuries European alchemy flourished and detailed manuscripts were widely circulated.

The account of a successful quest for alchemical knowledge from which the above quotation is taken was first printed in 1612, and was purportedly written by Nicholas Flamel (1330–1417), a wealthy Parisian "scrivener" – a preparer of legal documents. While Flamel was almost certainly a student of alchemical method, he may not have been the real author of the autobiographical account published in 1612. Several

It seems very likely that the so-called "alchemical autobiography" that has been attributed to Nicholas Flamel (pp.86-87) was an ingenious forgery manufactured on behalf of an enterprising French printer. The reasons why such a forgery should have been fathered on Flamel rather than some other fifteenth-century Parisian are apparent. The main one being that Flamel died a very rich man, and had made public his obsession with alchemy.

His interest in alchemy was proclaimed to the world in emblematic figures he had commissioned to be painted on an archway that he had donated to the great Parisian graveyard of the Holy Innocents. It was this public homage to alchemy, combined with his immense wealth, that convinced many people that he had been successful in his pursuit of the Philosopher's Stone – that elusive "medicine" that could turn base metal into gold (p.86).

→ ALCHEMICAL INSPIRATION ←

From the point of view of the occultist, as distinct from that of the historian, it does not greatly matter whether or not Flamel was the real author of the work attributed to him. The important thing is that for almost 400 years Flamel's supposed alchemical success has inspired many would-be imitators. The late Archibald Cockren, who died a few years after World War II ended, was one of the most remarkable of those twentieth-

Tree of Symbols
This depiction of the alchemical tree (right) – also known as the Philosopher's Tree and the Golden Herb – shows the magic fruits, including the golden and silver apples of the Sun and Moon. The seven symbolic designs encircling the tree represent the successive stages of the alchemical process. They are: calcination; solution; separation; conjunction; putrefaction; congelation; and finally, the making of the Philosopher's Stone.

Country Lore
From circa 1500–1800, it was commonplace for rural dwellers to compile books of country lore, such as the one below. Such books were filled with details of, for example, instructions for how to make remedies against the plague, and other lesser ills. The original formulae for most of the remedies in these books were derived from alchemical sources, although most of them were easy for the ordinary person to make.

century alchemists who have been inspired by such accounts of transmutation. Cockren was a London-based practitioner of complementary medicine who engaged in the manufacture of such alchemical remedies as "drinkable gold". He was reported to have succeeded in growing in his laboratory the "alchymical tree", also known as the "golden herb" – a curious creation that was reputed to combine the attributes of mineral and vegetable.

→ THE MYSTIC TREE ←

A mid-seventeenth-century translation of one of the treatises attributed to the sixteenth-century alchemical physician, Paracelsus, describes the mystic tree as follows:

"It is possible also that Gold ... may be so far exalted, that it may grow in a Glasse like a tree with many wonderful boughs, and leaves ... and so there is made of Gold a wonderful and pleasant shrub, which the Alchymists call their Golden hearb and the Philosopher's Tree ...."

The late C. R. Cammell, a poet with an interest in many obscure occult subjects, such as Enochian Magic (p.75) and the Golden Dawn's initiation ceremonies (p.76), was one of those who saw Cockren's mineral tree and observed it at various stages of its growth. Eventually, according to Cammell, it came to resemble a cactus cast in gold.

Cammell experimented with at least one of Cockren's alchemical medicines – a liquid that, while smelling and tasting of sweet flowers, was termed "potable elixir of gold". Taken in wine, reported Mr. Cammell, the elixir was most effective in countering mental and physical exhaustion; after taking a dose he claimed to need less food and sleep than usual and to feel "healthful and invigorated".

→ ALCHOHOLIC ELIXIR ←

It was significant that Cockren's elixir was taken in wine, for another of his alchemical potions was a "Philosophers' Wine" (the word "philosopher" in this context, and in the context of the "Philosopher's Stone" and the "Philosopher's Tree", is a synonym for alchemist) and many present-day alchemical elixirs consist largely of alcohol that has been imbued, so it is believed, with the subtle energy of a mineral or herbal substance.

The precise methods used by dedicated alchemists, both past and present, to manufacture vegetable and mineral elixirs tend to be complicated and expensive, making them unsuitable for amateur experimentation. The following process, however, is simple and inexpensive; and results in an elixir that, if alchemical theory of a particular type is to be believed, is saturated with the vital energies that, in traditional astrological belief (p.180), are often associated with the sun.

→ THE RECIPE ←

The ingredients from which the Solar Elixir are prepared are:

1 oz (25g) of coffee beans, preferably unroasted.

1 oz (25g) of sunflower seeds.

A handful of fresh vine leaves.

A bottle of strong, sweet red wine or a half bottle of brandy.

On any day between 22 March and 22 June, place all the ingredients in a transparent glass container. Tightly seal the container and place it in a position where it will be exposed to maximum possible sunlight at around noon and leave it in that position until 22 July. These dates apply if you live in the northern hemisphere – if your home is south of the equator, you should begin the process exactly six months later.

Secrets of the Solar Elixir
Vine leaves, coffee beans, sunflower seeds, and wine (below) are the ingredients of the Solar Elixir, which the reader can prepare by following the recipe on this page.

Alchemical Apparatus
In this engraving (below), a pair of alchemists are using an elaborate alchemical distillation apparatus of the type sometimes referred to as the "Serpent of Hermes".

On 22 July open the container and strain the contents. Carefully reserve the liquid for later use and thoroughly heat the solid matter in an old pan until it is reduced to ashes and a cindery residue – this will produce a great deal of smoke and a strong smell of burning, and should be done in the open air. Grind the ashes as finely as possible, add them to the reserved liquid and pour the mixture into a bottle. Seal the bottle and expose it to sunlight for six days, and then filter out the solids. The liquid that remains after filtering is the Solar Elixir.

If these instructions are followed carefully, the resulting elixir will be a perfectly harmless, oddly flavoured alcoholic drink; on a purely physical level it is no more than that – but it has supposed mystic properties. These, and the complex alchemical theories that dictated the way in which the elixir was made, are described in detail on page 91.

The ingredients of the Solar Elixir for which the recipe was given on the preceding page seem ordinary enough – and yet according to alchemical theory they are all subtly linked with metallic gold and, even more surprisingly, the sun and its energies.

An esoteric system of classification known as the "doctrine of correspondences", which links together seemingly dissimilar energies and material substances, is fundamental to both alchemy and the modern ritual magic with which it is often associated (pp.76-79). The doctrine of correspondences is one of the most difficult of occult theories for the modern student to understand, let alone to accept, for the way of

Alchemical Cosmos
An alchemical diagram (right) depicting the forces of nature in the innermost circle, and the influence of the stars – represented by the signs of the zodiac – in the outermost circle.

Transformation
This medieval illustration (below) is a symbolic depiction of the transformation of base matter into the so-called "Elixir of Life".

MVNDVS ELEMENTARIS 2

looking at reality that underlies the doctrine is at variance with assumptions that most people today take for granted – in other words, it is at odds with common sense.

⇥ A LITTLE COSMOS ⇤

Common sense would have it that each individual human being is a very tiny part of the universe. Alchemists and magicians who adhere to the doctrine of correspondences accept this, but argue that it is not the whole truth. Each human being, so they assert, is also a miniature universe in his or her own right. In the language of the alchemists of the Renaissance, a human being is a microcosm, a "little cosmos", which is a model of the macrocosm, "the great cosmos". It is not, of course, the physical body of a person that is primarily thought of as a microcosm, but the soul, of which the body is looked upon as being a particular manifestation. In the words of MacGregor Mathers (p.76) "the soul is a magical mirror of the universe".

⇥ THE INNER SUN ⇤

If MacGregor Mathers was right, it follows that every factor present in the macrocosm – the universe – is also present in the human soul. So, for example, the qualities of the sun around which our planet, Earth, revolves are also present in the psyche of every man and woman. These qualities should not be interpreted on a crudely physical level; no contemporary believer in the doctrine of correspondences would be likely to argue that in the centre of the human soul some sort of psychic hydrogen is fused into spiritual helium, in a similar fashion to the way in which fusion produces solar energy.

A modern alchemist would assert that the qualities that astrologers associate with the sun (p.180) manifest themselves in such various ways as atomic fusion and human vitality. Furthermore, so they would say, there are subtle links, not detectable by any of the methods of physical science preseently available, between every object that manifests such solar qualities. There are links, for example, between wine and coffee, both of which can be visualized as a physical glow of an essentially solar quality, and gold, which has been associated with the sun since classical times.

→ TABLES OF CORRESPONDENCES ←

Over the centuries, believers in the existence of subtle correspondences that link seemingly unrelated things have drawn up lists that endeavour to classify the proposed relationships. To the non-believer such "tables of correspondences" are bewildering, seeming almost arbitrary. It is difficult for the outsider to see, for example, the way in which the planet Mars, pentagons, tobacco, blood, and the Greek god, Aries, can be linked together as aspects of the same underlying reality. Nevertheless the correspondences are held by some to be real enough, however unlikely they may seem. It is interesting to note claims that experiments conducted by certain anthroposophical scientists (p.94) have provided some evidence, however debatable, of their objective existence.

All the ingredients in the recipe given on page 89 are held by most modern

Raw Material
Many alchemists shared the belief that by grinding and manipulating quartz (above), they would be able to produce the raw material of life – the Prime Matter.

Magic Fuel
Charcoal (top right) was the fuel that fired the alchemists' furnaces as they endeavoured to purify with heat what they regarded to be the "base minerals".

Hard Mineral
Malachite (above right), an intensely hard mineral, was used by alchemists to manufacture mortars and pestles. It was believed to have the property of clearing the mind of illusion.

Fool's Gold
Iron pyrite (left), known as Fool's Gold, is a compound of iron and sulphur. Many alchemists believed it could be transmuted into pure gold. Despite a lack of any real evidence, many actually believed they were successful.

alchemists and ritual magicians to correspond to the subtle energies of the sun. Their solar qualities are increased by exposure to sunlight, and the reduction of the solid components of the potion to ash is said to endow them with aspects of "elemental fire" that pertain to the sun. Although the ashes are filtered off, leaving only a few soluble salts in the liquid, the elixir has been endowed with a quality that some alchemists refer to as the "Sun-Fire process".

→ FIERY QUALITIES ←

The Solar Elixir, it is claimed, is a substance endowed with solar and fiery qualities that exist on a non-physical level and are therefore incapable of detection, even by chemical analysis. It is claimed that those who imbibe it in small quantities on a regular basis will be endowed with that psychic vitality that corresponds, in essence, to the golden power of solar energy. How much truth there is in these claims, I cannot say, other than that a substantial number of people claim to benefit from the effects of the elixir. The elixir's physical or spiritual merits can only be measured by its effects on its judge.

Students of alchemy can be found in almost every country of the world – but not all of these devotees of what has been called "occult chemistry" agree on the nature of the path that should be followed towards the desired end of transmuting base metals into gold.

Indeed, not all of them agree on what is indicated by the word "transmutation" in an alchemical context. Some modern schools of alchemy are concerned with the manipulation of physical substances, and the manufacture of elixirs that will prolong life and change the nature of metals; others look upon these goals as being of very little importance. These latter assert that the real laboratory in which serious alchemical experimentation is conducted is in the mind of the alchemist, and that the "lead" they aim to transmute into gold is the dross of everyday consciousness. This dull everyday lead is transformed into a "golden" consciousness, a new and "higher" awareness, which is capable of attaining to the world of spirit through modes of perception that are usually well beyond the reach of most human beings.

→ OLD IDEA ←
This interpretation of alchemy as an interior process is not a new one. It may well be implicit in some Renaissance alchemical texts; it was made explicit by the seventeenth-century German mystic, Jacob Boehme; and was proclaimed in the nineteenth century by the American writer, General E.A. Hitchcock.

It is, however, with the name of the psychoanalyst C.G. Jung (p.164) that the psychological interpretation of alchemy is today most closely associated. Jung seems to have become vaguely interested in alchemy at an early age, an interest that was heightened when he found that some of his patients who had never seen an alchemical text reported dreams incorporating obscure alchemical symbolism. These dreams might include such images as a dragon swallowing the

Important Visitor
The alchemist, Basil Valentine, receiving a visit from Cremer, the Abbot of Westminster (above, left).

Sun and Moon
These illustrations (left), showing the conjunction of the sun and moon, are taken from the book, Liber Mutus.

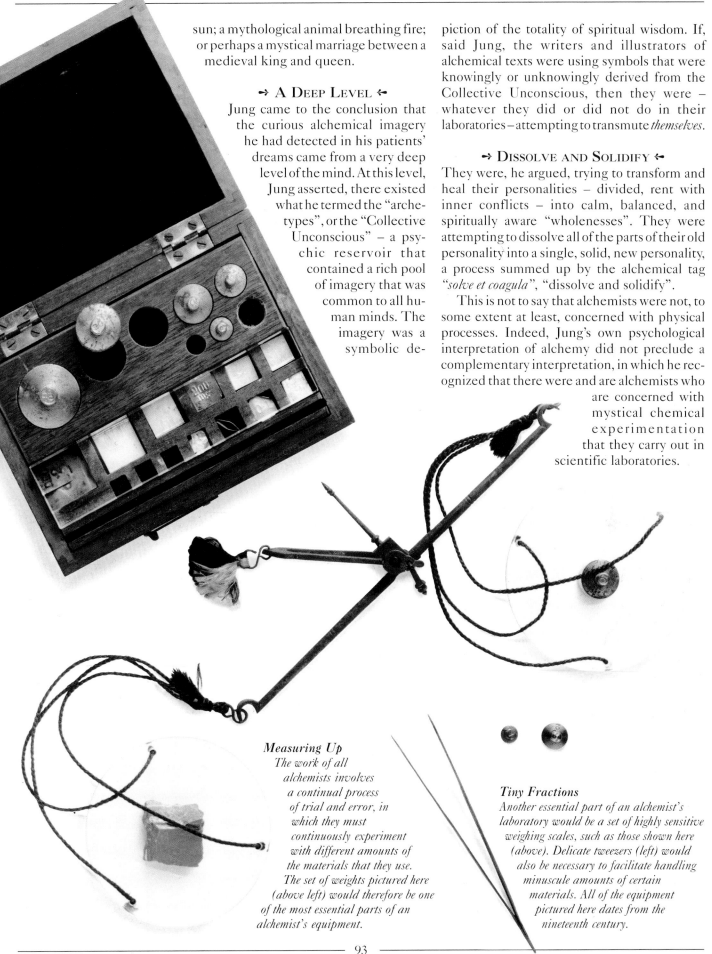

sun; a mythological animal breathing fire; or perhaps a mystical marriage between a medieval king and queen.

→ A DEEP LEVEL ←

Jung came to the conclusion that the curious alchemical imagery he had detected in his patients' dreams came from a very deep level of the mind. At this level, Jung asserted, there existed what he termed the "archetypes", or the "Collective Unconscious" – a psychic reservoir that contained a rich pool of imagery that was common to all human minds. The imagery was a symbolic depiction of the totality of spiritual wisdom. If, said Jung, the writers and illustrators of alchemical texts were using symbols that were knowingly or unknowingly derived from the Collective Unconscious, then they were – whatever they did or did not do in their laboratories – attempting to transmute *themselves*.

→ DISSOLVE AND SOLIDIFY ←

They were, he argued, trying to transform and heal their personalities – divided, rent with inner conflicts – into calm, balanced, and spiritually aware "wholenesses". They were attempting to dissolve all of the parts of their old personality into a single, solid, new personality, a process summed up by the alchemical tag "*solve et coagula*", "dissolve and solidify".

This is not to say that alchemists were not, to some extent at least, concerned with physical processes. Indeed, Jung's own psychological interpretation of alchemy did not preclude a complementary interpretation, in which he recognized that there were and are alchemists who are concerned with mystical chemical experimentation that they carry out in scientific laboratories.

Measuring Up
The work of all alchemists involves a continual process of trial and error, in which they must continuously experiment with different amounts of the materials that they use. The set of weights pictured here (above left) would therefore be one of the most essential parts of an alchemist's equipment.

Tiny Fractions
Another essential part of an alchemist's laboratory would be a set of highly sensitive weighing scales, such as those shown here (above). Delicate tweezers (left) would also be necessary to facilitate handling minuscule amounts of certain materials. All of the equipment pictured here dates from the nineteenth century.

MEDICINAL POISON

"Pure logical thinking cannot yield any knowledge of the empirical world"
Albert Einstein

HOMOEOPATHIC PREPARATIONS are so diluted that chemical analysis shows them to contain nothing more than lactose. Nevertheless, there is a good deal of evidence that these "remedies" can be therapeutically effective. Much of such evidence has been derived from reports made by homoeopathic physicians of their personal experiences with highly "potentized" (diluted) remedies rather than from controlled clinical trials; yet the sheer bulk of such evidence is impressive.

Why, then, have so few homoeopathic practitioners been prepared to take part in scientific testing of their potentized remedies, in which one group of patients receives a specific homoeopathic preparation and another, victims of the same complaint, receives either a placebo or an orthodox drug? The answer involves the whole philosophy of homoeopathy – the general attitude underlying the therapeutic approach of the practitioner to the patient. That attitude is well expressed in a phrase used by many holistic therapists: "We treat the patient, not the disease"; a phrase that has important practical implications for the homoeopath. He or she will know that for any particular physical disorder there are a number of remedies that

Natural Ability
Samuel Hahnemann (above) (1755–1843), known as the founder of homoeopathy, was an unsuccessful doctor when he came to formulate his own system of medicine. This system was based on the belief that people have the ability to heal themselves from within, and that a doctor's task is to stimulate this ability.

can be justified on the basis of the ancient Paracelsian principle of like-cures-like – the belief that certain drugs derived from natural sources and administered in tiny quantities will produce symptoms similar to those being suffered by the patient, and will stimulate a natural healing process. Which remedy is chosen depends upon the physical and psychological make-up of the individual patient. One patient suffering from hay fever, for example, may be prescribed a totally different remedy from another with the same complaint. This makes it impossible to carry out clinical trials to compare homoeopathic and orthodox remedies.

→ TRY IT FOR YOURSELF ←

Many highly potentized homoeopathic home remedies for common ailments are available in both pharmacies and healthfood stores. Some tend to alarm at first, for the raw materials from which they are made include such deadly mineral and vegetable poisons as arsenic and belladonna. Yet they are all quite safe – potentized to such high levels that not one molecule of the original material remains. In spite of the dilution to vanishing point of the original drug, many people regularly use homoeopathic preparations, finding them both effective and free from all side-effects. Readers might find the remedies opposite suitable for personal testing.

HAHNEMANN'S PROCESS

Homeopathy literally means "treatment by the same" – a drug or poison taken in large amounts will produce particular symptoms; but the same drug taken in small amounts will *cure* those symptoms. For example, tiny amounts of pollen are used to treat hay fever. Hahnemann's process, illustrated here (right), involved diluting the original ingredient with water; he would then shake the mixture by hand 100 times, and end by banging the sealed bottle down hard on an old leather-bound book. This process would be repeated again and again, each time further diluting the resultant mixture. One part of that resultant mixture would be added to 100 parts water. Today the homoeopathic remedies are shaken by machine.

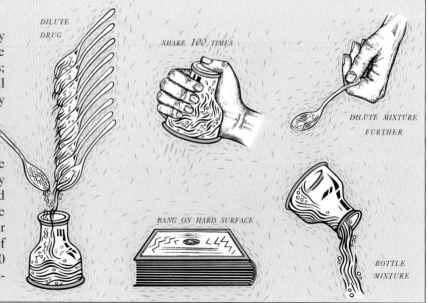

DILUTE DRUG

SHAKE 100 TIMES

DILUTE MIXTURE FURTHER

BANG ON HARD SURFACE

BOTTLE MIXTURE

ACONITE 6 – aconite at the "sixth centesimal potency", which means that for every part of aconite in the preparation there are no less than 9,999,999,999,999 parts of lactose. In practice, aconite 6 contains no aconite at all, yet it is used to treat shock and colds.

ARNICA 6 – said to aid recovery from bruises and shock.

ARSEN. ALB 6 – white arsenic, but absolutely harmless in this form. Used, on the principle of like-cures-like, for ailments with symptoms similar to those of arsenic poisoning, such as stomach pain.

BELLADONNA 6 – another poison in harmless, virtually non-existent, guise. This one is used as a home remedy for mild sore throats, "hot flushes", and even blushing.

CALC. CARB 6 – a homoeopathic preparation of chalk, thought to be effective against both cramp and depression.

CANTHARIS 6 – derived from the sinister irritant "Spanish fly". In this safe form it is used as an antidote to the effects of sunburn.

KALI. PHOS. 6 – diluted sodium phosphate that is used to counter mental exhaustion.

MIXED POLLEN 30 – a classic homoeopathic remedy for hay fever.

NAT. MUR. 6 – a potentized form of common salt; helpful to some victims of migraine.

RHUS. TOX. 6 – a homoeopathic derivative of poison ivy. Used to afford relief to sufferers of mild rheumatic aches.

SULPHUR 6 – thought to relieve the symptoms of dry and itchy skin.

THUJA 6 – used as a cure for warts.

It is fun, perhaps informative, certainly harmless, and may even be beneficial to experiment on oneself with these and any of the many other homoeopathic remedies that are available.

It is essential to remember, however, that medical advice should be sought about any ailment, however unimportant or minor it may seem, that persists for more than a few days.

Royal Favourite
King George VI of England was a life-long believer in homoeopathic medicine. He frequently used a remedy made from the hypericum plant (above). He even named one of his racehorses (below) Hypericum after the plant. Hypericum is used as a remedy for healing wounds and for alleviating the pain of rheumatism and headaches.

BY THEIR MAJESTIES' APPOINTMENT
During the long career of the homoeopathic physician, Sir John Weir, his patients included no less than four British monarchs – George V, Edward VIII, George VI, and Elizabeth II. Following Sir John's retirement in 1968, the appointment of a successor was announced in the London Gazette: "The Queen has graciously been pleased to appoint Margaret Grace Blackie, MD ... FFHOM." FFHOM stands for "Fellow of the Faculty of Homoeopaths". By appointing Dr. Blackie, the Queen was continuing a royal tradition that still abides – at the present day one of her personal physicians is the homoeopath, Dr. Ronald Davey.

Royal Racehorse *Hypericum (right), George VI's racehorse watched by Princess Elizabeth.*

How, then, can homoeopathic remedies possibly exert any physical influence upon patients? This question has long worried homeopathic practitioners. One rationale has been developed by anthroposophical physicians – practitioners of a system of holistic therapy based on teachings of the Austrian mystic, Rudolf Steiner. This incorporates the use of a modified homeopathic pharmacology. Steiner's indications depend for success on the use of tables of correspondences (p.91). Anthroposophic pharmacists and practitioners assert that the materials subjected to potentization are far more than just physical molecules; they are believed to carry within themselves the essence of the terrestrial and cosmic processes that brought these materials into existence.

They have, as it were, been imprinted with the mark of the forces that gave birth to them. This invisible "essence-of-process" is, it is claimed, imparted to the dilutants – in effect, the remedies – by the methods used in the manufacture of homoeopathic remedies.

→ SCIENTIST OF THE INVISIBLE ←

The teachings of Rudolf Steiner have inspired those who practise anthroposophical medicine. His system, anthroposophy, means "wisdom for the world". Yet in his lifetime he was the object of both intense admiration and near-pathological hostility. Steiner was the spiritual physician,

Spiritual Scientist
Rudolf Steiner (above) linked the world of natural science to that of the spirit. His Anthroposophical Society, founded in 1912, was devoted to the study of the interdependence of spirit and science.

Universal Man
Goethe (left), thinker, scientist, and poet, was fascinated by the occult. His philosophical and scientific ideas greatly influenced Rudolf Steiner and the foundation of the Anthroposophical Society. He was once described as "the last universal man".

said his followers, who could cure civilization of its ills. Steiner's opponents, and they were many, were agreed that they lived in a diseased society – but they regarded his teachings as symptoms of, rather than remedies for, humanity's spiritual sickness. The Nazis claimed he was the agent of a Jewish conspiracy; the Marxists claimed he was a capitalist conspirator who was attempting to slow down the progress of the revolutionary proletariat.

Today it is asserted by some that he was "a scientist of the invisible", a man possessed of faculties that enabled him to employ supernormal modes of perception in order to discern the spiritual realities that underlie the physical world. Others believe that Steiner was no more than a schizophrenic – the originator of a delusional system that has deceived many – or a charlatan. I find the last view untenable: Steiner's work and life indicate that he wholly believed in all that he taught.

STEINER AND KANDINSKY

Rudolph Steiner was born on February 27, 1861, the son of a railway official. He was to become a prolific teacher and in 1912, the founder of the Anthroposophical Society. Steiner's teachings – whether or not they derived, as he claimed, from the employment of modes of perception higher than the five senses – have not only survived but have grown more influential as the years have passed. They have influenced, for example, not only practitioners of holistic medicine but artists, architects, educationalists, and even some organic farmers. In particular, the Russian artist, Wassily Kandinsky, was deeply influenced by Steiner; most notably the latter's thoughts and writings on Johann Wolfgang von Goethe's work – *The Theory of Colour*.

Steiner claimed that he had clairvoyant powers that allowed him to see the solutions to artistic, political, and social problems. He stated that to solve such problems was the most important aim of the Anthroposophical Society. He once said: "anthroposophy has its roots in the perceptions ... yet the branches ... and fruit ... grow into all the fields of human life and action."

In the years prior to his death in 1925, Steiner was lecturing on mathematics, theology, medicine, philosophy, drama, and many more subjects. His ideas on medicine are based largely on magical theories: syphilis, for instance, was considered a punishment for lack of love. His farming theories mainly concern planting crops in accordance with the phases of the moon. Steiner was, without doubt, one of the most remarkable minds of his generation. Yet even though he faced intense opposition in his lifetime (in fact the Anthroposophical Society headquarters were burned to the ground), his influence, particularly in the field of education, is today as strong as ever.

Anthroposophical Art
Steiner's theories on colour can be seen in Wassily Kandinsky's painting All Saints' Day *(1911).*

There are, of course, many similarities between Steiner's anthroposophy and Hahnemann's homoeopathy, but one of the greatest differences is in public acceptance. Homoeopathic treatments are used by millions around the world, and homoeopathy is practised by many conventionally trained doctors; whereas anthroposophy has always attracted some hostility.

This is not surprising, for any esoteric group or movement with an ideology that runs counter to the prevailing orthodoxy tends to be subjected to attacks – often wholly untrue – claiming that that group's leading figures are financially dubious, immoral, or insane. Nevertheless, the nature of the attacks on Rudolf Steiner and the movement that grew up around the teachings to which he gave expression, was quite exceptional in its mendacity, virulence, and violence. Steiner and some of his closest associates were accused of sexual immorality and of "stealing souls". The infant Nazi Party described him as "a Galician Jew plotting against Germany", carried out an unsucessful attempt to murder one of his lieutenants, and may well have been responsible for the destruction by fire of the Anthroposophical Society's headquarters in Switzerland. After the Nazi's seizure of power in 1933, the German anthroposophical movement was subjected to savage persecution. Its schools were closed down, its publications suppressed, and most of its leaders were either forced to emigrate or sent to concentration camps.

What was the reason for this extraordinary hostility? No one knows for sure, but it seems likely that the Nazis saw Anthroposophy as a real threat, a "magic of light" that challenged the spiritual darkness of which they were a physical manifestation.

Head of Homoeopathy
Hahnemann (right), the Father of Homoeopathy, is considered by many to be the Father of western alternative medicine.

Pills
A single drop of a homoeopathic remedy, already diluted many times, is all that is added to a bottle of lactose pills.

Just a Drop
A homoeopath may prescribe just a drop a day of a remedy made by adding one part of the active ingredient to 100 parts water – it could be only one drop from a pipette (above). This is repeated until there is virtually nothing left of the ingredient.

Powdered Rhubarb Root

Rhubarb has been used for many years by practitioners of alternative medicine as a cure for constipation. Here (below), the root has been powdered.

Juniper Berries

The oil from juniper berries (below) is used to treat acne, diabetes, cirrhosis of the liver, dandruff, and much more.

Licorice Ailments

Licorice (below left) is one of the oldest medicines known to mankind. Although it is often used to flavour sweets, it has also been chewed by people from all over the world as a treatment for various ailments. Though has a pleasant calming effect on the user, its potent laxative properties tend to discourage over indulgence.

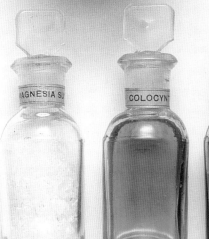

Nettle Tea

Nettle (Urtica dioica) is specifically recommended by herbalists as a treatment for nervous eczema and for children's eczema. It is suggested that the patient takes an infusion of nettle, three times a day. Dried nettle leaves (left) have become very popular as an invigoring herb tea.

Infusion Tool

Infusers (bottom left) are essential instruments for herbalists, as they are used to make herbal "teas" from various vegetable "drugs". You can use one to make your own herb teas.

Antiseptic

Marigold (left), also called Calendula, is a versatile herb. It has healing and antiseptic properties.

ABRA-MELIN

"I believe in the practice and philosophy of what we have agreed to call magic, and what I ... call the evocation of spirits"

W.B. Yeats

IN A CERTAIN SENSE, the life of the major poet W.B. Yeats was a quest for his "Real Self", a search into the inmost recesses of his soul in order to find unity with that divine spark that Yeats believed was at the core of his being.

Yeats' poetry was almost a by-product of that search: a welling-up of the waters of spiritual vitality from the "inner space" of his unconscious mind. And much of his poetry is *magical* in the sense both that it possesses the force of incantation, and that its inspiration is to be found in what the occultist Dion Fortune termed the "Western Esoteric Tradition".

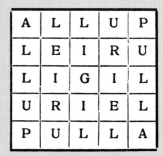

Aleister Crowley
In this rarely seen photograph (below), the magician, Aleister Crowley (facing the reader), performs magical rites in the tradition of Abra-melin. Crowley went on to devise a system of magic, known as Sex Magik, a synthesis of ritual magic and Tantrism (pp.200-201). As well as being a magician, Crowley was also an eccentric. When he was asked why he called himself "the Beast" he replied: "My mother called me the Beast".

MAGICAL BOXES

Abra-melin squares are not the meaningless groups of Roman letters that at first sight they appear to be. They are a reworking of a classical palindrome (a phrase that reads the same backwards as forwards). When ritually consecrated they are said to be capable of producing magic effects.

Squares of Power
Each Abra-melin square (below) acts as a talisman and can be used in the casting of magic spells.

A	L	L	U	P
L	E	I	R	U
L	I	G	I	L
U	R	I	E	L
P	U	L	L	A

M	E	L	A	M	M	E	D
E	R	I	F	O	I	S	E
L	I	S	I	L	L	I	M
A	F	I	R	E	L	O	M
M	O	L	E	R	I	F	A
M	I	L	L	I	S	I	L
E	S	I	O	F	I	R	E
D	E	M	M	A	L	E	M

E	K	D	I	L	U	N
K	L	I	S	A	T	U
D	I	N	A	N	A	L
I	S	A	G	A	S	I
L	A	N	A	N	I	D
U	T	A	S	I	L	K
N	U	L	I	D	K	E

In his notorious book, *Ideas of Good and Evil,* he wrote of his fundamental belief in magic (see opening quotation).

Yeats followed this affirmation of his belief by describing an experience with an experiment involving the use of Enochian tablets (pp.74-75) that resulted in his imagination beginning "to move of itself, and to bring before me vivid images ...."

→ THE MAGE ←

In view of Yeats' lifelong quest for his Real Self it is perhaps rather surprising that he never ventured to experiment with the technique of discovering what some occultists call "the Operation of Abra-melin". It is almost certain that Yeats knew of this technique; the manuscript that describes it was translated into English in the 1890s by his friend, MacGregor Mathers (pp.74-76).

Mathers published his translation of the manuscript, entitled *The Book of the Sacred Magic of Abra-melin the Mage,* in 1898. Financially it was a disaster, selling very slowly and not even recovering the costs of its printing and binding. This was probably because most serious occultists of the time thought of it as "just another grimoire and therefore not worth bothering about". A "grimoire" is a textbook of ritual magic dating from the Middle Ages to the early-nineteenth century. Most of these books are, indeed, "not worth bothering about", ranging from the sinister to the just plain silly – full of absurd spells, for instance to "hinder a sportsman from killing any game" and to have "carnal knowledge of any woman, whether she will or no".

→ HOLY GUARDIAN ANGEL ←

The Sacred Magic of Abra-melin the Mage, is, however, in a class of its own, teaching a yoga-like method of giving the aspirant a knowledge of the Real Self – which the author, using the terminology of his own time, calls the "Holy Guardian Angel".

Perhaps the reason why Yeats never attempted to carry out the Abra-melin experiment was simply that he considered it too time-consuming. The aspirant has to spend many months in prayer

Sacred Magic
Abra-melin's Book of the Sacred Magic *(below), attributed to a 15th-century Jew, reveals an extraordinary and quite unique system of magic. A magic sword, such as the one below, would have been used in ritual magic.*

and chaste solitude. At the end of this period, following white magical rites, the Holy Guardian Angel manifests itself. That is to say, the aspirant becomes at one with his or her own Higher Self – the spirit manifests itself in everyday life, the supernormal becomes part of material reality.

→ MIRACLE TALISMANS ←

This inner unity being achieved, the successful experimenter has the power to employ various lettered squares, "Abra-melin talismans", to perform miracles.

In recent years Mathers' translation of Abra-melin has been reprinted several times. I know several occultists who claim to have successfully performed the processes outlined in it. How seriously such claims should be taken is a matter of personal opinion.

THE BOOK OF THE SACRED MAGIC OF ABRA-MELIN THE MAGE

BY S. L. MACGREGOR-MATHERS

Translated from the Original Hebrew into the ... and now rendered into English from an ... and valuable MS. in the Bibliothèque de l'Arsenal at Paris.

... and copious Introduction and ... tes by the Translator and Numerous ... cal Squares of Letters.

New and ...

... of 500 copies

JOHN M. ...
21 Cecil Court, Charing ...

W.C.2

THE ROSICRUCIANS

"*Post Centum Viginti Annos Patebo*"
(After 120 years I shall reappear)

Fama Fraternitatis

IN 1614, THERE WAS PRINTED, at Kassel in Germany, a pamphlet entitled *Fama Fraternitatis*...("The Fame of the Brotherhood"), the contents of which caused excitement and controversy at the time and are still the subject of much dispute.

The *Fama* told the story of Christian Rosenkreuz, a noble German born in 1378, who had travelled to the East in search of hidden wisdom. Rosenkreuz was educated in a monastery where he learned Greek and Latin. As a young man he was taken by a monk on a pilgrimage to the Holy Sepulchre – the tomb in which Christ is believed to have been buried. However, the monk died before reaching Jerusalem, and so Rosenkreuz continued his journey alone. In Damascus he first learned of the secret wisdom to be found in the mysterious Arabian city of Damcar. Here he was taught much by the initiates of a mystical secret society, learned Arabic, and translated an unidentified book, the *Liber M.* From here he travelled to the North African city of Fez, in Morocco, where he learned to evoke the spirits of Fire, Earth, Air, and Water.

✦ THE MYSTIC VAULT ✦

He subsequently returned to Europe and, after further adventures, including five years spent in meditative solitude, he and four others founded the Rosicrucian Fraternity. The members of this society built a secret headquarters, the House of the Holy Spirit, invented a "magical language", and travelled Europe healing the sick and admitting carefully chosen recruits to their order.

In 1484, at the advanced age of 106, Christian Rosenkreuz died and was interred in a vault. The fraternity he had founded, the Rosicrucians, survived him, although the site of the burial place of its founder was forgotten. In 1604, 120 years later, members of the third generation of Rosicrucian adepts accidentally found

The Rose Cross
The Order of the Golden Dawn wore the symbol of the Rose Cross (above). The design was derived from the teachings of the Kabalah and MacGregor Mathers who believed that he had received its symbolism from his contact with the "Secret Chiefs". The 22 petals of the Rose Cross correspond to the 22 letters of the Hebrew alphabet. The cross in the centre is the Cross on which Christ died at Calvary. It is symbolic of death and spiritual renewal.

the forgotten vault. The body was incorrupt, and the chamber in which it lay was lit by "the sun of magi" – which seems to have been one of the everlasting lamps of medieval legend. The vault was decorated with mystic symbols and designs and, furthermore, contained manuscripts of hidden lore and secret wisdom.

The Rosicrucian fraternity, said the anonymous author of both the *Fama* and a sequel to it that was printed in 1615, felt it to be its duty to reveal these facts to the world and to indicate that candidates for Rosicrucian initiation were at liberty to apply. Unfortunately neither pamphlet gave any information as to where, or to whom, such application should be made.

✦ REAL OR HOAX? ✦

Reasonably enough this omission aroused suspicions. Some believed that the Rosicrucian society was non-existent outside the imagination of the author of the pamphlets and denounced him as a hoaxer. Others were convinced of the existence of the brotherhood and its secrets, and issued printed appeals for admission to its ranks. None of the latter seem to have received any response to their applications – or, if they did so, did not make it a matter of public knowledge.

A decade after controversy had died down, the whole matter was largely forgotten – although as late as the reign of Charles II (1649–1685), some occultists such as John Heydon asserted that they themselves were Rosicrucians.

✦ ESOTERIC MASONS ✦

In the eighteenth century, a number of allegedly Rosicrucian societies, most of which had some connection with the occult freemasonry that flourished at the time, were active in continental Europe, particularly within Germany. Whether any of these bodies had actual historic links with the original Rosicrucians, if *they* ever existed, has not be proven. What seems certain, however, is that one of the groups has exerted an abiding influence over modern societies.

The body in question was the "Golden and Rosy Cross", whose members were largely concerned with alchemy. The names of the grades, in which alchemical secrets were revealed to its members, are familiar to all who have made a study of modern esoteric societies. They were adopted by MacGregor Mathers and his associates for the Order of the Golden Dawn, which they led. From this Order the grade titles were passed down to organizations which are active today.

→ USE OF SYMBOLS ←

Mathers also employed symbols taken from a book compiled by spiritual heirs of the Rosicrucians, which was published at Altona in 1785. For example, he largely based the design of the cross worn on the breasts of initiates of the Golden Dawn's "Adeptus Minor" grade upon a drawing reproduced in the 1785 volume.

Via the Golden Dawn, eighteenth-century Rosicrucian symbolism has been passed down to a number of twentieth-century groups employing ritual initiation. The same groups are familiar with the contents of the original *Fama*, and more than one of them works a rite largely concerned with the symbolism of the vault in which the incorrupt body of Christian Rosenkreuz was found.

→ SPIRITUAL FORCE ←

Other twentieth-century occultists, notably those influenced by Rudolf Steiner (p.97), have regarded the story of Christian Rosenkreuz as more than legend or hoax. They see it as a factual account, albeit expressed in symbol, of an outpouring of spiritual force that took place

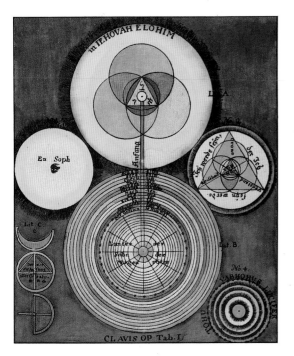

Favourite Subject
Like the Rosicrucian order itself, the symbols of the Rose and Cross (above) have obsessed artists since the 17th century.

Symbol of the Universe
In the Rosicrucian cosmological diagram (left), the glyph on the left represents the unmanifest, the basis of all being, from which emanates the universe as we know it.

in fifteenth-century Europe. In 1906, Steiner was the head of the "Mysteria Mystica Acterna" which was, loosely speaking, a masonic lodge. Steiner believed that Christian Rosenkreuz had indeed created a fifteenth-century brotherhood, but that his teachings had become known only in the eighteenth century. Goethe, for example, had been profoundly influenced by the ideas of Christian Rosenkreuz.

Today several modern esoteric orders claim Rosicrucian descent and knowledge of the secret wisdom. The most genuine are those associated with the Golden Dawn, although it is doubtful that their teachings and practices bear much resemblance to those of the original Rosicrucians.

THE MIDDLE PILLAR

"The Pillar of Severity is on our right side, the Pillar of Mercy is on our left, and the Pillar of Equilibrium in our midst"

Israel Regardie

ISRAEL REGARDIE, the practising alchemist who suffered a laboratory accident (p.86), was by profession both a psychotherapist and a chiropractor – a therapist who uses manipulation of the spinal column and other parts of the body as a method of treating disease.

His approach to the psychotherapeutic side of his healing activities was thoroughly eclectic for while he was a fully qualified practitioner of a form of analysis developed by Wilhelm Reich, a one-time pupil of Freud; he was also confident that Jungian theories proposing the existence of the "Collective Unconscious" were of much importance. In them he noted many resemblances to traditional beliefs associated with magic and mysticism.

➜ REICHIAN THERAPIST ⬅

Reich was a major influence on Regardie. He had been a practising Freudian analyst and had formulated the theory of "physiological armouring". By this Reich meant that various physical symptoms without any neurological cause, were the result of the body adopting a posture that, in reality, was caused by that person trying to communicate a psychological disorder. This theory had a very great influence on Israel Regardie in the formulation of his healing exercises.

➜ OCCULT EXPERT ⬅

Regardie was, in fact, an expert on almost every aspect of western occultism. He had been initiated into the *Stella Matutina*, a Rosicrucian offshoot of the Golden Dawn (pp.80-81) in the 1930s, and had subsequently edited and helped to publish many of the instructional manuscripts and pamphlets prepared by MacGregor Mathers and his associates – for example those that deal with Enochian Magic (pp.74-75).

Regardie was no mere theoretician. He had worked almost all of the practical techniques of western occultism: he had conducted rituals designed to charge his psyche with subtle energies; he had consecrated several of his own "magical implements"; and he had tried to make astral journeys. After his initiation

Mystic Healer
Rasputin (1872–1916), the last Russian Czarina's pet mystic (below), was an unsavoury character. As a young man he had been influenced by a heretical sect, the "Khlysty", who held the unorthodox belief that sinning was necessary for ultimate salvation. Rasputin's presence at court provoked an outrage among many members of the aristocracy, but he won the admiration and loyalty of the Imperial family by his ability to heal the haemophiliac Czarevitch, heir to the throne, of hitherto uncontrollable haemorrhages. Some present-day occultists attribute his strange powers to the use of a technique similar to that of the Middle Pillar.

Trying the Process

While the entirety of the Middle Pillar process is fairly complex, involving the use of not only creative visualization but also a technique called "the Vibration of Divine Names", there is no reason why readers should not experiment for themselves with a simplified version of it. For, unless you are suffering from a psychotic disorder, it can do you no possible harm and may well do you some good. It will also give you a better understanding of the nature of some of the esoteric psychic exercises used by western occultists. Experimenters should give the exercise a fair trial; for it to have any chance of having an effect you should practise the exercise for five to ten minutes each day for at least a month, as described below:

a) Sit alone in a relaxed position but with the spine kept erect. Breathe slowly and deeply and imagine a stream of energy pouring from above into a sphere of white light situated immediately above the head.

b) From this sphere visualize a stream of glowing energy flowing downwards – through the neck, down the spine, into the genitals, and then down to the feet.

c) From the feet imagine the energy stream turning upon itself and flowing up the front of the body and returning to its source above the head. A continuous flow must be imagined with the energy moving simultaneously upwards and downwards.

If the full exercise is carried out, Regardie believed, an individual experimenter would be helped with breathing and relaxation, as well as having a life-enhancing energy released. Other effects might well be the ability to heal others and to perform magic. Regardie himself found that his abilities as a healer were very much enhanced by the Middle Pillar exercise. Interested readers can continue with the more advanced experiments detailed by the late Dr. Regardie in his book *The Middle Pillar*.

---

into a grade of the *Stella Matutina* rather pompously termed "Lord of the Portal", Regardie had become acquainted with a magical technique known as the Middle Pillar exercise. This was taught to Regardie as a method of energizing centres of psychic force that, it is claimed by occultists, exist in the astral and other subtle "bodies" that underlie the physical bodies of human beings.

→ Linked Spheres ←

Regardie and other initiates of his grade were instructed to think of these centres as corresponding to the centre column of the kabalistic Tree of Life (p.106), which comprises three rows of linked spheres. The middle row of circles – the Middle Pillar – are the spheres of Beauty, Foundation, Kingdom, and the Supreme Crown: collectively, the Pillar of Equilibrium.

The initiates were told that they should visualize the Middle Pillar first. They should stand up and imagine a brilliant light shining above their heads. They should then visualize this light descending to the nape of the neck, then moving down to the heart, and from there to the hips and then down to the feet – all regions of the body that are thought to be centres of spiritual energy. The initiate should recite the Hebrew names for God, which correspond to each energy centre. In this way, the cosmic forces symbolized by the various spheres of the Tree of Life, would be made available to the corresponding aspects of the spiritual core of the individual initiate. The initiates would be able to utilize these cosmic forces to enhance their spiritual being.

Eclectic Inspiration
Israel Regardie drew upon the teachings of an astonishing collection of writers, including C.G. Jung, Aleister Crowley, H.P. Blavatsky, and D.H. Lawrence (above). Like Regardie, Lawrence believed in the existence of subtle psychic centres associated with the head, the solar plexus and the genitals. Lawrence was a believer in all things psychic for most of his adult life. Indeed, even as he lay dying in a sanatorium in Venice, he claimed that he had an out-of-the-body-experience in which he floated above his bed and saw himself with Maria Huxley, who was by his bedside.

Israel Regardie claimed that he practised the Middle Pillar exercise at least once a day. According to his own account he found the exercises to be extremely effective. Not only did he feel better mentally, he said, with an enormous improvement in the harmony of the various components of his mind and emotions, but he also felt charged with an increased vitality that made it easier for him to cope with the stresses and strains of everyday life.

For the rest of his life Israel Regardie employed the Middle Pillar exercise. After he had gone into practice as a chiropractor, the alchemist and mystic developed certain methods that he believed gave him the power to transfer to his patients some of the vast cosmic energies that he professed to have tapped by his continual use of the exercise.

→ Eastern Traditions ←

While the Middle Pillar technique is unquestionably of western origin – being, as we have seen, the development of a complex Golden Dawn process for projecting the kabalistic Tree of Life as a column of spheres – the theories underlying its use have a marked resemblance to concepts associated with Indian and Tibetan yoga. The psychic centres of the Tree of Life, supposedly vivified by the use of the Middle Pillar exercise, correlate well with the chakras that are believed to be energized by the practitioners of the Kundalini yoga of Bengal. There are of course differences between the two techniques, perhaps the most vital difference being that the Kundali and Middle Pillar energy flows rotate in opposite directions.

THE MYSTICAL KABALAH

"The modern occultist ... uses a philosophical conception of the Tree to interpret what it represents to his conscious mind, and he uses a magical ... application of its symbolism to link it up with his subconscious mind"

THE "TREE" referred to in the above passage, written by the magician and psychotherapist Dion Fortune (p.77) in 1934, is the most important of the many symbolic diagrams employed by modern students of the mystical kabalah – in particular by devotees of the particular version of it that derives from MacGregor Mathers and his successors.

The word "kabalah" (also spelt Cabbala and Qabalah) is derived from an Aramaic Chaldee term meaning, very roughly, "oral tradition". Originally it was purely Jewish, a system of mystical philosophy and practical technique that, according to legend, had been transmitted to Moses by the archangel Metatron. Its real beginnings seem to have been less miraculous: it was the creation of medieval Rabbinical mystics who had been influenced by a number of ancient traditions, not all of them Jewish.

→ ETERNAL QUESTIONS ←
The Rabbis who created the kabalah combined old teachings, for example those concerning numbers and letters that were already to be found in the ancient *Sepher Yetzirah* (Book of Formation), with their own intuitive and rational endeavours to answer eternal spiritual questions. Questions such as: if the universe is under the control of a Supreme Being who is utterly benevolent, how is the existence of evil to be explained? If that Being exists outside the world of space and time how can He be concerned with it and involve Himself in it? And how, if at all, can humanity, trapped in the

The Tree of Life
The spheres in this symbolic diagram are used to represent the ten aspects of God. The right side is male, the left female, and the centre column harmonizes them. To kabalists these spheres were also centres of power, accessible to man.

material world of time and matter, approach the Eternal and share in its mode of consciousness?

The answers given by the Rabbinical kabalists to these and similar questions bore a strong resemblance to those given by the adherents of many other mystical philosophies, from Christian Gnosticism to Taoism (p.184).

→ CHRISTIAN CREEDS ←
The Supreme Power, the Rabbis asserted, is totality – in the last analysis everything from an archangel to a louse, while not being exactly part of the Eternal, emanates from It. Those readers who are familiar with the formulae of the historical Christian creeds can consider the verb "proceeding" as it is used in reference to the Holy Spirit ("proceeding from the Father and the Son") as an equivalent for the verb "emanating" as it is used by the kabalists.

As everything emanates from the Eternal, said the Rabbinical kabalists, the totality of things is a unity that subsumes seeming opposites, such as mercy and severity, or love and hatred. It is possible, they said, for human beings to so change their modes of consciousness that they progress upwards through the successive emanations of the Eternal, and, ultimately attain to a unity in which the opposites resolve into one; in other words the human soul directly apprehends the divine.

The kabalists classified the emanations as ten Sephiroth (numbers) linked to one another by 22 Paths, each one corresponding to a particular letter of the Hebrew alphabet. The Tree of Life was intended as a diagrammatic representation of this classification. Over the centuries the kabalists revised and developed their mystical system, and by the sixteenth century a Christianized form of it had developed. Some Christian scholars interpreted alchemical symbolism in kabalistic terms; others, such as Cornelius Agrippa, found in the kabalah the key to the doctrine of correspondences (p.90).

The Creator
The Head (right) of Macroprosopus, the "Vast Countenance", which in kabalistic law symbolizes God as Creator – the attributes of which are described at length in the treatise known as "Sepher Yetzirah". In kabalistic writings, "create" means to "emanate"; therefore "created by God" should be read as "emanated from God". Emanation provides a way of linking the spiritual world with the physical world; to the kabalists it also indicates the completeness of the Divine Being, as opposed to the nothingness of the Divine Non-being.

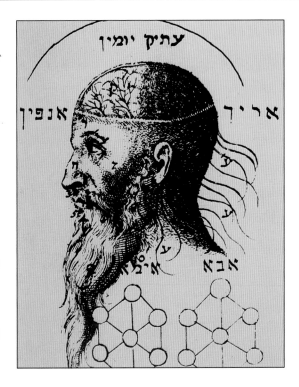

Towards the end of the last century MacGregor Mathers and other western occultists began to concern themselves with the kabalah generally, and Agrippa's version of it in particular. They interpreted it in terms of their own occult beliefs and, in the case of Mathers, the wisdom he had acquired, so he believed, from his Masters.

Mathers' synthesis of all varieties of western occultism – that which Dion Fortune referred to as the Western Esoteric Tradition – was for this reason given a kabalistic core. Thus, for example, the grades of initiation of the order that Mathers led were thought of as corresponding to the five lower Sephiroth of the Tree of Life and the "paths" associated with them. Consequently the rituals with which these grades were conferred, incorporated much kabalistic symbolism.

The influence of Mathers' version of kabalism has proved to be an abiding one, and most modern esoteric societies have incorporated it into their teachings and their ceremonies.

CORNELIUS AGRIPPA

Cornelius Agrippa (1486–1535) was in some ways an unlikely character, a one-time professional soldier who became an accomplished physician and a student of alchemy, kabalism, and white magic. In his day, he was famous at the courts and universities of Europe. Unlikely stories grew around him even in his own lifetime. It was said, for example, that in the presence of the scholar Erasmus and the Ruler of Saxony, he had summoned from Hades the spirit of the Roman orator, Tully.

After his death the stories grew wilder. It was asserted that he had sold his soul to Lucifer, practised necromancy, witchcraft, and other dark sciences, and had always been accompanied by one of Satan's imps in the form of a black dog.

Agrippa believed that the universe is one spiritual whole. To him, the practice of magic, open to very few, was a way of investigating the universe. He wrote in his *Occult Philosophy*:

"Therefore man ... hath in himself all that is contained in the greater world, so that there remaineth nothing which is not found even truly and really in man himself ...."

Still Influential
The influence of Cornelius Agrippa (right) is still potent today on contemporary occultists who engage in "ceremonial workings".

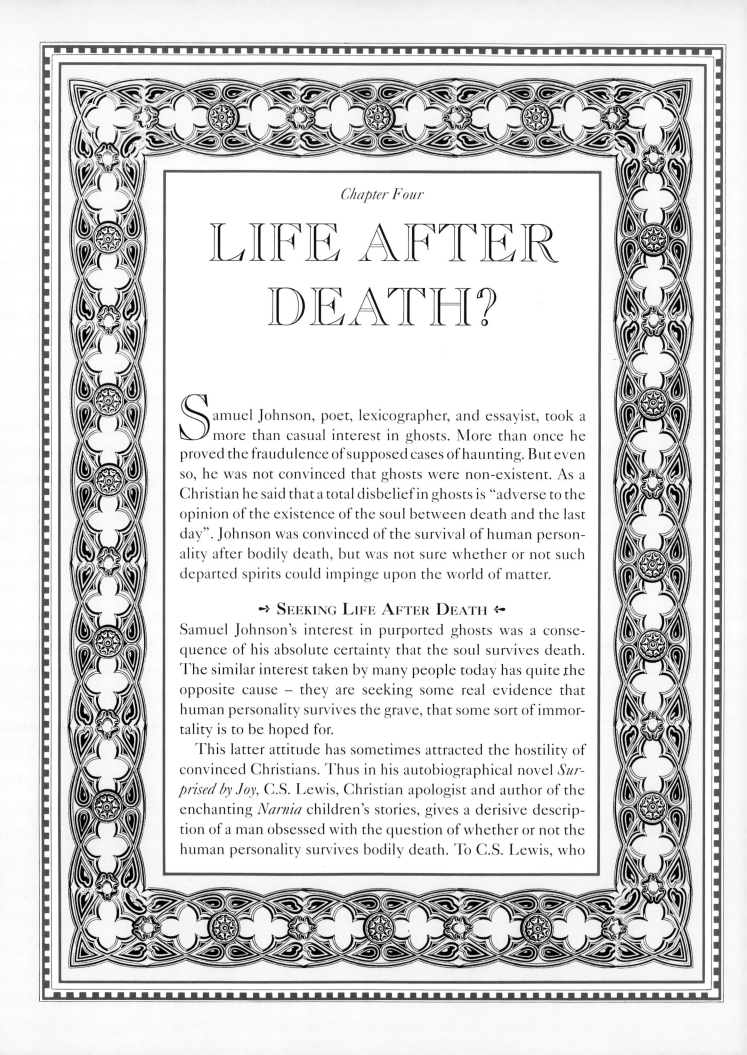

Chapter Four

LIFE AFTER DEATH?

Samuel Johnson, poet, lexicographer, and essayist, took a more than casual interest in ghosts. More than once he proved the fraudulence of supposed cases of haunting. But even so, he was not convinced that ghosts were non-existent. As a Christian he said that a total disbelief in ghosts is "adverse to the opinion of the existence of the soul between death and the last day". Johnson was convinced of the survival of human personality after bodily death, but was not sure whether or not such departed spirits could impinge upon the world of matter.

→ SEEKING LIFE AFTER DEATH ←

Samuel Johnson's interest in purported ghosts was a consequence of his absolute certainty that the soul survives death. The similar interest taken by many people today has quite the opposite cause – they are seeking some real evidence that human personality survives the grave, that some sort of immortality is to be hoped for.

This latter attitude has sometimes attracted the hostility of convinced Christians. Thus in his autobiographical novel *Surprised by Joy*, C.S. Lewis, Christian apologist and author of the enchanting *Narnia* children's stories, gives a derisive description of a man obsessed with the question of whether or not the human personality survives bodily death. To C.S. Lewis, who

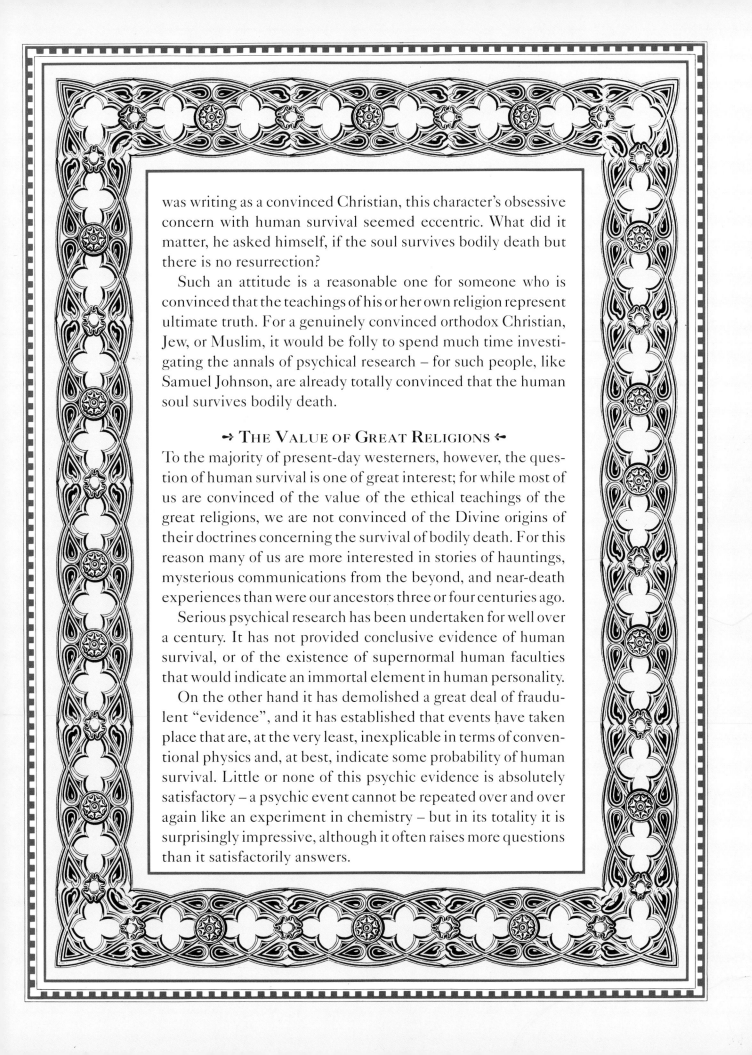

was writing as a convinced Christian, this character's obsessive concern with human survival seemed eccentric. What did it matter, he asked himself, if the soul survives bodily death but there is no resurrection?

Such an attitude is a reasonable one for someone who is convinced that the teachings of his or her own religion represent ultimate truth. For a genuinely convinced orthodox Christian, Jew, or Muslim, it would be folly to spend much time investigating the annals of psychical research – for such people, like Samuel Johnson, are already totally convinced that the human soul survives bodily death.

→ The Value of Great Religions ←

To the majority of present-day westerners, however, the question of human survival is one of great interest; for while most of us are convinced of the value of the ethical teachings of the great religions, we are not convinced of the Divine origins of their doctrines concerning the survival of bodily death. For this reason many of us are more interested in stories of hauntings, mysterious communications from the beyond, and near-death experiences than were our ancestors three or four centuries ago.

Serious psychical research has been undertaken for well over a century. It has not provided conclusive evidence of human survival, or of the existence of supernormal human faculties that would indicate an immortal element in human personality.

On the other hand it has demolished a great deal of fraudulent "evidence", and it has established that events have taken place that are, at the very least, inexplicable in terms of conventional physics and, at best, indicate some probability of human survival. Little or none of this psychic evidence is absolutely satisfactory – a psychic event cannot be repeated over and over again like an experiment in chemistry – but in its totality it is surprisingly impressive, although it often raises more questions than it satisfactorily answers.

SPIRIT GODS

"Bushmen are more aware of ghosts than they are of gods, and the ghosts of dead people are closer to them than some deity who lives far away in the sky"

James Wellard

AT THE BEGINNING of the sixteenth century, Arab traders attacked villages in West Africa and bound the captive tribesmen in chains, to be transported and sold as slaves in South America. Many of those villagers had never seen the sea and, crammed in the terrible rolling darkness of the ship's hull, they mumbled prayers begging Iemanja, the mother of all spirits and goddess of the sea, to spare their lives.

Arriving safely on the Brazilian shore, the tribesmen were convinced their goddess had delivered them from a watery grave. At night they erected altars in her honour and beat drums in candlelit ceremonies, a practice initially tolerated by their Portuguese masters.

Visiting Catholic priests, however, were determined to wipe out "spiritism", the worshipping of spirits as gods. In much the same way as the pagan feast days of Europe had been ousted by their Christian counterparts, the slaves were encouraged to worship the saints rather than their own "spirit gods", and the Virgin Mary rather than Iemanja.

→ SPIRITS AND SAINTS ←

The priests were only partly successful; what actually occurred was that the saints and spirits became fused into one in the minds of the spiritists. They were more than happy to worship the powerful white man's saints, but only as images of their own spirit gods. Idols of the Virgin Mary were worshipped *as* Iemanja; Oxalus, the god of purity and goodness, merged easily with Jesus; and St. John the Baptist was fused with Xango, the spirit of the wilderness. A more ironic fusion was that of St. Patrick who, due to the popular story telling of his "expulsion" of the snakes from Ireland, became identified

with the serpent god Damballah. So it was that spiritism first displayed its syncretistic versatility – its capacity to absorb other diverse faiths and yet remain fundamentally unchanged.

"Macumba" is one of the many eclectic derivatives of spiritism to be found today. It absorbed sources ranging from European spiritualism, as presented in *The Spirit's Book* of the nineteenth-century French spiritualist, Allen Kardec, to popular Catholicism and the shamanistic beliefs of the American Indians.

→ VOODOO AND OBEAH ←

A similar mix characterizes many other cults that have sizeable followings in the Americas and the Caribbean. The most notable of these are the Obeah cult of Jamaica and the Voodoo cult of Haiti – which again originated in West Africa and was carried by the slave trade to Haiti.

Haitian Voodoo has acquired a certain notoriety – so much so that the word "Voodoo" is quite often, and incorrectly, used synonymously with witchcraft and black magic. Yet similar cults and religions that are widely spread throughout the Americas are little known outside the local areas where they flourish.

Cuba, for example, has its own cults of spirit possession essentially identical to Voodoo, which, in spite of attracting the hostility of the ruling communist regime, continue to be practised in a semi-clandestine fashion. And not only

"Go Away Evil!"
A rather bizarre air freshener, "Kitamal" (below) is sold throughout the Americas. Kitamal is Spanish for, "go away evil". The spray is used by some as a do-it-yourself exorcism. The geomantic "bones" (below left), are actually wooden; they are used for fortune telling by followers of Obeah.

KITAMAL
LOS 7 PODERES INDIOS
AROMA REFRESCANTE PARA CUARTOS
Tabaco

in rural areas but, if some reports are to be believed, under the noses of Castro's brutal secret police in Havana and other urban districts.

As with the spirit possession cults of Brazil, Haiti, Jamaica, and some areas of the southern United States, those of Cuba are characterized by the synthesis of originally unrelated elements into a harmonious unity, albeit a unity confusing to the outsider.

→ WILLINGLY POSSESSED ←

Both Voodoo and Obeah are, in fact, perfectly respectable religio-spiritual cults, in spite of the common belief that their priests practise black magic – their ritual animal sacrifices and their frenzied dancing to invoke spirits, are simply too far removed from "civilized" religious practice. Devotees of spiritism, however, say that it is the civilized religions that are "too far removed" from the gods *they* worship, claiming such intimate contact with their own gods that on occasions they are willingly possessed by them. Within the context of spiritism, there is nothing unusual about a

Rum and Chillies
Rum and chillies (left) are credited with magical properties in certain spiritist religions, and, like garlic in medieval Christianity, are used to ward off evil. Unlike the more sophisticated religions, Voodoo and Obeah have preserved a strong faith in everyday folk-magic.

Voodoo Dance *Worshippers dance to an increasingly frenzied drum beat until a dancer is "possessed".*

man or woman in the throes of possession by a god – or, at least, behaving as though he or she were possessed by a god. For the central religious experience of the more "primitive" spiritists is the achievement of a form of what a psychologist would term "dissociation of consciousness". In lay terms this means that a *segment* of the mind of a particular individual takes over his or her *entire* mind – suppressing into the unconscious all other segments and seizing control of the body (p.117) – and directs it into unusual and uncharacteristic patterns of behaviour.

→ THE OLD BLACK SLAVE ←

In Macumba and Voodoo, such dissociation takes the form of possession by a god who exerts his powers for the benefit of either the person possessed or other devotees. The "Old Black Slave" god is believed to have the ability to heal those who come to him. Whether this healing is psychosomatic – the influence of the mind over the body – or whether there are genuinely supernatural forces at work is not proven.

It is not only for their supposed power to heal; to bring luck, love, and money; and to bring about the defeat of one's enemies that the deities of Macumba and Voodoo

Thunder Staff
Shango, the spirit of
thunder and lightning, is
considered to be one of the most
formidable spirits. His cult is
associated with the axe-shaped
baton (left) that symbolizes
power. The cult originated in
Nigeria where neolithic axe-
heads, dug up all over
Yorubaland, were thought by the
spiritists to be thunderbolts hurled
to earth by the angry spirit. The
figure depicted is a Shango worshipper
– always represented by a woman.

are worshipped by those persons whom they possess. They are also regarded as protectors against the sinister supernatural influences that are hostile to humanity; against, for example, Quimbanda, which is a form of Brazilian black magic; against the Haitian sorcerers who are believed to have the power to transform people into mindless zombies; and against the *"loup-garou"* of Haitian folklore – a vampire that sucks blood from its victims.

So just how much is folklore, and how much fact? It is interesting to note that it is not only spiritists who believe that they are literally possessed or, in Voodoo terminology, "ridden by divine horsemen". Some Catholic priests believe that misguided practitioners open their souls to possession, but insist that the possessors are demons and not gods (pp.140-143). Whatever the truth, it remains a fact that every New Year's Eve, large crowds still gather on the Copacabana beach, Rio de Janeiro, to prostrate themselves before Iemanja, who protected the slaves on their perilous voyage to the New World, nearly five hundred years ago.

SPIRIT CULTS

All spiritist cults are characterized by their ability to "absorb" originally unrelated elements taken from other religions into their own system of beliefs.

In these spirit cults, taking a notable example, the saints of the Catholic Church are looked upon as particular embodiments of the same cosmic forces that manifest themselves as both the spirits of deceased ancestors and as the gods and goddesses of African and American Indian origin.

↦ SOUL TRAIN ↤

Similarly, many techniques used to obtain that dissociation of consciousness that indicates possession by gods, ancestral spirits, and saints are a blend of very diverse methods derived from Africa, Europe, and native American sources. Some even believed in possession by machines: there is a recorded instance, dating from the 1920s, of a devotee believing that he was possessed by the "soul" of a steam locomotive.

↦ WITCH DOCTORS ↤

Some of the trance-inducing techniques utilized by spiritists are derived from the American Indian and African variants of shamanism. A shaman is a medium/priest/magician, referred to as a "medicine man" in an American Indian context and a "witch doctor" in an African one. The witch doctor has the power to commune with the spirits and to travel at will into the astral plane (pp.244-245). He is often the most powerful member of the tribe. Anthropological studies, such as those referred to in Sigmund Freud's *Totem and Taboo* have revealed the surprising fact that the chief of a tribe was often little more than a scapegoat to be sacrificed to the spirits when things were going badly. The witch doctor, who decided when the spirits were angry, was therefore responsible for the fate of the chief.

Possessed

A Voodoo priestess is willingly possessed by a spirit-god during a ritual (right). Devotees describe their bodies as being "ridden by divine horsemen"; Christian priests, however, claim practitioners open their souls to demonic possession.

Old Black Slave

Contrary to popular opinion, Voodoo is actually used to counter evil forces, such as the Haitian sorcerers who turn people into zombies, and the blood-sucking loup-garou. The witch doctor (below) "consults" the spirit of the "Old Black Slave", in order to heal his patient's injury.

CREATURES OF THE NIGHT

"*What manner of man is this, or what manner of creature is it in the semblance of man?*"

Bram Stoker *Dracula*

MOST OF US ARE FAMILIAR with the concept of the vampire: the sinister "undead" man or woman who slowly bleeds his or her victim to death, at the same time infecting them with unclean longings. Belief in the existence of such malignant and powerful individuals is worldwide. In Europe, the most famous vampire of all is to be found in fiction, in Bram Stoker's *Dracula*, a novel inspired by the real-life exploits of a sadistic fifteenth-century Romanian nobleman, Vlad the Impaler.

While gory tales of Vlad and Dracula caught the public imagination and fuelled fears of vampirism, the roots of such beliefs already existed. Stories of evil, blood-sucking demons are to be found in the Roman, Arabic, and Hebrew legends of antiquity. Some occultists believe that vampire legends were based on even older beliefs in werewolves – men who turn into vicious wolf-like creatures on nights with a full moon. For many centuries all over the world, belief in such creatures kept primitive people in fear; in parts of Africa, the peasant population

In Wolf's Clothing
Belief in werewolves – men that turn into savage, wolf-like creatures at night – has existed for centuries. Werewolves, (like the one depicted in the woodcut above) are usually described as being extremely hairy with long fang-like teeth. Some, even when in wolf form, retain human hands and feet, while others develop long claws. They all have a craving for human flesh.

firmly believed in the existence of were-leopards; reports of weretigers were common in areas of India for hundreds of years; and in certain areas of pre-communist China, it was widely accepted that some women had the power to transform themselves into foxes.

→ FANGS AND CLAWS ←

On the surface it might seem that vampires and werewolves are very different types of supernatural creature, but there are many similarities. Both are nocturnal and half-human. Both are "shape changers" – possessing the ability to transform themselves physically. For instance, vampires are usually ascribed the ability to take the form of wolves or bats. And indeed the sharp canine teeth and the claw-like nails of Bram Stoker's Count Dracula are decidedly wolf-like.

Despite their widespread notoriety (both being well-known to the modern public on account of their appearances in numerous horror films), belief in vampires and

Vlad the Impaler
Dracula was modelled on this evil Romanian nobleman (left).

Warding Off Wolves
According to werewolf lore, the only way to kill a werewolf is to shoot it with silver bullets (top). If you want to deter a werewolf from coming near, the plant wolfsbane (directly above), will keep it at bay.

Anti-Vampire Kit
*Vampires are tough creatures to get the better of.
Initially it may be hard even to identify one.
One sure way would be to look for a vampire's
reflection in a mirror – if there is no reflection
then you are truly in the presence of a vampire.
You will probably then want to keep it away from
you – garlic or a crucifix will do the trick. To kill a
vampire is more difficult: a
stake must be driven
through its heart.*

werewolves has virtually
died out in the West.
However, up until the end
of the eighteenth century,
people in the West genuinely
feared these evil creatures.
Evidence of their existence was seen
in, for instance, a corpse that, when
exhumed, seemed to have moved since its
burial. In reality, a corpse that had apparently
moved, and had, for instance, bloodied fingertips, could be explained by the gruesome fact
that people were sometimes buried alive – the
unfortunate victim had probably tried desperately to claw his or her way out of the coffin.

While tales of physical transformations and
the existence of blood-sucking vampires are
hard to believe, some occultists do believe in the
possibility of etheric
vampirism, or psychic transformations – the ability of
some people to absorb the
psychic energies of others.
One occultist claimed to have
transformed herself on a
psychic level into a wolf, which
seemed to have a will of its own.
As its will was to do evil, the
occultist needed all her powers of
creative visualization (pp.54-55) to
reabsorb the creature into herself.

→ MONSTERS OF THE MIND ←
Today, many people consider vampires and
werewolves to be monsters of the subconscious rather than the conscious mind.
Advances in the science of psychology are at
the root of this change of opinion: such phenomena as schizophrenia are put forward as
more credible explanations for the existence
of men who become monsters.

AUTOMATIC ART

"If ... painting becomes the habitual mode of expression, taking up the materials and beginning work (may) act suggestively and ... evoke a flight into a higher state"

Robert Henri *The Art Spirit*

THROUGHOUT HIS LIFE, the English psychic, Matthew Manning, has had uncanny experiences (p.136). He is also possessed of an unusual artistic talent. Not only is he a very competent painter in his own right, but at times he has produced drawings in the style of such legendary artists as Aubrey Beardsley, Pablo Picasso, and Albrecht Dürer.

Picasso died in April 1973. Three months later it would appear that he – or a non-human entity – psychically transmitted drawings and paintings through the hand of Matthew Manning. To all appearances these were late Picassos, showing the disregard for academic technique and conventional aesthetic sensibility that typified Picasso's work from *Guernica* until the end of his life – paintings for which art collectors paid large sums of money.

→ SPIRIT PAINTING ←

In his book, *The Link*, Manning told how he went about contacting the spirits of Picasso and other artists. He would sit with an ordinary felt-tip pen in his hand, concentrating his thoughts on a particular artist or illustrator. Almost immediately – in a state of consciousness rather than in a trance, as might be expected – he would feel his hand moving of its own volition. His hand would produce a drawing or picture in what was recognizably the style of, for example, Monet or Beardsley. Many of these paintings were signed with an authentic-looking signature or, as in the case of Beardsley, a monogram. Some were not, and Manning conjectured that these were the work of other deceased artists using his hand in order to pay homage to painters they admired.

Some believers in spiritualism have asserted that when Manning produced his works of "automatic art" his hand was under the control of the spirits of the artists whose styles they resembled. If so, there were either difficulties in transmission from the world of spirit to Manning's mind and body, or the technical standards of the artists had dropped since they left their physical bodies. For instance, the Manning "Monet", although recognizable as the style of Monet, is a very poor "Monet" indeed. This is not to doubt that Manning's automatic art was produced as he said it was – without his conscious volition. Those who know Manning have all been convinced of his sincerity. There are, however, various explanations of how he came to produce his automatic drawings that do not involve authentic communication with the spirits of dead art masters.

→ ASTRAL ART ←

One explanation is offered by occultists who have made a serious study of automatic art and of the various literary works attributed to great writers, such as Shakespeare and Charles Dickens, which have been received through the agency of spiritualist mediums. The astral plane (p.48), say such occultists, has a very mixed population of spirits – beneficent ones; minor demons of the sort that possess men and women (p.142); and entities that are neither really good nor bad, but are essentially

After Beardsley
This ink drawing (above), by Matthew Manning, depicts Salome after her notorious "dance of the seven veils", holding the head of John the Baptist. It is drawn after the style of the British Art Nouveau artist, Aubrey Beardsley. Manning believed that he was in contact with the spirit of Beardsley, who guided his hand to produce drawings. Manning also produced drawings in the style of Francisco de Goya, Pablo Picasso, and Albrecht Dürer. Manning's fascinating powers originally manifested themselves when he was only eleven years old, and continued throughout his lifetime.

mischievous, delighting in practical jokes. These latter are often referred to as "elementals", a word coined by the sixteenth-century alchemist, Paracelsus, and which, strictly speaking, should be applied only to the classes of discarnate beings known as sylphs, salamanders, undines, and gnomes. It is suggested that these astral hoaxers exert their influence on psychics, enabling them to produce excellent imitations of the works of famous artists and writers.

⇢ ART AND THE UNCONSCIOUS ⇠

Another hypothesis explaining automatic art has been put forward by a number of psychiatrists, and concerns the dissociation of consciousness (p.110). What takes over the mind and hand of the psychic who produces automatic drawings, poetry, or music, is not, they argue, a discarnate spirit of any sort, but a segment of the psychic's own unconscious mind.

This segment is concerned with particular artists and writers with whose work the psychic is familiar, and with whom he actually identifies himself. When a medium or psychic becomes dissociated, therefore, and is taken over by the art segment of the unconscious, he or she produces work derivative of the style of a particular artist or writer. In many ways this is a very convincing theory – but, as is shown on the following pages, it still leaves a great many questions unanswered.

Spirit Picture
This picture (above) is allegedly a "precipitated" photograph mysteriously produced by an American medium. Evidence has emerged for the influence of the mind on matter, and at early seances some mediums produced objects out of thin air.

A Sad Note
This snatch of old French (left) was produced automatically in 1988 by a medium called "Katie". Such writings often reveal unhappiness, perhaps welling up from a level of the subconscious from which knowledge, not available to the conscious mind, is somehow tapped.

Par faim la
Pray Fera
loup
Prisonnier,
extreme
detresse,
la

AUTISTIC ARTISTS

The very existence of autistic children – children who are of normal or high intelligence but who are largely unable to communicate with others – was unsuspected until a few decades ago. People were, of course, aware that there were children who were cut off from the world around them; but it was assumed that they were of low intelligence. Today autism is a recognized condition. Autistic children have been closely observed, and it has been noted that some of them display considerable artistic or mathematical ability. There is, for example, an autistic child, Stephen Wiltshire, who is able to draw with incredible accuracy the architectural details of historic buildings.

Could it be that the artistic skills of autistic children such as this are in some way related to the temporary trance states experienced by automatic artists?

SPIRIT CONVERSATIONS

*"There needs no ghost, my lord,
Come from the grave,
To tell us this"*

William Shakespeare *Hamlet*

IN HIS BOOK, *Folklore of China*, published in 1870, the writer, Nicholas B. Dennys, described a method used by Chinese mediums of getting messages from the spirit world. A medium is a psychic who supposedly acts as a channel between the worlds of spirit and matter. The oriental medium would hold a pointed, T-shaped stick over a table covered with a thin layer of sand. The crossbar of the T would be balanced on the palms of his hands, the pointed end would rest on the sand table, and the point

Ectoplasm
In the early days of the spiritualist movement some mediums caused excitement by producing ectoplasm – a peculiar, pasty, substance exuding from the mouth or body during a state of trance. In this case, the hands of the medium, Dorothy Henderson (below), are held by sitters on either side. Few researchers take ectoplasm seriously and believe that it was produced fraudulently.

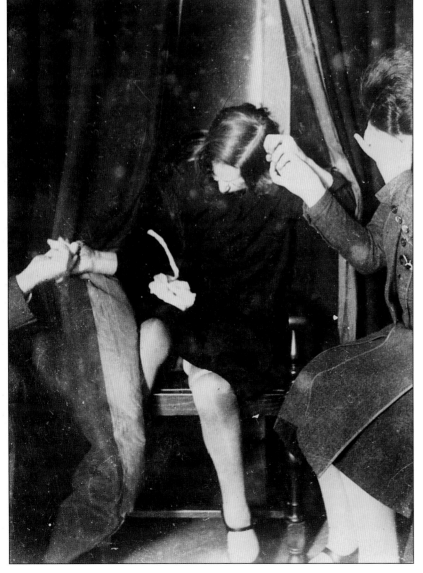

would move, tracing out Chinese characters conveying advice to the medium's clients. Dennys had an unsympathetic approach to matters psychic but, on the basis of his own observations, he was sure that these mediums did not consciously exert any muscular force.

➔ PATIENCE WORTH ←

In the early decades of the twentieth century, two mediums living in St. Louis, Missouri – a Mrs. Curran and a Mrs. Hutchings – used a similar method in an attempt to develop their own powers. The early communications they received were unimpressive, but very quickly Curran developed extraordinary psychic abilities and, over the next 25 years, produced some of the most remarkable mediumistic writings in the history of psychic research.

The entity who made these communications through the mediumship of Curran called herself "Patience Worth", and claimed to be the spirit of a seventeenth-century Dorset girl who had emigrated to America and been murdered by Indians. It is unclear whether Patience was the spirit of someone who had once lived on earth, a hoaxing elemental (p.117), or a fully developed secondary personality (p.57) of Curran. One thing, however, is absolutely certain – she was a talented and prolific writer. Over a period of five years she communicated 1,600,000 words through Curran's mediumship.

➔ HISTORICAL NOVELS ←

Most communications of this sort lack any literary merit whatsoever – they are of interest only because they are supposedly communications from the world of spirit. This is not the case with the writings dictated to Curran by Patience Worth, many of which took the form of historical novels. Indeed one of the novels she wrote in this way, *Hope Trueblood*, was published in Britain with no indication that there was any psychic element in its composition, and was reviewed favourably by several newspapers.

Hope Trueblood was set in mid-nineteenth century Britain. Patience Worth seems to have known an extraordinary amount about the social life of this period. Even more surprising was the knowledge revealed by Curran's communicator in *The Sorry Tale*, a story that related the life of one of the two thieves who were crucified with Jesus. The author of the book clearly had considerable historical knowledge of the social and political life of Palestine around the time of Jesus, and of the domestic arrangements of both the Greeks and the Hellenized Jews.

Such knowledge is very difficult to explain away on the hypothesis that it was already present in a segment of Curran's own mind. It is even more difficult to explain it on the basis of the spirit of a seventeenth-century Dorset peasant girl communicating through a powerful medium. How could Patience Worth know about the life of ancient Palestine? Perhaps Curran, or Patience Worth, was unconsciously in telepathic contact with spirits who had lived at those times? Or, as some occultists would argue, Curran was reading "astral records" (p.246)?

An unusual aspect of this case is that there was nothing at all unusual about Mrs. Curran prior to 1913, when Patience Worth first contacted her. She seems to have been a typical, perfectly respectable American housewife. And yet, for a period of 25 years or so, she claimed she was in contact with a discarnate being.

"Voices in my Ear"
Doris Stokes (below) wrote several best-selling books, such as Voices in my Ear, *on her life as a medium.*

Dead Poets
Mrs. Pearl Curran (above), a prolific automatist, produced writings of an extremely high quality. She had the uncanny ability of producing beautiful poetry instantly upon the proposal of a topic. One of her novels won a Pulitzer prize.

Automatic Writing
Countless cases of automatic writing (left) have been recorded over the centuries. Sometimes the writings are in a language unknown to the automatist, which presents a strong case for spiritual intervention as opposed to subconscious activity.

The nineteenth-century medium D.D. Home, for example, was denounced by the poet, Robert Browning, as a fraud and nicknamed, "Mr. Sludge the Medium". Subsequently Home was forced by legal action to return a substantial sum of money to an elderly female admirer. This makes Home sound dubious, yet there was no hard evidence that any of the extraordinary events that took place at his seances were fraudulent. Most of the evidence indicates that Home possessed supernormal powers.

→ THE FIRE-PROOF LEVITATOR ←

People whose opinions would have been accepted without question on any matter other than the supernatural, affirmed that they had witnessed Home perform seemingly impossible feats. These included laying his head in a fierce fire without injury, and floating in mid-air like a human balloon.

One witness of a levitation incident was the Reverend C.M. Davies who, in an article published in 1873, categorically asserted that he had seen Home float in the air of Mr. Samuel Carter Hall's drawing room for five minutes. Furthermore, he had checked "above and below" Home's body in order to ascertain whether the medium was suspended by some trick mechanism. He was not.

If Davies had been gullible where spiritualism was concerned, one would be inclined to dismiss his account as delusion or invention. He was, however, something of a sceptic. He considered a well-known medium of the day, Florence Cook, to be fraudulent even though she had convinced the scientist, Sir William Crookes, of her genuineness.

→ ASTRAL PROJECTIONS ←

Mr. Hall's own accounts of Home's levitations were quite specific. He had seen, he said, the medium float "in through the window, round the house, and out again".

What explanation can there be for such apparently impossible physical feats? Could it be that what Mr. Hall and others witnessed was not Home's "physical" body at all, but a projection of his astral body, not subject to this plane's laws of gravity or combustion?

Many spiritualists claim that we all have latent mediumistic powers of greater or lesser intensity. If so, can we bring our dormant powers into action? Can we carry out a sort of "psychical culture" that will have an effect upon our minds similar to that which physical exercise has upon our bodies? Convinced spiritualists tend to think that we can, but give two

D.D. Home
The Scottish psychic, Daniel Dunglas Home (right), is depicted levitating (above) at a seance in London. His extensive psychic abilities began with prophetic visions that foretold the death of his closest childhood friend and of his mother.

Mrs Curran's "normality" is, by no means, characteristic of all mediums, some of whom have been, in the phrase of the psychic researcher Dr. E.J. Dingwall, "human oddities". This has particularly applied to mediums associated with such psychic phenomena as the materialization of spirits; the spontaneous and inexplicable movement of heavy objects; and also the transportation of objects and even people, through solid matter.

warnings to those wishing to develop their psychic powers. First, no one should attempt to develop mediumship before reaching physical and psychological maturity. When the immature concern themselves with matters psychic, they tend to become neurotic and develop a one-sided attitude towards the occult that hinders their progression to full adulthood.

→ HEALTHY MIND ←

Second, no one should develop psychism who feels any doubt about their mental health; psychiatrists often encounter patients who have mistaken disordered messages from the depth of their own minds for spiritual revelations.

One of the simplest methods of developing any psychic powers you feel you may possess is to join a "development circle". Many local spiritualist groups in both Europe and the USA run such circles for would-be mediums. Those who are not interested in joining an organized group can still test their psychic powers by experimenting with automatic writing (p.116). All you need to do is sit down for a few minutes each day with a clear mind, and hold a pencil over a blank piece of paper. Sooner or later the pencil will move, seemingly independently of your own volition, and drawings, random words, and, eventually, meaningful sentences will be written, or images that are recognizable will be drawn. Whether these writings come from the spirit world or the unconscious mind is debatable – but those who produce them are manifesting what spiritualists would take to be mediumship.

Spirit Meetings
For centuries people have attempted to communicate with the spirits at meetings known as seances – taken from the French word for "sitting". One of the most popular types of seance (below) finds a group of spiritualists seated around a circular table. Spirits respond to questions asked by "rapping", turning, or even, on extreme occasions, levitating the table. The presence of a "medium" – a man or woman particularly sensitive to psychic influences – is usually beneficial, though not always essential, to the success of the sitting.

Joining Hands
The joining of hands (left) is often considered to be essential to the success of a seance. It is believed that the spirits use the combined psychic energy, contained within every living being, to produce physical effects upon our material plane. This could explain why the people taking part often feel drained after a seance.

THE SPIRIT WORLD

"The dissolution of our time-bound form in eternity brings no loss of meaning"

Carl Jung

Frederick Myers
F.W.H. Myers (left), a founder member of the "Society for Psychical Research" and author of Human Personality and the Survival of Bodily Death, *conspired with colleagues to provide "irrefutable proof" of life after death.*

Edmund Gurney
Edmund Gurney (below), 1847–1888, communicated with Mrs. Fleming, the sister of Rudyard Kipling, after his death.

Henry Sidgwick
Prof. Sidgwick (below), died one year before his friend, F. Myers, in 1900.

THERE ARE MANY DOUBTS about the genuineness of the purely physical phenomena associated with spiritualist mediumship, so much so that many serious psychical researchers have concluded that encroachments of the spirit world upon the dense matter of the physical are non-existent – the result of delusion or fraud.

→ DISCARNATE ENTITIES ←

On the other hand, it would be foolish to deny the existence of the mental phenomena of mediumship. There seems to be overwhelming evidence that natural psychics, such as Matthew Manning (p.116) and Mrs. Curran (p.118), attain curious and highly unusual psychological states in which, to all appearances, their minds and possibly their bodies are controlled by outside personalities – discarnate entities.

Is there, however, any evidence that these outside personalities are what mediums often claim they are – the spirits of the deceased? Have any of the phenomena associated with spiritualism been of such a nature that they have proved, or at least indicated a strong

THE SURVIVAL OF THE SOUL

The belief that human beings are possessed of souls is ancient. Indeed, there is some evidence to support the theory that this belief is almost as ancient as mankind's capacity for tool making – human bones dating back to the Stone Age have been found painted with red ochre. Archaeologists believe that this was probably an attempt to ensure the survival of the souls of the deceased by magically endowing them with eternal life – symbolized by the colour red, which represented fresh blood.

It may be that only chieftains or other prominent individuals had their bones painted red and were thought to possess souls that could survive death. Certainly in ancient Egypt it was believed that only the souls of the great survived and went to join the sun god (above). It was later accepted that everyone's soul survives death – some to be punished, others rewarded.

possibility of, human survival after bodily death? Few unprejudiced psychic researchers would claim that the reality of life after death has been proved – but most would be prepared to admit that it is difficult to explain some psychic phenomena, except on the hypothesis that men and women continue to exist after their bodies have died and have been buried, cremated, or otherwise disposed of.

➜ THE CROSS-CORRESPONDENCES ←

A good example of such mental mediumistic evidence for the survival of the human soul was provided by what are usually referred to as the "cross-correspondences". They came to light as a result of messages communicated to a number of psychics by three "spirits" who claimed to be deceased members of the Society for Psychical Research. Namely, Mr. Edmund Gurney, Professor Henry Sidgwick, and Mr. Frederick Myers. The psychics who received the purported spirit messages were not professional mediums who might have been induced by some financial motive to engage in an elaborate fraud. They were middle-class amateur researchers and included Mrs. Fleming, the sister of Rudyard Kipling, and Mrs. Verrall, a highly respectable woman who taught classical languages at the University of Cambridge.

These two ladies and other psychics received complex messages that made very little sense at all, unless they were related together. To take an actual example, on May 7, 1907, a Boston medium received a clear message, "I want to say thanatos". Some three weeks earlier, on April 17, she had psychically "heard" the last word as "tanatos". On the previous day, May 6, in India, Kipling's sister had received, supposedly from the same spirit communicator, a very garbled phrase: "Maurice Morris Mors. And the shadow of death fell on his limbs."

➜ SHAKESPEARE AND DEATH ←

"Thanatos" is classical Greek for "death", and "mors" is its exact Latin equivalent. Thirteen days after the Mors message had been received, Mrs. Verrall, the Cambridge classicist, received a series of disjointed phrases that included "the fire of life ... fades and I am ready to depart .... Come away, come away, pallida mors."

"Pallida mors" is Latin for "pale death"; "Come away, come away" are the four opening words of a song in Shakespeare's *Twelfth Night* – the fifth word is "death". None of the three messages received by the psychics (one in the

Planchette
The planchette (below) is sometimes used to assist automatic art or writing. The board is used to hold a pencil and is supported on small wheels that allow for easy movement. The medium simply places his or her hand on the board, which is then manipulated by a spirit. Sceptics attribute the movement to the subconscious.

USA, one in India, and one in England) meant much by itself. Considered all together, however, it could have been that the same discarnate human intelligence was endeavouring to prove its survival by making Greek, Latin, and Shakespearean references to death – a "cross-correspondence".

➜ AN IMPOSSIBLE COINCIDENCE ←

If there had been only one cross-correspondence, it would have been foolish to regard it as anything save coincidence. There were, however, hundreds of cross-correspondences, received over a period of 30 years by the psychics who were in touch with the originators of the messages. The sheer volume would seem impossible to explain away as multiple coincidences or the consequences of mere chance. The cumulative evidence of the cross-correspondences is extremely weighty, despite the fact that no individual example is impressive by itself.

In India, on March 11, 1906, Alice Fleming, the amateur medium and sister of Rudyard Kipling, received a spirit message from one of the cross-correspondence communicators. It told her to ask the husband of the Cambridge psychic, Mrs. Verrall, the meaning of the date May 26, 1894, to both him and the late Frederick Myers – to which the communicator added, "I do not think they will find it hard to recall, but if so, let them ask Nora". By "Nora" the communicator was referring to a woman well-known to Mrs. Verrall and her husband – the widow of the psychical researcher Henry Sidgwick.

➜ THE NUMBER OF THE BEAST ←

Alice Fleming wrote to Mrs. Verrall to pass on the communicator's question, but only three days later – before her letter could have reached England, let alone been answered – she received another psychic message. It seemed obscure to the point of being meaningless; yet it was soon to prove of great significance. It read:

"18, 15, 4, 5, 14. 14, 15, 5, 12. Not to be taken as they stand. See Revelation 13, 18, but only the central eight words, not the whole passage."

It was obvious to Alice Fleming that "Revelation 13, 18" was a reference to a biblical text – Chapter 13, Verse 18 of the Revelation of St. John, also known as the Apocalypse, the last book of the New Testament. The verse in

Mrs. Sidgewick
Mrs. Eleanor Sidgewick (1845–1936), was Principal of Newnham College, Cambridge, and President of the Society for Psychical Research, (1908–1909). The aim of the society, founded in 1882, has always been "to examine without prejudice ... those faculties of man ... which appear to be inexplicable on any generally recognized hypothesis."

question reads, in the Authorized Version: "Here is wisdom. Let him that hath understanding count the number of the beast: for it is the number of a man; and his number is six hundred threescore and six."

➜ RODEN NOEL ←

Alice Fleming could make nothing of this; it appeared to have no relevance to any message previously received by her or any of the other psychics who were involved in the unravelling of the cross-correspondences. Nevertheless, she forwarded the message to England where it was examined by Miss Johnson, an enthusiastic psychical researcher.

Miss Johnson realized that the "central eight words" of the message could be interpreted in two ways: either literally to produce the meaningless phrase, "of the beast: for it is the number"; or by taking it less literally and looking at the punctuation and meaning of the verse, which produces "for it is the number of a man". Could the numbers that formed the two opening sentences of the message be equated with names, she wondered?

They could. When she consecutively numbered the letters of the alphabet from 1 to 26 and translated the numbers of the two sentences into letters, she got a name: "Roden Noel". So who was Roden Noel, and what relation was there between this person and the date referred to in the first message received by Alice Fleming. Roden Noel, a minor poet, was a good friend of Frederick Myers

FEAR OF NIGHT

One of the oldest of human terrors is fear of the dark and of the forces that lurk unseen in the night. Since very early times night has been personified in female form as the mother of both the joys and the horrors of darkness – as depicted here by Michelangelo in his figure of *Night* in the sacristy of San Lorenzo in Florence.

In the eighth century BC, the Greek writer, Hesiod, describing how the world came into being, wrote that Darkness and Night emerged from the primeval chaos. From their intermingling, Day and Sleep were born, as were Dreams and Pleasure of Love. Death and the tribe of other black horrors were also born of the union. Death has long been seen as the first cousin of Sleep.

Peaceful Night
Michelangelo's sculpture, Night, *in the sacristy of San Lorenzo, Florence, depicts peaceful sleep.*

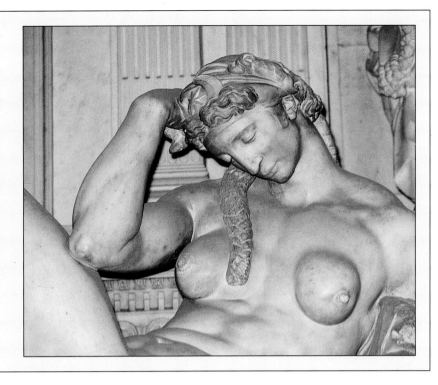

Mystifying Oracle
The Ouija Board (below) is used by spiritualists to make contact with the "other side". At one time sold on a commercial basis, the board has been taken off world markets because of the "disturbing and dangerous psychological effect" it has been known to have on inexperienced people.

and Mrs. Verrall's husband. He had died on May 26, 1894 – the date given in the first message received by Alice Fleming. Miss Johnson observed another cross-correspondence. Three days before Alice Fleming had received this first communication concerning Roden Noel – the one giving the date that proved to be that of the poet's death – Mrs. Verrall in Cambridge had reproduced by automatic writing a line from Noel's poem *Tintagel* – a poem which she had never read before.

→ THREE POSSIBILITIES ←

In judging the authenticity of the Roden Noel cross-correspondence, and hundreds of similar ones that came to light over a period of more than a quarter of a century, the student of matters psychic must consider three possibilities.

First, that the whole thing was an extended and rather pointless practical joke played by such respectable English ladies as Mrs. Fleming and Mrs. Verrall who, conspiring with others, such as the American medium, Mrs. Piper, were determined to waste the time of psychical researchers. There are those who seriously argue that this highly improbable theory was the most likely explanation for the phenomenon of the cross-correspondences.

Second, that the various psychics who received the cross-correspondences were in unconscious telepathic contact with one another – a contact so close that their minds partially merged to form a "group mind" that, for some mysterious reason, decided to purport to be Myers and other members of the Society for Psychical Research. This also seems improbable.

The third is that human beings survive bodily death and exist elsewhere than in the space and time of the universe of matter, and that human consciousness survives physical dissolution. In short, that death is not the end.

→ PROVING IMMORTALITY ←

The last possibility is not only the most exciting but, as far as most occultists are concerned, the most likely. For there are serious philosophical and physical objections to the idea that the widely separated and sharply differentiated minds of the mediums concerned could have merged into one, while the humourless seriousness of Mrs. Piper and the other sensitives involved makes it seem extremely improbable that they indulged in anything so frivolous as a practical joke. Nor is there the slightest indication that these thoroughly respectable ladies were so anxious to prove human survival that they were prepared to fake the evidence.

HEAVEN AND HELL

"Many of those who sleep in the dust shall awake, some to everlasting life, and some to shame and everlasting contempt"

The Book of Daniel

MOST RELIGIONS have their own view of heaven and hell. To Christians, heaven is everlasting bliss, while hell is everlasting spiritual agony. God and His angels sit in glory in Heaven, Satan and his devils occupy hell. The universe in which we physically live is the battlefield between the forces of heaven and hell – each of which strives to "occupy" the souls of men and women. Although early and medieval Christians saw heaven and hell as physical places to be enjoyed or endured for eternity, from the very beginnings of Christianity the idea existed that true hell was the spiritual agony of being cut off from God, and true heaven was the ecstasy of being in God's Kingdom.

↠ VIEWS OF HEAVEN ↞

One of the earliest civilizations to have believed in an afterlife was that of ancient Egypt. They concentrated on the rewards enjoyed in the afterlife, rather than the punishments.

Other religions have their own view of heaven and hell. For Buddhists and Hindus, for example, hell and heaven are not eternal states; rather they are part of a cycle of rebirth. In Islam, heaven is seen as a place of unlimited food, wine, and sensual delight. The Red Indians of America believe in the "happy hunting

Hell's Mouth
Demons torment the souls of the damned in a typically horrifying portrayal of the Christian concept of Hell as a place of physical torture (below).

ground" to which all the dead will go and which represents a better way of life than that on earth. In the minds of most believers, ideas of hell and heaven were part of folklore. If a good man or woman had an unexplained run of bad luck, it would invariably be blamed on Satan or on one of his imps. If a house was "troubled" by what would now be termed poltergeist phenomena, then blame would be laid on one of Satan's dark angels or, maybe, one of Satan's many allies such as a witch. Ghostly phenomena and

Just Desserts
The Ascent of the Prophet Muhammed to Heaven *(above) portrays the prophet being greeted by angels bearing gifts. The idea of heaven being a place where the just get their reward is an idea common to many, though by no means all, world religions.*

uncanny happenings associated with death, corpses, and funerals, were almost invariably looked upon as the work of God or the Devil. Sometimes, however, they resulted from the activities of the spirits of the dead who sought the prayers of saintly men.

→ A DREADFUL SPECTRE ←

A story was told concerning such prayer-seeking ghosts in a biography of Germanus, Bishop of Auxerre, who lived in the fifth century AD. The Bishop, visiting a remote part of his episcopal see in the company of some of his subordinates, stayed the night at an abandoned and reputedly haunted house. As one of the party read aloud to the others from a pious book:

"... there appeared ... a dreadful spectre ... while the walls were pelted with a shower of stones ... the Bishop ... fixed his eyes upon the fearful apparition ... he ordered it to declare who it was .... At once it lost its terrifying demeanour, and, speaking low ... said that he and a companion ... were lying unburied ... and disturbed the living because they themselves had no rest."

The Bishop ordered his men to search for the bodies and, after they were found, he ordered their Christian burial. Thereafter, the house ceased to be haunted.

Throughout the Middle Ages it was generally believed that such troubled spirits were in purgatory, suffering temporal punishment for their sins; when the purging was completed, they would attain to heaven. Other visitors, the saints, were thought of as being already in heaven, and when they approached human beings it was not to beseech prayers or Christian burial, but to warn, help, or even complain.

→ MOANING SPIRITS ←

Complaints from the saints could be about very minor things, suggesting that, although in heaven, they were still very concerned with earthly matters. For example, there are several medieval tales of a saint manifesting him or herself to grumble about the muddy footwear of pilgrims on his or her tomb. Somewhat more dramatic is a tale told by Gregory of Tours in his *Book of the Glory of the Blessed Martyrs* who reported that, when a thief opened the tomb of a saint at Lyons, the saint reanimated his own corpse, which grasped the would-be robber in its arms. Only when help arrived did the sanctified corpse loosen its grip.

Christian Heaven
The Virgin of the Lilies, *by Carlos Schwabe (left), is a typical depiction of the Christian idea of heaven.*

DEVILS AND ANGELS

*"**B**e thou a spirit of health or goblin damn'd. Bring with thee airs from heaven or blasts from hell"*

William Shakespeare *Hamlet*

ALTHOUGH DEVILS AND ANGELS belong primarily to the regions of hell and heaven, they do, according to folklore, occasionally stray into the mortal world. In medieval England, for instance, it was believed it was possible to summon devils, or even the Devil himself. If a knight wished to challenge a devil to a duel, he had to wait until there was a full moon and then ride into a particular fort and call for the devil to appear. A demon would then manifest itself in human form as a knight ready for battle.

According to the medieval *Gesta Romanorum* (*Stories of the Romans*), a warrior named Albert managed to defeat a spectral visitant from hell

The Furies
This detail from the Doré illustration to Dante's Inferno *(below) depicts "the furies", implacable she-devils who wreaked terrible revenge when summoned by Fate. These ugly sisters were born from the blood of Uranus who was castrated with a sickle by his youngest son, Cronus. The chief task of the furies was to exact revenge against the "betrayers of blood kinship". They did not harm Cronus who acted on his mother's wishes against his tyrant father.*

and temporarily capture his steed. At dawn the latter, "foaming and ... furiously striking the ground" managed to escape. It was pursued but "vanished in an instant". It is by no means clear whether the phantom knight was a true demon – a devil who had followed Lucifer in his rebellion against God – or a lost soul, a human being who had been damned and had taken on demonic attributes. Such an ambiguity was very common in medieval and Renaissance accounts of supernatural phenomena.

→ WANDERING SOULS ←

There were good theological reasons for such an approach to ghostly manifestations. Many were doubtful as to whether it was really possible for souls in purgatory to visit the earth, and, after the Reformation, some denied the existence of purgatory. These latter held that the souls of the

When the time comes for an evil man to die, LILITH appears to him and induces him to sin with her, and during his sin she kills him

however, it was diabolic rather than angelic intervention that was most in evidence in human affairs, and numerous pious individuals were subjected to devilish persecutions and assaults. For instance, one victim of infernal malevolence and ingenuity was an ecclesiastic named Richalmus, a man who saw demons everywhere. He even attributed the flatulence, accompanied by belching, and other unpleasant symptoms that oppressed him during the performance of his religious duties, to the activities of Satan and his minions

⤍ DEMONIC INFLUENCE ⬰

By the middle of the nineteenth century, few people believed that indigestion was hellish in the literal sense of the word. Yet large numbers of people observed what they believed to be new manifestations of both angelic and demonic influence – the phenomena associated with spiritualism. The spiritualist, Frederick Hockley, believed that he was in psychic communication with a being known as the "Crowned Angel", and some spiritualists attribute obscenities in automatic writing to demons.

The latter half of the twentieth century has witnessed a surprisingly widespread revival of belief in angels and demons; even such a middle-of-the-road evangelist as Billy Graham has asserted the reality of both, and expounded upon the nature of the influences he believes them to exert upon the human soul.

departed were either in heaven or in hell, and would never be allowed to leave their home. Amongst the great Doctors of the Church who asserted that the spirits of the dead did not normally manifest themselves to humanity was St. Augustine of Hippo. He accepted that on rare occasions, with divine permission, ghosts had genuinely appeared to men and women.

He believed, however, that the overwhelming majority of alleged ghosts were demons in disguise. He felt sure, he said, that if the spirits of the dead were all free to visit the living, then he would have seen the ghost of his dead mother, and many more people would have seen ghosts.

Until very recent times most Christians were as convinced as St. Augustine both of the reality of angels and demons and of their ability to intervene in human affairs. On the whole,

Lilith
Queen of the demons, Lilith seduces men in their dreams and sucks their blood. In the picture above she tempts a dying man to sin while Lucifer waits to steal his soul.

The Fall
The Fall of the Rebel Angels *(right) by Gustav Doré, from Milton's* Paradise Lost, *shows Lucifer and his legions being cast down into hell,* "there to dwell in adamantine chains and penal fire".

PHOTOGENIC PHANTOMS

"To explain this negative it is necessary to look in another direction than fraud or double exposure"

Emile le Roux

A VERY LARGE NUMBER of alleged spirit photographs – photographs purporting to show ghosts – survive in the archives of the Society for Psychical Research and in private collections. Most of them are obviously fraudulent, produced for gain by unscrupulous photographers desirous of making money out of the grief of those who had lost their loved ones. Most of these frauds were eventually exposed as tricksters, and some were the subjects of criminal prosecutions.

Amongst these was one of the earliest spirit-photographers, William H. Mumber, who had begun his career in Boston in 1861 but had subsequently moved his studio to New York's Broadway. Mumber's photographs of supposed

Cottingley Fairies
One of the most well-known "fairy stories" of all time is probably that of the Cottingley fairies (below). Between 1917 and 1921 two girls, Elsie Wright and Frances Griffiths, took what they purported to be photographs of fairies they had seen in Cottingley in Yorkshire, England. Years later, the girls admitted that the photographs were fake, made by pinning cut-out pictures of fairies to greenery. They maintained, however, that they had actually seen, and unsuccessfully attempted to photograph, real fairies.

spirits seem to have been produced by fairly simple trickery involving double-exposure and the substitution of a previously prepared plate for a sealed one. Nevertheless, in 1869 a New York jury acquitted him of a charge of obtaining money by false pretences. It must be presumed that the jury gave the verdict they did, which was against the weight of the evidence, because they were overawed by the testimony of a number of prominent individuals – the eminent banker Charles Livermore, for example – who swore to their belief in the genuineness of Mumber's productions.

➜ UNINTENTIONAL DISCOVERIES ←

On the whole, the most impressive spirit photographs have been taken by people who have had no intention of doing so. They have simply taken a photograph of a person or a place and subsequently found that unexplained "extras" had appeared on the print.

GROUP PHOTOGRAPH

In 1975 a retired R.A.F. officer, Sir Victor Goddard, published a description of a photograph that stood on his desk. It was meant to show the members of his squadron, who had survived World War I. However, it included the face of Freddy Jackson, an air mechanic, whose funeral had taken place on the day the photograph was taken; he had been killed by an aircraft propeller two days earlier. Sir Victor suggested that maybe Jackson was unaware of his death and so turned up for the photograph. Others have suggested that his face is actually no more than a blemish on the film, which bears an uncanny resemblance to the dead man's face.

Face in the Background
The face of a dead air mechanic, Freddy Jackson, appears in the group photograph (right) in the back row, fourth from the left.

Spectral Snap
An English photographer named Boursnell produced this photograph in 1890. It purports to show a spectral figure standing behind the somewhat sinister looking person in the foreground. What exactly a ghost is, and – depending on what it is – whether it could conceivably appear in a photograph, are puzzling questions. Spirit photographers were at work in the United States and Britain from the 1850s, but most were exposed as fraudulent. The phenomenon was related to the claims that early mediums could conjure up the spirits of the departed in visible and tangible form. This created great interest at the time – but the idea is now regarded with some suspicion. Trick photography, dirty lenses, or accidents in developing the film, are often blamed.

Many of the supposed spirit extras no doubt resulted from accidental double exposures of particular negatives. Others seem to have resulted from other factors that may have been, in essence, supernormal.

→ SEMI-TRANSPARENT FIGURE ←

For example, in 1891, Miss Sybell Corbet took a photograph of the library at Combermere Abbey, a magnificent country house in Cheshire, England. When it came to be developed the plate showed not only the library but what appeared to be the semi-transparent figure of the late Lord Combermere, whose funeral was taking place at the very time at which Miss Corbet was taking her picture.

It could have been a simple case of double exposure. Nevertheless, it proved impossible for investigators to identify any occasion on which Miss Corbet could have photographed Lord Combermere during his lifetime. This incident is curious, and like almost all purported instances of spirit photography, raises questions that are impossible to answer.

Could Miss Corbet have had such a strong will to believe in human survival that she engaged in unconscious fraud, making a double exposure but remembering nothing of it? Or, more likely, could some hoaxer have obtained access to her camera and inserted a previously exposed film inside it?

GHOSTLY ENCOUNTERS

*"Let the earth hide thee
Thy bones are marrowless,
thy blood is cold"*

William Shakespeare *Macbeth*

ONE DAY IN FEBRUARY 1907, Police Constable 265T was on duty at London's Hampton Court, a palace built by Henry VIII's Chancellor, Cardinal Wolsey, for himself. In 1529, however, Wolsey fell from grace when he failed to obtain papal consent for the king's divorce from his first wife. The palace was subsequently taken over by the king, who, with characteristic nonchalance, seized all Wolsey's property and condemned him to death.

As the policeman patrolled Ditton Walk, one of the paths that crisscross the grounds of Hampton Court, he saw a group of people approaching him – two or three men, rather formally dressed, and seven or eight women wearing long dresses. The group turned off from Ditton Walk, formed itself into a two-deep procession, and headed for the Flower Pot Gate, one of the exits from the palace grounds to the road that runs from the town of Kingston to the village – now London suburb – of Hampton.

As PC 265T watched this unusual procession, it vanished suddenly from sight. In the words of that respected and sceptical ghost-hunter, Peter Underwood, writing in 1977:

"One moment they were there, lifelike and looking absolutely natural and normal; the next moment they had completely disappeared." The official report of this incident is still preserved in the station occurrence book.

The Great Hall
Hampton Court, in London, has a rich history, and has been connected with many bloody events. It was built in 1514 by Cardinal Wolsey, Henry VIII's Chancellor. Later, when Wolsey fell out of the king's favour, it was taken over by the king himself. Like many stately homes it is said to be haunted. Ghosts have been seen in the grounds, in the gallery, and in the Great Hall (above).

THE SCREAMING QUEEN

This curious event may well have been the result of hallucination – but a surprisingly large number of individuals have had curious experiences at Hampton Court. For example, in the 1960s an actor, Leslie Finch, saw a "grey misty figure in Tudor costume". According to the folklorist, Christina Hole, many residents of the palace have heard terrified screams from the gallery, which is supposedly haunted by Queen Catherine Howard, who was executed by Henry VIII in 1542.

Ghosts seem most at home in ancient buildings that have been the scene of bloody and terrible events. It is almost as though such places absorbed the unpleasant emotions of those who suffered and passed away within their walls, subsequently playing them back in the form of "hauntings" – uncanny feelings and psychic re-enactments giving rise to overpowering terror.

Some ghosts, however, have manifested themselves in extremely prosaic surroundings. General Andrew Jackson (1767–1845), later to become the seventh president of the United States, had an extraordinary encounter with a ghost in the roadway leading to the front entrance of the home of a Tennessee plantation owner.

At the time the future president was driving a wagon pulled by a team of army horses. Suddenly it stopped, as though fixed to the ground. The horses strained against their harnesses, but the wagon remained immobile. The startled General Jackson called out "By the Eternal ... it's a witch", and received a reply from an incisive but disembodied voice, "All right, General, let the wagon move", at which words the wagon, so Andrew Jackson affirmed, once more moved forward.

⇥ IN BED WITH A GHOST ⇤

At the time when Andrew Jackson is reputed to have had his encounter with the ghost who immobilized his wagon, he was staying on the plantation of a close friend, John Bell. The plantation was notorious for the loathsome activities of a ghost, nick-named the "Bell Witch".

According to Richard Bell, a young son of John Bell, the phenomena associated with the haunting attracted the attention of numerous amateur investigators, all of whom met with "egregious defeat". Amongst these

MADAME LA GUILLOTINE

During times of great violence, subliminal fears about the dead often come to the forefront of the minds of the people who are living the events. So much blood was spilled in the Terror during the French Revolution and so many victims went to feel the bite of *Madame la Guillotine*, that a feeling grew among the general population that blood would have blood, that the restless ghosts of the dead would take their revenge.

Bloody Death (below) The creator of the Terror, Maximilien Robespierre was eventually guillotined.

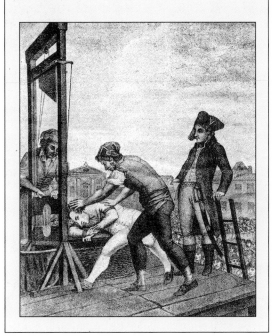

Two Presidents
Andrew Jackson's (above) story of his encounter with a murderous spirit on the Tennessee plantation of his friend, John Bell, gained credence from his reputation for toughness, and straightforwardness. A lawyer and soldier, he became president of the United States in 1828. He was not the only US President to have had uncanny experiences. Abraham Lincoln seems to have been fascinated by occult phenomena and attended a number of seances. At one of these, a supposed spirit, speaking through the body of the young medium, Nettie Colburn Maynard, is reported to have lectured him on the importance of the abolition of slavery. At another he and his bodyguard were supposedly levitated along with the piano on which they were sitting. Lincoln once recounted a vivid dream in which his body was laid out in state. Several days later he was assassinated.

investigators was William Porter, a neighbour who spent a night in the house and, according to his own account, had the unpleasant experience of the ghost getting into bed with him, rolling the bed-clothes into a tight ball, and giving forth a loathsome stench.

Porter seized the bed-clothes, which seemed to have become preternaturally weighty, with the intention of burning them, and staggered halfway across the room with them. He did not get very far, however; he recorded that they:

"got so heavy and became so offensive that I was compelled to drop them ... and rush out of doors for a breath of fresh air. The odour ... was the most offensive stench I ever smelled."

⇥ HAUNTED TO DEATH ⇤

The ghostly nuisance continued to produce this and other even more startling phenomena, for example the vomiting of pins and needles by one of the children, for a period of four years from 1817 until 1821. In that year, some three months after the mysterious death by poisoning of John Bell, a ball of glowing plasma rolled out of the chimney and burst apart while a voice declaimed "I'm going and will be gone for seven years". I should think the remaining family breathed a huge sigh of relief. Nandor Fodor, a Freudian psychotherapist, pointed out the most unusual feature about the case of the Bell Witch:

"Modern poltergeists, no matter how much mischief and destruction they wreak, stop short of murder. The Bell ... (poltergiest) did not, and it only ceased its activities after the death by poisoning of John Bell ... whom it tortured and persecuted with a fury of unrelenting savagery."

⇥ A CLEVER VENTRILOQUIST? ⇤

Like all poltergeist cases there are other possible explanations of the Bell phenomena that do not involve the supernatural. The voice of the supposed spirit could have been produced by ventriloquism; the physical phenomena, most of which took place in lamplit rooms rather than broad daylight, could have been fraudulent; John Bell could have committed suicide or, more probably, been the victim of a murder carried out by a close relation.

The basic question remains: is the Bell case best explained on the hypotheses of fraud, murder, and hysteria? Or was John Bell in truth the unfortunate victim of an executioner from the world of the unseen?

Willington Mill, near the English town of Newcastle-upon-Tyne, was built by a Quaker family named Procter at around the beginning of the nineteenth century.

Unlike Hampton Court (p.132), nothing very dramatic seems to have taken place within its walls – so it was an unlikely place for spectres to haunt. Yet by the 1840s it was sufficiently notorious as a site of ghostly phenomena for a Mr. Drury, an amateur ghost hunter, to seek the permission of the Procter family to spend a night in the mill.

➜ BUMPS IN THE NIGHT ←

Rather surprisingly, the Procters agreed to this request, and Drury, accompanied by a friend, carried out his investigation. The results exceeded his expectations. At midnight, the traditional hour for apparitions to manifest themselves, Drury heard the sounds of footsteps, a rattling cough, repeated knocking on the floor, and someone rushing up the stairs.

There could well have been nothing in the least supernatural about these sound effects. Perhaps

Indian Braves
Many spiritualist mediums have claimed a special relationship with a spirit "guide" or "control" from the world beyond death, a go-between who puts the medium in touch with other departed spirits who have messages for the living. In quite a number of cases in the United States, the control was believed to have been in life an American Indian, like these Chickasaw braves from an early illustration (below). American Indian "shamans" were believed to have the power to leave their bodies and penetrate the world of the spirits, so making appropriate "guides".

the Procter family were playing a practical joke upon their intrusive visitors, but an hour later both Drury and his friend witnessed less easily explicable happenings. A grey-clad woman appeared as if from nowhere, pointed with her finger to the floor, and advanced towards Drury's sleeping friend. The latter awoke and hurled himself towards the ghost which, said Drury, immediately dematerialized.

Other visitors to Willington Mill recorded even stranger apparitions. Two women reported an eyeless figure of "a bluish-grey hue" walking through a wall, while a married couple and their daughter saw a robed, half-transparent figure, which dimmed, turned blue, and slowly vanished, starting with its head.

By the 1850s, the Procters had endured quite enough of this spectacular (although apparently pointless) haunting and put their home up for sale. Throughout the course of these spectral episodes, which seem to have extended over a period of more than ten years, the ghost, or ghosts, of Willington Mill never gave the slightest indication of why they were haunting the Procters' rather than their own home, and no historical reason is evident. It is possible, as some contemporary occultists would conjecture, that some member of the family was an unconscious medium, leaking uncontrolled psychic energies that produced auditory and visual hallucinations in other people's minds.

➜ POTATOES AND PURGATORY ←

Not all nineteenth-century ghosts were as seemingly unmotivated as those that haunted Willington Mill. Some were reported to be concerned about serious matters: others with the minutiae of everyday life. A good example of the latter is provided by the case of the ghost of Henry Duty, who died in 1855. Apparently Duty was a keen gardener. According to William White, who succeeded Duty in the tenancy of his Sussex cottage, the deceased gardener materialized in the kitchen of his former home, indicated the whereabouts of some seed potatoes, and vanished away.

A German ghost of much the same period had a more serious desire – he came to beg the prayers of the faithful that he might be released from the fires of purgatory. This ghost was a thoroughly traditional one. His materializations were invariably accompanied by a smell of the grave, his touch was cold, and he alternately

The Crypt – Glamis Castle
There is a legend that Glamis Castle in Scotland
(above) contains a secret room inhabited by a monster.

Sir Oliver Lodge
Sir Oliver Lodge (right), the distinguished physicist,
was a member of the Society for Psychical Research.

wept boiling and freezing tears. All these
phenomena were described in medieval
reports of hauntings, as were requests for
prayers for release from purgatory.

⇢ REVEREND CHRISTMAS ⇠

Nineteenth-century Protestants found
such accounts, whether medieval or
modern, impossible to believe, and the
Reverend H. Christmas, an Anglican
priest with considerable scientific
knowledge, commented upon the
idea that: "the spirits of the dead
should be permitted to return to earth
... to support the doctrines of Masses
for the dead, purgatory and ... penance ...
is worthy of the darkest ... days of heathenism."
Clearly the Reverend Christmas believed that

those who claimed to have encountered "ghosts
from purgatory" were lying or deluded. The
member of the Society for Psychical Research,
to whom the potato-obsessed ghost of Henry
Duty was reported, came to much the same sort
of conclusion about his informant.

Many such siting s of ghosts or spirits cannot
be so easily explained. But if not delusion or
prevarication, then what? It is possible to advance another explanation for unlikely tales of
ghosts and hauntings.

If ghosts exist at all, they are, by definition,
living in some world other than the world of
matter. Those who perceive them, therefore,
must be using some mode of perception other
than that of the five senses.

Ordinary people, however, can rarely
understand anything outside their normal
perception and usual range of beliefs and
activities. As a result, so it has been argued,
spirit communications are often received in
garbled form, so a believing Catholic "sees"
spirits from purgatory, while an enthusiastic
gardener, however bizarre it may seem, will
probably "hear" messages about something very
dear to him – such as potatoes.

MISCHIEVOUS SPIRITS

"This is the very Mab that plats the manes of horses in the night; And bakes the elf-locks in foul sluttish hairs"

William Shakespeare *Romeo and Juliet*

IN 1967, AT THE AGE OF ELEVEN, Matthew Manning, the psychic artist who later "received" works of art from dead painters such as Beardsley and Picasso (p.116), was at the centre of the first of a string of odd events.

At first the events involved no more than the mysterious movement of lightweight objects, nothing that could not be explained as the antics of a mischievous child. For example, a silver tankard would be moved from a shelf to the floor, or a coffee table would be found a few metres away from its usual position. Subsequently the phenomena became less easy to explain. For example, taps, creaks, and dull knockings were heard by both night and day in various parts of the Mannings' home.

The disturbances were persistent enough for Matthew's parents to seek the advice of Dr. A.R.G. Owen, a Cambridge psychical researcher. He told them that the events that had

Haunted House
Borley Rectory in Essex, England (below), has been described as the "most haunted house in England". Apparitions that have been seen there include headless men, a girl in white, and a nun. In the 1930s, the house became the scene of spectacular poltergeist phenomena. Objects flew through the air, strange noises were heard, and doors locked and unlocked themselves. The house was investigated by researchers. Whilst some concluded that there was no real evidence to support any of the claims, others believed that the house had been a centre of supernatural activity. The controversy still reigns, although the rectory was burned down in 1948.

taken place were typical of those associated with what is now generally termed "poltergeist activity". The word "poltergeist" is derived from a German term meaning "noisy (or knocking) spirit". There have been reports of the supposed activities of these mischievous entities since classical times. "Mischievous" is more appropriate than "malignant" as poltergeist phenomena are rarely associated with physical injury to their victims. For example, heavy objects appear to levitate and crash to the ground, but usually without hitting anyone close to the scene of the disturbance.

→ CHILDREN AND ADOLESCENTS ←

Dr. Owen told the Mannings not only that poltergeist activity appeared to be at work, but that it is difficult to bring such phenomena to an end save by removing the person who seems to be the focus of the disturbances, usually a child or an adolescent, from the home in which the disturbances manifest themselves.

Accordingly, the Manning children were sent to stay with relatives and, later on, Matthew was sent away to school. For a time, the Mannings' home was free of mysterious noises and

37 Abbot Road
Unlike the Transylvanian castles and grim, pinnacled fortresses popularly believed to be the haunts of vampires, perfectly ordinary houses such as 37 Abbot Road, (right) are the more likely scene of poltergeist attacks. Investigations suggest that these curious cases are unconsciously caused by disturbed children or adolescents.

Spirit Vandals
Poltergeist attacks are a kind of psychic vandalism, in which bedding is ripped up and ornaments smashed – as shown here (below) in part of what seems like a childish tantrum. The missing "motive" may simply be that the child, or child-like spirit, is seeking attention. Reports of anyone actually seeing the spirit are very rare.

perambulating coffee tables. When Matthew returned, however, the disturbances resumed with greater intensity. Was Matthew a disturbed adolescent playing, perhaps unconsciously, a series of tiresome practical jokes on his family?

It would seem not, for some of the observed phenomena, such as the manifestation of sudden and inexplicable temperature differentials between one part of a room and another, would have been difficult for anyone to produce by trickery without the use of sophisticated equipment – and almost impossible for a teenage boy under, as he was, fairly constant observation by either members of his own family or independent outside observers.

⇥ A CHILDISH TANTRUM ⇤

Of course, some supposed poltergeists really are naughty children. On the other hand, however, it is difficult to explain many accounts of poltergeist activity save on the hypothesis that some children and adolescents spontaneously induce "psychic phenomena" that are attributable to the activities of disembodied spirits.

Poltergeist phenomena are sometimes spectacular and frequently alarming to those who witness them, but there is often a certain pointlessness about them. The poltergeist seems to behave like a child in a tantrum, making much fuss and noise but achieving nothing.

Adolescent Link
*The German psychical
researcher and professor
of psychology, Hans
Bender (right),
investigated a number of
poltergeist cases in the
1950s and '60s. In one of
them, nails and clothes-
pegs flew about of their
own accord in the house of
the Mayor of Neudorf.
When touched, the objects
were warm. The incidents
occurred only when the
mayor's 13-year-old son
was present. In another
case, in a Bremen china
shop, glasses and crockery
stopped flying off the
shelves only when a 15-
year-old apprentice left.*

In the eighteenth century, the Wesley family,
supporters of King George I, came to the conclusion that the spirit who apparently afflicted
their household was a Jacobite, that is to say, a
political supporter of the exiled House of Stuart,
one who believed that King George I was not
the rightful King of England. The Wesleys
arrived at that conclusion because the poltergeist
knockings of "Old Jefferey" were typically at
their worst when the family,
including all the ser-
vants, were present

at prayers for King George I. A possible clue as
to the origins of this "Jacobite poltergeist" was
provided by John Wesley himself, who wrote:

"My mother did not say amen to the prayer
for the king ... she did not believe ... [King
George I] was king. [My father] vowed he
would never cohabit with her till she did ... He
... [continued] as before. But I fear his vow was
not forgotten before God."

If, as has been argued, psychic forces can be
derived from explosive human situations, then
Old Jefferey may have been an unconscious
psychic projection of the Jacobitism of Mrs.
Wesley or one of her children.

↠ NO VISIBLE POWER ↞

Family tensions may also have been responsible for the psychic phenomena that in the
early 1850s manifested themselves in the home
of the Reverend Diakim Phelps in Stamford,
England . These were far more spectacular than
those that had plagued the Manning (p.136) or
the Wesley households, and were described by
one observer as follows:

"Bags of salt, tin ware, and heavier culinary
articles were thrown ... with a loud and startling
noise .... The large knocker ... would thunder ...
unmindful of the vain but
rigid scrutiny to which it was
subjected .... Heavy marble-
top tables would poise
themselves upon two
legs, and then fall
with their contents
to the floor ..., no-
body being with-
in six feet of
them." Inevitably
one theory was that
these phenomena

Ghost Film
*One object
that seems to
be a common
target of
poltergeist
activity is the
camera. Cine
cameras (right)
have been known
to start and run
apparently of their
own accord. However
much of the film shot in
this way, and that which
purports to show spirits, has
been proved to be fake.*

were the result of childish trickery, and it was pointed out that an 11-year-old son of the family was almost invariably present when the disturbances occurred. Rev. Phelps rebutted this suggestion in a letter to his friend, Asa Mahan, President of Oberlin College in the USA. He had witnessed the phenomena, he said, "hundreds and hundreds of times", and many of them took place "where there was no visible power by which motion could have been produced". The idea that the children were playing tricks was, according to their father, "as stupid as it is false and injurious".

⇥ THE CASE OF HENRI ⇤

It is difficult for the present-day student of poltergeist phenomena to make up his or her mind about the paranormal events that plagued the Wesley and Phelps households, for those who witnessed them were not trained observers and had no access to the sophisticated equipment used by modern psychical researchers.

This was not a problem in the 1980s' investigation of a French poltergeist, nicknamed "Henri". The leading researcher in the "Henri" case was Professor Hans Bender, Chief of the Institute of Border Psychology at the University

Poltergeist – the Movie
The phenomenon of poltergeists has been explored both in real life and in the realm of fiction. In the highly successful film, Poltergeist *(above), directed by Steven Spielberg, a very ordinary surburban family with young children are plagued by the activities of evil spirits who destroy family life, as well as their home. Despite the implausible special effects of this film, there are many real-life cases of supposed hauntings that are similar in many respects, for example, the ordinariness of the family and their home, and the fact that there are children present when the events occur, and that these children are the focus of the activity.*

of Freiburg in southern Germany. Professor Bender first had his attention drawn to the case in November 1980 by a physicist, Dr. Fleury, who had for some time been investigating a poltergeist at Mulhouse in France. For three years, Professor Bender was told, the Thierrys' ground floor apartment had been afflicted with dancing tables, the sounds of non-existent car crashes and abrupt changes of temperature.

Dr. Fleury installed a chart recorder in the Thierrys' apartment to log temperature changes. The results were baffling, with the machine recording not only inexplicably high temperatures but also curious broken and horizontal lines that were "technically impossible".

Professor Bender and the other investigators from Freiburg University were totally unable to find a rational explanation either for the curious behaviour of the scientific apparatus, or for the other phenomena that followed, such as the spontaneous activation of a cine camera that had been placed in a locked room. What seemed certain was that Mme. Thierry was the focus of the phenomena. It has been suggested she exerted an uncontrolled psychic force upon her environment, or, perhaps, she was possessed by a malignant spirit.

DEMONIC POSSESSION

"All spirits are enslaved which serve things evil"

Percy Bysshe Shelley

WHILE SOME CASES of demonic possession seem genuine enough, others, however, must be considered extremely dubious, probably the result of deliberate fraud. One such dubious case spawned a best-selling book, a very successful horror film, and two sequels.

The story behind *The Amityville Horror* by Jay Anson, and later the film of the same name, seems to be based on very thin evidence. The facts are that in November 1974, Ronald DeFeo, living at 112 Ocean Avenue, Amityville, Long Island, ran screaming into a bar; he told the startled barman that a homicidal maniac had broken into his home and shot his father, his mother, and his four brothers and sisters.

Salem Witch Trials
(Below) In 1692, in Massachusetts, USA, some children from a small village began to behave in a strange way, throwing violent fits and imitating animals. Satanism was suspected, and under questioning some of the children accused various people from the village of bewitching them. The children's accusations led to over 200 Salem residents being arrested; 20 residents were executed. Later, as the list of accused grew, great doubt was thrown on the children's stories.

The police, finding no evidence of a break-in, but indications that Ronald DeFeo had killed his own family in order to claim a substantial sum in life insurance, charged DeFeo with murder. He was subsequently found guilty and given six separate life sentences. His home was purchased by a young couple, George and Kathy Lutz, who occupied it from December 18, 1975 to January 14, 1976, a total of 26 days.

→ **A MALIGNANT ENTITY** ←

If the accounts Mr. and Mrs. Lutz gave to both Paul Hoffman, who published their story in the April 1977 issue of the US magazine *Good Housekeeping*, and to Jay Anson, the author of *The Amityville Horror*, are to be believed, the Ocean Avenue house was occupied by a malignant entity that endeavoured to take over the bodies of George and Kathy Lutz. Mr. Lutz's symptoms of possession were very alarming indeed:

Cleansing the Soul
St. Francis (above) expels hordes of demons from his birthplace, the Italian town of Assisi. The episode is almost certainly metaphorical, referring to the saint's attempt to cleanse the soul of the Church, which he believed had strayed from the path that Jesus had intended. At the ruined chapel of San Damiano outside the gate of Assisi, he heard a voice urging him: "Go, Francis, and repair my house, which, as you see, is well-nigh in ruins." Francis at first took this literally and determined to repair the chapel. He realized, however, that the True Church could only be constructed in the soul of Man. He set the same example as Christ by living selflessly.

his facial appearance changed in such a way that he began physically to resemble the condemned murderer. Then on January 10, 1976, George Lutz awoke to find that his sleeping wife had taken on the appearance of a dribbling, dirty-haired, 90-year-old woman. Although she remained in this state for several hours, her husband did not see fit to seek medical help.

↣ COLLECTIVE HALLUCINATION ↤

In 1978, when *The Amityville Horror* was published, Mrs. Lutz remembered her experience differently; it took place, she claimed, on January 7, lasted only a few minutes and was preceded by her levitating. There is little reason to suppose that Mr. and Mrs. Lutz were lying. It does seem likely, however, that they were the victims of collective hallucination rather than of possession. For, in the words of Dr. Kaplan, Director of the Parapsychology at the Insitute of America:

"We found no evidence ... of a "haunted house" ... a couple had purchased a house that they economically could not afford. It is our professional opinion that the story of its haunting is mostly fiction."

A DICTATOR POSSESSED?

The speeches of Adolf Hitler (1889–1945) were described by many of those who heard them as delivered "by a man possessed".

He always began his speeches hesitatingly, almost as if he had never before spoken in public. After a few minutes he would get into his stride, the tone and volume of his voice would rise, and he would speak with increasing confidence until he had aroused his audience to frenzied enthusiasm. At this point he and those who listened to him became almost as one – it was as if the words he spoke were an expression of all the most savage and evil emotions buried in the minds of those people to whom he spoke.

Was this result of an orator's trick? Or was Hitler literally possessed? Perhaps by some hellish entities who used him as their mouthpiece? It has been suggested that Hitler was in truth "a servant of Satan", a man whose body was taken over by devils. Indeed, it has been asserted by such writers as Trevor Ravenscroft that Adolf Hitler was an initiate of an ancient satanic cult, and willingly gave his body to be possessed by his master, Lucifer.

Spokesman for the Devil? Adolf Hitler (below) was believed by some to be possessed by the Devil.

The investigation of cases of alleged demonic possession is very often a frustrating business, for what, on the face of it, seem to be proven incidents of the "taking over" of a person by a demonic, or other, form of non-human entity, can usually be explained on the basis of hysteria and other mental disorders. If such interpretations do not fully explain the available evidence, it almost invariably transpires that the alleged demonic possession took place so long ago that there was no trained investigator to question eye witnesses.

A startling exception to this took place in the American Midwest during the present century, a well-authenticated case recorded by a Catholic priest, Father John Nicola, in his book *Diabolical Possession and Exorcism*.

The victim of the supposed possessing demon was "Mary"; her real identity has never been revealed. She was born in 1888, and by 1902 she was exhibiting symptoms of the type traditionally associated with possession. For example, she heard voices making blasphemous and obscene suggestions, foamed at the mouth when blessed by a priest, and displayed a supernormal ability to know whether an object, such as a rosary, had been sprinkled with Holy Water.

An hysteric or schizophrenic? Seemingly not, for several medical examinations not only failed to provide any evidence of physical abnormality, but seemed to show that, on a psychological

The Rite of Exorcism
The exorcist holds a crucifix (left) over the victim of possession, while reciting prayers from the Greek New Testament (far left). The use of the crucifix and the prayers are the two main elements in the exorcism.

level at least, Mary was "normal in the fullest sense". In the year 1928, Mary was exorcized at a community of Poor Clares (women following the rule of life laid down by St. Francis of Assisi) in Earling, Iowa. The exorcist was Father Theophilus, a Capuchin friar, who was assisted by an old friend, Father Joseph Steiger, and several nuns from the Poor Clares' community.

Candles and Bells
A bell (right) is rung several times, at strategic points during the ritual of exorcism. Sanctified candles (below) are also used.

⇢ HYSTERIA OR POSSESSION ⇠

The priests carried out a number of exorcisms, which took place over several days and were accompanied by startling physical phenomena. For example, Mary, or the demon who spoke through her, was able to make loud noises and utter comprehensible sentences without using her mouth. Even more alarmingly, she vomited and excreted substantial quantities of noxious substances although, throughout the entire period of the exorcisms, she took little nourishment save milk.

Mary also exhibited supernormal modes of perception, demonstrating knowledge of certain matters that she should not have known. Under the pains inflicted on them, Mary's demons were induced to give their names:

Holy Water
Sanctified water, known as Holy Water (right) is used to expel evil spirits from the souls of the possessed. A drop of the water is said to torment the demons.

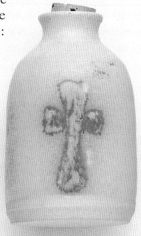

Beelzebub, Lord of the Flies, Jacob, Mina, and Judas. They all took an especial dislike to Father Steiger and, through Mary, threatened his life.

Shortly afterwards, Father Steiger was driving his car when, as he approached a bridge, a black cloud seemed to descend. He could see nothing, hit the railing of the bridge and, although he himself suffered only shock and bruising, his car was completely wrecked.

⇢ THE LION OF JUDAH ⇠

On the priest's return to the convent, one of Mary's demons taunted him:

"What about your new auto ... smashed to smithereens .... Our aim was to get you ... but [St. Joseph] ... prevented us from harming you."

In spite of the demons' ability, or so the priests believed, almost to kill one of the exorcists who were tormenting them, the minions of Satan were eventually defeated.

After over three weeks of exorcism, on December 23, 1928, Father Theophilus uttered the resounding command: "Depart ye fiends of Hell. Begone Satan, the Lion of Judah reigns." Mary's possessors screamed aloud, "Hell, Hell, Hell" and departed to their infernal abode.

Mary sat up, cried out, "Praise be to Jesus Christ", and from then onwards, so it has been asserted, lived a perfectly normal life, free of vomitings and obscene temptations.

OUT OF THE BODY

"I ... realized that my consciousness was separating from another consciousness, which was also me"

Lord Geddes

THOSE WHOSE RELIGIOUS BELIEFS are generally in line with one of the world's three great monotheistic faiths, Judaism, Christianity, and Islam, would probably not use quasi-psychological terminology, such as "the permanent cessation of consciousness" to define death.

Instead they might give an essentially religious definition implying belief in a number of complex theological concepts; for example, that death means that one leaves the body, is judged by God, and is sent to heaven or hell. Or simply, that death is the soul leaving the body.

→ FREE OF THE BODY ←

It is possible, however, for a person to have an "out-of-the-body experience", generally referred to by psychic investigators as an OOBE. An OOBE is a change of consciousness in which the soul appears to be free of the physical body *without* actually dying. After the experience normal consciousness is restored, although the experience is remembered.

Jack London
The American novelist Jack London was one of several famous writers who recorded their out-of-the-body experiences. London was influenced by his spiritualist mother.

Aerial View
A clear aerial view of the city of London was the extraordinary result of one person's OOBE.

Sometimes OOBEs are deliberately induced (p.48 and pp.246-247), and when this happens they are generally referred to by occultists as "astral projections". Others, perhaps more significant in relation to human survival of bodily death, are totally unexpected by the men and women who experience them.

Involuntary OOBEs are triggered by near-death, a life-threatening illness or a physical injury received in battle, for example. The American writer, Ernest Hemingway, and the late A.J. Ayer, Wykeham Professor of Logic at Oxford, both experienced states of non-physical consciousness induced in this fashion.

Hemingway had his OOBE on the Italian-Austrian front during World War I when, long before he wrote such best sellers as *For Whom The Bell Tolls* and *The Old Man and the Sea*, he was hit by shrapnel. Years after suffering his wounds he described the experience as: "my soul ... coming right out of my body, like you'd pull a silk handkerchief out of a pocket by one corner. It flew round and then came back and went in again, and I wasn't dead any more."

→ A RED GLOW ←

Professor Ayer's experience, which seems to have taken place in hospital as he was being resuscitated following a heart attack, was equally curious. He found himself first drifting towards a red glow, and then drifting away from it, back to his body and normal consciousness. He seems to have found his experience a significant one, one that cast slight doubts on his deep convictions that God was non-existent and that, as far as the individual human being was concerned, death was the end of everything.

Lord Geddes, a distinguished surgeon and diplomat, gives a very convincing account of an OOBE. After being accidentally poisoned, he describes how his projected consciousness was aware of the activities of the physician who was treating him. He described himself as *seeing his doctor think*, "He is almost gone", hearing the doctor asking questions but being unable to reply because "I was not in touch with the body", and his anger at being "pulled back" by the medical treatment he was receiving.

Coming from Lord Geddes, a man who had been a member of the British cabinet, and had been Ambassador to Washington, this testimony to the reality of OOBE was, and still is, one of the most impressive ever given.

PEACOCK

PHOENIX

PELICAN

PIEBALD MAGPIE

SPIDER

Proud Peacock and Pious Pelican

In Christian symbolism the peacock is an emblem of the immortality of the soul, because of the old belief that the bird's flesh does not decay. However, it could also stand for strutting vanity, and the "eyes" in its tail could suggest the "all-seeing eyes" of the church. As early as the first century AD, the story of the phoenix, the mythical bird that renewed its youth in fire every 500 years, was being used as a symbol of life after death. In the image of "the pelican in her piety", the young chicks represent human souls nourished on the redeeming blood of Christ's willing sacrifice and his suffering on the cross. The spider, on the other hand, is representative of an instrument of the Devil, spinning his webs to entrap sinning souls like flies. The piebald magpie, a notorious scavenger and thief, is another symbol representing Satan.

FLIGHTS OF FANCY?

There are hundreds of descriptions of "near death" and other out-of-the-body experiences given by men and women who, if anything, were biased against accepting the reality of such experiences. These are both impressive and surprising. For example, the hard-drinking, macho writer, Ernest Hemingway's account of his soul coming out of his body "like a silk handkerchief" carries weight because he was one of the most unlikely writers of his generation to have claimed to have undergone such an experience.

Hemingway's experience of his soul "leaving his body" was unaccompanied by any conventionally religious experience – he did not, for example, see a vision of the Blessed Virgin, as some have claimed. This, however, is not necessarily surprising. It would seem that those who undergo such experiences have visions of this nature only if they are predisposed to do so. A convinced Christian, for example, is more likely to see Christian imagery, whereas a convinced atheist is not likely to see much more than, for example, the red glow that was discerned by the philosopher A.J. Ayer, upon the occasion of his own near-death experience.

Vivid Account The writer, Ernest Hemingway (below), gave a description of his own OOBE.

Spiritual Awakening
A.J. Ayer (above),
Professor of Logic at
Oxford, experienced an
involuntary out-of-the-
body experience when he
was in hospital recovering
from a heart attack. He
felt himself drifting
towards a red glow, and
then drifting away from
it, back to normal
consciousness. This
experience had a profound
effect on Ayer, who had up
to that point been a
convinced atheist. It also
led him to believe that,
contrary to all his
previous beliefs, death
was not the end of life.

In the 1950s an American nurse, Mrs. Gussie Dowell, of De Lion, Texas, wrote to Dr. Robert Crookall, an English physical scientist making a study of astral projection, describing an out-of-the-body experience (OOBE) she had undergone at the age of eleven.

She had been stung by a noxious insect and had reacted by going first into shock and then into a full coma. She wrote:

"As long as I could feel anything, I suffered intensely. Then ... I looked down and could see my body .... I went to a place, through a veil of mist, high above the earth. I went to the men who were standing about the entrance, but was told to come [sic] back and live the rest of my life .... I started back and it was not long before I awoke in my physical body."

Mrs. Dowell's full account gave the interesting detail: the place "high above the earth" to which she travelled in spirit was surrounded by "pearly and translucent" walls. It all sounds like a child's idea of heaven, derived from the imagery of hymns and gospel music.

The use of naive symbolism does not, however, invalidate Mrs. Dowell's account, nor does it give any cause for it to be regarded as childish invention (p.147).

→ A SCEPTIC CONVERTED ←

In his book *Escape to the Sea*, the small-boat yachtsman, Fred Rebell, described how two OOBE experiences in the course of an ocean voyage converted him from scepticism to a belief in the reality of the astral world. On the occasion of the first of these experiences, Rebell "dreamed" that he was floating:

"... above the dark ocean. I knew myself to be roughly a hundred miles NNE of my boat's present position .... I saw a curious hull .... I made it out to be a ship with a stumpy mast and the captain's bridge aft resembling a hencoop .... The next morning ... I saw, about a mile ahead, the very duplicate of the ship ...."

Fred Rebell's second experience of leaving his body left him with a sense of mystical ecstasy. He seemed to be floating above the deck of his boat, *Elaine*, when he was seized, as though by the hands of some friendly giant, and carried high above the clouds, experiencing a feeling of utter happiness in which he wanted to "remain for ever".

Some kind of a bond, however, seemed to hold him fast to his earthly existence; in the adventurer's own words, "I felt I had still something to do in the world". He felt himself returning to his body and found himself, once again, in his bunk aboard the *Elaine*.

→ LOST FOR WORDS ←

There was a certain flatness in Fred Rebell's account of his out-of-the-body experiences; it was almost as though whatever happened to him was so mysterious and wonderful that he was lost for words with which he could properly convey its nature to his readers. The same is true of almost all other accounts of spontaneous out-of-the-body experiences with which I am familiar. From Mrs. Dowell with her "heaven", complete with pearly walls, to Ernest Hemingway describing his soul as an astral silk handkerchief (p.144), those who have endeavoured to recount their sensations and experiences have done so rather tritely. This may be because it is impossible to convey the nature of the experiences, which are, by definition, mysteries that must be experienced to be properly understood.

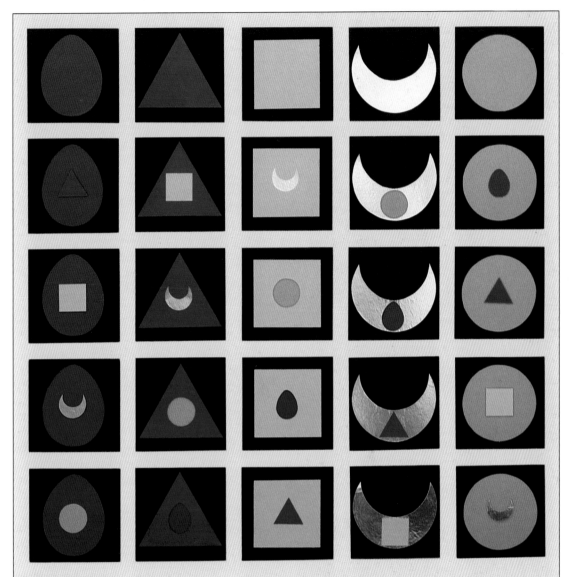

Sylvan Muldoon
The American writer Sylvan Muldoon (above) had several out-of-the-body experiences. Muldoon had his first experience as a child of twelve, when he was with his mother on a visit to a spiritualists' meeting. Muldoon awoke in the night, to find himself floating above his normal body, although he remained attached to it by what he described as a "thin silver cord", rather like an umbilical cord. Later on, Muldoon wrote that he believed this cord to be the only connection between the astral and physical body. If it was severed, the traveller would die. Muldoon's first experience was followed by hundreds of others, many of which were recorded in a book, The Projection of the Astral Body, written by the psychical researcher, Hereward Carrington. Both Muldoon and Carrington believed that astral travel was open to anyone who desired the experience. They laid out rules for experimenters to follow, such as instructions on how to achieve different speeds while travelling on the astral plane.

ASTRAL FORCES

In the 1880s, the Theosophical Society – the occult society founded in 1875 by H.P. Blavatsky – published a book by a Bengali scholar named Rama Prasad. The book, *Nature's Finer Forces*, was couched in obscure language, derived from a treatise in circulation among adepts of a Bengali cult, and was concerned with the permutations of five astral forces symbolized by a yellow square, an indigo oval, a red triangle, a silver crescent, and a blue circle – respectively representative of earth, ether, fire, water, and air.

Two of the book's readers, J.W. Brodie-Innes and S.L. MacGregor Mathers, both leading members of the Golden Dawn, took it very seriously indeed, believing that they discerned beneath its confused and confusing prose, esoteric teachings of both antiquity and importance. On the basis of their detailed researches the two men devised a method of using the five symbols, and twenty further combinations described in *Nature's Finer Forces*, in order to deliberately induce out-of-the-body experiences of a very specific nature. The soul of the experimenter, so they claimed, would be able to direct itself by the use of this method to the particular part of the astral plane symbolized by the geometric symbol, or a combination of symbols, employed.

Their method involves the experimenter concentrating on a chosen symbol until it is imprinted on the mind, to the exclusion of all other thoughts. The symbol is then visualized as a closed door. Finally, after further concentration, the experimenter imagines that the door swings open and that admission to the astral world is given.

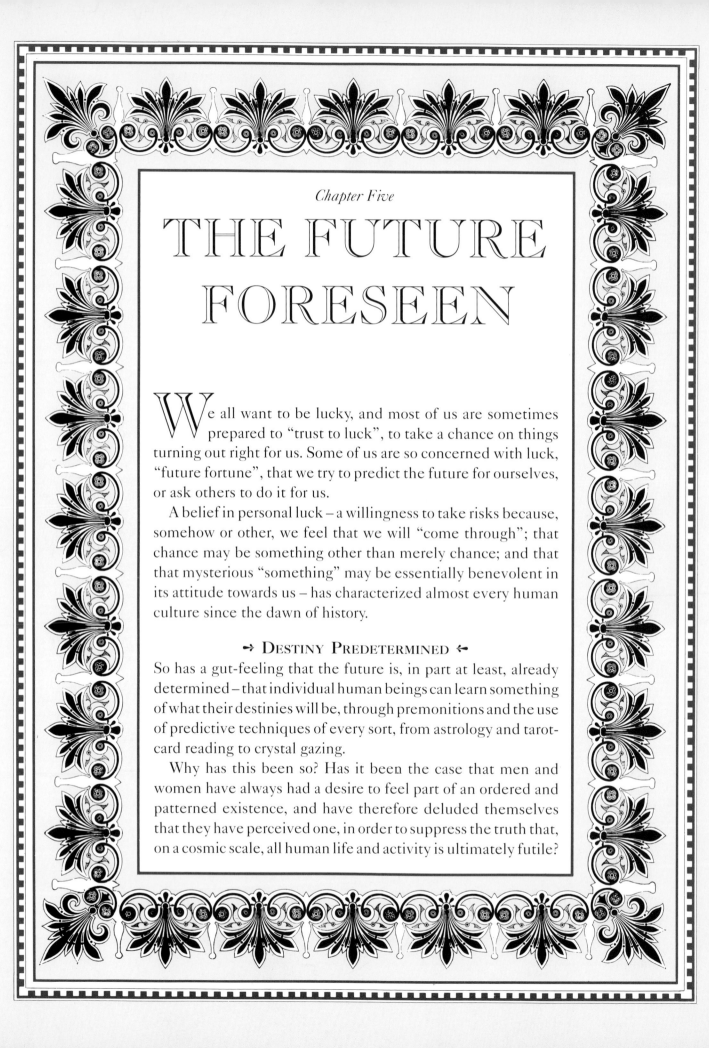

Chapter Five

THE FUTURE FORESEEN

We all want to be lucky, and most of us are sometimes prepared to "trust to luck", to take a chance on things turning out right for us. Some of us are so concerned with luck, "future fortune", that we try to predict the future for ourselves, or ask others to do it for us.

A belief in personal luck – a willingness to take risks because, somehow or other, we feel that we will "come through"; that chance may be something other than merely chance; and that that mysterious "something" may be essentially benevolent in its attitude towards us – has characterized almost every human culture since the dawn of history.

➔ DESTINY PREDETERMINED ←

So has a gut-feeling that the future is, in part at least, already determined – that individual human beings can learn something of what their destinies will be, through premonitions and the use of predictive techniques of every sort, from astrology and tarot-card reading to crystal gazing.

Why has this been so? Has it been the case that men and women have always had a desire to feel part of an ordered and patterned existence, and have therefore deluded themselves that they have perceived one, in order to suppress the truth that, on a cosmic scale, all human life and activity is ultimately futile?

Or is it that there is some evidence that, from time to time, human beings have genuinely seen into the future, and sensed the existence of a cosmic order that is beyond both space and time as we know them?

The old-fashioned materialist is forced to answer "yes" to the first question and "no" to the second. He or she may be giving a verdict that is not fully in accord with the evidence; for a very large number of people, now and in the past, have claimed to have had personal experiences that have convinced them of the existence of a vast cosmic plan, of which their own lives have been tiny details. Perhaps the most common of such experiences has been the "meaningful coincidence".

A meaningful coincidence is experienced when two or more events take place at the same time that, while they are not causally related, are significant in relation to one another. By "not causally related" is meant that none of the events caused another of them, and that, as far as we know, the events were not produced by the same exterior force.

↠ Chance and Fortune ↞

An example of a meaningful coincidence is provided by the old folk-story of the fisherman who loses a valuable ring or jewel in the sea and, months or years later, catches a fish that proves to have the lost treasure in its belly. It is perhaps significant that some version of this tale is told in almost every country of the world. This may mean that it is a psychological archetype – that on an unconscious level we all feel that the meaningful coincidence is more than *just* coincidence – that some power outside the full comprehension of humanity is manipulating events for its own purpose, good or ill.

Whether any fisherman has ever found something he has lost inside the belly of a fish is of no great importance, for a great many other meaningful and far more improbable coincidences are well authenticated, and some of them are in this chapter.

CRYSTAL MAGIC

"It was a maxim both in ancient India and ancient Greece not to look at one's reflection in water ... the Greeks regarded it as an omen of death if a man dreamed of seeing himself so reflected"

Sir James Frazer

THERE IS STILL A WIDESPREAD BELIEF in the magic of gems and other natural crystals. For example, some gems are considered unlucky, while others are believed to have healing powers; and many people believe that a polished globe of rock crystal possesses "occult virtues" that enable its user to see visions of the future.

Roman Cult
The bronze hand (below), dates from the late Roman Empire, when all forms of divination, from scrying to astrology, flourished. The hand bears the symbols, such as a cockerel's head and a pine cone, of the Roman mystery cult of Dionysus. Worshippers of Dionysus would work themselves into a frenzy, in which they might see visions of the future.

Anyone who wishes to try "crystal gazing", which has been considered an occult art since ancient times, may find it prohibitively expensive – a crystal ball is a very costly item. However, most people who have experimented with crystal gazing find that effective substitutes include a pool of black ink, a piece of concave glass painted matt black, a bowl of water, or even a polished piece of black coal.

→ POLISHED COAL ←

Interestingly enough, the sixteenth-century crystal gazer, Edward Kelley, used just such a piece of polished coal in his supposed reception of the visions that revealed the mysterious "Enochian language" to him (pp.74-75) and enabled him to correctly foretell the execution of Mary Queen of Scots.

Obviously, a piece of coal is not possessed of any inherent mystic properties – so how could it be possible for a crystal gazer to glimpse the future simply by concentrating upon it?

The answer given to this question by most psychics and occultists who have concerned themselves with scrying (the use of crystals, pools of ink, and the like, as aids to clairvoyance) can be split into three points.

→ THE SCRYER'S ANSWER ←

a) It is unlikely that there are any inherent "occult virtues" in precious stones or crystals. If they have any influence on those who wear or use them, it is likely to be psychological in origin. In other words, if someone believes that it is unlucky to wear opals, it is probable that if they do so they will feel stressed and, as a consequence of this feeling, make mistakes. Similarly, if a clairvoyant believes that he or she will achieve better results by using an expensive globe of rock crystal than, for instance, a glass of water as a tool for looking into the future, it is likely that the clairvoyant in question will get the expected improved results.

b) The only objective function of the central feature of any variety of scrying is to induce a state of trance, a "dissociation of consciousness".

c) In this state of dissociation, the clairvoyant faculty comes into its own and is freed from the bonds of time and space.

Whether or not the last assertion is correct, or whether the supposed visions of the scryer are no more than eruptions of symbol and fantasy from the volcano of the unconscious mind, is a matter for debate. There is no doubt, however, that the majority of people who experiment with scrying over an extended period do experience abnormal – perhaps supernormal – states of consciousness in which "visions" are seen with the mind's eye.

➔ AN EXPERIMENT WITH TIME ←

Any reader of this book who wishes to experiment can do so easily by patiently employing the technique outlined below – but no one should do so who is not mature and well balanced, for it is possible that certain people may think that their visions are revelations given to them by spirits or superhuman beings, when, in fact, they may well be no more than quasi-visual representations of their own unconscious desires and beliefs.

a) Unless you have a crystal ball, choose a substitute – a glass ball, a glass of water, or a small dish filled with ink or some other black liquid, are all equally suitable.

b) Sit in a quiet place in a fairly dim light for a regular period of time, 15 minutes to three quarters of an hour each day.

c) Stare into the "crystal", endeavouring to make your mind as blank as possible, unconscious of its physical surroundings. At first you are unlikely to "see" anything, and may begin to feel that the whole experiment is futile. After some time – days, weeks, or even months – it is probable that you will begin to discern something in your substitute crystal: usually no more than clouds, which may be of any colour but are said to be usually white, grey, or silver.

d) Eventually the clouds disperse and you will see pictures, sometimes static like a photograph, sometimes dynamic – almost as though you were watching a miniature television.

e) Make a careful note of what you "see" and endeavour to come to some conclusion as to whether you have been undergoing a psychic experience – genuinely sensing something that occurred in the distant past or obtaining a glimpse of the future – or just getting better acquainted with the contents of your own unconscious mind.

If you think you are seeing glimpses of the future, keep a careful note of the things you have seen. You may begin to notice events occurring that you have foreseen in your crystal. But, it is important to realize, you are likely to be subconsciously *looking* for events in your life that even remotely tie in with your visions.

Looking Ahead
The crystal ball (above) is the classic tool of the fortune teller, used throughout history by scryers of all nationalities, and used today by serious and fairground fortune tellers alike. Indeed, occultists believe it to be the oldest method of fortune telling, existing even before the invention of writing, by the shamans (wise men) of ancient tribes. The ancient method of gazing into a crystal to induce visions is identical to the one used today. But the beginner is unlikely to use a real crystal ball as they are prohibitively expensive. Instead, a polished piece of coal or a rounded piece of glass will do. In Arab countries, the traditional medium is a pool of black ink or oil in the palm of the hand (left).

CONJURING-UP SPIRITS

*"**B**e thou willing and ready to come to me whenever conjured to do so by the sacred rites of magic"*

Magic Rite: David Conway *Magic*

THOMAS HEARNE (1678–1735), at one time second keeper of Oxford's Bodleian Library, was a considerable scholar, a fiery Jacobite, the writer of an often scabrous journal in which he recorded the failings of his contemporaries with more wit than kindness, and an avid collector of medals, coins, books, and manuscripts.

One of his acquisitions was a manuscript, now in the Bodleian, entitled, *A treatise on the conjuration of Angels with experiments in crystal and directions for fumigation;* in this sense, the word "fumigation" means incense burning.

Hearne's manuscript seems to have been written by a late seventeenth-century "cunning man" (white magician), named Moses Long. But Hearne believed – probably correctly – that most or all of it was a transcript of an earlier document, dating from the early years of the reign of Queen Elizabeth I. The manuscript contains details of a magic rite that involves the calling up of spirits – the use of incense was, and still is, an integral part of many such occult rituals.

As soon as the spirits appear, they are asked questions. The rite is essentially one of prophecy – enacted to find the answer to questions that the earthly participants could not possibly know. An important

Umbrella
Traditionally it is thought to be unlucky to open an umbrella (above) indoors.

Lucky Hair-Cut
A person who wishes to attract good luck should have a hair-cut (left) on a night of the full moon.

A Singing Robin
If you should hear a robin (right) singing near your home, then your house will be blessed with good luck. If the robin is actually perched on your window sill, then you will soon find true love.

Chance Meeting
It is considered lucky to meet the same person twice on any one day (left). It is even luckier to meet the same person as you set out, and again on your return.

preliminary to the performance of the rite was the cutting of three rods from a palm tree – not, one would imagine, a particularly readily available commodity in Elizabethan England. Each rod was then to be wrapped in a piece of parchment inscribed with the name of one of three prophetic spirits – Darus, Artus, and Aebedel. For three successive nights, an incantation was said over each rod, followed by an invocation of the three spirits.

➤ THREE BEAUTIFUL LADIES ←

Whoever composed the invocation obviously suspected, or perhaps knew, that the spirits invoked were not of a celestial nature, and that they might appear in an unpleasant form. They were commanded to come, "gently and peaceably in the form of three beautiful ladies".

When the "beautiful ladies" appeared (supposedly this would take place at the conclusion of the third nightly invocation) the experimenter was instructed to charge them to "Truly tell ... the truth of all my requests and demands without any lying or deceit or delays." The rite seems innocent enough, and as the

researcher who transcribed the manuscript, Katon Shual, has remarked, behind it "is the essential rubric of a powerful invocation".

It is perhaps significant, however, that in the manuscript another hand than that of its compiler has inserted an incomplete sentence in relation to this rite:

"Therefore because I know now whether they be good or evil, I advise not to meddle with them, as I have advised others so in these ..."

The reasons why this curious addition to the manuscript was written, and why it was broken off in mid-sentence, can only be conjectured – but it sounds very much as if some experimenter with the process had had an unpleasant psychic experience. Katon Shaul has explained that the ritual outlined above concludes with a warning of the dangers of communicating with spirits. People tend to disregard this sort of advice, feeling that they are immune from danger – but there is quite a lot of anecdotal evidence that rituals, whether conducted for healing or prophetic purposes, can be dangerous when supposed contact with spirits is involved. The experimenter cannot be quite sure with whom or what he is dealing – in the words of the

commentator upon the Hearne manuscript, "whether they be good or evil". Whether the spirits evoked have an objective existence, and are beings that exist outside the mind of the magician, or whether they are dissociated elements of the magician's mind, lurking in the unconscious, is neither here not there. Whatever the nature of the spirits that were consulted, some of them, so the occult tradition avers, can be destructive.

⇝ ANTHONY OF PRAGUE ⇜

The tales of such destructive spirits, inflicting mental or physical damage upon those who have unwisely evoked them into consciousness, are many. A typical one is told in the introduction to one eighteenth-century occult text. The tale concerns a certain Anthony of Prague who communed with evil spirits some three centuries earlier; for a while he prospered – but eventually his spirit companion turned against him and hurled him from a great height; "his body was mangled and the street curs licked his blood".

A better authenticated story concerns the minor poet, Victor Neuburg, who is today best remembered as the man responsible for the first publication of the early works of the Welsh poet, Dylan Thomas. In 1912 Neuburg invoked the spirit of the war

Birds, Bees, and Beds
If you wish to keep a secret, tell it to the bees, renowned in folklore for their wisdom. If you tell it to bees in a beehive, the secret will remain even more hidden. A crow can foretell of good or bad luck depending on how many you see. For example: one crow signifies good luck; two, bad luck; three a wedding; four a burying; five for speed; and six means bountiful good luck. There are many superstitious beliefs concerned with the four points of the compass: east, west, north, and south. For example, if one's bed faces north it means a short life; if it faces south, it means a long life; if it faces east, great riches will be bestowed; if it faces the west, travel is indicated.

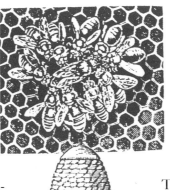

Good and Bad
Spiders (right) are nearly always associated with good luck – that is unless you kill one inside a house. To cross a black cat (left) in the street can foretell of either good or bad luck. Some people believe that the Devil takes the form of a cat, whereas others believe the cat to be sacred.

god, Mars. Subsequently Neuburg behaved in such a totally atypical and aggressive manner that a friend's suicide resulted. When he realized what he had done, Neuburg was so traumatized that for eighteen years after, he endured what would seem to have been a profound depressive illness. Whether or not the spirit Neuburg invoked came from within or without him, there seems no doubt that it half destroyed him.

⇝ FOLKLORE ⇜

While the Hearne manuscript describes rituals of a sophisticated nature, there are many other rituals designed to find answers to particular questions that have become part of popular culture. Many such rituals are known as superstitions, many of which are designed to ask questions about love – the future of a love affair, for instance, or the name of the future husband or wife. For example, there is a prophetic ritual to ensure that the object of one's desire responds. This ritual involves a mandrake plant (often associated with madness and sorcery) and should take place under a waxing moon. The mandrake should be fashioned to rsemble the loved one, buried, and a mixture of milk and a drop or two of the magician's own blood is then poured over the soil covering the mandrake. The magician must then recites the words:

"Blood and milk upon the grave
Will make X evermore my slave."

Then the mandrake is dug up and dried. More magic words are spoken over it. They are:

"This fruit is scorched by that same heat
Which warms my heart with every beat."

Finally the magician pierces the mandrake at the point that represents the heart of the loved one. The pin-pricked mandrake is them left on the window sill in full view of the moon. The magician then has to wait to see how efficacious his or her spell has been.

Rituals of this kind are more effective psychologically than magically. If a person pining for unrequited love truly believes in the ritual, he or she will be given renewed hope by the possession of the magically consecrated mandrake.

LUCKY CHARMS AND TALISMANS

> "*If you find an ash leaf or a four-leaved clover, you'll see your true love 'ere the day be over*"
>
> Anonymous

NO MATTER HOW HARD WE TRY, in this "space age" of ours, to eradicate the element of chance from our lives, we never seem to be quite able to convince ourselves that our scrupulous scientific methodology is ever quite enough. For example, the men of science who use micro-technology to send satellites into orbit are still heard to say such things as, "well, we have done all we can, now we can do nothing but cross our fingers and hope for the best". Bobby Robson, the former manager of England's international football team, would not dream of placing total

Lucky Boots
Pat Leahy (below), a football player with the New York Jets, is convinced of the power of his "lucky boots" to ensure he plays a better game. Because of some psychological need, many of us confer magical virtues upon objects that are not generally regarded as luck-bringing. However, perhaps it would be advisable to wear a "lucky suit of armour" if you intend to tell Pat Leahy that he is just being silly.

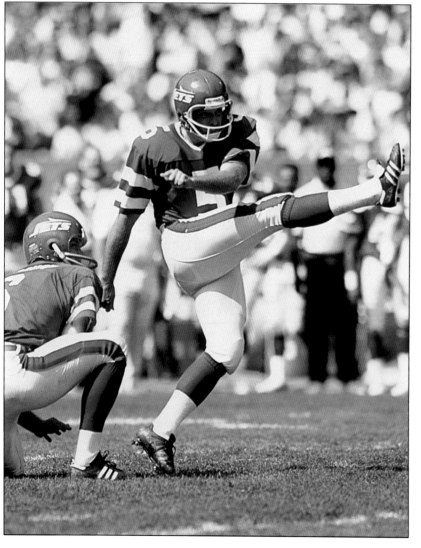

credit for his team's success in the 1990 World Cup on his managerial talents, or even the combined talents of his players: some of the credit must go to another influence – his "lucky scarf".

No matter how much faith we have in our own abilities, we always keep a healthy and cautious respect for "Lady Luck", whose whims can thwart even our very best laid plans.

In fact, nowadays, few wearers of charms, whether a footballer's "lucky boots" or a more conventional talisman such as a horseshoe, consciously think of them as anything other than amusing personal ornaments. Most would deny, for instance, that they believe they are likelier to be any safer on journeys than their fellows because they wear a St. Christopher medallion. It is possible, however, that some or all of those who wear such objects are unconscious believers in the efficacy of charms and that, as a consequence of this, their lives are better than would otherwise be the case. Unconsciously, they believe that their charms ward off bad luck, which causes an increase in confidence, which enables them to handle difficult situations more easily.

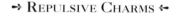

→ REPULSIVE CHARMS ←

Charms are not always pretty, and some are positively repulsive; one eighteenth-century French text urged those who wished to be successful gamblers to carry in their pockets a linen sachet containing various objects including a dried toad and the tooth of an executed felon. A more pleasant alternative to this was a four-leaved clover or a twig of rowan.

The supposed luck in owning a four-leaved clover may originate from the fact that there exist relatively few amongst the thousands of standard three-leaved clovers; simply finding one could be thought of as a lucky chance. The fortuitous "properties" are bestowed upon many other objects, however, is not always so easily explained. There is no very obvious reason, for example, why a horseshoe should be regarded as lucky. Nevertheless, this fact has not deterred many eminent folklorists from providing us with confident explanations as to why it is so. It has been said, for instance, that a horseshoe's shape symbolizes the crescent of the moon goddess, and the womb of a prehistoric mother goddess, giver of good fortune and fertility.

No explanation, perhaps, will ever sound totally convincing. But that is the very reason why it is called "superstition" and not "science".

Crosses and Coins

To many people, a silver dollar or a new penny (below) are both lucky charms. One of the most popular "charms" is the cross. The one shown here has a phial of water from the Holy Land.

Day-of-the-Dead Head

In Mexico, home-made "Day-of-the-Dead" skulls such as this one (below) are considered powerful good-luck charms.

Lucky Find

Finding a four-leaved clover (above) is considered to be exceptionally lucky. To achieve its greatest effectiveness, the four-leaved clover should be picked at midnight. Dill (above, top) is used as a charm against witches and is renowned, even today, for its ability to calm fretful babies. Its name derives from the old Norse, Dilla, to lull. A charm bracelet (right) is a decorative, though often expensive, way to attract good luck.

Little Buddha

Pocket-size Buddhas are one of the most popular talismans in the world.

Just the Ticket

Lottery tickets (above) are a popular method of people testing their luck. Although the chances of winning a lottery are very slim, it is a relatively cheap form of gambling.

Nelson's Charm

The horseshoe has long been associated with good luck. Admiral Nelson nailed a horseshoe to the mast of his ship.

Unlikely Charms

There are some very unlikely lucky charms, such as a champagne cork with a coin (left). For some people using a particular pen, (right) for example, during an exam, will ensure them success. A pebble is often used as a charm (far right). More specifically, pieces of coal are thought lucky if they are found on the street. Finding a pebble with a hole is thought very lucky.

Icons

An icon (right, and inside horseshoe) – an image of a sacred person – is considered sacred in itself. Some people believe that an icon will protect them from misfortune. The icon's power is derived from the sacredness of the image.

MAGIC CURES

"Go away death! Go away death!
Life from the flame
Give new breath!"

Rhyme to heal the sick

WE ALL HAVE OUR OWN personal rituals – particular ways of doing things – and these bring order into our lives and make us more efficient because we are following a regular pattern. To some extent we go "automatic", the unconscious mind partially takes over, and we can do things without concentrating our thoughts on unimportant aspects of the task in hand.

Cured by a Toad
Toads (below) are believed to have many magical properties, several of them connected to Black Magic. In the main toads are considered repugnant and potentially dangerous creatures. However, it was once believed that a toad-shaped stone – known as a toadstone – had the power of curing poisonous bites and stings.

We invent such personal rituals – particular ways of doing things – and they become so familiar to us that we do not usually think of them as rituals, just as the sensible way of doing something. Occult rituals, of course, tend to be more complex than personal rituals, but in the last analysis, they have the same purpose – to impose an ordered pattern that makes it much easier to achieve the intended result.

Many occult rituals are "rituals of cure" – for example, rituals designed to bring about a cure to a specific malady, or to bring general good health. It is important to note that however harmless many of these rituals appear, they all share the same disadvantage – they may lead an over-enthusiastic person to rely on healing rituals when he or she should be consulting an orthodox practitioner.

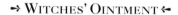

➤ WITCHES' OINTMENT ➤

Many rituals of cure involve the use of herbs; it is believed that their mixture of natural and healing properties is remarkably effective for some cures. One such ritual cure is known as "Witches' Ointment". This cure is supposed to be prepared when the moon is waxing and is in one of the astrological earth or air signs – Taurus, Gemini, Virgo, Libra, Capricorn, or Aquarius. When the time is appropriate, an ointment is made from a combination of hemlock, poplar leaves, wolf's bane, and soot.

SNAKES AND SKIN

The shamans of Indian tribes in California had a close relationship with rattlesnakes, with whom they communicated in their dreams. In springtime, the shamans would go out and catch rattlers and bring them back to the village in sacks and then play with the captives, allowing the snakes to bite their hands. Then the snakes were placed in a hole. This ensured that for the coming year the snakes would rattle if anyone came near, instead of striking without warning.

Many societies thought that snakes had magical powers. In England, in the Middle Ages, it was thought that if the skin of an adder, or viper, was placed outside the front door, then all the members of the household would be protected from harm. Powdered adder skin was a powerful "cure-all".

Snakes have appeared in myths and legends of almost all societies throughout history. Because snakes slough their skin, they have been associated with longevity, immortality, and eternal youth. Their phallic shape has ensured their frequent association with sexuality. The snake is also frequently associated with Satan, because the Devil is supposed to have taken the shape of a serpent when tempting Eve.

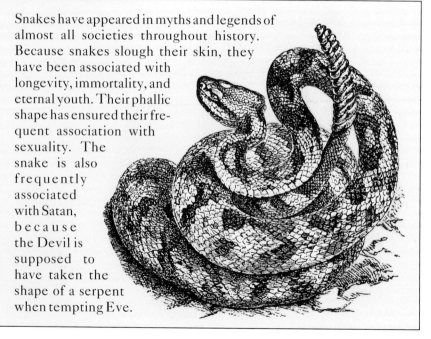

There are numerous rituals of cure that amount to no more than popular superstitions; for example, some people believe that if the head of their bed is placed towards the north, they will have a short life; if it faces the south, they will have a long life; or they may believe that should they see a grave digger coming towards them, they may soon fall ill.

Another popular belief is that the wearing of a ritually consecrated talisman or amulet will bring good luck and good health. For example, the ancient Egyptians believed that a talisman representing the shape of a frog would ensure continuing good health.

→ THE ROSE-CROSS RITUAL ←

There are also rituals of cure that pertain to psychic healing. These are more complicated and less well known. I will outline the Rose-Cross ritual for you to try:

a) Go to the south-east corner of a large room. With outstretched right arm trace a large cross and circle with your fingers. As you draw the figure, visualize it as being outlined in the air by light streaming from your fingertips.

b) Walk clockwise round the room, pausing in the south-west, north-west, and north-east corners to make a cross and circle in each.

c) On completing the circuit move back to the south-east side of the room and visualize the cross that you drew there, then bring your fingers inwards to its centre.

d) Holding your hand high, go diagonally to the room's centre and trace another cross and circle above your head.

e) Continue diagonally to the north-west corner of the room. Bring your hand to the centre of the visualized cross and circle that you had drawn previously.

f) Return diagonally to the centre of the room, and with your arm pointing downwards, make the shape of a cross and circle towards the floor, visualizing it being traced in glowing light beneath your feet.

g) With arm raised, walk diagonally to the room's centre, visualizing the cross and circle.

h) Face north-east and move diagonally to the north-east corner; bring your hand to the centre of the visualized cross and circle.

i) Move diagonally to the south-western corner, pausing in the room's centre to visualize the cross and circle beneath your feet; bring your hand to the centre of that cross and circle.

j) Move clockwise around the perimeter of the room until you reach the south-east; pause at the north-west and north-east corners and visualize the glowing fingers.

k) When you reach the south-east retrace the original cross and circle, making it much larger than on the first occasion.

l) Return diagonally to the centre of the room. Stand for a few minutes visualizing the six glowing crosses and circles. This concludes the rite.

The Rose Cross ritual is more in the nature of prevention than cure. To get any real effects from it, you need to experiment with it for a month or so on a daily basis. It can do no harm and it is claimed that it helps to establish an inner peace and a psychic harmony in which the experimenter is to some extent protected against physical and psychological disorders. If the ritual works it is because, say occultists, the rites enacted are actually already known in what Jung termed the "collective unconscious". They already exist in the hidden part of every individual's mind. This is because the rite has probably been enacted for many hundreds, if not thousands, of years.

→ ORNATE RITUALS ←

There are other even more complex rituals, such as those associated with the Hermetic Order of the Golden Dawn (pp.76-79). These are elaborate in the extreme, made as impressive as possible by the use of ornate language and eye-catching furniture decorated with symbolic designs. Yet these could be, and often have been, dispensed with. In such cases, the chief initiating officer of the rite can recite a simple formula that allows him to dispense with some of the more flamboyant aspects of the rite.

Ritual Adornment
Many rituals involve the wearing of special vestments, which may have been ritually consecrated. For example, the African head-dress (right), may have been worn by a shaman or witchdoctor when performing healing rituals and ceremonies.

MEANINGFUL COINCIDENCE

"*A 'strange coincidence' to use a phrase
by which such things are settled
now-a-days*"

Lord Byron

IN THE AUTUMN OF 1967, a London police officer named Peter Moscardi was told by a close friend that he had tried to telephone him at work but had been unable to get through. Constable Moscardi explained that his number had been changed a day or two earlier, and gave his friend what he thought was the new number. In fact, however, the number he gave was wrong: he told his friend that the last three digits were 116, instead of the correct 166.

Shared Life
There are many well-known stories of seemingly impossible coincidences. One well-documented case concerned two men – Dr. Reisneren and Mr. Armstrong. They met and found to their mutual astonishment that not only did they look alike, but that they shared the same birthdate. A further astonishing coincidence occured when they both died at the same time (right): their cars collided.

Nepalese Mandala
This 16th-century Nepalese "Mandala", or mystical diagram (left), is a symbol of enlightenment used for meditation. Carl Jung believed that concentrating on such symbols would develop a person's intuitive powers.

A few days later, shortly before midnight, Constable Moscardi was patrolling an industrial estate. He noticed an unsecured door and entered the office, unoccupied for the night, of a light industrial unit. As he went in, the telephone rang and, on impulse, he answered it. To his astonishment the caller was his friend endeavouring to contact his (Moscardi's) work number. The friend had rung the number Moscardi had given him, which was, of course, the wrong number – yet by some amazing coincidence Moscardi was standing by the right telephone at the right time.

The writer Arthur Koestler was extremely impressed by the seeming purposefulness of this coincidence, which he described in one of his books. It was almost as though some unseen power had determined that Constable Moscardi should speak to his friend at a particular time on a particular date and had fixed things – a wrongly given number, a carelessly unsecured door – so that it was brought about.

If an unseen power really did arrange that Moscardi should be rung at a particular time by a particular person its purpose is, like the nature of the song the sirens sang, beyond conjecture.

Fickle Fortune

Cleromonacy is the name given to divination by lots – whether it be by throwing dice, drawing sticks, or similar means. Dice (below) were used in gambling games, and for telling fortunes, even by ancient Egyptians and Romans, who made them of bone or ivory.

Dual Purpose

Cards (above, right, and below) are used both for telling fortunes and for gambling games, such as Black Jack and poker.

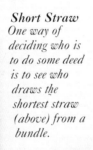

Short Straw

One way of deciding who is to do some deed is to see who draws the shortest straw (above) from a bundle.

Heads or Tails?

Tossing a coin (above) to see whether it will fall head or tail up is an age-old way of deciding an issue or predicting fate.

But who knows what might have happened to Moscardi had he not stopped to answer the call, and chatted for a while to his friend. That some disaster should befall him would be no more remarkable than that which actually occurred.

The purpose of other, equally improbable coincidences are often more apparent – simply, to return lost goods to their owners, for example. The film star, Anthony Hopkins, has experienced just such a coincidence.

→ THE GIRL FROM PETROVKA ←

In 1971 George Feifer's personal copy of his novel *The Girl From Petrovka*, heavily annotated in the margins, had been stolen from a car parked in London. Two years later the film rights of the novel had been sold and Mr. Feifer travelled to Vienna to meet Anthony Hopkins, who was to star in the movie.

Mr. Hopkins told him the story of a strange coincidence that he had experienced. Having signed a contract to appear in *The Girl From Petrovka*, he had gone out to buy the book, but was unable to find a copy. On his way home he noticed an open parcel on a seat in London's Leicester Square underground station. He looked at it carefully and found that it was not, as he had half suspected, a bomb, but a copy of the George Feifer novel had been looking for.

He produced the book for Mr. Feifer's inspection; it was the author's own annotated copy, stolen some two years earlier.

→ THE EMPTY CHURCH ←

In 1950, a seemingly purposeful series of small coincidences affected the destiny of the entire choir of a church in Beatrice, Nebraska. On March 1 of that year, choir practice had been scheduled to begin at 7.20 pm. At that time neither the minister nor his wife and daughter, all members of the choir, had arrived. They were running late – the minister's wife had run into a tricky problem in pressing her daughter's dress. Two other members of the choir were intending to be late because they wanted to listen to a particular radio program. Another, a young girl, was still at home desperately trying to solve a maths problem, while a husband and wife had found that their car would not start … and so on.

Not one member of the choir arrived at the church until at least ten minutes after he or she should have been there. Exactly five minutes after the time at which choir practice should have begun, the empty church was completely destroyed by a gas explosion.

The twentieth-century psychologist most intrigued by meaningful coincidences was Carl Jung, founder of the school of depth psychology associated with his name.

Born in 1875, the son of a Swiss pastor, Jung qualified as a physician and began to specialize in neurology. Subsequently, he studied the writings of Sigmund Freud, founder of psycho-analysis, and between 1907 and 1913 was generally looked upon as Freud's favourite pupil, the "Crown Prince" of Freud's analytical kingdom. Jung said that throughout his entire life he directly experienced seemingly meaningful coincidences – the juxtaposition of causally unrelated events that were significant only in their relationship to one another.

One of these took place in 1909 and involved Freud. The two psychologists had been discussing psychic phenomena and Freud had expressed his scepticism as to their genuineness. An explosive noise was heard by both men. Freud continued the conversation until it was interrupted by another inexplicable explosive sound, clearly having its origin in the room in which the conversation was taking place. Freud looked upset and brought the meeting to an end, complaining of the noises, which he attributed to the expansion and contraction of the pipes of his heating system.

Jung, on the other hand, referred to the explosions as "catalytic exteriorization phenomena". Quite what he meant by this is uncertain, but it seems likely that he was implying a belief that he himself was responsible for the phenomena, either by unconscious mediumship or by

All the Popes
A series of prophetic mottoes – brief Latin tags – surfaced in the 16th century. They pertain to future Popes, including Pope Paul IV (above). Their origin is uncertain, although they have been attributed to Saint Malachy. However, it is more probable that they were compiled by Don Arnold de Wyon in the same century. Oddly enough, perhaps as the result of coincidence, these tags have fitted the Popes remarkably well. Only one such motto remains – perhaps the next Pope will prove to be the last.

JUNG AND PSYCHIC TRUTHS

In a certain sense it would be true to say that the psychologist, Carl Jung, "made the occult respectable". He took ancient, traditional beliefs, re-examined them in the light of the psychological concepts he had developed, and proclaimed that at least some of them were "psychic truths". By this, Jung meant that certain concepts might or might not be objectively true, but, in either case, they are psychologically true for human beings – the minds of men and women operate as if such statements are objectively true.

For example, whether the gods of force and war – Thor with his hammer and his thunderbolts, Ares with his sword and his spear – enjoy an objective existence, in the same way that either you, I, or anyone else enjoys an objective existence, is neither here nor there. According

to Jung, these gods exist as "psychic truths" in the "collective unconscious" minds of all Europeans and can erupt from there with an absolutely terrifying destructive force.

In his *Essays on Contemporary Events* Jung interpreted the rise of the Nazi party in accordance with this theory. The Nazis, he argued, were men and women possessed by the dark and adverse aspects of the Teutonic gods; through them a berserk Thor found an outlet into the world of matter, their hands wielded his hammer and with it, they had smashed the Cathedrals of Christendom.

Jung's writings on Nazism, not entirely surprisingly, have been much misunderstood. Indeed, some commentators have adopted the line that Jung actually supported the Nazis. This, in fact, is not true. He simply endeavoured to understand their popularity in occult somehow producing a meaningful coincidence. After Jung's break with Freud in 1913 he underwent a prolonged inner crisis that involved either almost unbelievable coincidences or psychic phenomena (or possibly both). For example, Jung's electric doorbell was afflicted by some untraceable fault in its circuitry that caused it to ring of its own accord; these mysterious peals invariably took place at times when Jung was feeling "something is about to happen".

Jung overcame his crisis after he had written a very strange inspirational work entitled *Sermons to the Dead*, but he continued to experience curious coincidences in relation to his analytical work. On one occasion, for example, a patient was talking about the symbolism of beetles when a very large and brilliantly coloured beetle, somewhat resembling an Egyptian scarab, flew into the room.

→ CHANCE AND SYNCHRONICITY ←

Not all coincidences that strike people as remarkable are quite as extraordinay as they may seem. Suppose, for example, that you are a New Yorker visiting London and stand in Oxford Street or some other well-known shopping centre. Suddenly you see an old acquaintance from Brooklyn whom you have not seen for years. You greet each other warmly, exchange news, and express your astonishment at the way chance has brought you together.

In reality there is nothing particularly odd in the two of you encountering one another over 3000 km (2000 miles) from home. Literally hundreds of New Yorkers walk along London's main shopping streets every day of the week, just as hundreds of Londoners walk along Fifth Avenue. A New Yorker's chances of meeting someone from home when he or she is visiting London are quite high.

Not all coincidences are so easily explained away. It is difficult, for example, for most of us to believe that nothing more than blind chance and a double coincidence led to the recovery of George Feifer's stolen novel (p.159).

Jung was not a believer in unalloyed chance. In 1952 he explained that he had studied the horoscopes of 180 married couples and had become convinced that while there were no causal links between astrological factors and human destinies, there were "coincidental" links. The correlations between the rules of traditional astrology and the lives of those whose horoscopes Jung had studied were so marked that the chance of them not being meaningful was very small indeed.

This led Jung to formulate the theory of synchronicity – the word synchronicity literally means "at the same time", but Jung used it to indicate what he termed "the equal significance of parallel events". He asserted that everything that takes place at a particular moment of time has the qualities of that moment, and that all events taking place at the same time are linked.

terms. He wrote that he wanted the German people to be led by a "God-possessed man" rather than the savage Teutonic gods who had possessed the mind of the mass of Germans, and who had led them towards the horrifying evils of Nazism.

Jung's belief in psychic truths attracted the hostility of both materialists and occultists. The former argued that a "psychic truth" could be a truth only if it was objectively true – if this was not the case then it was the very opposite – a psychic delusion.

A very similar criticism was made by some occultists, notably Rudolf Steiner (pp.96-97), who asserted that the gods of evil, such as Lucifer and Ahriman, really did enjoy an objective existence, and continually endeavoured to frustrate the necessary spiritual evolution of humanity.

Henry Fielding
The 18th-century novelist, Henry Fielding (above), was the subject of a strange coincidence. A well-known occultist and psychical researcher of the pre-1914 period approached a friend and asked after their mutual acquaintance "Have you seen Fielding?" At exactly the same time, the friend enquired, "Have you seen Tom Jones?" Tom Jones is, of course, the name of Fielding's most poular fictional hero. Was it a coincidence, or was it in fact the result of some form of telepathy?

Pure Chance
Many gambling games, such as roulette (left), are based on pure chance. By using a probability theory, it is possible to work out the precise odds in favour of the Bank. Over time, however, the Bank – to the chagrin of most gamblers – almost invariably does better than predicted. Why is this? No sure answer is known. Similarly, many gamblers work out what they consider to be foolproof systems based on the laws of probability. Invariably, these systems break down. Very few gamblers, who play games of pure chance, win.

Chives
The smallest, and perhaps the most delicately flavoured, member of the onion family are chives (left). According to English country lore chickens, geese, and turkeys will thrive if chives are mixed with their food.

Garlic
Apart from its legendary capacity to keep vampires at bay, garlic (below) is reputed to confer valour upon cockerels who are fed upon it, becoming "most stout to fight and so are horses". Other strange properties attributed to it include driving moles from gardens, curing warts, and conferring endurance upon long distance runners.

Blood-Red Rose
According to classical legend, the first red rose plant (below) sprang from the blood of the slain demi-god, Adonis. It has since become the symbol of love, Venus, and the Blessed Virgin.

Alchemilla
The name of this plant (below right) is derived from the Arabic word for alchemy. The name was conferred because of the wonder-working powers of dew condensed upon its leaves.

Catnip
It is said that chewing catnip root (right) makes the most gentle person fierce and quarrelsome. Perhaps that is why rats supposedly fear it and, while usually omniverous, will not eat it, even when famished.

THE POWER OF PLANTS

THROUGHOUT HISTORY, plants have been universally exploited by mankind for the infinitely varied "powers" they contain, powers that can be used for good or evil depending on the will of the user. Plants can be used, to kill or to cure; for their scent to attract lovers or repel enemies; in ointments for effects as various as curing a wound, to supposedly endowing supernatural powers. A good example of the latter is the notorious "witches' flying ointment", the main ingredient of which is said to be the lethal belladonna. Many plants also have symbolic signifcance.

Sunflower Seeds
Bruised sunflower seeds (right) are reputed to increase human sexual potency.

Bay Leaves
Priestesses of Apollo used bay (right) to induce prophetic trance.

Rue
(above right) According to one Elizabethan herbalist, "if a man be anointed with the juice of rue, the poison of wolf's bane ... todestooles, the biting of serpents, stinging of scorpions, spiders, bees, hornets and wasps will not hurt him". Rue is also reputed, "to hinder witches from their will".

Valerian
The root of valerian (left) has been long valued for its diuretic qualities and its usefulness in the treatment of epilepsy. So prized were its medicinal qualities that it was formerly named "All Heal".

Marjoram
An oil derived from marjoram (right) was an ancient remedy for sprains. Used as an incense it is said to be useful in "evoking spirits".

Lavender
According to Salmon, a famous seventeenth-century herbalist, the sweetly scented lavender (above) is very effective "against the bitings of serpents, mad dogs and other venemous creatures, being given inwardly and applied poultice wise".

DOOM, DEATH, AND DISASTER

"The blood of the just shall be required of London, Burned by lightening in thrice twenty and six ..."

Nostradamus

THE HISTORY OF HUMANITY in modern times has been such that anyone who has predicted that a major war would break out "in the next twenty-five years" has almost always been right. Their success has been almost inevitable, and the same goes for anyone who has had premonitions of war. It is only very detailed premonitions of military events that are worth taking seriously, and these have been few in number. One such was reported by the Dutch psychic researcher, Professor Tenhaeff.

➺ PREMONITIONS OF DOOM ➻
In 1929, one of the psychics whom he studied visited someone, whom the Professor disguised under the name of "Mrs. W.R.", at her home at Oosterbeek, near Arnhem. The psychic became very upset, had premonitions of doom, death, and disaster and had visionary "flashes" of soldiers in an unfamiliar uniform. His warning sixth sense gave him no idea of the time scale involved and, assuming the event was going to take place in the very near future, he begged Mrs. W.R. and her family to pack their most

Man of Miracles
Edgat Cayce (above) was a psychic healer and a clairvoyant. Cayce would go into a trance in order to make diagnoses of his patient's illnesses. One time, when he was in a trance, he discovered the identity of a murderer. After this chilling experience, Cayce was called upon several times to help the police trace criminals. He also often helped relatives of those missing in World War I to trace their loved ones.

treasured possessions and leave their home. They disregarded the advice, which was all to the good, for it was not until fifteen years later, in 1944, that Oosterbeek became the centre of exceptionally bloody conflict between allied paratroops who had landed at Arnhem and the German soldiers of an S.S. Panzer division.

➺ THE SINKING OF THE TITANIC ➻
The problem in all instances of supposed premonition is to decide whether some genuine psychic sense was at work or whether the correspondence between a supposed premonition and an actual event was the result of an extraordinary coincidence. It is ultimately impossible to know.

Take, for example, the case of a writer named Morgan Robertson who, in 1898, published a novel recounting the story of the destruction of a supposedly unsinkable ocean liner named SS *Titan*. Using his imagination, he gave the displacement of the fictional liner as 70,000 tons. This was, in fact, a ludicrously large figure at the time Robertson was writing. Robertson also described how the ship hit an iceberg on her maiden voyage across the Atlantic. The majority of the 2,500 passengers on the fictional ship were drowned because the *Titan* had only 24 lifeboats – a figure that fell well short of the ship's requirements.

The Seer
Nostradamus (left), was born in St. Rémy de Provence, France. He was an extremely intelligent child who readily absorbed Hebrew, Latin, and Greek. As a young man he discovered that he possessed healing and precognitive powers. It was not until 1555, when Nostradamus was 52 years old, that he published his first yearly Almanac. His prophecies made him famous and he was summoned to an audience with the French royal family, whose horoscopes he was asked to compose.

NOSTRADAMUS
Some people seem to be able to induce a state of consciousness, in which they can literally see into the future. One such may have been the French seer, Nostradamus (1503–1566), some of whose predictions were very precise, giving specific dates for coming events. None of the predictive techniques with fixed rules, such as astrology (pp.180–183), can produce such exact results. One such date was rather cryptically given in a verse that has been interpreted as prophesying the Great Fire of London in 1666: "The blood of the just shall be required of London, Burned by lightening in thrice twenty and six, The ancient lady shall fall from her high place, And many of the same sect shall be destroyed." Students of Nostradamus interpret the "blood of the just" as that of the martyred King Charles, executed in London 17 years before the Great Fire, while the "ancient Lady"

In April 1912, the real-life *Titan* – which was, of course, the SS *Titanic* – with a displacement of 66,000 tons, hit an iceberg on its maiden trans-atlantic voyage and sank. The majority of its 2,224 passengers were drowned, largely because the ship had only 20 lifeboats, about half the number required for safety.

Robertson was almost or completely right about practically everything. Did he have a premonition – his mind picking up from the future signals of psychic distress from the doomed passengers? Or should one just ascribe this uncanny resemblance between fiction and fact to coincidence?

⇢ THE PRUDENT PARENT ⇠

In 1978, the wife of a Spanish hotel executive named Jaime Castell became pregnant. Señor Castell was delighted, looking forward with the greatest enthusiasm to the prospect of fatherhood. In 1979, however, three months before the baby was due to be born, Jaime Castell had a warning dream in which a disembodied voice told him that he would die before the birth took place.

Most people would have either disregarded the dream or have worried about it without taking any action. Señor Castell, however, was a man of exceptional prudence and practicality. He approached an insurance company and took out a life policy on which the sum assured was payable only on death.

A few weeks later he was driving along the highway at the prudent speed of 80 km/h (50 m.p.h.) when a driver travelling at twice the speed in the opposite direction lost control, hit the highway's central barrier, turned upside down and landed on top of Señor Castell's vehicle. Both drivers were killed instantly: Señor Castell's dream was tragically realized.

⇢ BEYOND SUSPICION ⇠

The insurance company paid up without demur, its spokesman explaining that it would normally carry out a full investigation of a death taking place so soon after a policy had been taken out but it was not doing so because "this incredible accident rules out suspicion ... a second either way and he would have escaped".

An impressive example of a premonitory dream fulfilled – but it would only be really convincing if one could be sure that hundreds of other nervous fathers-to-be had not had similar, but unfulfilled, premonitions of disaster. Again we are faced with the problem of deducing whether such events are the result of real premonitions or are in fact coincidences.

(la dame antique) is thought to mean St. Paul's Cathedral, which was destroyed in the fire together with dozens of other churches – an interpretation of "many of the same sect".

An even more remarkable hit by Nostradamus involves a verse mentioning a period of 290 years. One commentator, as early as the eighteenth century, suggested that this period had begun in 1649, and that in 1939, some event would take place that would be of major importance in British history. In 1922, this suggestion was amplified by H.H. Kitzinger, author of *Mysteries of the Sun and the Soul*, who interpreted the verse as a specific prophecy of a major international crisis in 1939, which would involve Poland, Britain, and Germany.

On September 1, 1939, Germany invaded its weaker neighbour, Poland; two days later Britain and France went to Poland's aid. The Second World War had begun.

Biblical Prophets
The Old Testament prophets depicted above hold scrolls on which are written their Divine messages. Primarily the prophets acted as an intermediary between God and Man, receiving, interpreting, and passing on messages from God to humankind. Some of these messages foretold of the future. According to biblical tradition, prophets would receive messages while in a trance-like state, or in dreams. Sometimes prophetic messages were not absolute – certain actions would have to be carried out by those who received the prophecy.

In early December 1978, a man named Edward Pearson was charged before a Scottish court with travelling on the railway without a ticket. Mr. Pearson, who gave his occupation as "unemployed Welsh prophet", explained to the court that he had been on his way to London to see the Minister of the Environment. He had wanted to warn the British government of a coming minor earthquake in Scotland, so that it could advise the local people to take protective measures. He had, so he said, considered the matter to be of sufficient urgency to justify his decision to travel by train, although he was without enough money to buy a ticket.

The court and those members of the public who read reports of its deliberations were amused but not impressed – an earthquake in Scotland big enough to be detected without the

Lost Continent
An artist's depiction of the Great Metropolis (above), the capital of the lost continent of Atlantis. Occultists believe that Atlantis was a perfect world, peopled by a race possessing visionary powers.

The Oracle at Delphi
The ancient Greek prophetesses uttered their solemn pronouncements at the Temple of Apollo, at Delphi (left). Each prophecy was revealed in a trance.

use of complex seismic measuring devices would be very rare. Three weeks later, Scotland was hit by a small earthquake, which shook some people from their beds and caused minor structural damage in Glasgow and other places. Perhaps, Mr. Pearson had a genuine premonition of danger – such forewarnings of unpleasant events seem to be surprisingly common.

Indeed, it has been suggested that we all experience premonitions but only on a subconcious level, so that we are not fully aware of them. If so, considering how much subconscious motivations affect our everyday actions, it seems possible that we sometimes avoid dangers that we have unconsciously sensed.

→ STATISTICAL ANALYSIS ←

There is some scientific evidence to support this. In the late 1970s, a large number of major railway accidents were subjected to a detailed statistical analysis by W.J. Cox. The analysis involved comparing the number of passengers on a train involved in an accident, with the number on the same scheduled train on the same day in earlier weeks.

The differences between the numbers were statistically significant – on average there were fewer passengers on the accident runs than on the incident-free runs of the same scheduled trains. Coincidence? Or were the missing passengers induced to avoid the risks of injury and death by unconscious premonition?

Premonitions of one kind or another play a large part in the Bible in both the Old and New Testaments. Biblical premonitions are termed prophecies, and are interpreted as Divine revelations – messages passed from God to Man. Like the premonitions of Mr. Pearson, biblical prophecies tend to be concerned with death, disaster, and, in particular, the end of the world. However, biblical prophets tend not to have "automatic" revelations; rather they go and seek them intentionally, by, for example, going into a trance.

→ THE BOOK OF REVELATION ←

Some of the most analysed of all prophecies are those that are found in *The Book of Revelation*, which was, for many years, the most popular book of the Bible. Commentators have argued over the exact meaning of the sometimes complicated imagery in which the revelations are couched. However it is generally accepted that they refer to the conflict between good and evil, and the eventual triumph of good. When this triumph occurs:

"There shall be no more of anything accursed, but the throne of God and of the Lamb shall be in it, and his servants shall worship him; and they shall see his face, and his name shall be on their foreheads. And night shall be no more, they need no light of lamp or sun, for the Lord God shall be their light, and they shall reign for ever and ever."

Commentators have argued as to when this final and everlasting triumph will occur. Not surprisingly readers have tended to apply it to their own particular age. It is also not clear who actually received these Divine revelations, although most commentators believe it was the author of the fourth gospel, St. John, who was one of Christ's disciples.

→ 1999, THE END OF THE WORLD ←

Nearly all cultures have some sort of concept of the impermanence of the world, and to many, such an end is, in fact, a beginning of a new, purer life. It is not surprising, then, that a constant preoccupation of people who have premonitions is suggesting a date for the end of the world. According to the Bible, the world will end in terrible famine and wars. As nearly every age has seen such catastrophes, there is a tendency for people to believe that "the end of the world is nigh". One prophecy made by a

renowned seer, Nostradamus (p.164) stated that the world would end in 1999. Another, the famous fifteenth-century seer, Mother Shipton, believed 1881 to be the final year.

There are still people today who walk round with banners declaring that the end of the world is imminent. This is often less of a reminder of biblical prophecies than a look at the current state of the world, where the potential devastation caused by man, through his new weapons of war, and industrial waste and pollution, is on a scale hitherto unknown. Indeed, it is not only the "prophets" amongst us, but also some scientists, who are predicting doom and disaster.

It is almost impossible to ascertain whether or not people really do have unconscious or even, indeed, conscious powers of prediction, and one of the major problems with trying to identify whether or not a particular prophecy has actually come true, is the vagueness in which they are told. It is only too easy to fit the event to the prophecy, as detractors of Nostradamus have sometimes claimed.

The Sibyls
The figure of the sibyl, or prophetess, is frequently found in religious art. The Renaissance genius, Michelangelo, adorned the ceiling of the Sistine Chapel in Rome with five frescoes of sibyls, including the Libyan Sibyl *(above). Sibyls were prophetesses of the ancient world – a world that considered prophecy to be a gift peculiar to women. The sibyls' prophecies were interpreted as foretelling the coming of Christ. There were a total of five major sibyls, each representing an ancient civilization: Rome, Greece, Africa, Persia (Iran), and Turkey.*

READING THE LINES

"If a man look sharply, and attentively, he shall see Fortune: for though she be blind, yet she is not invisible"

Francis Bacon

THE IDEA THAT ONE'S character and, possibly, one's destiny, is written in the lines of the hand is a very old one. There is, for example, an ancient Chinese system of palmistry, and references to palmistry can be found in ancient Jewish texts. Some palmists claim that their art is validated by an Old Testament text (Job Ch. 37 v. 7) which declares that God "... sealeth up the hand of every man; that all men whom He hath made may know it".

The palm contains numerous lines, any one of which may be found on some – or most – human hands. Three of these lines, however, are considered to be of much greater importance than all of the rest, and, apart from one or two exceptional, and usually pathological, conditions, are to be found in the hands of each and every human being.

These lines are the Head Line, the Heart Line, and the Life Line. While the lines are usually in the positions shown on the opposite page, they can vary from these positions very considerably. They can also extend more or less, at either end, than is shown in the illustration. So, for example, the Life Line can extend back to the bracelets, or can begin 3 cm ($1\frac{1}{4}$ in) away from the wrist in the direction of the fingers. Similarly, it can end well before the edge of the palm or it can go over that edge.

Japanese Palmistry
While some Japanese palmists (above) have displayed an interest in western chiromancy, most of them use a system derived from China. In recent years, some western occultists have studied this oriental occult art, which ultimately stems from Taoist polarity theory, and have claimed that it admirably complements occidental palmistry.

↠ A LOOK AT THE LINES ↞

THE LIFE LINE: If this extends to the Mount of Jupiter – the fleshy pad below the forefinger – it is believed to indicate an ambitious nature, one showing an excessive ambition, marked by a lack of a sense of proportion and, perhaps, selfish egotism. Lines cutting the Life Line and running up to the Mount of Jupiter also show, it is thought, ambition – but of a more balanced sort. If the Life Line is joined to the Head Line, forking from it, the "life energy" will be under the control of the reasoning faculty. If the line forks between, and runs up to, both the thumb and forefinger, then reason and the life energy should be admirably balanced. If the Head Line begins well below the Life Line, an impulsive character is indicated.

A HEAD FOR CHARACTER

Phrenology enjoyed a period of popularity and esteem in the nineteenth century as a way of measuring mental ability and character from the shape of the skull. Subjects were solemnly diagnosed as having a "bump of generosity" or "organ of acquisitiveness, secretiveness, or self-confidence", or whatever it might be, and plaster skulls were made with areas of the head designated by character traits.

The founder of the "science" was a distinguished Austrian physician, Franz Joseph Gall. Queen Victoria and Prince Albert had the royal children's heads measured by George Coombe, the noted Scottish phrenologist. In America, reading people's bumps became part of the stock in trade of the travelling showman and patent medicine seller. In Germany in the 1920s and 1930s some occult groups became interested in phrenology as a way to measure "racial purity".

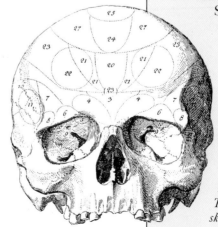

Phrenology Skull
The diagram (left) shows sections of a skull that control aspects of character.

THE MOUNTS

As well as the major lines on a hand, there are other features that palmists study. The mounts of Jupiter, Saturn, Venus, Mercury, Mars, and the Moon (shown in the diagram of a hand, right) are used to shed further light on a person's destiny.

JUPITER: Strongly developed, this mount indicates ambition, success, and riches. If the mount of Jupiter is excessive, the person will be over ambitious, even ruthless.

SATURN: A strongly developed mount of Saturn indicates a practical, careful, and hard-working personality.

VENUS: This mount indicates a sympathetic, warm-hearted person.

MERCURY: This mount shows a person's ability to communicate with others.

MARS: There are actually two mounts of Mars: one is positive (positioned above the mount of Venus), the other negative (positioned above the mount of the Moon). If the mounts of Mars are strongly developed, it shows the person to be aggressive to an extreme degree. If they are underdeveloped, the person will be shy.

MOON: This mount is connected to a person's imaginative power. If the mount is overdeveloped, it means that the person lives in a fantasy world. If it is underdeveloped, the person is likely to be rather dull.

Lines of Destiny
The model of the hand (left) shows the "major lines". These are the Heart Line, the Head Line, and the Life Line. Interpreting these lines can reveal a person's destiny.

THE HEAD LINE: In the diagram above, this line is shown extending almost right across the palm. However, it can stop anywhere across the palm and it can curve abruptly towards the wrist, ending somewhere in the Mount of the Moon, which is the fleshy pad near the wrist on the side opposite to the thumb. Such a curve is thought to indicate a sensitive and creative personality; however, if the curve continues through the Mount of the Moon until it almost reaches the wrist, the sensitivity can be extreme, often resulting in excessive introversion and, sometimes, a tendency towards depression.

A long, well-defined, and reasonably straight Head Line was traditionally associated with an excellent retentive memory and "mental toughness"; a fork at the end of the line that is furthest away from the thumb is taken as an indicator of literary or oratorical ability; and a Head Line which actually crosses the Life Line – unusual, but not excessively so – is held to correlate with a choleric, ill tempered personality.

THE HEART LINE: As is suggested by its name, this line is taken as an indicator of the emotions and sexuality – the lower it is on the palm and the more curved its structure, the stronger the sexual drive of the person on whose hand it appears. If, on the contrary, it is high on the palm and one end finishes towards the wrist, rather than towards the Mount of Jupiter (see diagram), then inhibition, emotional and sexual, is indicated.

If the Head and Heart Lines are close to one another, the emotions are usually under the control of the mind; the opposite is thought to be indicative of the emotions being uncontrolled by common sense – a situation that can often lead to trouble.

DEALING WITH FORTUNE

*"For I dipt into the future,
Far as human eye can see"*

Sir James Frazer

AN ORDINARY DECK of western playing cards, such as is used to play bridge or poker, has oriental analogues; there are surviving decks of medieval Persian, Chinese, and Indian playing cards. However, it seems unlikely that the western decks are directly derived from oriental sources. Apparently the 52-card western deck is a simplified version of the tarot.

Like the tarot, ordinary playing cards have been, and still are, used for fortune telling. However, the divinatory meaning generally attached to an ordinary playing card is often different to that given to its tarot forerunner.

For example, cartomancers give the ordinary Nine of Hearts a different meaning to its ancestor, the tarot Nine of Cups.

Oriental Cards
These cards (below and left) are analogous to, but not the exact equivalent of, the tarot and standard playing-card decks of the West. As illustrated, some oriental cards depict elegant courtesans.

French Fortunes
The cards at the bottom of this page are of French origin and depict various distinguished courtly figures from the country's colourful history.

Heraldic Cards

(below and left) Throughout the eighteenth and nineteenth centuries, educational decks, dealing with subjects ranging from zoology and botany to geography and history, were produced in large numbers.

Cards of Love

An early nineteenth-century deck (right), in which each card was correlated with human emotions of one sort or another. Some similar decks were less innocent.

Court Cards

The court cards of the suit of Diamonds (right) correspond to, and are derived from, the suit of Wands in the tarot deck. There are many different ways of interpreting the four suits in a playing-card deck. One popular way is to equate each suit with one of the four elements: Diamonds to fire, Clubs to earth, Hearts to water, and Spades to air.

Feminist Cards

This eighteenth-century deck (right) devotes each card to a major female historical figure, such as England's Elizabeth I.

ON THE CARDS

"*Nothing more certain than uncertainties; Fortune is full of...variety: constant in nothing but inconstancy*"

Richard Barnfield

CARTOMANCY – THE USE of ordinary playing cards or tarot decks in order to obtain answers to questions, analyse the nature of a situation, or to learn the general nature of what the future holds in store – is one of the most popular methods of fortune telling. It is not, however, a particularly easy one. The good cartomancer has to try to let his or her intuitive faculty have full play, and to use a card spread in order to build, on the basis of such "cook book" interpretations as those given here, the outline of a story that gives the truth about a confusing situation, or provides a glimpse of the future.

There are many cartomantic spreads – ways of laying out the cards in order to tell fortunes – and some of them are of such complexity that it takes many hours of manipulating the cards and endeavouring to intuitively discern their meaning, to "read" them adequately.

→ CARTOMANCY EXPERIMENT ←

Here are some simple spreads with which readers of this book can experiment. The simplest spread – the two card spread – requires just two cards, one to symbolize the past, the other the future; it is said to be adequate to answer a simple question such as "Will my love life improve over the next year?" Shuffle the cards – this must always precede the laying out of a spread – and deal the top two. That on the left is the past; that on the right is the future. Try to answer the question by elaborating the keywords given on the facing page. If the question was that given as an example above, and the two cards dealt were the Four of Clubs and the Six of Spades, this answer, derived from the keywords, could be something like "In the past you have been more successful in your financial affairs than in the life of the emotions, but over the next twelve months your love life is likely to improve as the result of you taking a journey – going on holiday perhaps".

An excellent method of analysing a complex situation is given in the following spread. Deal the top five cards of the pack in the order shown in the diagram (above). Take Card

```
    3
1   2   5
    4
```

Tarot Cards

The minor arcana (below left) form the bulk of the tarot card pack. They include all the cards except for the tarot trumps, which are known as the major arcana. Most modern packs give the novice some idea of each card's symbolic meaning on the card itself. For example, as shown here, the ace of swords, is given the meaning of a card that, in some way, assists and modifies all the other cards around it. So, if it appeared next to a card with a negative meaning, the ace of swords could be seen as having a modifying influence on the negativity of the adjacent card.

3 as the dominant influence in the situation as it is at the present; take Cards 1 and 2 as representing coming influences; Card 4 shows the true nature of hidden influences affecting the situation; Card 5 shows how all the factors combine and how the situation will be resolved.

Another popular spread is the "clock spread". Deal the top twelve cards in the form of a clock – the first card on one o'clock, the last on twelve o'clock. The keywords of the twelve cards indicate the general nature of the enquirer's life over the next twelve months. The one o'clock card representing the first month, and so on, round the clock, to the twelfth card, which represents the last month of the coming year.

To actually read any of these spreads, you need to

A powerful card. Materially helps the cards surrounding it.

MINOR ARCANA

The loss of a lover. Sorrow and disappointments.

THE THREE OF SWORDS

Great disillusionment. Disorder and confusion.

MINOR ARCANA

acquaint yourself with each card's meaning. A brief summary of card meanings is as follows:

SUIT OF HEARTS (Cups in tarot decks) – Ace; good luck: 2; deep love: 3; successful endings: 4; tensions and difficulties: 5; disappointments and partings: 6; final success through struggle: 7; deceit: 8; self fulfilment: 9; health and prosperity: 10; much success: Jack (or tarot Page); dreaminess: Knight (in tarot); a message: Queen; light-heartedness: King; hostility and severity.

SUIT OF CLUBS (Pentacles or Discs in tarot decks) – Ace; material success: 2; abrupt change: 3; improvement: 4; financially beneficial news: 5; material worries: 6; prosperity: 7; financial mistakes: 8; small improvements: 9; prosperity achieved: 10; material prosperity from hard work or inheritance: Jack (tarot Page); prudence: Knight (tarot only); usefulness: Queen; generosity: King; quiet energy.

SUIT OF SPADES (Swords in tarot decks) – Ace; tension and virility: 2; harmony and balanced force: 3; separations: 4; peace: 5; failure and bad news: 6; happy journeys: 7; unresolved situations: 8; crisis: 9; ill fortune: 10; sorrow: Jack (tarot Page); subtlety: Knight (tarot decks only); personal enmity: Queen; loneliness: King; responsibility and authority.

SUIT OF DIAMONDS (Wands, Staves, or Batons in tarot decks) – Ace; renewal: 2; power and wealth: 3; material success: 4; happy endings: 5; struggle: 6; success through effort: 7; great risks and danger involved: 8; urgency: 9; persistence, doggedness: 10; misused energy: Jack (tarot Page); reliable partners: Knight (tarot decks only); undue haste: Queen; financial success: King; happy love or money inherited.

↝ HIGH-POWERED CARDS ↜

Within the tarot-card deck is a group of cards known as the tarot trumps. When these 21 cards are dealt in spreads they indicate events and emotions of a particularly powerful, and sometimes philosophical, and spiritual nature. The meanings attributed to the tarot trumps are subtle, and each reader must draw his or her conclusions as to their deeper meaning. However, a rough guide is as follows:

FOOL; unexpected events, eccentricity, folly.
MAGICIAN OR JUGGLER; risk, adaptability.
PRIESTESS; intuition, secrets.
EMPRESS; creativity, luck.
EMPEROR; ambition, success, authority.
HIGH PRIEST; advice, assistance, the occult.
LOVERS; love, sexuality, choices offered/made.
CHARIOT; final success, obstacles overcome.
JUSTICE; decisions, patience needed.

The Future in Verse
These cards (below) each bear a prophetic rhyme.

Pack Variety
Although there are several established tarot card packs, such as the Aleister Crowley pack, there are numerous variations. In addition to the many types of tarot packs, there are other cards designed with fortune telling rather than card playing in mind. For example, these cards (right) are not, strictly speaking, tarot cards, yet they can be used in the same way. At one time, Tarot cards were looked upon with some suspicion, but not so any more. If used properly, under guidance, they are not in any way sinister. To be dealt the Death card is not, as once was thought, indicative of the death of a relation or, indeed, of the enquirer; rather it may indicate some kind of spiritual death.

HERMIT; wise and careful guidance, tact, reclusiveness.

WHEEL OF FORTUNE; inevitable change, good fortune, financial success, improvements.

STRENGTH; courage, fortitude.

HANGED MAN; setbacks, suffering, self sacrifice.

DEATH; failure, partings, losses.

TEMPERANCE; good health, wise management, successful partnerships.

DEVIL; sexuality, material possessions, choice between the spirit and the flesh.

TOWER; destruction, conflicts, losses.

STAR; unexpected help, pleasant surprises.

MOON; risks, adventure, puzzlement.

SUN; prosperity, happiness, love.

LAST JUDGEMENT; fresh starts, reunions, important decisions.

UNIVERSE; certain success, happy journeys.

The important thing to remember about any card reading is that the meaning of the cards (as given above) is not by any means the only interpretation possible. An experienced reader will make as much use of his or her intuition, as they will of the hand that is dealt.

ON THE CARDS

"*Madame Sosostris, famous clairvoyante, has a bad cold, nevertheless is known to be the wisest woman in Europe, with a wicked pack of cards*"

T.S. Eliot *The Waste Land*

THERE ARE AN enormous variety of tarot decks available today. They range from modern reproductions of eighteenth-century cards – originally printed from crude woodblocks and then coloured by hand – to "esoteric decks" designed to convey the teachings of particular western occult groups under the guise of symbol.

The design and manufacture of such esoteric tarot decks owes its origins to the theories of an eighteenth-century French scholar, Court de Gablin, who argued that the tarot was of ancient Egyptian origin, and that the designs of the 22 cards of the "major arcana" – the tarot trumps, usually numbered from 0 to 21 – were degenerate versions of the secret symbols of the priests of the Egyptian deities, Thoth, Isis, and Osiris. De Geblin's ideas were enthusiastically adopted by a

fortune teller who called himself "Etteilla" (the reverse of his real name, which was Alliette) and who, with more enthusiasm than knowledge or judgement, designed a rectified deck, replete with mangled Egyptian images, which is still made at the present day.

Where Etteilla led, others have followed. In the 1850s, the French ritual magician, Eliphas Levi, produced modified versions of some of the trumps; thirty years later these were the basis on which, with the aid of his own psychic experiments, S.L. MacGregor Mathers designed a deck that was used by W.B. Yeats and other initiates of the "Order of the Red Rose and the Cross of Gold".

Love Cards
The tarot suit of cups (above) symbolizes love and friendship.

Ace of Wands

Force for Change
The suit of wands in the tarot deck represents change – for better or worse. These particular cards (above) are taken from the deck designed by the ritual magician, Aleister Crowley.

Cards of Conflict
These cards (left) are from the suit of swords. They are used to represent conflict and strife.

Cards for Colouring
These cards (right), from
a 1960's black-and-white
deck, intended for hand-
colouring, are influenced
by Aleister Crowley. The
card most prominently
shown here, The Blasted
Tower, is also known as
The House of God. It is
generally held to
correspond to the
planet Mars and the
forces of destruction.

THE BLASTED TOWER XVI

Lord of the Hosts of the Mighty

TEN OF PENTACLES

PRINCESS OF PENTACLES

Princess of the Echoing Hills

Popular Deck
The "major arcana" – tarot trumps – were
first issued in 1910. The deck (below)
was designed by the mystical writer,
A.E. Waite. It is one of the
most widely used, and many
other tarot decks owe their
design to it.

THE FOOL

JUSTICE.
THE HANGED MAN.
DEATH.
TEMPERANCE.
THE DEVIL.
THE TOWER.
THE STAR.
THE MOON.
THE SUN.
JUDGEMENT.
THE WORLD.

THE MAGICIAN.
THE HIGH PRIESTESS
THE EMPRESS.
THE EMPEROR.
THE HIEROPHANT
THE LOVERS.

WHEEL of F
THE
ST
THE

Divine Folly
Another A.E.
Waite design,
this tarot trump
(above) is
numbered 0 and is
named The Fool.
Waite saw this card
as symbolizing, not
foolishness, but divine
folly – an expression of
spiritual wisdom.

8
9
10

20.
FORTUNE
FORTUNE

JUGMENTATION INCREASE

17
DECES
DEATH

INCAPACITE INCAPACITY

VERTU
VIRTUE
DAME

DEVOUEMENT DEVO

13
MARIAGE
MARRIAGE

LIAISON
LOVE AFFAIR

Knight of Wands
Queen of Wands
Prince of Wands
Princess of Wan

Fortune
This card (above),
from a modern deck,
represents fortune.

Modern Version
These modern versions of Marriage (left),
Death, and Virtue (above) are derived
from the 18th-century Etteilla deck.

THE MAGIC OF NUMBERS

"Number is the ruler of forms and ideas, and is the cause of gods and demons"

Pythagorus

A GOOD MANY PEOPLE are fascinated by numbers, and for centuries they have been manipulated by occultists in order to predict the future. The physicist, Isaac Newton, for example, spent more of his time studying the numbers mentioned in the Old Testament Book of Daniel in the hope that he could thus discover the exact date at which the world would come to an end, than he did in developing his theory of gravity. However despite the apparent absurdity of such an occupation, it has to be admitted that ancient systems of calculating numbers, supposedly significant in relation to the character and life of an individual, are sometimes productive of intriguing results.

⇢ NUMBERS IN NAMES ⇠

In many of the world's ancient alphabets, the symbols used for letters also have a numerical significance. In Hebrew, for example, the first letter of the alphabet, Aleph, also represents the number 1, and the second letter, Beth,

A; I; Q; J; Y	1
B; K; R	2
C; G; L; S	3
D; M; T	4
E; H; N	5
U; V; W; X	6
O; Z	7
F; P	8

Letters and Numbers
Greek and Hebrew letters had a numerical equivalent. In the chart above, one version of the letter/number equivalences is given (it is important to note that there are other versions). To work out a person's key number – that is, the number that will help numerologists to understand a person's personality – the numerical equivalent of each letter of the name is added up (p.177). The resulting number is then interpreted (p.179).

Albert Einstein
The name of the mathematical physicist and genius, Albert Einstein (left), numerologically adds up to forty-six. If four and six are then added, the total is ten. If the one and nought are then added together, the number reduces to one. One is the number associated with single mindedness, ambition, concentration, and creativity. These are all qualities with which Einstein was associated. The planet Mercury is said to influence the number one. Mercury is associated with the brain and intellectual activity.

THEIR NUMBER'S UP

Some of numerology's hits and misses can be illustrated by considering how famous dictators measure up numerologically. The name, Joseph Stalin (above), adds up to 1 – the number of egotism – while Stalin alone adds up to 8, as does Uncle Joe, the nickname by which the Soviet dictator was widely known in the West during the Second World War. The number 8 suggests worldly success and power, which seems appropriate, and the late President Ceausescu of Romania adds up to 8 too, which can also be indicative of a dramatic fall fom power. On the other hand, the one-time Chinese leader, Mao Tse Tung, yields the number 6, which, improbably in this case, signifies a placid, unadventurous temperament and a certain feminine domesticity.

Hitler's name adds up to 2, which is satisfactory, since 2 is fundamentally the number of evil and the devil. If Hitler's title "Der Fuhrer" is analysed, it turns out to contain too many 5s – four of them in ten letters – which suggests mental instability and arrogance of psychopathic proportions. However, if the name Adolf Hitler is taken, the number is 7, the number of occult gifts.

represents the number 2. Any word written in one of these alphabets has a numerical as well as a literal significance, and the same applies to personal names and titles.

In modern alphabets letters do not have numerical equivalents, but numerologists – believers in the supposed mystic significance of numbers – have adapted the number values of Greek and Hebrew letters to the letters used in English, and other similar present-day alphabets. This has resulted in the use of the letter/number equivalences given on page 176.

These are used by contemporary numerologists in order to find "names in numbers". For example the letters in "George Bush" (3+5+7+2+3+5 2+6+3+6) add up to 41 – but numerologists usually employ addition in order to reduce all double-digit numbers (i.e. numbers over 10) to a single figure number. In the case of George Bush the reduction is to 5 (4+1). If a double-digit number had resulted, a further addition would have been made. If, for example, a name added up to 48 it would first be reduced to 12 (4+8), and then to 3 (1+2). The final single figure number is termed the Key Number. The supposed basic attributes of these as a guide to character and, to a lesser extent, destiny, are given on page 179. George Bush would therefore appear to be a 5 – which is hardly how he appears to those who know him as a President of the USA.

⇝ THE PRESIDENT AND THE MAN ⇜

This raises an important point in relation to number-in-name characterology; it is not the legal name that matters, but the name generally used. This can vary – the same person can be known by a number of different names in different circumstances. If a man or woman is known by one form of name in his or her professional life, and another in his or her personal life, that man or woman is likely to have two Key Numbers – thus reflecting the differences between their private and public personalities. So when thinking of George Bush as a President, not as a private person, a numerologist considers his title in his official capacity – usually as President Bush, sometimes as President George Bush. The former adds up, using the same letter/number technique as that which was outlined earlier, to 53, which reduces to 8, the latter to to 78, which further reduces to 6 (7+8 = 15; then 1+5 = 6).

As will be seen by reference to page 179, either of these Key Numbers is admirably consonant with a President's public life and to the attitudes displayed by Bush. The number-

Billie Holliday
The numerical equivalents of the vowels and consonants of the name of the late singer, Billie Holliday (above), add up to forty. Four added to nought reduces to four, Billie Holliday's Key Number. In life, Billie Holliday seems to have displayed many of the negative qualities of the "four", including bouts of rage or exhiliration, alternating with deep depression. However like many "fours", she was hardworking, and achieved fame and respect through her career as a singer. Her personal life was, however, always difficult, which accounts for her moods.

from-your-name technique described on this page is used to calculate the Key Number of the name by which someone is known, and this number supposedly indicates the general character of the named individual.

Two other numbers are derived from a personal name or names – these are the Personality Numbers and the Heart Numbers.

The former is derived from the consonants of the name and is supposedly an indicator of the nature of the personality. The word "personality" is used here in its old-fashioned sense, derived from the Greek, "a mask". In other words, the Personality Number represents the mask that the individual presents to the outside world – how he or she wishes to be perceived, and commonly is perceived, by others, and not the "real" or "inner" person. However, the mask presented to outsiders can be an expression of the inmost self, the real desires, of a man or woman. In this case the Heart Number, which is derived from the vowels of a name and supposedly signifies the inner nature of the bearer of that name, will be the same as the Personality Number. In most cases, however, the numbers differ and, so numerologists assert, a consideration of the Personality and Heart Numbers in relation to one another provides a method of comparing the outer and inner natures of a given individual.

As an actual example of how this can be done, consider the name "Marilyn Monroe". This actress has intrigued the general public by her unusually complicated personality. Using the method outlined on page 177 this gives a Key Number of 2, a Personality Number of 8, and a Heart Number of 3. Thus:

MARILYN MONROE

4 1 2 1 3 1 5   4 7 5 2 7 5

Marilyn's numbers add up to 47, and should be further subdivided to find the key number:

4+7 = 11, and 1+1 = 2 (the Key Number)

The vowels of the name add up to 21, so the Heart Number is 3 (2+1), and the consonants of the name add up to 26, so the Personality

Marilyn Monroe

The American movie star, Marilyn Monroe's (below left) key number was two – the number of femininity. Her feminine charms cannot be doubted and few women have exploited their beauty – or been exploited because of their beauty – to the same extent. "Twos", however, also tend to be unsure of themselves, and although this was not the self she showed to the world, those who came to know Marilyn Monroe well were surprised by her quite astonishing inferiority complex and emotional instability.

George Bush

The numerical equivalents of the letters of George Bush's name (above) add up to a number that reduces to five. George Bush is not a typical five – but he does possess the first-class intelligence and the capacity to take risks that are sometimes associated with that number. However, if we take his name and title together – President George Bush – his key number is a six. "Sixes" are known for their ability to be successful in any career they choose to follow – surely true of a President of the United States.

Number is 8 (2+6). These three numbers – Key 2, Heart 3, and Personal, 8 – seem to have fitted Marilyn Monroe very well. Her Key Number was that of femininity, so was obviously very appropriate, and while her career dominated her life, she does seem to have had the 2 desire for a settled domesticity, although she never achieved a happy marriage. Her Heart Number was 3, and she seems to have been possessed of both the negative qualities of that number – showiness and conceit – and some of the positive ones, especially adaptability and quick thinking.

Marilyn Monroe's Personality – "mask" – Number was 8, that of material success attained through unremitting effort. And that was exactly how her character came over to those who knew her in the context of her working life.

→ Number Meanings ←

ONE; the number of ambition; personal energy directed mainly to self-advancement, and – if the negative aspects of the number are dominant – selfishness. *Ones* can be strong forces for good, but if they allow their egotism full play, they can be dominating and inconsiderate, even, in extreme cases, tyrannical.

TWO; the number of femininity in the old-fashioned sense of the word. The number often typifies the follower, not the leader, and *twos* can tend to be much too easy-going. They are usually good natured, if a trifle placid. *Twos* can be over-secretive and somewhat malicious.

THREE; the number of integration, harmony, and wholeness. A typical *three* is outgoing, adaptable, popular, and fast-thinking. In general they are fortunate and envied by others. They can be showy and conceited.

FOUR; the number of reliability and steady application. *Fours* tend to proceed slowly but unstoppably through life, eventually achieving all they want – but often not until middle life. One of their faults is a tendency to bottle up their true emotions.

FIVE; the number of mystery and the inexplicable; *fives* often conceal their true selves from others, sometimes living a life that is externally at odds with what is going on inside their heads. Many *fives* are attracted to things psychic; some of them can be reckless.

SIX; the number of reliability, loyalty, and abiding affection. The personality of the *six* – neither as stolid as that of the *four* nor as flashy as that of some *threes*, but often combining the best elements of both – usually leads to success.

SEVEN; the number of profound thought and creative imagination. *Sevens* are often more interested in their inner than their outer lives.

David Bowie
The numerical counterpart of the name, David Bowie (above), is thirty-seven, which like the name Albert Einstein (p.176) reduces to the number one. Although the world of show business is very different from that of mathematics, both men have exhibited "one" characteristics. However, like many people in show business, David Bowie is just a stage name. The singer's real name was David Jones. This name also reduces to the number, one, suggesting that the private David Bowie is much the same as the public David Bowie.

They sometimes strike others as being a little withdrawn, and have great difficulty in communicating with their fellow men. Like *fives*, they are attracted by the occult, although usually on a more serious level.

EIGHT; the number of unremitting effort, practical success and, sometimes, disastrous material failure. The typical *eight* is a tireless and dedicated worker and thus achieves success; but a tendency to occasional recklessness can sometimes result in the loss of all that has been attained. As a consequence of this, some *eights* can become extremely bitter characters.

NINE; the number of success on every level, and, sooner or later, *nines* get what they want out of life – materially, intellectually, and emotionally – and attain to great happiness. They must, however, guard against a tendency to try to dominate the lives of others. They also have a tendency to be over enthusiastic and may be a little whimsical about their aims in life.

THE ASTRAL INFLUENCE

"Astrology is the language of individuality and uniqueness"

Caroline Casey

MANY OF US SAY we know our astrological sign – meaning the zodiacal sign the sun is in on our birthdays. These sun signs are: Aries; March 21–April 20. Taurus; April 21–May 21. Gemini; May 22–June 22. Cancer; June 23–July 23. Leo; July 24–August 23. Virgo; August 24–September 23. Libra; September 24–October 23. Scorpio; October 24–November 22. Sagittarius; November 23–December 22. Capricorn; December 23–January 19. Aquarius; January 20–February 19. Pisces; February 20–March 20.

While we say, for example, that we are Cancerians if we are born between June 23 and July 23, our personalities, astrologers say, will only be very strongly Cancerian if we have "Cancer ascendants" as well as having the sun in that sign on our birthdays.

CANCER
JUNE 23 - JULY 23

LEO
JULY 24 - AUGUST 23

VIRGO
AUG. 24 - SEPT. 23

LIBRA
SEPT. 24 - OCT. 23

SCORPIO
OCT. 24 - NOV. 22

SAGITTARIUS
NOV. 23 - DEC. 22

ARIES
MARCH 21 – APRIL 20

TAURUS
APRIL 21 – MAY 21

 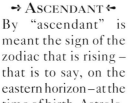

GEMINI
MAY 22 – JUNE 22

→ ASCENDANT ←

By "ascendant" is meant the sign of the zodiac that is rising – that is to say, on the eastern horizon – at the time of birth. Astrologers consider that the ascendant sign is quite as important as the sun sign in determining the likely character and destiny of an individual. If, for example, someone is born with the sun in Capricorn but with Leo on the ascendant, he or she is most unlikely to display the characteristics of the archetypal Capricornian – a plodding slow-but-sure approach to life, and a tendency to achieve success in the later rather than the earlier part of life.

Instead the Capricornian with a Leo ascendant is likely to display some of the characteristics of both signs; perhaps to combine the sometimes grim, dogged determination of the pure Capricornian with the fiery glowing personality of the archetypal Leo.

To calculate an ascendant accurately, complex tables are required, and one has to know the exact time of birth. Rather than explain it here, the reader would be advised to seek the advice of a professional astrologer.

→ THE FIRST ASTROLOGERS ←

So where and when did belief in the influence of the stars begin? Astrology seems to have first evolved in ancient Mesopotamia, where it was practised by priests. They concerned themselves with the prediction of major events, such as a good harvest, and the destinies of kings and princes. By classical times, however, the mathematicians – the Greek and Chaldean professional astrologers who had plied their trade in the Roman Empire – had turned their attention to delineating the characters of ordinary folk, and such matters have occupied astrologers ever since.

CAPRICORN
DEC. 23 - JAN. 19

AQUARIUS
JAN. 20 - FEB. 19

PISCES
FEB. 20 - MARCH 20.

Such astrologers have almost invariably taken it for granted that astrological factors decisively influence the personality and fate of the individual, and often surprise people by the accuracy of their descriptions of characters. Other astrologers see their art as an expression of an all-embracing philosophy that satisfactorily explains not just the lives of individuals but the nature of, for example, the great upheavals of time, which have led to the rise and fall of civilizations. Those astrologers who try to predict the future of nations rather than individuals, still exist – although their prophecies rarely seem to be of notable accuracy. Perhaps those of their fellows who confine themselves to lesser, more precise, matters, are wise so to do.

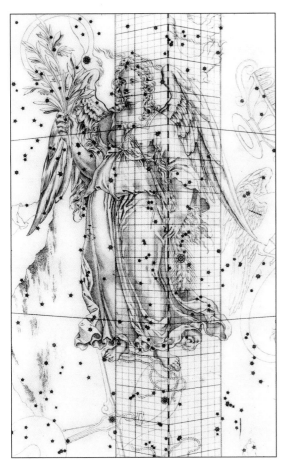

Aries represents the head; Taurus represents the neck and shoulders; Gemini represents the arms; Cancer represents the upper chest; Leo is associated with the heart and solar plexus; Virgo represents the stomach; Libra represents the bowels; Scorpio represents the genitals; Sagittarius represents the thighs; Capricorn is associated with the knees; Aquarius represents the shins; and, finally, Pisces represents the feet.

This particular classification, however beautiful some of its portrayals, such as that reproduced on page 183, is a very crude one. Apparently all that was

Virgo
The astrological sign of Virgo (left) is ruled by the planet Mercury, which governs the mind. Virgo is depicted as a maiden carrying a wheat sheaf, symbolizing fertility and abundance.

From ancient Rome to present-day San Francisco, the twelve signs of the zodiac have been used as a system of classification – endeavours have been made to find a correspondence between each sign and each particular material thing (for example, a plant), as well each non-material aspect of reality (for example, an emotion).

↠ **CHAINS OF BEING** ↞
An example of such a system of classification can be provided by the traditional attributions of the signs of the zodiac to particular parts of the human body. Both Medieval and Renaissance astrologers were generally in agreement with one another as to precisely how each of the classifications should be made. The following list represents these astrological associations:

Pendants
Most people are aware of their star sign; some proclaim it to the world by wearing symbolic pendants (above).

originally done to arrive at such associations seems to have been to draw a human figure and to write upon it the names of the signs of the zodiac at roughly equal intervals from the head to the feet.

More subtle types of twelvefold classification are of greater interest. Take, for example, some of the things supposedly "ruled" – that is to say, in correspondence with – the sign Scorpio. These include not only the genitals but the emotions, pleasures, vices, and even places associated with the genitals. Thus lust and

Necklaces
The garnet necklace (top) is associated with Scorpio; the blue lapis lazuli necklace (second), with Aquarius; the amethyst (third), is Piscean.

lechery are held to be ruled by Scorpio, and so are what our Victorian ancestors referred to as "houses of ill repute"; interestingly, I know of at least one modern astrologer who claims that strip clubs and pornographic videos are ruled by the star-sign of Scorpio.

Fantastic as this attribution may seem to the non-astrologer, it makes perfectly good sense within the context of astrology considered not only as an empirical

method of classification, but as a particular example of a general mode of thinking within the entire philosophy of the zodiac.

This mode of thinking is derivative of a Medieval and Renaissance concept that scholars term "the chain of being" – the belief that nothing is separate, totally independent, but instead is a link in "chains" between earth and Heaven. If one accepts the truth of this concept there is nothing unreasonable in thinking of brothels and the sign of Scorpio as linked in a particular chain of associated things.

Rings
From left to right, the main stones in each ring (above) are: dark sapphire, which is the birthstone of Capricorn; moonstone, which is normally associated with people born under the star sign, Cancer; the third ring is of tourmaline, the birthstone of the sun sign Gemini; and the ring on the forefinger contains Zircon, the stone that astrologers claim is suited to people born under Aries. As well as stones, colours and numbers are linked to signs.

Three Stones
This citrine necklace (left) should be worn by those born under the sign of Virgo, say astrologers. The ruby earrings that are resting on the citrine necklace (above) should be worn by people born under the Leo star sign; and these lovely opal earrings (above) should be worn by Librans.

Emerald Earrings
Emeralds, such as the stones in these earrings (above) are the birthstone of those born under Taurus. If Sagittarian believers wear turqoise jewellery, such as this pendant (left), it is claimed they will feel more confident in life.

STAR SIGNS AND THEIR MEANINGS

ARIES: The pure Arian is desirous of command and control. In personal relationships Arians like to be the boss. In their careers they are usually successful, but they find it hard to be subordinates. They are initiators rather than administrators, practical as opposed to intellectual.

TAURUS: The typical Taurean is slow but sure, pressing implacably onwards towards their goals. They enjoy all material pleasures and are prepared to work hard to get them. Generous and imaginative; in love, they tend to be jealous but caring.

GEMINI: Because of an unusual capacity to see both sides of an argument, Geminians are seemingly inconsistent. They tend to be witty, good communicators, and to have the ability to fascinate others, particularly where the emotions are concerned. However they have a reputation for being fickle in love.

CANCER: Cancer is the sign of the Crab, and pure Cancerians, like crabs, have a hard exterior but are soft inside. They are much more sensitive than most of those who know them suspect. A tough appearance hides a caring nature. Never criticize a Cancerian – they are likely to take it badly.

LEO: This is the sign of the Lion, and pure Leos want to be monarchs of all they survey. They are often well equipped to do so – extremely efficient and living in a blaze of glory that lights up the lives of others. They are often very charismatic; although they can be demanding friends, they are very loyal.

VIRGO: This is the sign of efficient planning, and Virgoans tend to have an ability to impose order upon chaos. They plan every aspect of their lives – material and emotional – and thus achieve success. They tend to keep a tight rein on their emotions – this is because, when unleashed, they are powerful.

LIBRA: "Balance" is the keyword of the pure Libran character and Librans want

The Ruling Stars
This illustration from a fifteenth-century prayer book (above), displays the twelve signs of the zodiac and the parts of the body that they rule. Aries rules the brain; Taurus rules the throat and neck; Gemini rules the shoulders, arms, and lungs; Cancer rules the chest and the stomach; Leo rules the heart; Virgo rules the abdomen and intestines; Libra rules the kidneys and skin; Scorpio rules the genitals; Sagittarius rules the hips, thighs and arteries; Capricorn rules the knees; Aquarius rules the legs and ankles; Pisces rules the feet and toes.

everyone to be as just and fair as themselves. They are sometimes indecisive although, paradoxically enough, easily influenced by others. Librans hate to be alone. Because of their need to have a partner, they often form very unsatisfactory relationships.

SCORPIO: This is traditionally seen to be the sign of violence and debauchery – an exaggeration, perhaps, but those people who are most strongly Scorpionic tend to be more abrupt, strongly willed, and erotically inclined than the rest of us. They can also be self-destructive.

SAGITTARIUS: A lucky sign, and archetypal Sagittarians tend to rely on their luck and take risks. They usually achieve emotional happiness and material success – their luck sees them through. Sometimes, however, their luck fails them; they court disaster.

CAPRICORN: The pure Capricornian often strikes others as plodding, dull, and boring. He or she certainly does not sparkle, but often turns out to be the tortoise that overtakes the hare and achieves success in later life. Although they may hide it, many Capricorns are desirous of prestige and power throughout their life – they may "marry for money".

AQUARIUS: The Aquarian is idealistic, and freedom-loving. Aquarians tend to be humanitarians, deeply concerned about the welfare of others. They are unconventional, often to the point of eccentricity. They are forward thinkers with independant minds but may be wary of emotional commitments.

PISCES: This has been described as "the sign of the poet" – which is a polite way of saying that very strongly Piscean personalities are sometimes so unworldly that although they are loveable, they are also exasperating. Pisceans tend to be a little vague in practical matters. Pisces is the sign of the "healer" and indeed the typical Piscean will probably be attracted to one of the caring professions.

Chapter Six

THE EASTERN PERSPECTIVE

A century ago there were very strong distinctions between the magics of East and West. For example, most western occult students disbelieved in reincarnation, generally accepted throughout the Far East. Since then there has been a considerable cross-cultural interchange between the mysticism of Occident and Orient, and western occultists who are disbelievers in reincarnation are now the exception rather than the norm.

↠ THE INFLUENCE OF THE WEST ↞

West has affected East as well – thus the traditional medicine of India has been influenced by homeopathy, and the Cao-Dai cult of Vietnam combines Buddhist beliefs with the European spiritualist techniques. Nevertheless, the main flow of esotericism has been from, and not to, India, China, and Japan.

Yet there is still a distinct difference of emphasis between East and West: that of the concept of duality – of complementary "pairs of opposites" – which has had a much greater influence on the techniques associated with, for example, Taoism and tantrism, than it has had on their western equivalents.

In spite of the profound philosophical differences that separate the great religions of the East, such as Buddhism, Taoism, and the Hindu faiths, they are united in their perception of spiritual and material reality exhibiting a consistent duality.

This duality manifests itself as pairs of opposites – dark and light, force and form, spirit and matter, and so on. They are not normally equated with a fundamental opposition between good and evil. Instead they are seen as mutually dependent upon one another, one impossible to even conceive of as existing without the other – just as no two-dimensional object could possibly exist without having length as well as breadth.

The pairs of opposites are regarded as particular expressions of a cosmic polarity – of two eternal principles that contrast with, but are complementary to, one another. Beyond the duality is discerned an eternal unity that manifests itself as "twoness". This unity is conceived of as having separated itself into the opposites before time began. It can only be approached by the human being who is capable of, firstly, bringing the opposites into harmony with one another in his or her own inmost self, and, secondly, "slaying them". That is to say, bringing the opposites into a union that destroys them by getting beyond them, uniting the consciousness of the individual with that of the mode of "super existence" of which existence, as we know it, is but a dim and distorted reflection.

→ DIFFERENT TERMINOLOGY ←

The early stages of the mystic path are the same for the Buddhist monk, the Taoist holy man, and the tantric yogi – a recognition of the pairs of opposites. Only the terminology differs – Buddhists call the cosmic principles "voidness" and "non-voidness"; Taoists, yin and yang; and tantrics, Shiva and Shakti. The whole cosmos, which for the oriental mystic includes the world of spirit as well as the world of matter, is thought of as pulsating with subtle forces that exist as a consequence of the actions and reactions of the two great polarities.

It is these energies that are manipulated by the oriental mystic and psychic, be he or she a Hindu tantric, a Chinese practitioner of the martial arts, or a Japanese Zen Buddhist.

THE BOOK OF CHANGE

"Never-Changing, the Ever-Changing ... Nothing lies outside it; there is nothing which does not contain all of it"

John Blofeld

THE *I CHING*, THE BOOK OF CHANGE, is an ancient Chinese oracle – a book used to answer questions about the future. Many books that have been used as oracles employ a simple consultation technique: the book is opened at random, a finger is jabbed at the open page, and the sentence upon which it falls is taken as being the answer, literal or symbolic, to the proposed question. The *I Ching*, however, is different from other oracles in two important ways.

First, it does not give specific answers to questions; rather it provides detailed analyses of the situations about which questions are asked, as they are at the time of asking. Second, it is far more than merely an oracle – it is a divinatory expression of a philosophical system. The *I Ching* has profoundly influenced both Chinese Buddhism and the two great religions that China has given to the world: the magical and mystical Taoist faith, and the austere teachings of Confucius – who once said that if another fifty years could be added to his life, he would devote them all to the study of the *I Ching*.

The philosophy to be found in the *I Ching* is a Chinese version of the polarity theory of duality that underlies all the great religions of the Orient (p.185). It proposes a positive and dynamic principle, "Yang", and a negative, form principle, "Yin". The two opposites complement one another, and are both manifestations of the eternal and infinite T'ai Chi.

➙ FINDING A HEXAGRAM ➚

The permutations of Yin and Yang are represented in the *I Ching* by the interaction of broken lines (- -) for Yin and whole lines (—) for Yang. These are used to form eight three-line figures (trigrams), for example:

These are permuted to form 64 six-line figures, hexagrams. The complete version of the *I Ching* gives readings for each hexagram, and for each individual line of every situation concerning which advice has been sought.

Yin and Yang
The entire philosophy of the I Ching *is based on the ancient duality theories represented by the above symbol. All pairs of opposites in nature, eg. male and female or black and white, each contain the seed of the other, and continually turn into each other, creating order within chaos.*

When using the original Chinese text, which is couched in symbolic language that relates to traditional Chinese folklore, the task of interpretation requires a good deal of intuition. For example, the advice might be to approach your problem "the way wild foxes are believed to run across frozen lakes".

The traditional method of selecting a hexagram is complex, involving fifty dried yarrow stalks, and a much simpler technique involving three coins was evolved by Chinese diviners. An even simpler method uses dice.

Pearl Harbor
The decision to launch the sudden attack on American warships at Pearl Harbor (below), in December 1941, was made only after experts had consulted the I Ching. *Its use spread to Japan from China, where it was used as a matter of course to predict the changes and chances of war. In the 1960s, when Chinese armies menaced India and all the media predicted an invasion, the* I Ching *expert, John Blofeld, consulted the oracle, which correctly forecast that the threat would come to nothing.*

To obtain a hexagram and consult the wisdom of the *I Ching* using a die, proceed as follows:

a) Clearly formulate your question about a situation and how that situation should be best resolved, and write it down.

b) Throw a die six times and make a note of each of the numbers thrown in a vertical column, with the first number at the bottom and the last number at the top. If, for example, you threw the numbers 1, 6, 4, 4, 3, and 5, you would note them down as illustrated below.

c) Draw a line by the side of each number – a broken line for an even number and an unbroken line for an odd number; for example:

5 ⎫
3 ⎬ upper
4 ⎭ trigram

4 ⎫
6 ⎬ lower
1 ⎭ trigram

d) Look at the top three lines of your hexagram – these represent a trigram. Find your particular trigram in the top horizontal line of the diagram on page 188, which shows the eight upper trigrams of the *I Ching*. The next step is to find the bottom three lines of your hexagram in the left-hand vertical column showing the eight lower trigrams. Run a finger down from your top-row trigram and another finger across from your left-hand trigram to the point where they meet. The number on which you find your finger is that of the indicated hexagram that you will find listed overleaf on page 189. In the case of our example hexagram, you will find that the number represented is 42.

e) Read the brief divinatory interpretation of the relevant hexagram, and try to fathom intuitively its meaning in the context of the question, and the situation from which the question arose. Some advice on interpretation of the *I Ching* is given on the following page.

UPPER TRIGRAM / LOWER TRIGRAM	☰	☱	☲	☳	☴	☵	☶	☷
☰	1	34	5	26	11	9	14	43
☳	25	51	3	27	24	42	21	17
☵	6	40	29	4	7	59	64	47
☶	33	62	39	52	15	53	56	31
☷	12	16	8	23	2	20	35	45
☴	44	32	48	18	46	57	50	28
☲	13	55	63	22	36	37	30	49
☱	10	54	60	41	19	61	38	58

It is common practice in the East for scholars of the *I Ching* to learn "by heart" the entire text and the meaning of its sequence long before attempting to interpret the hexagrams. This, of course, would be most impractical for less serious students, who would be well-advised to try an alternative method that involves learning as you go – a trial and error approach.

→ CONSULTING THE ORACLE ←

Each time you consult the oracle, make a note of the advice given to you from the panel opposite. Interpret the advice as you see fit and make a rough note of your ideas. Be as precise as possible with your questions; the more vague a question is, the more vague the answer will be. After the situation in question has resolved itself, return to your notes. You may then be able to re-evaluate your original interpretation. If you cannot discover any immediate relevance in a given response remember that you will be limited by your expectations; you may later see the sense in a very unexpected outcome.

It has been said that the *I Ching* has a "personality" of its own and even a "sense of humour"; you will grow more familiar with the character of the oracle as you practise your divination. If you feel that you are making progress, you may then wish to study the Blofeld edition, which is more or less a direct translation from the Chinese. The study of eastern folklore and symbolism, interesting in itself, would undoubtedly increase your understanding of, or affinity with, the *Book of Change*.

The Hexagrams

The above diagram illustrates the eight elemental trigrams representing (from left to right, or top to bottom) heaven, lake, fire, thunder, wind, water, mountain, and earth. The student of the I Ching *must first become familiar with the various attributes of each of these elements; for example, where fire, springing from the Yang polarity, represents illumination and clarity, or where water, offspring of Yin, represents mystery and profundity. Numerically represented in the diagram are the sixty-four hexagrams, all possible dualities of the eight basic elements, eg. fire and water, or heaven and thunder. Each combination relates to the interaction of cosmic forces as they relate to human affairs, and also the duality within the self; eg. subconscious against conscious and instinct against reason.*

Magic Wands

Dried yarrow sticks (left) were originally employed in consulting the I Ching *of ancient China and this is the oldest method of divination used to construct a hexagram. Fifty wands are used in this complicated system but it is hailed by experts to be the best. Those wishing to learn this way should consult John Blofeld's edition. Other systems have involved fewer wands, coloured beads, or even "preprogrammed calculators and computers". The simplest methods, however, involve the throwing of coins or dice; but any system can be chosen that is capable of "creating randomness" and contains symbols representing Yin and Yang. The language of the* I Ching *is purposefully obscure and paradoxical. Ultimately, as in many other systems of fortune-telling, the only real way to interpret the symbols is through "intuitive understanding". This objective is best served by the type of confusing terminology that mystics of all countries and all times have employed in order to communicate meanings impossible to express in the language of reason.*

THE SIXTY-FOUR HEXAGRAMS

1: Be bold but do not be reckless, and all should end happily and well.

2: Intense and unrelaxing effort is required.

3: Make haste slowly; call upon others' help.

4: Make up your mind; the time has come to make decisions. Learn from experience.

5: A combination of decision, persistence, and sincerity will ensure your success.

6: Be cautious; do not take risks and do not trust to luck. Your plans may lead to conflict.

7: Well-considered action will lead to success.

8: You should try to give as well as take; work out another hexagram.

9: Be happy with small successes. Be responsive to other people's wishes.

10: A problem can be overcome by enterprise and doggedness.

11: Good fortune is on the way in this matter.

12: Things are not what they seem; do not take risks or follow others' advice.

13: Things will end well if you consider others' interests; do not procrastinate.

14: Seek the assistance of others. Be prepared for the unexpected!

15. Remain calm, do what seems correct, and all should end satisfactorily.

16: Avoid misunderstandings by explaining your point of view. Seek assistance.

17: Keep a low profile or things will go badly.

18: The situation is muddled; patiently try to unmuddle it. Do not be lazy.

19: A mixed situation, with both good and evil forces stirring; try to nip the latter in the bud.

20: Avoid being too hasty; consider every factor involved very carefully.

21: Take positive, forceful action and push yourself forward briskly.

22: Stick to the rules; do not do anything to which others can make objections.

23: Draw in your horns and remain calm. Take no action. A time for patience and prudence.

24: Experiment with the new; at all costs avoid clinging to the old.

25: Act in accordance with your inmost desires. Act spontaneously.

26: Work! Play! Be thoroughly extrovert. A time for great energy.

27: Take care! Concentrate on major matters, not trivialities. Do not discourage others.

28: A time for sustained, planned effort.

29: Do not compromise; stick to your principles, and things will end well.

30: Come to terms with reality – you cannot have everything.

31: Good fortune is with you – but avoid being too complacent. Do not miss the tide!

32: A time to accept the blows of fortune. Be humble, like the reed that bows in the wind.

33: A time for orderly retreat and inactivity.

34: Provided you do the morally right thing the situation should end well for you.

35: If you use your influence for good you will control the situation.

36: Do not be depressed; keep cool and calm amidst the muddle and confusion.

37: A time for loyalty, and for fulfilling all of your obligations.

38: Compromise and good will are called for.

39: Avoid disputes, seek friends' help; also, consult hexagram 33.

40: A time for boldness, for forgetting about the past and thinking about the future.

41: Be prudent; draw on your inner strength.

42: Be bold; make major changes in your life – but consider others' interests.

43: Be firm, show good will, and do not act recklessly. Be resolute.

44: Rely on your own judgement; make your own decisions and act on them.

45: Try not to be too self-reliant; seek the help and advice of others.

46: Be adaptable, prepared to think and act quickly, and to take advice.

47: A very difficult situation; be resilient.

48: Try to behave as would be expected of you; call upon your inner strength.

49: A rapidly changing situation. You should be ready to change with it.

50: The situation is unpromising; keep a low profile and take no action.

51: Surprises abound, on the whole unpleasant ones. Think extremely carefully before you make any moves.

52: You need inner strength; calm self-examination is called for.

53: Avoid being overly hasty; allow things to develop at their own pace.

54: Do not take chances; be very careful; avoid giving offence.

55: Enjoy what happens. Just relax.

56: Nothing is certain at the moment; you must be patient.

57: Do not make any moves without first considering all the implications.

58: Be generous, consider all new ideas, and co-operate with others.

59: Be careful, proceed selflessly. Be sure that your motives are honest.

60: You are at an important turning point; accept any constraints upon your actions.

61: Do not lose your temper; explain all your actions very fully.

62: Concentrate upon minor problems; do not try to resolve major ones.

63: Be prepared for the totally unexpected. You will emerge strengthened.

64: Success comes from caution; you are treading on very thin ice.

THE LUNAR CALENDAR

"Everything that takes place at a particular moment of time has a quality associated with that moment"

Carl Jung

CHINESE "ASTROLOGY" is not astrology at all in the western or Indian sense of that word. It is not based upon the apparent movements of the sun, moon, and planets through the signs of the zodiac. Rather, it is concerned with time; it is measured by the 60-year cycle of the traditional Chinese lunar calendar, which was ancient before the Incas rose to power in Peru, or the Romans withdrew their legions from Britain.

It classifies human beings into 60 categories according to the lunar years in which they were born, attributing traits of character to each category. It relates to astrology only in the sense that it is an expression of C.G. Jung's dictum that every moment of time has a certain "quality" associated with it.

The 60-year cycle of the Chinese lunar calendar classifies the years of the twentieth century as shown on the table on page 193. Find the lunar year of a birth in this, and note the "type", for example, Fire Sheep, which follows it. The type is made up of a Chinese "element", for example, Wood or Water, followed by one of twelve animals, real or imaginary. First read the full animal characterization, then read the elemental modification that follows it, and draw your own conclusions from this.

→ **ANIMALS AND ELEMENTS** ←

RAT: A hard-working and thrifty animal, the Rat is practical, extremely ambitious, and wants to accumulate money and things. Rats are avid collectors. They conceal their emotions, but sometimes fall deeply in love.

Metal Rats are dominating and emotional; Water Rats tend to be intellectuals; Wood Rats are unconventional; Fire Rats are independent and enthusiastic; Earth Rats are stable.

Ox: Even more hardworking than the Rat, the Ox is both stubborn and intelligent. Ox passions are not easily aroused, but when Oxen

Astrological Chart (Above) Like its western counterpart, Chinese astrology divides human beings into twelve basic personality types. In China, however, they are connected with twelve animals, eleven of which are real, plus the dragon. Each animal type is then subdivided into five – the five elements of fire, water, earth, wood, and metal, of which, in Chinese theory, all things are composed.

Horse People (Right) People classified as horses according to the Chinese system are, like the animal itself, greatly loved by those who are closest to them and liked well enough by everyone else. They dislike being tied down or reined in, preferring the freedom of the gallop in open country. They are notoriously unpredictable.

fall in love their feelings endure. They can often be deeply introverted characters. Metal Oxen are both artistic and argumentative; Water Oxen are intensely rational, but often fail to allow for irrational behaviour in others; Wood Oxen share the feelings of others; Fire Oxen tend to rudeness; Earth Oxen are exceptionally stolid and stubborn.

TIGER: "Born lucky" is a fair description of most Tigers – and they need luck because they take undue risks. They are sensual, restless, and unpredictable. They are often very enthusiastic, and impulsive. They can be very difficult to live with.

Metal Tigers are extrovert; Water Tigers are usually placid but sometimes explode into rage; Wood Tigers are agreeable, like contented cats; Fire Tigers are dominating; Earth Tigers are the most practical.

RABBIT: These are even luckier than Tigers. They are generous, thoughtful, artistic, and intelligent, but inclined to abrupt mood changes. They like an easy life and tend to look for partners who will provide one.

Metal Rabbits are both more emotional and more devious than the rest of the clan; Water Rabbits tend to introversion; Wood Rabbits are sometimes excessively generous; Fire Rabbits are more commanding than most; Earth Rabbits are more serious and some are intellectual.

DRAGON: All Dragons are energetic, strong-willed, and suitably fiery towards those they feel threaten their interests. Their personalities

tend to make them successful. Usually they marry young or remain single throughout life.

Metal Dragons are the toughest of the tough; Water Dragons are more capable of compromise than most; Wood Dragons are more creative; Fire Dragons are excessively active; Earth Dragons are the most stable of their clan.

SNAKE: Snakes tend to secretiveness. They are self-reliant, tenacious, and as energetic as Dragons, although subtler and more tactful. They are pleasure loving and have the abilities to get the luxury they crave. They are highly sexed and sometimes promiscuous.

Metal Snakes are extremely logical; Water Snakes are both artistic and practical; Wood Snakes are the kindest of their tribe; Fire Snakes are too much concerned with power and money; Earth Snakes are slower but more likeable.

HORSE: Horses are liked by most people and loved by those who know them well. They are freedom-loving, generous, normally cheerful, and somewhat unpredictable.

Metal Horses are more adventurous and egotistic than other Horses; Water Horses are notable for their wit; Wood Horses try their best to control their unpredictability; Fire Horses

The Dragon

The dragon (above) is an extremely powerful figure – both in eastern and western mythology. In China, however, the dragon is considered to be a benevolent creature, unlike the harmful beast portrayed in western folklore. In Chinese astrology, someone born in the year of the dragon is believed to possess many desirable qualities. He or she is said to have a tremendous zest for life, and is both charismatic and powerful. Dragons are also said to be very considerate and helpful – though they can be somewhat arrogant at times. "Fire Dragons" are incredibly vigorous and gay characters, though they can sometimes have fiery tempers.

are intelligent, passionate, and bad tempered; Earth Horses are the least temperamental.

SHEEP: Sheep are gentle, considerate, and sympathetic. Their feelings are easily hurt, and when this happens they tend to extremes of depression. In their love lives Sheep get on best with people who are neither so gentle nor so trusting as they are themselves.

Metal Sheep are a little tougher than other Sheep; Water Sheep are the gentlest of all; Wood Sheep are more outgoing than their fellows; Fire Sheep are a mite more combative; Earth Sheep are fanatically hard workers.

MONKEY: Monkeys are often conceited, but their outstanding charm usually makes up for this. They are extremely resourceful and are sometimes deceptive. They tend to promiscuity in the early part of life, but most of them eventually settle down.

Metal Monkeys are the fiercest; Water Monkeys are the most sensitive; Wood Monkeys are the most communicative of a communicative tribe; Fire Monkeys often take foolish risks; and Earth Monkeys are the most placid.

COCK: Witty, with a distinct bite to their wit, Cocks are often tactless in their dealings with

others. They have disciplined minds and are good at organizing the lives of both themselves and others. Some of them are a little eccentric.

Metal Cocks find compromise difficult; Water Cocks are more intellectual than most; Wood Cocks are gentler than most; Fire Cocks are always "performing", and many people find their company rather exhausting; Earth Cocks are the most practical and the least flamboyant.

DOG: Dogs are notable for their honesty, capacity for strong affection, objectivity, and intelligence. They are slow to give their love but, once given, it is usually life-long.

Metal Dogs are exceptionally inflexible – they make good friends but dangerous enemies; Water Dogs are the most contemplative and Wood Dogs the most flexible; Fire Dogs are born "leaders of the pack"; Earth Dogs have enormous practical ability.

BOAR: Boars are loyal, utterly reliable, and sociable – thoroughly pleasant people whose decency atones for their occasional tactlessness. The physical side of love is of exceptional importance to almost all of the Boars.

The Metal Boar is "pushy" and tends to be outgoing; Water Boars find it difficult to keep their physical and emotional appetites under control; Wood

Serious Business
Women (above) make figures of horses and other creatures related to the Chinese system of horoscopes. Astrology is taken more seriously in the East than by most people in the West, and people's awareness of their sign is greater.

Beast of Burden
The ox (below) is a patient beast of burden in the East. People born in a year of the ox are expected to be strong, stolid, and stubborn. They work hard, are deeply introverted, and difficult to get to know well.

ASTROLOGY AND TAO

The cycle of animal years leads to a twelvefold recurrence; and the five elemental factors lead to a sixtyfold recurrence. So, the Year of the Rat, comes round every twelve years, whereas the Year of the Metal Rat comes around only every sixty years. It does not end there: Chinese astrology is further complicated by the attribution of a positive or negative aspect to each elemental animal.

⇢ TUG OF WAR ⇠

These aspects are not to be equated with good and evil, rather they should be thought of as the positive (Yang) and negative (Yin) aspects of reality that, according to Taoist philsosophy, oppose and support one another. Consider two equally balanced tug-o'-war teams: they oppose each other with all their strength, yet it is that equal strength that supports them both. Or consider an arch: each side of an arch is essential for the other, and for the arch itself, to stand.

Of the twelve animal symbols, six are always positive (rat, tiger, dragon, horse, monkey, and dog), the other six are always negative. Generally speaking, Positive people will thrive by leading a thrusting, positive life, and by actively seeking whatever they want; Negative people, on the other hand, will get on better by not being too combative.

⇢ HOURS AND DAYS ⇠

Each year is divided into twelve periods that roughly coincide with the star signs of western astrology. They are: Rat – Sagittarius; Ox – Capricorn; Tiger – Aquarius; Rabbit – Pisces; Dragon – Aries; Snake – Taurus; Horse – Gemini; Sheep – Cancer; Monkey – Leo; Rooster – Virgo; Dog – Libra; Boar – Scorpio. Similarly, each day is divided into 12 animal sections: Rat – 11pm to 1am; Ox – 1am to 3am; Tiger – 3am to 5am; Rabbit – 5am to 7am; Dragon – 7am to 9am; Snake – 9am to 11am; Horse – 11am to 1 pm; Sheep – 1pm to 3pm; Monkey – 3pm to 5pm; Rooster – 5pm to 7pm; Dog – 7pm to 9pm; and finally, the Boar – 9pm to 11pm.

It is possible, then, for a person born in the Year of the Metal Rat (positive), in the month of the Dog, in the hours of the Ox, with the astrological sun sign, Libra. When reading a person's character, all of this has to be considered.

1886-1946	1946-2006	
08.1.86-23.1.87	02.2.46-21.1.47	Fire Dog
21.1.87-11.2.88	22.1.47-09.2.48	Fire Boar
12.2.88-30.1.89	10.2.48-28.1.49	Earth Rat
31.1.89-20.1.90	29.1.49-16.2.50	Earth Ox
21.1.90-08.2.91	17.2.50-05.2.51	Metal Tiger
09.2.91-29.1.92	06.2.51-26.1.52	Metal Rabbit
30.1.92-16.2.93	27.1.52-13.2.53	Water Dragon
17.2.93-05.2.94	14.2.53-02.2.54	Water Snake
06.2.94-25.1.95	03.2.54-23.1.55	Wood Horse
26.1.95-13.2.96	24.1.55-11.2.56	Wood Sheep
14.2.96-01.2.97	12.2.56-30.1.57	Fire Monkey
02.2.97-21.1.98	31.1.57-17.2.58	Fire Cock
22.1.98-09.2.99	18.2.58-07.2.59	Earth Dog
10.2.99-30.1.00	08.2.59-27.1.60	Earth Boar
31.1.00-18.2.01	28.1.60-14.2.61	Metal Rat
19.2.01-07.2.02	15.2.61-04.2.62	Metal Ox
08.2.02-28.1.03	01.2.62-24.1.63	Water Tiger
29.1.03-15.2.04	25.1.63-12.2.64	Water Rabbit
16.2.04-03.2.05	13.2.64-01.2.65	Wood Dragon
04.2.05-24.1.06	02.2.65-20.1.66	Wood Snake
25.1.06-21.1.07	21.1.66-08.2.67	Fire Horse
13.2.07-01.2.08	09.2.67-29.1.68	Fire Sheep
02.2.08-21.1.09	30.1.68-16.2.69	Earth Monkey
22.1.09-09.2.10	17.2.69-05.2.70	Earth Cock
10.2.10-29.1.11	26.2.70-26.1.71	Metal Dog
30.1.11-17.2.12	27.1.71-15.1.72	Metal Boar
18.2.12-05.2.13	16.1.72-02.2.73	Water Rat
06.2.13-25.1.14	03.2.73-22.1.74	Water Ox
26.1.14-13.2.15	23.1.74-10.2.75	Wood Tiger
14.2.15-02.2.16	11.2.75-30.1.76	Wood Rabbit
03.2.16-22.1.17	31.1.76-17.2.77	Fire Dragon
23.1.17-10.2.18	18.2.77-06.2.78	Fire Snake
11.2.18-31.1.19	07.2.78-27.1.79	Earth Horse
01.2.19-19.2.20	28.1.79-15.2.80	Earth Sheep
20.2.20-07.2.21	16.2.80-04.2.81	Metal Monkey
08.2.21-27.1.22	05.2.81-24.1.82	Metal Cock
28.1.22-15.1.23	25.1.82-12.2.83	Water Dog
16.2.23-04.2.24	13.2.83-01.2.84	Water Boar
05.2.24-24.1.25	02.2.84-19.2.85	Wood Rat
25.1.25-12.2.26	20.2.85-08.2.86	Wood Ox
13.2.26-01.2.27	09.2.86-28.1.87	Fire Tiger
02.2.27-22.1.28	29.1.87-16.2.88	Fire Rabbit
23.1.28-09.2.29	17.2.88-05.2.89	Earth Dragon
10.2.29-29.1.30	06.2.89-26.1.90	Earth Snake
30.1.30-16.2.31	27.1.90-14.2.91	Metal Horse
17.2.31-05.2.32	15.2.91-03.2.92	Metal Sheep
06.2.32-25.1.33	04.2.92-22.1.93	Water Monkey
26.1.33-13.2.34	23.1.93-09.2.94	Water Cock
14.2.34-03.2.35	10.2.94-30.1.95	Wood Dog
04.2.35-23.1.36	31.1.95-18.2.96	Wood Boar
24.1.36-10.2.37	19.2.96-07.2.97	Fire Rat
11.2.37-30.1.38	08.2.97-27.1.98	Fire Ox
31.1.38-18.2.39	28.1.98-05.2.99	Earth Tiger
19.2.39-07.2.40	06.2.99-27.1.00	Earth Rabbit
08.2.40-26.1.41	28.1.00-04.2.01	Metal Dragon
27.1.41-14.2.42	24.1.01-11.2.02	Metal Snake
15.2.42-04.2.43	12.2.02-31.1.03	Water Horse
05.2.43-24.1.44	01.2.03-21.1.04	Water Sheep
25.1.44-12.2.45	22.1.04-08.2.05	Wood Monkey
13.2.45-01.2.46	09.2.05-28.1.06	Wood Cock

Boars tend to a more subtle approach than the rest of their tribe; Fire Boars can be reckless; Earth Boars can be slothful characters.

→ MANY VARIATIONS ←

Chinese astrology is a very complex system. The character types I have given here are simplified. Like western astrology, there are other factors, apart from the year and month of birth, that can be taken into consideration. For example, the time of birth also adds another dimension to the calculation of an individual's astrological chart; this is known as the companion sign. In addition to this, the Chinese astrological calendar can be superimposed on the western astrological chart (pp.180-183) to achieve an even fuller picture of an individual's birth chart.

A Dog's Life
The vase below is adorned with hounds. Dogs are regarded as lovable, loyal, and affectionate animals in China, as in the West. Those born in one of the years of the dog can expect to share these canine character traits. Honest to a fault and thoroughly reliable, they are the most dependable of friends and they always aim to please. On the other hand, they can make the most determined and dangerous enemies.

THE SLEEPING SERPENT

"*Disciplined action, study of the self, and surrender to the Lord, constitute the practice of Yoga*"

Yoga Sutra II. I

MANY, PERHAPS MOST, westerners tend to think of yoga as no more than an unusual type of physical culture, characterized by strange postures and breathing exercises.

In reality this physical yoga – hatha yoga – is vastly more complex than is generally appreciated, there being a great deal more to it than its purely physical components. In any case it is only one variety of the numerous systems of mystical technique collectively termed yoga.

→ THE GROUND OF ALL BEING ←

"Yoga" means "union", and the object of all its serious practitioners is the achievement of the union of the mind and soul of the individual human being with a cosmic entity greater than his or her self. This cosmic entity has been given many names over the millennia through which yoga has been practised – Brahma, Krishna, Shakti, Shiva, God, the Absolute, and even "the Void"; but the essence of what a yogi aims to achieve has always remained the same: unity with the "Ground of All Being", the underlying reality that upholds and created, or perhaps emanated, the universe.

One of the most commonly practised forms of yoga in India is that of the kundalini, or "serpent fire", also known as "layayoga", which means, roughly, "centre yoga". This technique has its rationale in what could be called occult physiology. Its teachings concern the existence of chakras, centres of psychic energy. These chakras are held to be associated with, but not a part of, various physical segments of each and every human body.

→ KUNDALINI YOGA ←

Some ancient Indian treatises on these chakras and their interconnections go into mindbending detail, listing literally thousands of them. Mercifully, kundalini yoga is largely concerned with only the seven major chakras. These are the following:

1) The *Muladhara* chakra: the perineum, situated between the genitals and anus.

2) The *Svadisthana* chakra: the pubic area.

3) The *Manipura* chakra: the solar plexus.

4) The *Anahata* chakra: associated with the cardiac plexus, the region of the heart.

5) The *Vishuddha* chakra: larynx and pharynx.

6) The *Ajna* chakra: area from the middle of the eyebrows to halfway down the nose.

7) The *Sahasrara* chakra: associated with the area immediately above the crown of the head.

→ THE COILED ONE ←

None of the above, nor what follows, should be taken too literally. In any attempted description of psychic centres in everyday and, inevitably, materialistic, language, an element of symbolism and analogy has to be employed.

It is supposed by practitioners of kundalini yoga that all human beings have a latent reservoir of psychic energy; this is symbolically thought of as a coiled serpent (the word kundalini literally means "the coiled one") that lies sleeping in the *Muladhara* chakra.

The techniques of kundalini yoga are designed to arouse the dormant powers of this sleeping serpent by, firstly, awakening it from torpor and then getting it to raise its body upwards through each of the chakras until its head is in the ultimate *Sahasrara* chakra. It is believed that as the head of the serpent reaches the successive chakras, the latter are vivified,

Absolute Union
Yoga (above) is a way of preparing oneself mentally and physically for union with the Absolute, or God, or whatever term is used to describe something that is indescribable. In the West it is seen mainly as a system of exercises, of which there are more than a thousand asanas, or postures. The postures are named after animals, plants, or objects, whose qualities, it is believed, can be assimilated by the yogi who assumes each position. There are asanas named after the lion, the plough, the camel, the locust, the lotus, the sun, the thunderbolt, and hundreds more. Standing on one's head is an asana recommended for clearing the mind and, at the same time, clearing the sinuses.

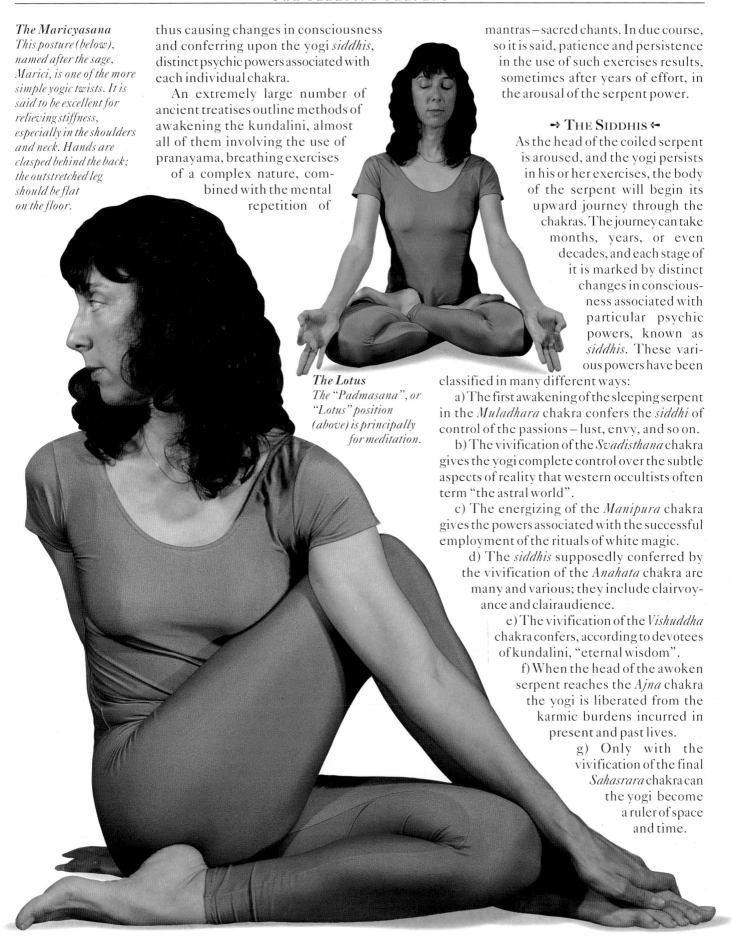

The Maricyasana
This posture (below), named after the sage, Marici, is one of the more simple yogic twists. It is said to be excellent for relieving stiffness, especially in the shoulders and neck. Hands are clasped behind the back; the outstretched leg should be flat on the floor.

thus causing changes in consciousness and conferring upon the yogi *siddhis*, distinct psychic powers associated with each individual chakra.

An extremely large number of ancient treatises outline methods of awakening the kundalini, almost all of them involving the use of pranayama, breathing exercises of a complex nature, combined with the mental repetition of

The Lotus
The "Padmasana", or "Lotus" position (above) is principally for meditation.

mantras – sacred chants. In due course, so it is said, patience and persistence in the use of such exercises results, sometimes after years of effort, in the arousal of the serpent power.

→ THE SIDDHIS ←

As the head of the coiled serpent is aroused, and the yogi persists in his or her exercises, the body of the serpent will begin its upward journey through the chakras. The journey can take months, years, or even decades, and each stage of it is marked by distinct changes in consciousness associated with particular psychic powers, known as *siddhis*. These various powers have been classified in many different ways:

a) The first awakening of the sleeping serpent in the *Muladhara* chakra confers the *siddhi* of control of the passions – lust, envy, and so on.

b) The vivification of the *Svadisthana* chakra gives the yogi complete control over the subtle aspects of reality that western occultists often term "the astral world".

c) The energizing of the *Manipura* chakra gives the powers associated with the successful employment of the rituals of white magic.

d) The *siddhis* supposedly conferred by the vivification of the *Anahata* chakra are many and various; they include clairvoyance and clairaudience.

e) The vivification of the *Vishuddha* chakra confers, according to devotees of kundalini, "eternal wisdom".

f) When the head of the awoken serpent reaches the *Ajna* chakra the yogi is liberated from the karmic burdens incurred in present and past lives.

g) Only with the vivification of the final *Sahasrara* chakra can the yogi become a ruler of space and time.

The *siddhis*, those occult powers supposedly gained by successful practitioners of kundalini yoga (see preceding page), are not, if yogic treatises are to be believed, by any means the monopoly of any particular technique. For example, hatha yoga is sometimes referred to as the "yoga of power" because of the psychic powers alleged to be obtained by its adepts.

⇢ SPIRITUAL ILLUMINATIONS ⇠

However, a number of people who have advanced far along the yogic path, experimenting with such disciplines as kundalini yoga, hatha yoga, and the Tibetan Buddhist "yoga of the Void", have stated that, while they have experienced both extraordinary changes of consciousness and what they have considered to be spiritual illuminations, they have *not*, on the other hand, obtained any specific psychic powers, such as telepathy.

Such people have tended not to deny that some yogis may have acquired *siddhis*, but simply assert that it is possible to travel far along the yogic path without experiencing any phenomena that are exterior to the mind and spirit.

The Chakras Diagram
The chakras associated with the human body are represented in this diagram (right). These are not physical organs of the body, but focuses of psychic energy linked with the heart (below), larynx, the crown of the head, and other parts of the human frame. The kundalini, or serpent, which lies in the lowest chakra, can be aroused by certain techniques. As it uncoils and rises like a rearing cobra up the spine, the successive chakras are energized, conferring various powers on the yogi.

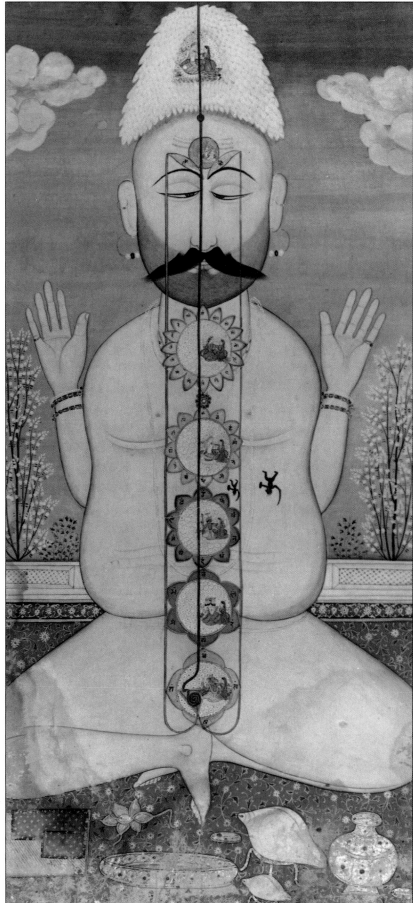

Body Control
Most Indian yogis are not contortionists, but some contrive to fold themselves into weird shapes and postures in their drive to assume the rarer asanas (below). It is generally considered to be essential that the practitioner be comfortable in the position he has assumed. All sorts of supernormal powers are believed to accrue to the yogi and the asanas, from the mental powers of telepathy and clairvoyance, to physical powers such as levitation and the ability to walk on water. With controlled breathing techniques, the posture may be held for an extremely long time.

What then, is one to make of the claims concerning occult powers made in some yogic literature? One possibility is that some of these claims are to be taken literally, while others are intended to be interpreted only allegorically or, at any rate, half allegorically.

⇝ ROADS TO UNION ⇜

Perhaps the best attitude to be adopted towards the *siddhis* is the same as that which western mystics have generally adopted towards the physical phenomena of mysticism, that is, in no way to seek after them but, if they are experienced, to look upon them as unimportant diversions from the true goal of all mystics, East or West. That goal is the transcending of everyday consciousness and the union of the soul with the "Ground of All Being".

There are many yogic disciplines, "roads to union", which, so it is affirmed, can enable the seeker to reach this ultimate goal of transcending everyday consciousness. They include:

a) Bhakta yoga, the yoga of devotion, in which the aspirant concentrates his or her love on a god or goddess. Eventually, consumed by the fire of divine love, he or she becomes at one with the object of love or, perhaps, the cosmic principle personified by the particular deity.

b) Gnana yoga, the yoga of knowledge, in which philosophical or religious learning provides the key to open the doors that lead to a transformation of consciousness.

c) Karma yoga, the yoga of the deed or destiny, in which the seeker after union accepts the burdens of destiny, practises good works, and thus eventually attains to spiritual liberation.

d) Raja yoga, the "royal yoga" – union through moral, mental, and physical discipline.

e) Mantra yoga, the yoga of "spells" – rhythmic chants of a sacred nature.

All the above, and most other forms of yoga, have their western analogues. Thus, for example, bhakta yoga is very close indeed to the devotional mysticism of such medieval personalities as

Margery Kempe, Richard Rolle, and Walter Hilton; the techniques of raja yoga have a certain affinity to the training methods evolved by Saint Ignatius Loyola in the sixteenth century; karma yoga is in essence identical with the "practical mysticism" of such saints as Vincent de Paul; hatha yoga has some similarity with a particular mystical school associated with the ancient Orthodox churches – a form of mysticism known as Heychasm.

→ HEYCHASM ←

The basic texts of Heychast mysticism are to be found in the *Philokalia*, first printed in 1782, but containing material dating back to the fourth century AD. Space does not allow anything approaching even a very brief summary of the mass of material contained in this vast compilation; it suffices to say that particular bodily postures are advised, as are certain modes of breathing, and that the ceaseless repetition of a particular prayer, combined with concentration upon a psychic centre corresponding with the *Manipura* chakra, is the core of Heychasm.

It could be argued that Heychasm is Christian hatha yoga. Westerners tend to either think of yoga as a curious variety of physical culture, only marginally associated with mysticism and

Meditation
An Indian sadhu, or holy man (below), meditates quietly in the Lotus position, legs crossed and hands resting on the knees. The Hindu and Buddhist traditions place a particularly high value on the practice of meditation, but it has its place also in Christianity, Judaism, Islam, and other religious systems. Broadly speaking, the purpose is to detach oneself from the everyday hustle and bustle of life, and to seek a communion with something greater than the self that lies behind the world of fleeting appearances. It is not a loss of consciousness, as in trance, but an expansion of one's consciousness. There are numerous reports of supernormal powers being released. Many consider it to be a trigger of psychic abilities.

religion, or to assume that any religious component of yoga is exclusively Hindu. This last misconception is largely a result of an historical accident; the first Europeans who encountered yoga in modern times met with it in one or other of its Hindu manifestations. Yet most of the yogis with whom the ancient Greeks came into contact, referred to as gymnosophists – "wisdom athletes" – in classical literature, may well have been Buddhists, and in precommunist Tibet there was a well-developed tradition of Buddhist yoga.

In general, Buddhist yogis have tended to be less concerned with wonder working and the attainment of quasi-magical powers than have some Hindu practitioners of this variety of mysticism. Indeed, there is a Buddhist tradition that those who seek miraculous powers over the physical world for their own sake are wasting their time – one should use material means in order to bring about material effects. In this connection, a traditional story told of Sakyamuni Buddha is of some relevance. According to this tale the Buddha encountered on his travels a yogi living by a wide and fast flowing river. "After 25 years of spiritual exercises, meditation, and austerity", boasted the yogi, "I have achieved the power of levitating across the river". "Surely", replied the Buddha, "it would have been quicker to build a bridge?"

This anecdote has a universal validity. There is a curious human tendency to be unduly complex; to do things the hard, rather than the easy, way. We often tend to seek out wisdom from afar when what is, in essence, the same wisdom, may be discovered close at hand, on offer to anyone who chooses to ask for it.

→ YOGI MILLIONAIRES ←

For a century or more this tendency has resulted in some seekers after spiritual truth wasting a great deal of time and money on purchasing "spiritual teachings" from self-styled holy men who have often proved to be, at best, incompetent, and sometimes mentally ill or fraudulent. For instance, in the 1930s one Indian "Perfect Master" received large sums of money from gullible Americans and Europeans who considered him extremely wise and spiritually advanced because he never spoke but communicated to his disciples by pointing at letters painted on a board. More recently another became a multi-millionaire and acquired a fleet of Rolls-Royce motor cars by the simple expedient of assuring people that they were practising "tantric yoga" when they indulged their physical appetites. One very simple

conclusion can be drawn from a consideration of the careers of these and similar supposed "Masters of Wisdom" – it is inadvisable to pay money for spiritual instruction to a man or woman from whom no sensible person would buy a second-hand automobile.

⇝ First Steps ⇜

People whose interest in yoga is confined largely to those aspects of it that are concerned with improving physical health can find guidance in a number of easily available step-by-step guides to hatha yoga. Those whose concern is with yoga in its fullest sense, union with the "Divine Otherness", the goal of all mystics at all times in all places, also have a wide variety of texts at their disposal. Each of these alternative texts has its admirers, although it is apparent that some are of much greater importance than others. Two classical yoga texts are quite outstanding, and are available in numerous translations. They are the *Yoga Sutras of Patanjali* and the *Bhagavad Gita*. Both texts are of extremely ancient origin and convey to the reader the essential theory and core techniques of yoga with conciseness and clarity.

In using them, however, it must be kept in mind that they were written in a society that was not advanced technologically; much of the instruction given in them cannot, therefore, be followed literally in the present day and must be adapted to modern conditions. Thus, for example, advice to carry out certain meditations sitting on a mat in a lonely forest can be adapted to any quiet sitting room – even if it were in an apartment in New York or London.

Tibetan Monks

Monks and nuns in pre-communist Tibet may have totalled no less than five to ten per cent of the entire population. Only a small number of these were primarily concerned with meditation, yogic exercises, and other activities relating to the pure life of the spirit. Most of them carried out duties of a somewhat secular nature concerned with keeping their own monasteries, some containing as many inhabitants as a small town, and were centres of economic prosperity.

Such monks and nuns engaged themselves in farming, horticulture, cleaning and maintenance, and even – armed with huge clubs – in defence and security. However secular the duties of most monks and nuns (above), the core activities of all Tibetan religious houses were the study of the Buddhist scriptures, the performance of religious ceremonies, and the pursuit of spiritual enlightenment. It is claimed that the "lamas", the Tibetan monks, acquire many magical powers in the course of their "pursuit", though the attainment of these powers is not an end in itself.

Bed of nails
Imperviousness to pain is one of the remarkable physical powers widely attributed to holy men. The oriental sadhu, or fakir, who has trained himself, can loll casually on his bed of sharp nails (below) without the slightest discomfort. Sadhu is the general term for Hindu ascetics and miracle workers. They belong to many different groups and schools of practice. On initiation into an order at the age of twelve or over, a sadhu abandons his name and takes a new one, as a sign of a new identity. Some sadhus go naked, some wear clothes. This one is holding a "mala" of beads, which in the West would be called a rosary, used for keeping count of how many times a mantra or prayer has been repeated. A sadhu may live by begging, by telling fortunes, selling lucky charms, or giving conjuring performances. Some are solitary, some live in communities.

THE WAY OF ACTION

"In wandering, I've visited all kinds of Tantric meeting places, but never have I found another holy place as blissful as my own body"

Saraha – Tantric Poet

TANTRISM IS THE "WAY OF ACTION": in essence it is a practical spiritual discipline rather than a body of doctrine. The concern of those who would follow its precepts is to slay the duality of the "pairs of opposites" (p.185) by uniting them in an explosive spiritual marriage.

As an essentially pragmatic discipline, one that asks to be judged on its results and is not greatly concerned with the exact religious affiliations of those who seek to achieve them, tantrism straddles many of the world's religious boundaries. There are Buddhist tantrics, Jain tantrics, Hindu tantrics, and neo-Gnostic tantrics. There are also Taoist adepts who, while they do not call themselves tantrics, follow a path with a great deal of similarities to particular tantric disciplines.

Tantric Holy Family
This Indian miniature (below) of Mount Kalasa (Everest), shows the holy family of Shiva and Shakti.

These diverse religions are united in their belief that the totality of things expresses an underlying duality, a fundamental "twoness", which can be discerned in everything. For tantrics, the duality of the universe is, at its root, divine.

→ SHIVA AND SHAKTI ←
There is a god and there is a goddess; one emanates the form aspect of perceived reality, the other its force aspect. All gods are aspects of one god, in India termed Shiva; all goddesses are aspects of one goddess, who in India is generally known as Shakti.

The tantric identifies the principles of maleness and femaleness with the complementary dualities of all manifested reality; material,

Tantric Eroticism
An erotic stone-carving (above) from the Hindu temple, Khajuraho. Tantric "eroticism" causes much controversy amongst religious sects, many of whom consider its rituals too open to misuse. Exponents, however, assert that such rituals fuse spiritual and physical love, supporting the tantric poet, Saraha's, view that the body, far from being "unclean", is the ultimate temple.

mental, and spiritual. It is through the male/female polarity that the would-be adept endeavours to transcend that duality, to get beyond it, to enter a state of trans-formed consciousness by means of a union be-tween the Divine and the human.

Even though the highest purpose of tantric rituals is the conventional Bud-dhist goal of attaining enlightenment, many orthodox Hindus and Buddhists look upon tantrism with some sus-picion. They tend to think of it as a sex cult, a pseudo-mystical cloak veiling licentiousness and even perversity.

However, only "left-hand" tantrics incorporate physical sexuality into their rites. The majority of tantrics are of the "right-hand" persuasion and are extremely dubious of the legitimacy of left-handed tantrism, feeling that, at best, it verges upon sorcery. The sexuality involved in right-handed rites is purely symbolic and those who participate in them no more take part in collective immorality than those who drink wine at a Christian celebration of Holy Communion take part in collective drunkenness.

⇢ THE EMBRACE OF THE GODDESS ⇠
In India the major tantric rite is *chakra puja*, circle worship. The ceremony begins with the priest and priestess in the midst of a circle of seated male and female partners, each man having the female tantric with whom he cus-tomarily works at his right hand, hence the phrase "right-handed tantra"; in tantric cults where physical sexuality is employed in the rites, the female adept sits on her partner's left.

The priest stands while the priestess lies on a mat on which a triangular diagram symboliz-ing the goddess Shakti has been drawn. It is the priestess upon whom the rite is centred. Men-tally identifying himself with Shiva, the priest chants mantras, rhythmic invocations, with the object of making the body of the priestess a temporary dwelling place of the great goddess. When the mantras are concluded, the priestess, or, rather, Shakti within her, is worshipped by

Circle of Perfection
This 11th-century statue (above) depicts the tantric god, Shiva, the "eternal being", dancing on the body of a dwarf demon. The surrounding circle represents the cycle of creation, destruction, and rebirth. In the tantric ceremony the circle has an important symbolic place, with the priest and priestess, representing Shiva and Shakti, sitting in the midst of a circle of seated male and female partners. The circle is the symbol of perfection – "Here there is no beginning, no middle, no end, no samsara, no nirvana. In this state of supreme bliss, there is no self and no other."

the entire assembly while the priest pours libations of coconut milk and holy water at her feet. The priest then hands the priestess a flower or, sometimes, chas-tely embraces her. In either case the act is a symbolic portrayal of the eternal coupling of Shiva and Shakti, the interplay of the positive and nega-tive that perpetually recreates the cosmos.

In left-handed tantra, of course, the symbolic portrayal is much more specific and direct in its nature. Once they have witnessed the symbolic marriage of force and form, of Shakti and Shiva, all the participants in the ceremony take part in a feast that concludes with each man emulating the priest and gently embracing his partner or, perhaps, presenting her with a flower.

Like the priest's action, this symbolizes the union of the polarities, but, if the whole rite has been correctly performed, the symbol becomes, so tantrics aver, a reality for the participants in the ceremony: the men feel "the embrace of the goddess": the women that of the god. In other words, there is a genuine mystical union of the human and the Divine.

⇢ TWILIGHT SPEECH ⇠
Tantric masters originally compiled the tantric rites as aids for initiates training under them. Not intended for public perusal, their secrets were safeguarded by an argot known as "twi-light speech". Many rituals made use of the "mantras", verses or words believed to be of "superhuman origin" received and spoken by inspired seers and poets. The mantras aided the participants of the tantric rituals to invoke the divinities in their meditations.

The "twilight speech" and mantras were often interpreted, amongst more orthodox sects, as more evidence of tantric sorcery whose devo-tees wallow in "the mud of the five lusts". Disciples of tantra, however, claim they control the passions by means of the passions. The Hevajra Tantra says "The expert in poison repels poison by that very poison...the world is bound by lust, and released by the same lust".

TAOISM - THE WAY

"The Holy Man's good works are as mighty as Heaven and Earth, yet he is not humane"

Lao Tzu

CHINESE TAOISM IS A MYSTICAL philosophy in which no statement is accepted as being absolutely true or absolutely false, no action either completely virtuous or completely lacking in merit. To the Taoist sage everything is in flux, always in the process of turning into its own opposite, and at the same time everything is immutable and eternal. A statement can be simultaneously true and false; an effect can precede the event that caused it; things can be in two places at the same time.

→ PHILOSOPHY AND PARADOX ←

A bizarre way of looking at reality, and yet, oddly enough, Taoist paradoxes about the nature of space and time, and the events that take place in them, are reminiscent of some of the theories associated with contemporary mathematical particle physics.

This similarity between an ancient mystical philosophy and modern concepts in the shadowy ghost world of sub-atomic reality, a field in which the distinction between physics and philosophy has blurred to vanishing point, makes it very difficult for the open-minded observer to reject Taoist philosophy as merely paradox built up into a system. Still less can we adopt the attitude of the nineteenth-century critics of Chinese culture, who dismissed Taoism as an absurd collection of superstitions derived from the musings of half-crazy mystics.

The central tenet of Taoist philosophy is the primary existence of the Tao. Although it remains untranslatable in its entirety of meanings, on one level it signifies the "Path" or the "Way".

Blessed Isles
A plate (below) depicting "Taoist deities" walking on the seas surrounding the "Blessed Isles of the West". "Taoist deity" is actually a contradiction in terms in the strictest sense of the words since, originally, Taoists recognized no god as such, but only the "Tao". Beliefs in gods came into being only with the emergence of "Popular Taoism", when supposed Taoist monks began practising alchemy and yoga, things that the original Taoists would perhaps have considered to be pointless divergences from the "Path". The beliefs of the Zen Buddhists (pp.204-207), resemble original Taoism more closely.

The Tao is a path in many senses. It is, for instance, the way that has to be followed by "the superior person", the literal translation of Chinese ideograms that convey the idea of a human being who lives in accordance with the laws of the great cosmic principles and the greater principle that subsumes them. It is also the way that leads from existence to a non-existence that, paradoxically, is more "real" than reality itself.

The Tao first manifested itself as pure and undifferentiated energy, "chi", which, as soon as it became manifest, divided into the primal pairs of opposites, yin and yang, form and force, cosmic "femininity" and cosmic "masculinity". Yang, the masculine, is associated with aggressive male characteristics, force instigating motion that causes change; Yin, the passive female, absorbs the force of Yang so that, in constantly changing, the whole remains the same. The paradox of the Tao has been likened to a wheel that spins – while there is constant motion, the centre is constantly still.

→ POPULAR TAOISM ←

There is no concept of hell in the Taoist religion, nor, strictly speaking, is man to be seen as fallen and in need of redemption. Rather, man is seen as having lost his way, and is in need of regaining his "path". All he has to do is lay down the burden of his desires and "the wandering thoughts" that obscure his view in order to see the "way" and be in harmony with the Tao. Many Taoist sages found the highly structured life of urban and cultivated rural China incompatible with the peace they desired. Consequently they retired into mountain wildernesses to practise yoga and regain the primal purity of the Tao.

Taoism, ironically, seems to have strayed enormously from its original "path". More superficial beliefs in

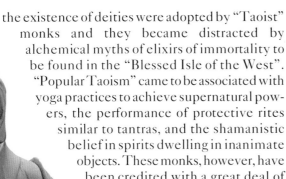

the existence of deities were adopted by "Taoist" monks and they became distracted by alchemical myths of elixirs of immortality to be found in the "Blessed Isle of the West". "Popular Taoism" came to be associated with yoga practices to achieve supernatural powers, the performance of protective rites similar to tantras, and the shamanistic belief in spirits dwelling in inanimate objects. These monks, however, have been credited with a great deal of success in their endeavours, particularly with regard to longevity, with reports of monks supposedly living for hundreds of years in their mountain retreats.

⇾ THE VOID ⇽

In its purest nature, Tao came to be one of the greatest influences of Zen Buddhism. The two religions share the belief that intuition is supreme. Essentially, harmony with the Tao – the "Void" in Zen – can be achieved *only* intuitively, not by any efforts of mental reasoning. "We shape clay into a pot, but it is the emptiness

Gods and Dragons
This mirror (above) depicts Taoist "deities", and dragons that symbolize benevolent power in the East.

inside that holds whatever we want" says the *Tao Te Ching*. Taoist teachings have had considerable impact in practical terms; for example, the idea that hardness is weakness, that weakness has its strengths, is incorporated in such unrelated disciplines as Chinese traditional medicine (p.212) and the martial arts (pp.210-211).

LAO TZU

The author of the *Tao Te Ching* is a nebulous character as far as historical records are concerned, with one outlandish legend stating that Lao Tzu (left), translated as "Old Child", remained 70 years in his mother's womb and was born with grey hair.

More realistic theories exist that the philosopher, a contemporary of Confucius, was a more or less anonymous archivist at the court of the declining Chou dynasty, although, this too, is far from certain. Legend has it that Lao Tzu set off on a journey to the West, to escape the decadence that had beset his country. On his way through the gates of the city, the gatekeeper pleaded with him to write down his ideas. The result was the *Tao Te Ching*: 81 paradoxical axioms of good-humoured, poetic, wisdom, as relevant today as they were two thousand years ago.

Another legend states that a meeting actually took place between Lao Tzu and Confucius, an irresistible idea in the context of the parallels that exist between them. Both men were aware of the irreversible corruption that was eating into the soul of their country. Confucius tried desperately to fight against it and, reluctantly but inevitably admitting defeat, set about another mammoth task of compiling codes of morality as a "seed" for future generations. Lao Tzu, with good-humoured irreverence, told Confucius he was a fool. The old Taoist's relatively tiny document, the *Tao Te Ching*, is testament to his intuitive faith that the "seed" already existed in the heart of man and the way of the Tao.

"Throw away morality and justice and the people will do the right thing ... (If not) just stay at the centre of the circle and let all things take their course."

ZEN BUDDHISM

"What is the most important principle or teaching of Buddhism?"

Emperor Wu

"VAST EMPTINESS", replied the Indian sage, Bodhidharma, to the above question.

In AD 480, Emperor Wu, noted for his pious Buddhism, invited Bodhidharma to his court. He told Bodhidharma of his many good works, of the holy men he had fed and clothed, of the monasteries he had founded, of the scriptures he had caused to be preserved and copied, and asked: "How much merit have I acquired?"

"None at all", replied Bodhidharma.

Bodhidharma's answer encapsulates the attitude of the masters of Chinese Ch'an Buddhism, better known in the West by its Japanese name, Zen, to the possibility of acquiring spiritual merit by carrying out virtuous actions. It is certain that Ch'an Buddhism was based on the Dhyana Buddhism of India; whether or not the story about the emperor and Bodhidharma is apocryphal and whether or not it was he who brought Ch'an Buddhism to China is open to speculation.

According to legend the originator of the Dhyana school was Gautama Buddha himself. Gautama gave a wordless "sermon" by simply holding aloft a golden flower. The onlookers were all puzzled save for Kasyapa, Gautama's most learned disciple, who suddenly broke into a smile of enlightenment: he had attained liberation from the wheel of unending birth and rebirth, he had himself become a buddha.

→ SHOW ME YOUR MIND ←

It is said that Kasyapa's smile, or rather, what it signified, passed down through 28 successive patriarchs of the Dhyana school. The last of these patriarchs was Bodhidharma, the sage who gave such a blunt reply to the Chinese emperor and whose dark, ferocious, features were carved upon the hilts of innumerable Japanese Samurai swords many centuries later. For Bodhidharma, so it is averred, was the founder not only of the Ch'an variant of Chinese Buddhism, but also of the school of boxing from which many of the oriental martial arts evolved (pp.208-211).

Emptying The Mind
Meditation (above) is central to the practice of Zen Buddhism. Followers of Zen are taught to empty their minds of all intellectual reasoning, thereby opening up their minds to higher levels of perception – known as intuition. For most westerners this is a difficult concept to grasp. However, it makes sense when the most basic principle of Zen is considered. According to Zen teaching, real understanding is possible only through intuition and not through any logical thinking process.

Bodhidharma, or perhaps the Buddhist school of which he may have been a personification rather than a patriarch, did not accept the truth of many of the teachings of other Buddhist sages. Rituals, and even the Buddhist scriptures, were looked upon as, at best, valueless in the quest for spiritual liberation, and probably as actual obstacles to it. Fasting to the point of near starvation and other forms of extreme asceticism were regarded as foolish. Even the question of the existence or non-existence of the individual mind, a subject of debate in many centres of Buddhist learning, was considered of no interest as exemplified in this story:

Bodhidharma was approached by one of his pupils who begged him, "Pacify my mind." The sage replied "Show me your mind", and, when the petitioner replied that he couldn't do so, said "There, I have pacified your mind".

→ FACING THE WALL ←

There is a meditation technique traditionally associated with Bodhidharma called "facing the wall". This method requires the aspirant to endeavour to cut off the mind from all desire, even the desire for spiritual enlightenment, as completely as someone who literally turns his or her face to the wall cuts off the mind from new visual perceptions.

In practice this implies a direct, intuitive meditation on nothing, on mere emptiness. The aspirant should thus be enabled to empty the mind of all ego consciousness, of all desire, of all spiritual ambition, and thereby attain to an intuitive awareness of the unity and all-inclusiveness of "the Buddha-nature".

To westerners, even to most oriental Buddhists, the idea of meditating on nothing seems very odd indeed. There are, however, certain similarities between Bodhidharma's "facing the wall" and an abiding current in the great river of Christian mysticism. This latter is termed the "*via negativa*", the "negative path".

The *via negativa*, which had its origins in the neo-Platonic mysticism of late classical times, is based on the premise that we cannot know God by His positive attributes, for these are utterly beyond human comprehension; we can only know, or understand, Him to any degree at all by meditating on what He is *not*.

ZEN GOES WEST

The Japanese scholar and disciple of Zen, D.T. Suzuki (1870–1966) (above), was a central figure in the process of introducing Zen Buddhism to the West. He was invited to America early in the twentieth century accompanied by two other disciples of Zen, both of whom remained to set up Zen groups such as the "First Zen Institute of America", founded, in New York, in 1930. Suzuki preferred to give lectures; his forceful personality, and his subsequent writings on the faith did much to promote Buddhism, and Zen in particular. Ironically, it was not until America's conflicts with two Buddhist countries, Korea and Vietnam, that Buddhism really began to attract much attention in the American media. The emergence of "hippies" in the 1960s provided the most striking evidence of Buddhist ifluence. Even though Buddhism is established in the West, its following remains relatively small, perhaps due to the fact that its teaching of contempt for material wealth is so strikingly at odds with western ideals.

He is not, for example, bound by time and space; by meditating on this negative attribute, we may be able intuitively to discern something of what He actually *is*.

↠ CAN NOTHING BE TAUGHT? ↞

It is difficult for the average occidental to take some aspects of Ch'an (Zen) Buddhism altogether seriously; certain of the paradoxical statements made by enlightened masters seem strange to the point of madness. Perhaps the greatest paradox of all is that faced by the Zen teachers who know that nothing of the Buddha-nature can be "taught" as we understand the word. Instead the "vast emptiness" must be revealed and comprehended intuitively.

The Grand Buddha
The Dafo (Grand) Buddha (above) is situated at Leshan, in China. It is the largest of all the millions of representations of the original Buddha, Guatama Buddha, in the world. Carved into a cliff face, the Dafo Buddha is 70m (26ft) long. The Dafo Buddha was designed by the Buddhist monk, Haitong, in AD 623; it was finally completed in AD 713.

or some of those who read or heard about the incident, would be jerked out of ordinary consciousness as a result of psychic shock, and would experience instant enlightenment that Japanese Zen Buddhists term *"satori"*. He hoped that his undignified eccentricity would result in some minds intuitively apprehending "the universality of the Buddha-nature".

→ MADNESS AND ILLUMINATION ←

Paradoxical actions, such as that of Teng Yingfen, rude replies to questions, like that given to the emperor by Bodhidharma (p.204), and meditation upon irrational concepts, for instance "the sound of one hand clapping", have long been a feature of Ch'an Buddhism and its Japanese variant, Zen Buddhism. Just as Teng Yingfen's unusual position was intended to shock, so were some of the statements made about the nature of Ch'an Buddhism by a number of Ch'an masters. For example, Hsuan-Chien, who lived a century or so before

A Zen Garden
To western eyes, a Zen garden (above) – an off-balance, naked landscape, made of rock and sand rather than vegetation – seems to be the very antithesis of what we would normally consider a garden. Like all Zen art, the garden reflects the emptiness that is the essence of Zen; the viewer is invited to "enter" the landscape and create his own garden, to sense the "hidden plenitude" in the empty spaces. For in Zen Buddhism, excessive interpretation is, as one follower put it, "a leech on the spirit of life".

What are we to make of the eighth-century teacher, Teng Yingfen, who, feeling that death was approaching, decided not to take to his bed but instead to stand upon his head until he died? It has been suggested that Teng Yingfen died in this strange posture because he wanted to shock his pupils by this reversal of normal behaviour. He wanted to subject his pupils to an abnormal experience, watching their revered teacher, a Ch'an sage, die standing upon his head, so that some of them,

Teng Yingfen said: "There are no Buddhas, no Patriarchs. Bodhidharma was only a bearded old barbarian ... the scriptures... [are] ... sheets of paper to wipe the pus from your boils."

Hsuan-Chien's deliberate and, in a Buddhist context, deeply disturbing, statements can be paralleled in other mystical traditions. There are recorded instances of heterodox Muslim mystics dismissing the Koran as meaningless nonsense, of Hindu tantric adepts urging their pupils to eat large quantities of beef, and of seventeenth-century mystics advocating beer and tobacco as an aid to achieving the unitive state.

The Art of Death
Samurai warriors carried two swords and a dagger (left), and wore a helmet (right) and a terrifying mask (below). Unafraid of Death, when Japan was threatened with invasion by Kublai Khan in 1281, the Samurai fearlessly held off the attack. The tradition continued into World War II, when Japanese pilots, known as Kamikaze, flew in suicide raids.

Warrior
This very colourful banner (below) depicts a Samurai warrior wielding his sword. Samurai swords were generally believed to possess souls of their own.

The purpose of all such injunctions and statements was probably the same; what today might be called "shock therapy", the administration of a metaphorical kick, in the hope that it might be effective in throwing the minds of some from one dimension into another.

➤ DIVINE FOLLY ←

The behaviour of some mystics, however, most notably Zen masters, has been such that even those sympathetic to mysticism have thought it symptomatic of insanity rather than of any spiritual illumination.

There is a perfectly respectable argument in favour of the ideas that, first, madness is akin to the "Divine folly" of Ch'an masters and Taoist adepts and, second, that both display a resemblance to a childlike attitude towards life – which is a very different thing to a childish one.

In his book *Zen and the Comic Spirit*, the American writer, M. Conrad Hyers, analysed and expounded the relationships he believed he had discerned existing between the child, the fool, the lunatic, and the Zen master.

The child, he said, has not yet learned the adult trick of arbitrary classification; that is, of first creating artificial categories for each aspect of reality and then having one's own personal behaviour and ways of thinking conditioned, or even controlled, by those same arbitrary and ultimately deceptive categories.

The fool, on the other hand, is fully aware of the generally accepted categories but chooses to disregard them – to wear socks on his hands instead of his feet, for example.

The lunatic is unaware of the distinctions between the categories accepted by the majority of human beings and behaves inappropriately.

The Zen adept, asserts Mr. Hyers, is perfectly well aware of the nature of the conventional categories, but has transcended them.

THE WAY OF THE WARRIOR

"*All martial arts known under Heaven began in Shaolin*"

Ancient Chinese Saying

WHILE WE CAN BE SURE that the countless Chinese and Japanese varieties of the art of hand-to-hand combat did not originate in any one place, it does, in fact, seem possible that a tradition derived from the Buddhist monastery of Shaolin played an important part in the early development of many of them.

The original Shaolin was built at the end of the fifth century AD on the instructions of the Emperor Hsiao-Wen (in later centuries many monasteries and temples of the same name were built). It was first occupied by Buddhist monks from India who, under the leadership of their Abbot, Batuo, dedicated their lives almost exclusively to the task of translating their ancient Buddhist scriptures into Chinese.

Star of the Orient
Jackie Chan (below), today almost as well-known amongst kung fu film fanatics as is the late Bruce Lee, has amassed a fortune from his incredible talents. He directs his own films which are becoming ever more popular in the West. Jackie Chan also performs all his own stunts, many of which are extremely dangerous.

According to tradition, the life of the monastery changed when the monk Bodhidharma (p.204) visited the Shaolin temple and taught its monks not only the "way of meditation" (Ch'an or Zen) but "*wu-te*", "martial virtue". Before the coming of Bodhidharma, Chinese warriors trained primarily to fight; they bullied the weak.

↠ WARRIOR MONKS ↞

Bodhidharma taught the monks the idea that the ultimate purpose of the martial arts is not to fight but to gain spiritual progress. In tribute, portrayals of the Zen patriarch, blue-eyed, bearded, often with protruding and broken front teeth, hang in almost every Japanese "dojo", martial arts training centre.

For centuries the warrior monks of Shaolin were revered by many and feared by some, and their temple was a uniquely important centre of

FISTS OF FURY

Until comparatively recently, Chinese martial arts, as distinct from their Japanese equivalents such as judo, were quite unknown to most westerners. Over the last thirty years or so, however, Chinese martial arts films, notably those starring Bruce Lee (right), have familiarized millions with kung fu and other Chinese fighting techniques. In films such as *Enter the Dragon* and *Fists of Fury*, Bruce Lee captured the imagination of the western world with his uncanny skills. Lee, who died in somewhat mysterious circumstances in 1973, possessed extraordinary abilities that were not easily explicable. On several occasions, for instance, he publicly demonstrated his power to send a man flying over two metres (six feet) with a blow extending over a distance of only one inch. He was capable of doing several "push-ups" on just one finger. Lee began practising "Wing-chun", in Hong Kong at the age of thirteen, because, he claimed, boys he used to bully had outgrown him. He was never interested in competition and claimed that the only belts he owned were the ones that he used to "hold up his trousers". He died of "cerebral oedema" (brain swelling) at the age of only thirty-three but rumours abound as to more mysterious causes.

the martial arts. By AD 700 there were about 500 of these Buddhist warriors, and as late as the 1670s there were 128 of them, all masters in the art of combat. This traditional and very precise enumeration may have a symbolic numerological significance – 128 is exactly twice the number of the *I Ching* hexagrams (p.187).

At this time the Shaolin monastery was an established centre of military excellence largely independent of imperial control. Towards the end of the seventeenth century, however, the reigning Manchu emperor decided that this independence was an intolerable affront to his undivided rule and sent his army to subdue Shaolin. Consequently, the temple was stormed and set on fire by the hordes of imperial soldiers and, according to the legend, 110 of Shaolin's 128 monks perished in the flames.

Self Defence
So-called "soft" martial arts (left), where the "victim" uses an opponent's strength to his or her own advantage, are especially suited to women against male aggressors.

Keep Your Head
Although developed independently of western influences, the head gear worn in Kendo (left) is surprisingly similar to that worn by European fencers.

Kendo
Kendo seems to have developed from a warrior's swordfighting technique into a method of spiritual elevation associated with Zen Buddhism during the three centuries preceeding the Meiji restoration of 1868. Followers of Zen seek to "raise" all artforms from the level of reason to the higher plane of intuition; the combatant seeks to "forget" techniques and rules and achieve an intuitive spontaneity. At first, Kendo fighters used a solid oak dummy sword, more or less the same weight as a metal one, and capable of inflicting serious physical harm, even death, upon an opponent. This was soon replaced, however, by the light bamboo (left) that is still used today. This "sword" is much more likely to hurt the ego and mortify the spirit than to wound the body.

Stick to It
Kendo literally means "the way of the sword" but the "sword" of Kendo (right) is actually made of split bamboo, is extra light, and is unlikely to deliver blows that are dangerous or even painful. The Kendo competent more or less flicks his "sword" at his opponent, a movement that would, in fact, be quite useless in authentic sword fighting.

The remaining 18 were protected by a golden curtain that the Buddha, responding to their pleas for help, wrapped around them. The surviving monks then proceeded to teach the martial arts to all those Chinese dedicated to the struggle against the alien Manchu dynasty that had overthrown the native rulers in 1644.

By the end of the seventeenth century, two forms of "hard" martial arts particularly associated with Shaolin were fairly widely disseminated.

→ KUNG FU ←

A "hard" martial art is one in which force is opposed by greater force, as in the Chinese fighting techniques collectively referred to as "kung fu". The "soft" martial arts are those where force is not met by an equivalent or greater force. The soft art's effectiveness comes from yielding to force. As an example of a hard technique being met by hard and, alternatively, soft responses, consider the following situation:

An attacker launches a kick at his opponent, a hard application of force. A hard response would be to avoid or deflect the kick and return it with a stronger one. A soft response, one of many possibilities, would be to avoid the kick, seize the opponent's foot while it is in forward motion, and push it further in the same direction in which it is actually going, thus causing the attacker to lose balance and fall upon his back.

The skilled soft martial artist uses curved movements that, it is claimed, can be observed in the movements of animals that fight in a soft way. Curved movements are used, as distinct from the linear motions, such as straight kicks or punches, associated with the hard arts.

→ THE DANCE OF PA-KUA ←

In the Yin and Yang terminology of polarity in China (pp.187 and 202), the hard martial arts pertain to Yang, the soft ones to Yin, although the Yang arts invariably incorporate certain Yin features and vice versa.

There are certainly dozens, perhaps even hundreds, of Yin fighting techniques, but the most widely used and typical of them are certainly Pa-Kua and T'ai Chi Ch'uan.

Pa-Kua is a martial expression of a particular design where the eight trigrams of the *I Ching* (p.202) are laid out in circular form, the four

T'ai Chi
While the Chinese communists have rejected Taoism as a "relic of feudal superstition" they have retained, rather surprisingly, a considerable respect for certain techniques that are ultimately derived from Taoist polarity and subtle energy concepts. They have encouraged Chinese traditional medicine, of which is inextricably intertwined with Taoism, and have endeavoured to get large numbers of people (left) to engage in collective T'ai Chi exercises that imitate the defensive movements of animals. As these are entirely derived from Yin/Yang spiritual-polarity theory, it is not clear how their employment can be reconciled with dialectical materialism.

strongly Yang trigrams (which contain only one or no broken line) facing the four Yin trigrams (which contain only one or no whole lines).

It is difficult for the western observer to appreciate that Pa-Kua is a martial art at all, for it seems more like an improvised dance. In a sense it is a dance, the dance of life as an expression of the interflow between the two eternal polarities of Yin and Yang.

Nevertheless, it is a also a martial art, one in which an attacked person continually circles his or her opponent at great speed, avoiding every blow or kick and, from time to time, dealing a devastating counter-blow which relies for its effect on the force of the attacker being diverted backwards to its origin.

➻ T'AI CHI ➸

"T'ai Chi Ch'uan" means "supreme pole fist". Like Pa-Kua it is a particular expression of complex concepts concerning polarity expressed in a simple circular diagram.

The diagram in question, T'ai Chi, appears on the flag of the Republic of Korea. It shows a circle, cut in two by an S-shape, one half black and one half white. But in the black half of the circle is a small white circle, and in the white half a small black circle.

The black half represents Yin, the white half, Yang; and the small circles in each half symbolize the fact that all Yin aspects of reality contain Yang elements and vice versa.

That T'ai Chi is a martial art is not immediately apparent; indeed, most people who practise it, whether western or eastern, look upon it as a specialized form of physical exercise, not only because T'ai Chi exercises contain no obvious fighting moves, but because they are generally intended to be performed with great deliberation, not at all the sort of thing one associates with hand-to-hand combat.

Nevertheless, expert analysis of the movements of T'ai Chi shows that they are slow, but highly stylized, throws, locks, blows, and so on. It is claimed that a true master of T'ai Chi is invincible in combat.

Suit of Armour
The breastplate (below) worn by Kendo combatants.

EASTERN REMEDIES

"When we summon the wisest of (doctors) we may be relying on a scientific truth, the error of which will be recognized in a few years time"

Marcel Proust

THIRTY OR FORTY YEARS AGO the general western attitude towards traditional oriental therapeutic systems was one of complete contempt. Few knew anything of the elaborate theoretical structures from which these systems derived their rationale and those who did tended to look upon them as superstitious relics of the past, destined to be swept away by the advance of modern medical science.

Pin-point Accuracy
The first Europeans to encounter acupuncture assumed that its practitioners inserted needles almost at random. In reality, however, the entry point is specifically chosen, in accordance with anaesthetic physiology concerned with subtle energy flows, known as meridians, some aspects of which are illustrated in the 18th-century Chinese medical chart, which is depicted below.

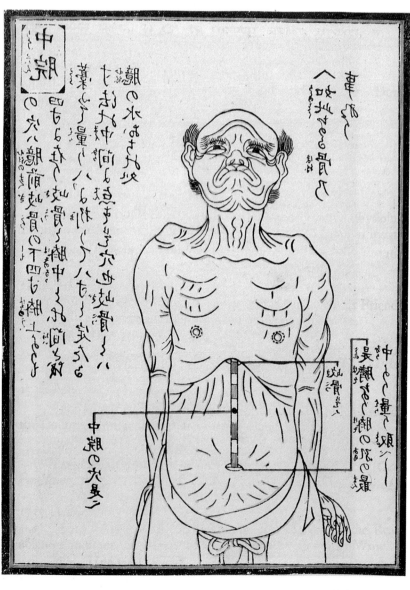

The present day situation is very different. While most people would not challenge the effectiveness of techniques associated with western medicine, many tend to be doubtful about its seeming inability to deal satisfactorily with a number of chronic ailments in which psychological as well as physical factors may be involved, such as some allergic reactions; it tends to neglect the spiritual factor in the human totality of body, mind, and spirit.

A consequence of this widespread, albeit often unexplained, public dissatisfaction with some aspects of "high-tech" western medicine has been a growth of interest in western systems of complementary medicine, such as homeopathy, and in traditional therapies of eastern origin – particularly those derived from China, such as acupuncture and acupressure.

It was in the seventeenth century that Europeans first became aware of the existence of acupuncture, a system of therapy based on the stimulation of bodily meridians (invisible currents of supposed subtle energies associated with the human body) by either the insertion of needles at vital points (nodes) on the meridians or the placing of smouldering herbal cones on those same points.

→ JESUITS AND TAOISTS ←

The Jesuit missionary priests who, almost three centuries ago, were the first Europeans to encounter acupuncture, were inclined to look upon it with considerable suspicion. Firstly, its techniques were entirely different from the heavy bloodletting and drastic purges associated with seventeenth-century European medicine. Secondly, the theoretical concepts that underlay both acupuncture and Chinese herbalism were inextricably linked with the mystical polarity philosophy of Taoism (pp.202-203). There was the same emphasis on the pairs of opposites and the importance that these, Yin and Yang, should be in equilibrium with one another.

Nevertheless, some Jesuit missionaries were prepared to admit that Chinese traditional medicine passed the empirical test – the proportion of patients treated by it who appeared to recover from illness seemed to be rather higher than the proportion of patients who recovered after the administration of western therapies. Acupuncture worked, they said, but the theories on which it was based were superstitious nonsense.

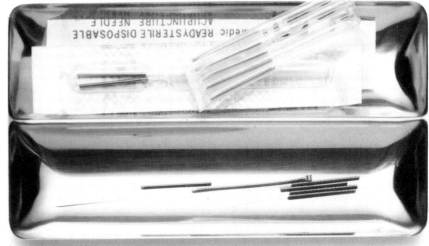

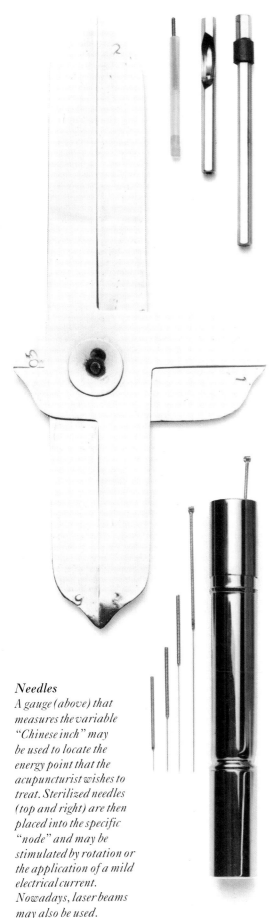

Present-day western physicians who have made a detailed study of acupuncture take a somewhat similar point of view.

Acupuncture, they say, is undoubtedly effective in the treatment of certain medical conditions, and in some cases *more* effective than western medicine. It has, for example, helped a great many people suffering from such chronic disorders as low back pain, migraine, arthritis, and addictions of one sort or another. On the other hand, so it is said, the traditional physiology that underlies acupuncture, with its meridians and nodes, is arrant nonsense.

→ The Placebo Effect ←

Some western physicians who take the point of view outlined in the above paragraph tend to explain the cures, or alleviations of physical discomfort, produced by acupuncture and other eastern therapeutic disciplines, as being the result of the "placebo effect" – the tendency for people to feel better when they are having some form of treatment that they consciously or unconsciously believe will make them feel better. In other words, they look upon acupuncture and allied disciplines as forms of autohypnosis.

Over the last forty years somewhere between two and three million surgical operations have been carried out in mainland Chinese hospitals with the patients fully conscious – sometimes

Needles
A gauge (above) that measures the variable "Chinese inch" may be used to locate the energy point that the acupuncturist wishes to treat. Sterilized needles (top and right) are then placed into the specific "node" and may be stimulated by rotation or the application of a mild electrical current. Nowadays, laser beams may also be used.

Pierced Ears
There are over 120 acupuncture points on the ear, as shown on the acupuncturist's model (above). Each point is said to have a reflex connection with other organs and specific parts of the body.

eating and drinking during the course of their operations – but seemingly without feeling pain, "anaesthetized" by needles inserted at particular nodes and rotated in them throughout the operation.

Somewhere around fifteen per cent of all surgical operations in mainland China – including major lung surgery – are reported as being carried out with the aid of acupuncture, and around three quarters of the patients concerned reported little or no pain. It seems too easy to believe that these patients responded as they did because they were self-hypnotized, although it has even been suggested that the patients on whom acupuncture is employed as a pain killer are carefully selected as "good hypnotic subjects" by their surgeons.

What seems to at least partially invalidate this theory as an explanation of acupuncture analgesia is that Chinese veterinary surgeons also commonly employ acupuncture when carrying out surgery on their animals. What is more, these animals seem to respond to the pain-killing properties of acupuncture better than their human

Marxist Medicine
The leaders of Communist China have encouraged the practice (above) of Taoist-derived traditional therapies.

equivalents – a fact that is difficult to explain as the result of autosuggestion. Perhaps it makes more sense to say that any pain felt by a human patient is likely to be the result of autosuggestion since we can associate surgery with pain whereas animals surely have no such preconceptions.

➳ MISSING THE POINT ✦

A less simplistic viewpoint has been adopted by other western medical practitioners who explain the successes of traditional Chinese therapies on a hypothesis that does not involve Taoist mystical concepts. Perhaps, they say, the needles and smouldering herbal cones of oriental medicine stimulate nerves which, in turn, send "healing messages" to the brain that are then transmitted, by means of the spinal cord, to the diseased areas of the body.

Such theories are interesting though not altogether satisfactory. Can they really explain the remarkable successes of Chinese surgeons, witnessed and filmed by many European and American medical practitioners, in conducting long and complex operations without even the use of any anaesthetics?

Moxibustion Cones
Herbal cones (below) are prepared using mugwort (left).

Acupuncture Alternative
Acupuncture literally means "puncture by a needle", but herbal cones (left) may be used in place of the needles with similar effectiveness. Known as "moxibustion", this method, though normally very gentle, can sometimes cause blistering. A gentler alternative is to apply finger pressure to the "nodal points" – those areas where energy enters and leaves the body.

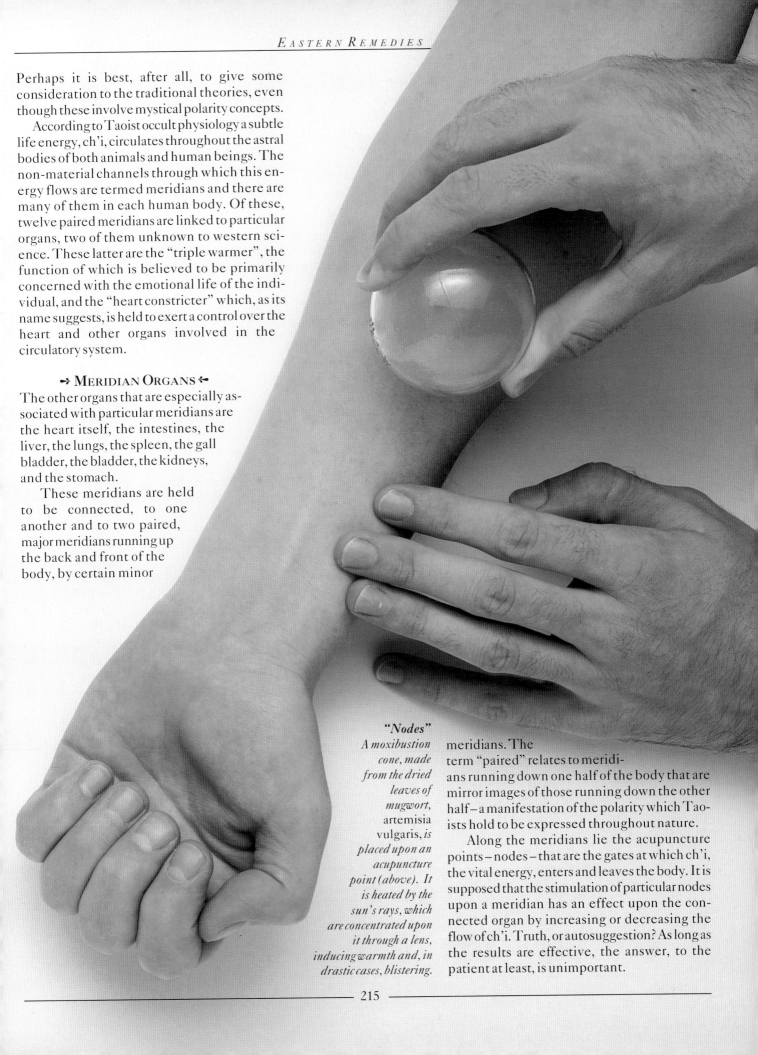

Perhaps it is best, after all, to give some consideration to the traditional theories, even though these involve mystical polarity concepts.

According to Taoist occult physiology a subtle life energy, ch'i, circulates throughout the astral bodies of both animals and human beings. The non-material channels through which this energy flows are termed meridians and there are many of them in each human body. Of these, twelve paired meridians are linked to particular organs, two of them unknown to western science. These latter are the "triple warmer", the function of which is believed to be primarily concerned with the emotional life of the individual, and the "heart constricter" which, as its name suggests, is held to exert a control over the heart and other organs involved in the circulatory system.

→ Meridian Organs ←

The other organs that are especially associated with particular meridians are the heart itself, the intestines, the liver, the lungs, the spleen, the gall bladder, the bladder, the kidneys, and the stomach.

These meridians are held to be connected, to one another and to two paired, major meridians running up the back and front of the body, by certain minor

"Nodes"
A moxibustion cone, made from the dried leaves of mugwort, artemisia vulgaris, *is placed upon an acupuncture point (above). It is heated by the sun's rays, which are concentrated upon it through a lens, inducing warmth and, in drastic cases, blistering.*

meridians. The term "paired" relates to meridians running down one half of the body that are mirror images of those running down the other half – a manifestation of the polarity which Taoists hold to be expressed throughout nature.

Along the meridians lie the acupuncture points – nodes – that are the gates at which ch'i, the vital energy, enters and leaves the body. It is supposed that the stimulation of particular nodes upon a meridian has an effect upon the connected organ by increasing or decreasing the flow of ch'i. Truth, or autosuggestion? As long as the results are effective, the answer, to the patient at least, is unimportant.

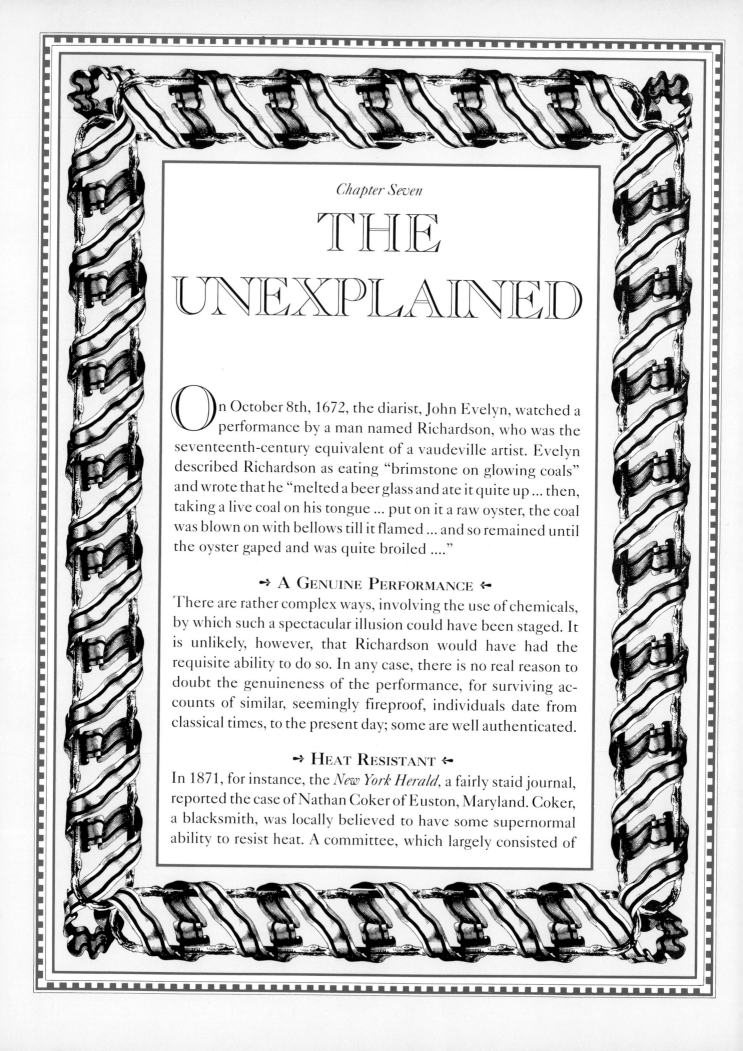

Chapter Seven

THE UNEXPLAINED

On October 8th, 1672, the diarist, John Evelyn, watched a performance by a man named Richardson, who was the seventeenth-century equivalent of a vaudeville artist. Evelyn described Richardson as eating "brimstone on glowing coals" and wrote that he "melted a beer glass and ate it quite up ... then, taking a live coal on his tongue ... put on it a raw oyster, the coal was blown on with bellows till it flamed ... and so remained until the oyster gaped and was quite broiled ...."

⇀ A GENUINE PERFORMANCE ↽

There are rather complex ways, involving the use of chemicals, by which such a spectacular illusion could have been staged. It is unlikely, however, that Richardson would have had the requisite ability to do so. In any case, there is no real reason to doubt the genuineness of the performance, for surviving accounts of similar, seemingly fireproof, individuals date from classical times, to the present day; some are well authenticated.

⇀ HEAT RESISTANT ↽

In 1871, for instance, the *New York Herald*, a fairly staid journal, reported the case of Nathan Coker of Euston, Maryland. Coker, a blacksmith, was locally believed to have some supernormal ability to resist heat. A committee, which largely consisted of solid local citizens, none of them inclined to a belief in the occult, asked Coker to demonstrate his powers. He agreed, remarking that "Since I was a little boy, I've never been afraid to handle fire". A shovel was heated until it glowed; the fire, resistant blacksmith removed his boots and "placed the hot shovel on the soles of his feet, and kept it there until the shovel became black". Coker proceeded to handle molten lead, glowing coals from his forge, and a piece of red hot iron.

Similar stories of human beings possessed of supernormal powers, from fire resistance and levitation to bilocation (the power of being in two places at the same time) have abounded. The alleged witnesses who claimed to have observed the activities of those with supernormal powers have often been reputable, honest, conservative people who have found it difficult to believe that what they saw really happened.

↦ WITNESSING THE IMPOSSIBLE ↤

Take, for example, the Victorian scientist, William Crookes. Told that a levitation that he had observed was "impossible", Crookes is reported to have replied, "I did not say it was possible, I said it happened". Crookes' statement echoed a paradox uttered by Tertullian, an early Christian apologist, in reference to his faith: "It is certain because it is impossible" – in other words, the whole Christian faith is so completely at variance with the world of common sense that it is unlikely to be based upon invention; anyone who wanted to tell lies would make statements more intrinsically believable than those enunciated in the Christian creeds.

One is inclined to feel much the same about many of the stories, seemingly well authenticated, regarding incorrupt bodies, miracles, supernatural healings, men who drink molten lead, and so on. In terms of our everyday experience such things are, quite clearly, impossible.

And yet sometimes, it would seem, they happen.

SPIRITUAL HEALING

"Spiritual healing is just a healer acting as a channel for the divine energy which is available from God"

Dr. Don Copland

IN 1900, A 23-YEAR-OLD Kentucky-born travelling salesman named Edgar Cayce suddenly became mute. A salesman without a voice is like a politician without a party, so the youthful Cayce sought medical assistance. Conventional treatment did not help, and he turned to unorthodox practitioners, from osteopaths to chiropractors and mesmerists; nothing worked. Finally, he consulted a hypnotist named Layne, who assured him that he possessed a peculiar psychological disposition that, while it allowed him to enter into a hypnotic trance, did not allow him to accept post-hypnotic suggestion from other people. This, said Layne, was why the hypnotists Cayce had previously consulted were unable to cure his speechlessness.

⇢ THE FAITH HEALER ⇠

Layne put his patient into a hypnotic trance and told him to attempt giving *himself* the post-hypnotic suggestion that he would recover his power of speech. This odd procedure worked – in effect, Cayce had healed himself. Now convinced that Cayce had the power of spiritual healing, Layne suggested that they

Healing Techniques
Traditional shamanistic healing techniques, employed in the Navaho and other American Indian cultures, include trance, prolonged drumming, and even the use of symbolic designs executed in sand (below).

In Africa
In sub-Saharan Africa, traditional healing techniques, involving the use of herbs, fetish dolls, and incantations, are still widely employed. According to some investigators the use of such methods can coincide with the spontaneous remission of both physical and mental disorders. A fetish doll, such as the one below, would be held by a pregnant woman.

should work together. Cayce, a Christian by faith, was dubious about the morality of spiritual healing and so refused. Immediately upon refusing, however, he once again lost the power of speech – a fact that persuaded him that God meant him to heal others.

For some time he worked with Layne. The hypnotist would put Cayce into a trance state in which he would diagnose and prescribe for those who came to see them. Before long, Cayce found that he did not even need to see his patients – Layne would give him their names and addresses and Cayce would, without hesitation, "... give the cause of ... ailments and suggest treatments to bring about a cure".

⇢ STRANGE FRUIT ⇠

A remarkable number of people claimed to have been cured of chronic illnesses by following Cayce's curious prescriptions, which included such remedies as consuming a particular fruit in large quantities and drinking Coca-Cola. By the end of 1911, he had acquired a national reputation as a spiritual healer.

Significantly, the best authenticated cases of his healings involved the cure of complaints in which psychological factors play a part: chronic indigestion, low back pain, and skin complaints. This suggests that at least some of Cayce's patients were healed, not by him, but by their belief in him and his supposed paranormal abilities. This theory is supported by Cayce's failings as a prophet.

Cayce undoubtedly believed in the genuineness of his psychic gifts and, when entranced, would sometimes prophesy.

Some of his more spectacular prophecies have not been fufilled – for example, the legendary Atlantis has not yet begun to rise again

Lourdes
While Lourdes (above) is the best known of the shrines at which healings have been reported to have taken place, it is by no means the only one. Some of the Lourdes healings are well authenticated, explained by sceptics only by their catch-all phrase "spontaneous remission". Indeed, the Catholic Church itself has been suprisingly sceptical about such healings, and has often taken years before agreeing that a healing is miraculous. Similar "miracles" have occurred at Fatima in Portugal, and Knock in Ireland.

from the Atlantic, nor has most of Japan yet been submerged under the Pacific. Despite this, he did score some remarkable successes.

On one occasion, for instance, he used clairvoyance to lead the police to the site of a concealed murder weapon, which resulted in the eventual conviction of a man for murder. On another occasion he prophesied to the vicepresident of a railroad company that unless a certain employee was dismissed, the man's negligence would cause a major accident. Cayce's advice was disregarded, the accident duly happened and, ironically, the vice-president was one of the victims.

Cayce died in 1945, and the source of his powers remains a mystery. In a state of normal consciousness he was inarticulate and unintelligent. When in a trance, however, he spoke as a man of wide-ranging knowledge – fluently, and using complex medical terminology. Perhaps some entity temporarily took over Cayce's

body in order to prescribe the odd remedies and treatments that restored many of his patients to health. Or was Cayce perhaps gifted with a mysterious "healing virtue", or, at least, did his patients believe this to be so?

The idea that Cayce was possessed of an inner healing virtue is not as unlikely as it may seem. The belief that some people, independently of their character or intelligence, have the ability to heal, can bring unwelcome attention to those thought to carry the gift.

For instance, in the early 1660s, King Charles II of England had a disturbing experience while walking through St. James's Park. He was accosted by an eccentric Welshman named Arise Evans who, according to John Aubrey:

"... had a fungous growth on his nose and it was revealed to him [perhaps in a dream] that the king's hand would cure him ... he kissed the king's hand and rubbed his nose with it, which disturbed the king, but cured him."

Soviet Faith

Dzhuna Davitashvili (right) is a Christian faith healer from Soviet Georgia. She had the unusual honour of being called in by the Soviet authorities to help prolong the life of the late President Brezhnev. According to the Sunday Times *(August 29, 1982) she has "testimonials from high Soviet officials thanking her for curing ... double pneumonia ... and malignancies". Here she is shown treating a young girl in a public display of her powers.*

For centuries people believed that the touch of the lawful English monarch could cure scrofula – tuberculosis of the lymphatic glands. As late as the reign of Queen Anne in the early eighteenth century, the monarch ceremonially touched the glands of men and women afflicted with scrofula. One of the very last of those favoured in this way was the great Dr. Samuel Johnson, who wore around his neck the thin gold "touch medal" given to him by the Queen, until the day of his death.

⇥ THE HEALING TOUCH ⇤

The idea that English kings and queens had healing powers may well have derived from Anglo-Saxon beliefs about the sanctity of royalty – Saxon kings who died by violence were almost invariably canonized. But quite ordinary people were sometimes believed to have the power of curing others by touching or stroking.

A well-known healer during the reign of Charles II was Valentine Greatrakes, an Irish Protestant country gentleman, who normally

SNAKE HANDLING

"They shall pick up serpents" wrote Saint Matthew in the New Testament. He was referring to "signs" that will "follow" true believers. In 1909, George Went Hensley, an American evangelist of the Holiness Church, decided that the gospels should be taken literally, and instructed devotees to handle serpents. The practice spread quickly through Tennesee and Kentucky, and then through neighbouring states. Today, several American states have banned the activities of the serpent-handling cults.

A service can last for three or four hours, although the snake-handling "event" rarely lasts longer than twenty minutes. It is preceded by the devotees kicking aound a large box. The box contains a knot of increasingly angry poisonous snakes. The snakes are angered before handling because the devotees believe that the greater the danger, the holier the participant. The first to put his or her hand into the box is held in great esteem by other members of the cult. Many devotees have been bitten and, although a large number of them have recovered, there have been several fatalities – including Hensley himself, who died of a snake's bite in 1955.

Snake-handling Cult
(Left) US insurance companies no longer treat death from a snake's bite in church as accidental.

made no charge for his services, and whose honesty and healing abilities were attested by many of the highest reputation.

Greatrakes was 33 when he first arrived at an inner conviction that he had the ability to cure scrofula by touch. He told his wife of his belief. She, sceptically, considered it a "strange imagination", but suggested that he should test his powers by attempting to heal a local sufferer, a boy named William Maher.

⇥ THE POWER OF PRAYER ⇤

Greatrakes prayed over the boy and stroked the affected glands; within a month the boy's swollen glands returned to normal. He then treated several other scrofulous patients by the same method. Some seemed to derive some benefit from Greatrakes' ministrations, others appeared to be completely cured. Eventually, Greatrakes became more ambitious and began to treat other diseases as well as scrofula, with equally satisfactory results.

Greatrakes was a typical spiritual healer: he prayed over his patients, many of whom recovered their health. His healing abilities puzzled and amazed many observers.

One of the more interesting suggestions regarding Greatrakes' cures was made by the poet, Henry More, who conjectured that there might be "very well a sanative and healing contagion, as well as a morbid and venomous" – in other words that Greatrakes "infected" others with his own excellent health.

St. Paul
St. Paul (left), pictured here healing the sick natives of the island of Melita after being shipwrecked there on a voyage bound for Italy. The chief of the island was called Publius, and his father lay "sick of fever and dysentry: unto whom Paul entered in, and laying his hands on him and healed him". After this miracle, all the diseased and dying on the island were brought to him and cured. St. Paul had himself been converted to Christianity by a miracle. Then called Saul, a fanatically orthodox Pharisaic Jew, he seems to have been present at the stoning to death of Stephen, the Church's first martyr, and had engaged in much "threatening and slaughter against the disciples of the Lord". He journeyed towards Damascus, with the intention of taking prisoner any Christians he found there. Nearing Damascus he was thrown to the ground as "there shone round about him a light out of Heaven". A voice, heard not only by Saul but also by his companions, said " I am Jesus, whom thou persecutest". Jesus told him to continue to Damascus where "it shall be told thee what thou must do". Saul arose from the ground completely blind, and remained so until he was baptised, in Damascus, some three days later. From then on Saul, now called Paul, performed miracles himself: striking blind a sorceror named Elymas; healing a congenital cripple; and casting out a spirit from a soothsaying maid.

CRYSTALS AND COLOUR

"*Marvel, O mortal! their hue, lustre, loveliness, Pure as a flower when its petals unfurl*"

Walter de la Mare

CRYSTALS HAVE LONG BEEN reputed to have magical powers. For instance, it has been said that to wear an emerald ring affords protection from poison, that rubies can be used as "shew-stones" in which things far off in time and space can be discerned by those gifted with psychic powers, and that a smoky quartz stone carried by a hunter will ensure that he finds an abundance of game.

In recent decades the ancient belief in the magic influences of gems and semi-precious stones has experienced a rebirth on the fringes of complementary medicine. Those crystals recommended by a practitioner of this sort of therapy are seldom selected on the basis of the particular physical or mental disorder from which the patient is suffering. Instead the particular crystal to be used is selected by a variant of dowsing in which a pendulum, composed of a crystal secured to a string, is swung over the patient's hand until a particular reaction is observed.

When the appropriate reaction has been obtained then the specific crystal that caused it is applied to effect a cure. Crystals and stones are said to contain energy, similar to that which forms the subtle "astral body" (pp.244-247) of all manner of life on the "material plane"; simply holding a crystal, some believe, can influence a persons health, beneficially or otherwise.

Green Goodness
Green crystals and stones, such as the five shown below, are often associated with the Anahata, or heart, chakra. As well as emerald – the most obvious green stone – malachite, and green or watermelon tourmaline, are all said to be especially beneficial to the healing process.

Crystal Power
A natural quartz crystal, whether rough (left) or cut (above left), is said to be particularly beneficial to the heart. Red semi-precious stones – these (above right) have been polished by "tumbling" – are said to be good for the circulation, for regenerating cells, and for renewing energy and vigour. Red stones are associated with the base chakra and should be used in this area.

Yellow Stone
Geode (above, top), is a natural circular formation that is usually hollow but in this case is totally filled with an agate-like substance. Geodes may contain almost anything from near gem-quality amethyst crystals to mica schist. This, and other yellow or orange stones (above) such as citrine, amber, or agate, is thought to be beneficial to the spleen – or the Svadisthana chakra. Yellow is also the colour of "inspiration".

Healing the Heart
Malachite (above, second from bottom), is said to be helpful for the psychological condition known as a "broken heart".

Soothing Blue

Blue stones (below), such as sapphire, aqua-marine, or lapis lazuli, are thought to be associated with the Visshuddha chakra, which affects the larynx and the pharynx. Sore throats and tonsilitis can supposedly be soothed when a healer uses one of these stones. A patient might be instructed to carry the stone around on his or her person for the period of their illness. Turquoise has even been attributed the power to provide a tongue-tied person with the gift of eloquence. This is an attribute similar to that of the Blarney Stone in Blarney Castle, Eire, which is said to bestow those who kiss it with "the gift of the gab".

Amethyst Powers

A natural selection of amethyst quartz, made up of hundreds of individual crystals and probably of South American origin (left). Now only a semi-precious stone, since the discovery of considerable deposits in Brazil relegated it from a higher status. At one time gem-quality, unflawed amethysts were almost as valuable as rubies. Amethysts are thought to improve powers of intuition. Crystals can be used to clear the energy lines – known to acupuncturists as "meridians" (pp.212-215). Lie down and place a crystal on the areas associated with each of the chakras (pp.194-197) in order to clear the channels. Alternatively, crystals can be carried by the user, or they may be held by a healer over the relevant part of the body and moved in a circular direction in order to cure a malady or simply in order to improve the "recipient's", or rather the patient's, general state of health.

Rose Quartz

Rose quartz (below) is believed to have a special link with subtle solar energies that make it particularly "receptive". Rose quartz is good for the skin, and is often used to ease the misery of menstrual pains.

Crystal Selection

A selection of crystals and tumble-polished stones (right), including white-banded amethyst and "Tiger's Eye", a yellow/black stone containing asbestos. Some contemporary admirers of the teachings of the occultist, Dion Fortune, assert that the asbestos content makes such stones particularly suitable as subjects for talismanic consecration due to the supposed linkage between asbestos and a "Venusian Master of Wisdom".

COMPLEMENTARY MEDICINE

"*We (live) in an age of alternatives– from alternative living to alternative comedy. And alternative health care is no joke*"

Elaine Farret

RECENT DECADES HAVE witnessed a tremendous increase in the popularity of alternative and complementary therapies: from commonly known and very popular therapies such as acupuncture and homeopathy, to less well-known treatments such as Rolfing and iridology, which are described later. Between these there are dozens, no, hundreds of "alternative" therapies – eastern and western, ancient and modern – so many that they would merit a book of their own for even a partial explanation of the methods they involve. The following few pages describe some of the more interesting therapies.

Homeopathy and its sister therapy, anthroposophy, are dealt with in some detail elsewhere in this book (pp.94-99), as is acupuncture (pp.212-213) – perhaps the eastern equivalent of homeopathy in terms of public awareness. Homeopathy and similar systems of medicine rely for success on the premise that "like treats

Iridology
Iridology, the diagnosis of physical conditions on the basis of the appearance of the patient's iris (right), was largely developed over a century ago by one Ignatz von Peczely, a Hungarian homeopathic practitioner. In the first two decades of the present century, iridology rather became the vogue amongst practitioners of naturopathic medicine, but was then almost forgotten until 1952, when the chiropractor, Bernard Jensen, published an important book on the subject.

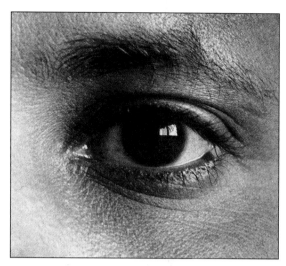

like". A homeopath will take a tiny amount of a poison – the effects of which are similar to the symptoms of a particular illness – and, after diluting the solution again and again until practically none of the original agent remains, use the resulting solution to treat that illness. It has been argued that the impressive success rate of homeopathy is largely due to the "placebo effect", wherein the patient thinks he or she is being treated, and therefore reaps therapeutic benefits; they are cured, we are told, by their own mind. Most alternative therapists would agree with this up to a point. In the case of

Blessed Pebble
A "consecrated pebble" being handled by its owner (right).

CRYSTAL THERAPY

Just as certain gems are linked with individual star signs, so professional crystal therapists link different stones with particular ailments; a patient will be prescribed a certain stone or gem to hold. Over the last two decades or so, the use of consecrated tumble-polished agate or other semi-precious stones, has become increasingly popular amongst practitioners operating on the wilder fringes of alternative medicine. Many recipients of such stones claim to have benefitted psychologically, and in some cases physically, from carrying one in their pocket or purse, and handling it just as the patient of a crystal therapist would.

At least one stone handler, however, was less fortunate; in 1990 Richard Cavendish, writing in London's *Literary Review*, reported that he had experienced an extraordinary run of bad luck until he threw his stone away.

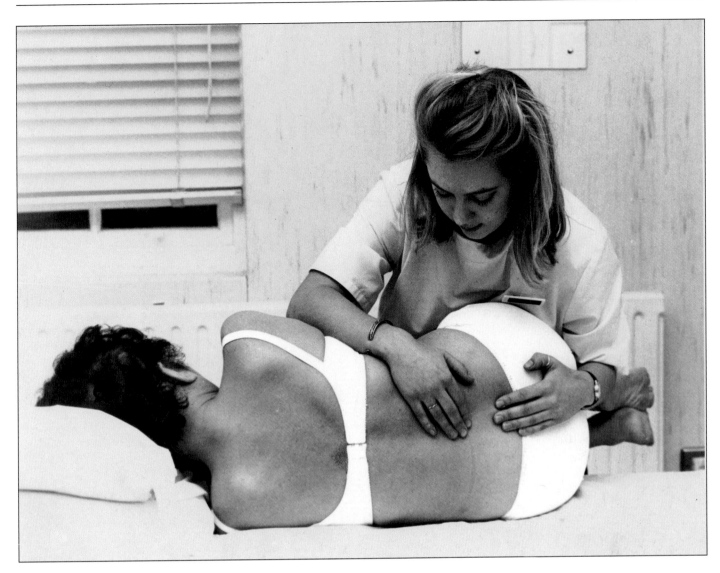

Osteopathy
Osteopathy (above) originated in the nineteenth century and, apart from herbalism, is the oldest form of complementary medicine to originate outside the medical profession – both nature cure and homeopathy were developed by orthodox physicians. At one time, osteopaths attempted to cure every sort of physical disorder, even infectious diseases, by manipulation, mainly of the spine. Today most osteopaths confine their attentions to medical conditions associated with joint and back pains, still by manipulation.

homeopathy, however, the argument falls down when you consider the impressive success rate of the increasing number of vets who use homeopathic treatments, where surely nobody can argue the case for a placebo effect.

Acupuncture, and its related oriental therapy, Shiatsu, share the fundamental belief that an energy, transmitted by the life force, is distributed through the body along a system of meridians, or invisible channels. When a person falls ill, it is because the harmony of the life force has been upset – there is an imbalance. In acupuncture, this is treated by inserting fine needles into specific points on the meridian, so restoring balance. With Shiatsu, also known as G-Jo, acupressure, and Jin Shin Do, a finger or knuckle is used to exert pressure on the point.

Manipulative therapies have become increasingly popular in the twentieth century, massage, osteopathy, and chiropractic being the best known. Osteopathy and chiropractic are both forms of massage – both are concerned

with the manipulation of joints, especially the spine. Their differences are mainly historical.

Rolfing, developed in the 1940s by the American doctor, Ida Rolf, concerns itself with tissue manipulation. Its aim is to liberate the physical structures of the body, allowing them to realign themselves properly "with gravity".

→ FLOWER POWER ←
Dr. Edward Bach, a London-born pathologist who qualified prior to the First World War, became a homeopath for a while, before he developed his 38 specially prepared remedies derived from the flowers of plants. Dr. Bach believed that by holding his hand above a flowering plant he could sense that plant's properties. He also believed that the underlying cause of any disorder is a negative emotional state. Bach isolated 38 flowers that could be used to treat various negative aspects, which he sub-divided into seven groups: fear; uncertainty; lack of interest in the present; despondency

and despair; over-concern for the welfare of others; loneliness; and, lastly, over-sensitivity. Herbalists share Bach's belief in the power of plants, but herbal remedies have been in use for centuries, in both the East and West. Herbalists argue that: just as animals and birds will know instinctively which plants to eat when they lack certain vitamins or trace minerals – and may even migrate to find them; so our primitive ancestors instinctively knew which herbs were beneficial and which were poisonous. Homeopaths, of course, argue that even poisonous herbs are beneficial with the right preparation, but that is another question. Herbalism is not really "alternative" at all:

Fidelity Symbol
The emblem of fidelity, rosemary (top left) was reputed to improve the memory. It would also be carried in neck pouches during times of plague, as it was thought to purify the air.

Immortal Holly
Long before holly (top left) became associated with Christmas, it was revered as a symbol of immortality. Today, herbalists infuse holly as a tea to treat rheumatism.

Old Meets New
Extract of evening primrose (left), long thought to have healing powers, is used in several modern drugs.

Head Help
In recent tests, 70 per cent of the migraine sufferers tested, experienced improvement after a daily helping of feverfew (left).

Sweetener
Santolina (above) was thought to kill intestinal worms, and infusions of santolina were taken to cleanse the kidneys. Today, however, this sweet-smelling daisy is used to repel insects.

Ancient Cure
One of the oldest known herbs; the Greeks revered chamomile (below left) as a cure-all. Today it is sold as a soothing tea and a tonic.

Plant Food
Nettles (left) were thought to have magical properties because other plants grow well in their vicinity. Rich in iron, nitrogen, and protein, cut nettles before they flower and soak them for a month to make a good plant food.

Sleepers
Poppy seeds can lie dormant for years, germinating when the soil is disturbed. The soldiers who dug the trenches during the First World War, created fields of poppies.

Balm
"Balm, given every morning, will renew youth, strengthen the brain and relieve languishing nature". This laudatory appraisal was in the London Dispensary in 1696.

Thyme Scales
These huge scales (below) were used by herbalists in the eighteenth century.

Holy Herb
17th-century herbalists thought that mint (right) could cure everything from venereal disease to colds. But mint has always been revered as a holy plant: the biblical Pharisees used to collect tythes in mint.

Herb Tree
Broom (left) is used in several medicines, including diuretics, yet is toxic.

Life or Death
Foxgloves (right) are highly toxic, but for centuries they have provided the main drug used to treat heart failure.

Essential Oil
Valued mainly for its fragrant essential oils, jasmine (right) has relaxant, sedative properties, and has been used to treat depression.

Cure-all
Eucalyptus (right) was once used as a cure for diorrhoea, colds, viruses, and wounds. Some of the plant's medicinal properties are still recognized today.

Indian Drug
In 1569, Dr. Monardes noted that the Indians used bergamot (right) as medicine. It contains thymol, an antiseptic.

A ROYAL BATH

In the Middle Ages, baths were considered as conferring both a physical and a ritual purity on their recipients. As a consequence of this, alchemical writers and illustrators used the bath as a symbol of the purification of base matter. Ceremonial bathing became a preliminary to admission to some chivalric orders, and those suffering from physical ailments would bathe in springs supposedly endowed with medicinal powers. The latter procedure was never completely abandoned and in the last century hydrotherapy became something of a cult, and is still in vogue today amongst believers in naturopathy.

Royal Bath A medieval woodcut (left) shows a queen taking a herbal bath, attended by physicians.

the medicinal properties of certain plants and herbs are widely recognized, and many modern drugs consist largely of such plant extracts.

Aromatherapy is another system of medicine that began in the East, only to become popular in the West many centuries later. Essential oils were used in China as far back as records go, and have been used there ever since. In fact aromatherapy was common to all ancient civilizations. In the distant past, aromas were ingested, whereas now aromatherapy describes the practice of rubbing aromatic oils into the skin, or of using them in baths and foot baths. Aromatherapy is aligned with "Nature Cures" such as hydrotherapy, naturotherapy, diets, and the more obscure ionization therapy.

→ NATURE CURES ←

The theory behind all of these is that, left to her own devices, Nature cures. Purists model their lifestyle as closely as possible on Nature's. They believe that by avoiding alchohol, drugs, and tobacco, and by getting as much fresh air and exercise as possible, then our body will look after itself. These days there are very few purists; most practioners believe that Nature Cure should be complemented by other treatments, homeopathy and manipulative therapy, for example.

There are hundreds of therapies of all kinds: apart from the Manipulative Therapies mentioned here, there are many others, including the Alexander technique,

Feldenkrais technique, reflexology, and applied kinesiology. There are movement therapies, including yoga, dance, and T'ai Chi; sensory therapies, including colour, art, aroma, and music therapy. There are many forms of psychotherapy, from biofeedback to hypnotherapy. Other therapies fall into the behaviourist, humanist, and transpersonal-psychology categories. There are also the paranormal therapies, many of which are dealt with in detail in this book, including: psychic surgery, past lives therapy, healing shrines, exorcism, hand healing, faith healing, and spiritual healing. Some of these so-called alternative therapies are purely physical; most of them, however, are thoroughly holistic, aimed

Aromatherapy
For centuries, vials of essential oils (below) have been used by aromatherapists for the treatment of various maladies. The natural aromatic oils are normally diluted and applied to the body externally – adding the beneficial qualities of massage to the treatment. Alternatively, they may be added to bathwater, or they might be inhaled.

PATCHOULI   ROSE   LEMON   LAVENDER

at treating the mind and spirit of the patient as well as his or her body. Such an approach can be, and often is, extremely successful, but in certain circumstances it can be dangerous. This is especially the case if the practitioner or doctor concentrates too much on the psychological and spiritual aspects of the patient's welfare, and neglects his or her physical and medical needs.

Modern medicine is much maligned by some, though not all, alternative therapists, to the point where it has been claimed that orthodox medical practitioners can be a threat to your health. Generally speaking, this is, of course, nonsense. It is much easier to criticize scientific medicine than to live without it; for us to complain about the failure of our medical advisers to cope with all our physical disabilities while we forget such triumphs of orthodoxy as the eradication of smallpox from the world.

When we complain about the sufferings of those who have developed allergies to modern drugs, such as penicillin, or children who are thought to have been brain damaged by vaccines, most of us tend to overlook or take for granted the benefits conferred on us by scientific medicine. We must try to bear in mind the hundreds of thousands – perhaps millions – of adults and children whose lives have been saved by antibiotics, vaccines, and other products of modern pharmacology. We ignore the fact that mental hospitals in the West no longer harbour tens of thousands of patients suffering from hopeless insanity resultant from tertiary syphilis; the reality that today a physician who tells a patient that he or she is tubercular is no longer pronouncing what was once tantamount to a death sentence.

Anyone who believes that the disadvantages of modern medicine and scientific pharmacology outweigh the benefits they have conferred upon humanity should, perhaps, try living without them. He or she is likely to find that with a pre-industrial way of life goes a pre-industrial way of death.

→ HEALTH WARNING ←

It is very important that, before turning to a practitioner of one variety or another of holistic medicine, you make sure that there is no physical disorder present that can easily and effectively be cured by orthodox treatment. It is all too easy for a person interested in psychic matters to attribute, for instance, pain in the upper thighs and physical exhaustion, to some profound psycho-spiritual malaise, when in fact it is caused by an inadequacy of the pancreas.

This having been said, it has to be admitted that there is no doubt at all that many people, suffering from an enormous variety of symptoms, have benefitted from alternative therapies of almost every kind. And indeed, many practitioners of orthodox medicine will quite happily advise their own patients to see one form or another of alternative practitioner, for *complementary* treatment. In truth, there is no justifiable reason why orthodox and alternative systems of medicine should not be capable of working side-by-side towards achieving their common aim – good health.

Oils
Bath oils, such as the capsules below, are a good example of aromatherapy in everyday use.

Incense Sticks
Originating in China, where relaxation is an artform, Joss sticks (far left) are becoming ever more popular in the West. Few doctors would dispute how essential relaxation is to good health. Stress related illnesses are all too familiar, and ever more people are turning to the soothing properties of incense to combat tension.

PSYCHIC SURGEONS

"Most ... things psychic surgeons do, ... involve manipulating invisible powers. (Actions) are strictly symbolic. That does not mean it is not effective"

Dr. Virginia Garrison

THERE IS NO FIELD of psychic activity more riddled with fraud than psychic surgery. People of all nationalities, suffering from chronic or terminal illness, have been cheated of large sums of money by self-proclaimed "psychic surgeons" who, in reality, are merely confidence tricksters using sleight of hand.

The typical fraudulent psychic surgeon carries out the deception with considerable skill. He or she appears to operate by pushing his hand directly inside some part of the patient's body – the abdomen, for example – and then withdrawing it, bloody and clutching supposedly diseased tissue. Traces of blood are then sponged

Trance Operation
An "operation" being performed by the English medium, George Chapman (below), who, when in trance, was supposedly possessed by the spirit of William Lang (1854-1937), in life a distinguished opthalmologist. Chapman's – or William Lang's – "operations" have always been carried out a few inches above the physical body of the patient; allegedly they have been on the "spirit body" that, once healed, has a permanent influence for the better on the patient's physical health.

away from the patient's skin and, to the amazement of those onlookers who are not accomplices, the flesh is seen to be unbroken.

"Operations" of this sort have been filmed, and a frame-by-frame examination has revealed the nature of the trick.

➳ ANIMAL TISSUE ➳

What happens is that the "psychic surgeon" has a piece of bloody tissue, usually from an animal source, concealed in his hand. He manipulates his fingers and the soft tissues of the patient's body so that the hand seems to enter the patient's body – in reality it has, with great dexterity, been doubled back upon itself.

At the end of the bogus operation the "diseased tissue" is taken away to be "ritually destroyed" – a histological examination would quickly reveal its animal origin and expose the fraudster. The grateful patient, who may feel temporarily better as an effect of psychological factors, is then pressed to make a substantial donation to enable the "surgeon" to carry on his or her beneficent activities.

➳ DOCTOR FRITZ ➳

The work of some psychic surgeons is not so easy to explain. Remarkable among these was the Brazilian, José Arigo, whose body was, apparently, often taken over by the spirit of a deceased German physician, "Doctor Fritz".

There seems to have been no question of sleight of hand being involved in the surgical operations carried out by Arigo in the period from 1950 to 1971. Wounds were left on his patients' bodies, which healed with unusual speed, but were undoubtedly genuine. The quickness of this healing was all the more remarkable in that Arigo – or "Doctor Fritz" – used unsterilized instruments. One observer, Judge Immesi, described a cataract operation carried out by Arigo as follows:

"I saw him pick up what looked like a pair of nail scissors. He wiped them on his sports shirt, and used no disinfectant of any kind. Then I saw him cut straight into the cornea of the patient's eye. She did not flinch, although she was fully conscious. The cataract was out in a matter of seconds.... Then Arigo said some sort of prayer as he held a piece of cotton in his hand. A few drops of liquid suddenly appeared on the cotton and he wiped the woman's eye with it.... She was cured."

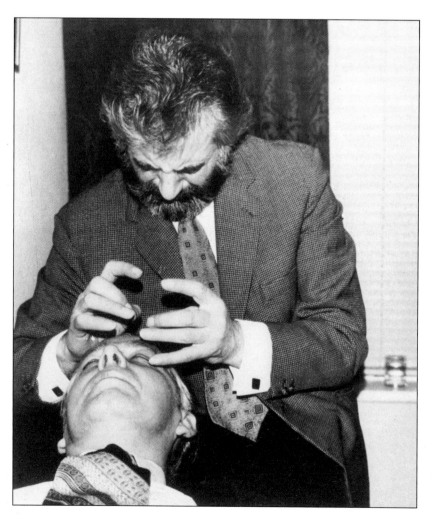

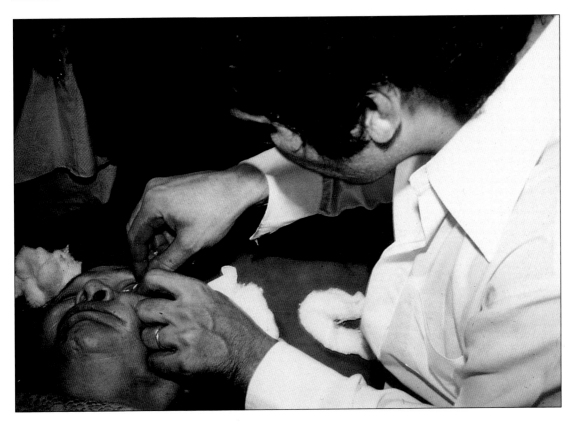

Bloody Fake?
The Brazilian psychic surgeon, Edivaldo Oliviera Silva (below), in action, performing what seems to all outward appearances to be a major, and rather bloody, abdominal operation on a child. While there is absolutely no doubt that many patients appear to have recovered from severe illnesses after having undergone such supposed operations, equally there can be no doubt that, while Silva may well be a genuine psychic, fraudulent psychic surgery has been widespread. A great deal of evidence has been gathered on how it can easily be faked, using sleight of hand and bloody animal tissue.

Another observer of Arigo described him removing a goitre – a diseased gland in the throat – slapping it into the fully conscious patient's hand, and wiping the wound, which hardly bled at all, with a piece of dirty cotton. The patient suffered no ill effects from this extraordinary treatment. Indeed, during the decades that Arigo practised his psychic, but very physical, surgery, there seem to have been no allegations that his treatment caused any harm. On the contrary, hundreds of grateful patients asserted that Arigo had cured them and he became a national hero, his "miracle healings" widely reported in the Brazilian press.

→ PSYCHIC MEDICINE ←

Arigo also practised psychic medicine and would prescribe drugs for his patients. No one seems to have suffered as a result of taking the drugs and some claimed considerable benefits, including cures for illnesses that had been described by conventional doctors as terminal.

It is unlikely that the extraordinary phenomena associated with Arigo's career as a psychic will ever be fully explained. There seems no doubt that he genuinely believed in the spirit of Doctor Fritz who at times controlled him and gave him paranormal powers. Was he deluded? Or was he an authentic medium who, through the intercession of some supernatural grace, was able to heal the sick and dying?

Ivan Trilha
Latin America is the world centre of psychic surgery. Why this should be the case is undetermined. One sociological explanation that has been put forward for this oddity is that South America's economic structure, in which modern technology and extremely primitive subsistence-farming exist side by side, creates expectations of medical help in sickness that cannot be met by modern, orthodox medicine. Paraguay, whose psychic surgeon, Ivan Trilha, is pictured above conducting an eye operation, provides a good example of such an unbalanced economy. A great many psychic surgeons are fakes, callously taking money from desperate people. Nevertheless, there are some who claim to have benefited from this branch of "medicine".

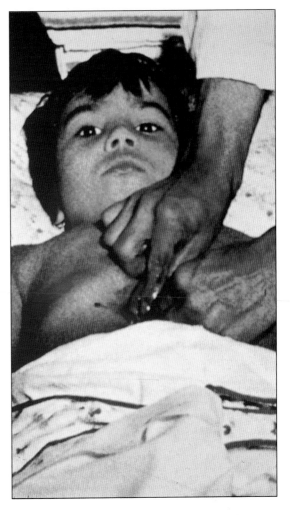

MIRACLES AND CURES

"*Daughter, be of good cheer; thy faith hath made thee whole*"

Matthew 9. 22

ON OCTOBER 8, 1982, *The Universe*, Britain's leading Catholic newspaper, reported that the Lourdes International Medical Commission had confirmed the miraculous nature of the sixty-fifth "scientifically inexplicable" cure at the shrine of the Blessed Virgin Mary at Lourdes, in South-West France.

The alleged miracle had taken place some seven years earlier when an eleven-year-old Sicilian girl, Delizia Ciroli, diagnosed as suffering from bone cancer, became free of all symptoms of the disease after bathing in the

Wesley and Graham Methodism is today a somewhat staid type of Christianity, but the careers of its eighteenth century founders were dramatic enough. John Wesley (below), its leading evangelist, was a strong believer in witchcraft, ghosts, and miracles. A substantial number of people were "cured miraculously" of their ills after hearing him preach. Billy Graham (right) is, perhaps, the most famous modern evangelist.

pool at Lourdes. The seven-year delay was by no means untypical; no Lourdes healing in the twentieth century has been officially recognized without numerous medical investigations extending over several years.

→ THE VISIONS OF BERNADETTE ←

It was in 1858 that, in the ninth of a series of eighteen visions of the Virgin, it was revealed to a young peasant girl, Bernadette Soubirous, that if she dug in the earth she would uncover a spring endowed with the power to heal. The source uncovered by Bernadette has flowed ever since, producing about 25,000 gallons of water a day. Apart from the 65 officially attested healings, tens of thousands of people claim to have benefited spiritually and physically by bathing in its waters. However, there are many other Lourdes pilgrims who have obtained no improvement in physical health.

"Outpourings of grace" associated with Roman Catholic shrines such as Lourdes in France and Knock in Ireland, where miracles or scientifically inexplicable healings actually take place, can be experienced at great distances from the shrines. This may be because water or earth act as physical channels through which healing energies are transmitted. For example, in 1881, the Archbishop of Hobart in Tasmania restored his failing sight by applying cement from the church at Knock to his eyes.

The Catholic church does not have a monopoly on miracles performed by the Virgin and saints. In 1968 apparitions of the Virgin were witnessed by thousands of Copts – Monophysite Christians whose belief that Christ had only one nature is regarded as heretical by the Catholic Church – at Zeitoun in Egypt.

➜ MIRACLES INVESTIGATED ←

A series of what were claimed to be miraculous healings followed, and an investigatory medical commission was appointed by Cyril VI of Alexandria, the international leader of Monophysitism. The commission reported that some of those who had seen the visions had been cured of illnesses including such physical conditions as blindness and cancer.

At the beginning of the eighteenth century, at the grave of François de Paris, in the Parisian cemetery of St. Medard, far more spectacular alleged miracles had been directly experienced by a number of Jansenists – adherents to the

St. Francis Xavier
The sixteenth-century Jesuit missionary, Saint Francis Xavier, was reported to have miraculously cured the blind and the sick in India. Parts of his allegedly incorruptible body are still annually displayed to the faithful.

Augustinian theology of Cornelius Jansen, Bishop of Ypres in the seventeenth century. François de Paris, a Jansenist noted for his personal holiness, was buried in May 1727. On that very day a healing miracle supposedly took place at his graveside and, over the next few years, numerous strange wonders followed, many of them well authenticated and not easily attributable to hysteria or suggestibility. For instance, one woman whose breast had largely been eaten away by a malignant ulcer not only had her skin healed but, incredibly, was also reported to have grown a replacement breast.

At St. Medard some devotees subjected themselves, for extended periods and without seeming to suffer any ill effects, to being beaten on the stomach with huge iron mallets and pestles. Others munched burning coals and laid their heads in fires so hot that their headgear was burned, although their hair and eyebrows were unsinged.

The events at St. Medard bewildered even the most hostile observers – the Jesuits, bitter opponents of Jansenism, were unable to detect any imposture, and assumed that the miracles were genuine, but of diabolical origin. Some people, however, remain sceptical.

A FUTURE SAINT?

On September 29th, 1929, Mary Therese Collins, a sixteen-year-old girl from the village of Drimoleague, Eire, calmly bid goodbye to her sister: she was, she told her, going to die that night. In life, there was little exceptional about Mary; she was described by friends as "radiant with goodness", but other than that, she was a normal, quiet young girl. The next morning she was indeed dead.

In 1981, some 52 years later, another Collins was to be buried in Mary's grave at Caheragh Old Cemetery. To the shock of the gravediggers, the coffin and Mary's body were both intact. Her hands, they said, were joined, as though in prayer, beneath her chin; her eyes were open and "shining like diamonds", and neither her flesh nor her clothing had suffered. Mary's grave soon became a place of pilgrimage, visited by thousands from all over Ireland; many "miraculous" cures have been claimed by pilgrims to her grave, and there is a movement petitioning for her canonization.

Saintly
Mary Collins' body was incorrupt some 50 years after her death.

The Cork

TUESDAY MORN

No. 49,835

HER BO

SIXTEEN-year-
Drimoleague, i
"always radia
September 29,
On April 22
opened and a
eye, the body
Even more
some, is the
that the ty
was still pe
girl.
Since th
body for e
discovery

One of those baffled by the phenomena reported by numerous observers at St. Medard was the Scottish philosopher David Hume, a man who shocked his contemporaries by declaring his disbelief in miracles. He remarked of the events that had taken place at the grave of François de Paris that "never was a greater number of miracles ascribed to one person" and that they "were immediately proved on the spot, before judges of unquestioned integrity, attested by witnesses of credit and distinction".

Despite this remark, Hume remained convinced that miracles were absolutely impossible and they could not have taken place at St. Medard, and that the witnesses were victims of undetectable deception.

➤ BIZARRE SPECTACLES ←

Inexplicable phenomena produced by the nineteenth-century medium, D.D. Home (p.120), provoked a similarly implacable and hostile response from some observers.

While Home, and others who shared his adventures, did not emulate the more extreme activities of the Jansenist wonder workers, their activities were often bizarre enough to alarm the conventional, and sufficiently inexplicable to infuriate sceptical philosophers.

D.D. Home was frequently accused of being an impostor, but there is no evidence of actual deception, although the lax conditions at many

JACINTA   FRANCISCO   LUCIA

Three Children
These three children (left) witnessed a series of apparitions of the Virgin Mary at Fatima, in Portugal. A similar vision was experienced by four children at Pontmain, in France, in 1871. In 1833, the Virgin Mary reportedly appeared to two children at La Salette, also in France, and made several prophecies that "plunged France into religious and political controversy". There have been hundreds of other "sightings" of the saint around the world.

LAZARUS

The Gospels record Jesus raising three people from the dead: the daughter of Jairus (Matthew XII); the son of a widowed inhabitant of Nain (Luke VII); and finally, Lazarus (John XI). The first two reported resurrections could be explained as recoveries from coma – Jesus actually said of the daughter of Jairus, "... the damsel is not dead but sleepeth". Lazarus, however, was decomposing; Martha, the dead man's sister, said, "Lord, by this time he stinketh: for he has been dead four days". Jesus ordered that the stone blocking the entrance of the tomb be removed and cried, "Come forth!" Lazarus emerged from the tomb, wrapped in a shroud.

Raising the Dead
Lazarus rising from his tomb, four days after his death – Jesus had brought him back to life (right).

Resurrection
The allegedly miraculous resurrection from the dead of Dr. Raymond (left) – one of a number of alleged cases of the same sort, for which the evidence is not altogether satisfactory. It is not only Roman Catholics who have allegedly been raised from the dead; in the 1860s an English girl named Lizzie Hatch was supposedly brought back to life by an Anglican deacon.

Weeping Virgin
An American image of the Blessed Virgin Mary (left) that allegedly produces of miraculous tears. Similar phenomena were reported at Prato, Italy, in 1484; at Goa, India, in 1636; at Ancona, Italy, in 1796; in the Italian diocese of Osimo in 1892; and at Templemore, Ireland, in 1920. Although some of the statues are clearly fakes, not all of them can be so easily discounted. An eager public makes even the most obvious fakes instantly a place of worship, and often cure – such is the power of faith.

of his seances would undoubtedly have facilitated fraud. Why, then, were so many accusations of fraud made against him? Probably because of homophobic suspicions, founded on his association with younger men.

➥ MIRACULOUS PHENOMENA ↩

One of these men was Lord Dunraven, an athletic young sportsman who spent almost two years in Home's company, living in the closest proximity to him. The two men lived together, travelled together, usually shared a bedroom and sometimes a bed. However, it was not uncommon for men of the Victorian era to sleep in one bed and it should not be assumed that they had a physical relationship.

Dunraven, who was no occultist, wrote a privately printed account of his remarkable experiences of "miraculous phenomena" during the two years of his companionship with Home. He saw, so he claimed until the end of his life, Home miraculously elongate, gaining height in an unbelievable, inexplicable way; he saw him handle red-hot coals without appearing to suffer any burns; he witnessed peculiar lights and heard puzzling sounds about the bed they shared; he saw Home levitate, on more than one occasion, above a London street.

Until the end of his life Dunraven insisted that his account was the unvarnished truth and, from what is known of his character and later life, it seems most improbable that he was deliberately lying. If Lord Dunraven was not lying, then was he the victim of a cunning fraud, or was he a man who had witnessed miracles?

Let us concentrate on just one of Home's miracles, which took place in a London apartment – an occasion on which, so Dunraven affirmed, Home floated out from the third-floor window of one room and floated in again at the window of another room. Perhaps Dunraven was drugged, or hallucinating. If the latter case were true, it must have been a collective hallucination, because two of Dunraven's friends, neither of them a convinced spiritualist, believed that they had also witnessed the events.

➥ LIKE A CIRCUS ACROBAT ↩

Home may have arranged an elaborate illusion. It has been suggested that he hung some kind of wire across the street and wriggled across it like a "circus acrobat". Possible, but improbable: Home was tubercular, took little exercise, and was physically frail. Such a feat would have been almost impossible for him to perform, and it is difficult to imagine a motive for such a physically dangerous and easily detectable fraud. Home was not being paid by any of the three witnesses, and he had no known reason to risk his life trying to impress them.

Perhaps Home genuinely performed a miracle. History supplies numerous instances of supposed human levitation, of which those of St. Joseph of Copertino in the seventeenth century are perhaps the best authenticated. On one occasion the saint was observed to fly about 11m (36 feet) through the air; on another he converted the Lutheran Duke of Brunswick to Roman Catholicism by levitating before him for a period of 15 minutes.

ARTIFICIAL HUMANS

"*The deformity of its aspect ... informed me that this was ... the filthy daemon to whom I had given life*"

Mary Shelley *Frankenstein*

MARY SHELLEY WROTE her famous novel, *Frankenstein*, after listening to a conversation between her husband and Lord Byron. They were discussing the experiments of Charles Darwin. He had preserved a piece of vermicelli in a jar "until it moved of its own accord".

Mary Shelley's fertile imagination began to ponder on the possibility of reanimating a human corpse, or perhaps, creating a "superhuman" from several corpses, and giving it life. This is, of course, exactly what occurs in her story.

But Frankenstein's monster is not the only artificially created human in historical legend. There are many references to the homunculi, the man-made men of ancient alchemy, dating from Arnold of Villanova in the 13th century, to Count John Ferdinand of Kufstein, in the Tyrol, in the 18th century. In *Frankenstein*, the misguided doctor develops his perverted interest in natural science through reading the works of Paracelsus, a 16th-century alchemist. Parcelsus is perhaps the best known "manufacturer" of a humunculus. He claimed to have successfully "grown" a human from a man's semen, which he had sealed in a jar and then "magnetized" by burying it in horse manure for forty days, after which it resembled a human form. The humunculus, he tells us, should then be kept at the

"*It*"
The film industry, and the cinema-going public, is obsessed with humanoid "creatures" such as the tree-man from the film, It *(below). There have been several films based on the Jewish legend of the Golem, including* Prague Nights *(bottom right) and* The Golem. *Frankenstein, though, has been in more films than all of the other creatures combined. To date, he has been the subject of an astonishing 110 films.*

FRANKENSTEIN

Frankenstein written by Mary Shelley, the wife of the poet, Percy Bysshe Shelley, is thought of as being one of the greatest of supernatural novels. Yet *Frankenstein* is not an occult novel, for it contains no explicitly supernatural elements. Rather, it is an example of early science fiction, for its protagonist, the young Baron Frankenstein, constructs what would today be termed an android from human remains and endows it with life by the use of electricity, not by the use of magical rituals such as those associated with the legend of the Golem.

In spite of its lack of overtly supernatural elements, there seems to be no doubt that this theme appeals to, and is derived from, the same unconscious archetypes that inspired legends of wonder working Rabbis creating artificial life forms to serve the Jewish citizens of medieval Prague; of alchemists manufacturing homunculi, small and imperfect human forms; and learned Friars, such as Roger Bacon, endowing brazen heads with the powers of speech. These archetypes are concerned with a desire that occasionally manifests itself amongst some mystics to emulate God by ceasing to be a creature and becoming a life creator.

Frankenstein's Monster One of the many cinematic versions of "The Creature" (left).

constant temperature of a mare's womb for forty weeks, during which time it should be fed on human blood until it grows into a normal human child. It is claimed that some ancient alchemists and philosophers were born in this manner.

Jewish legend has it that certain rabbis had the power to create a human slave from clay – the Golem. Golems are never allowed to leave the house of the rabbi, and are controlled by having the word "emeth" (truth) written on their forehead. Golems do not stop growing, and some, it is said, grew so big that they endangered the rabbis and their families; at this point the rabbi removes the "E" from emeth, leaving "meth" (he is dead), and the golem returns to clay. One Golem had grown so large that the collapsing clay crushed its master to death.

The Golem
The Hebrew legend of the Golem (right), derived from a medieval Jewish mystical ceremony, in which the adept symbolically endowed an earthen image with life.

SACRED WOUNDS

"Alas, O Lord to what a state dost thou bring those who love thee!"

St. Teresa of Avila

WRITING IN 1229, Thomas Celano, the first biographer of St. Francis of Assisi, who had died some three years earlier, described the strange wounds on St. Francis's body:

"His hands and feet seemed pierced in the midst by nails, the heads of the nails appearing in the inner part of the hands and in the upper part of the feet.... his right side, as if it had been pierced by a lance, was overlaid with a scar, and often shed forth blood...."

In other words, St. Francis bore upon his body wounds identical to those inflicted upon Jesus at his crucifixion at Golgotha – the stigmata. He had acquired the stigmata in 1224 when, in the course of a spiritual retreat on Mount Alvernus, he had suddenly fallen unconscious while praying. When he had recovered from his swoon, the five wounds were found imprinted upon his body, "marvellously wrought by the

The True Christian
St. Francis of Assisi (left) was transformed from a "soldier and a reveller" into the most Christ-like of men. His vocation was to follow the teachings of Christ literally and in absolute poverty. He despised the rules and regulations of the organized church and flatly refused to set up his own order, remaining always uncompromising in his insistance that Christ's example was the law, the will of God. His unique sense of brotherhood with all creatures made him a most endearing character. For this reason he is especially popular with young children.

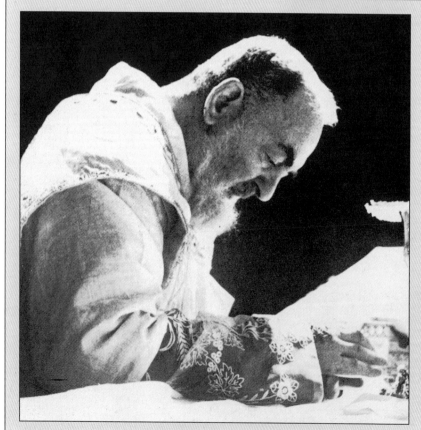

PADRE PIO

Dedicated admirers of Francesco Forgione, better known as Padre Pio da Pietralcini, are today busily engaged in "promoting his cause". Like Saint Francis of Assissi, the founder of the order to which he belonged, Padre Pio was imprinted with the stigmata. His followers are urging, firstly, his beatification, and subsequently, his canonization. It will be interesting to note whether, in the promotion of Padre Pio's cause, his body will be exhumed and, if so, whether it will appear uncorrupted – as have the bodies of several other known stigmatics. The body of Saint Theresa was brought up smelling, not of the grave, but of fresh violets. During his life, Padre Pio was credited with remarkable powers of precognition and clairvoyance. Despite his own attempts to avoid the public eye, and the reserved attitude of the Catholic Church, people flocked to see him.

The Capuchin Friar
Padre Pio received the stigmata in 1918 at the age of 28. He had his agonizing wounds for 50 years – until his death on September 28th, 1968. .

Antonio Ruffini

Reports of the sudden appearance of the five wounds of Christ upon the bodies of otherwise perfectly healthy people have been reported many times since Francis of Assisi was stigmatized in in 1224. Antonio Ruffini (below) is a modern day stigmatic. Whether such wounds are miraculous or – psychologically or otherwise – self-afflicted, is open to speculation.

Tears of Blood

Teresa Neumann (right) was one of the most notable of modern stigmatics. Born the child of a poor Bavarian family, she was a victim of numerous physical disorders, probably psychosomatic in origin, until 1926, when these disappeared and the marks of the stigmata appeared on her body. For the rest of her life blood flowed from her hands, feet, and side on most Fridays. She frequently went into deep trances in which she was reported to have spoken in fluent Aramaic, the language of Palestine in the first century AD. She was also frequently seen weeping copious tears of blood (right). For the last 35 years of her life she was never once seen to eat solid food.

power of God". This was the first recorded instance of the stigmata; there have been hundreds since. Writing in the 1950s, Father Herbert Thurston estimated that the number might well be approaching 400, although he admitted that some cases had been obviously fraudulent and others poorly authenticated.

→ ACID BURNS ←

Typical of a fraudulent stigmatic was Sister Jeanne of the Angels, an Ursuline nun who, after proclaiming that she had been bewitched by a priest named Grandier, posed as a saint and artificially impressed the stigmata on her body, probably using acid for the purpose. The unfortunate Grandier, as a result, was condemned to be burned at the stake in 1634.

Just as the discovery of forged money does not disprove the existence of real bank notes, similarly, the undoubted deceptions practised by some stigmatics should not discredit other perfectly genuine cases of men and women spontaneously developing wounds in their hands, feet, and side, corresponding to the five wounds inflicted on Jesus.

Curiously enough, stigmatization is and has been far more common among women than men. Indeed, the only well-authenticated cases of full stigmatization (that is, all five wounds being reproduced) in men are those of St. Francis and of Padre Pio, an Italian friar.

Padre Pio exhibited – perhaps "suffered" would be a better description – the first symptoms of stigmatization, pains in his palms, in 1915; but it was not until 1918, in dramatic circumstances, that he became fully stigmatized. He was celebrating the Festival of St. Francis when he suddenly, and for no apparent reason, collapsed. Picked up from the ground, he was found to be bleeding from hands, feet, and side. From then until his death in 1968 these wounds bled each day. He seems to have tried to conceal it from public view, even going to the length of wearing gloves when celebrating Mass.

The Church, wary of both fraud and delusion, keeps a close eye on purported stigmatics and their activities, and Padre Pio was kept under regular observation by some, including medical practitioners, acting on behalf of his ecclesiastical superiors. No evidence of fraud was ever found, there was never a sign of the ever-open wounds becoming infected and, since Padre Pio's death, there has been a campaign to canonize him. This canonization would be an acceptance by the church that his stigmatization, like that of St. Francis, was genuinely miraculous.

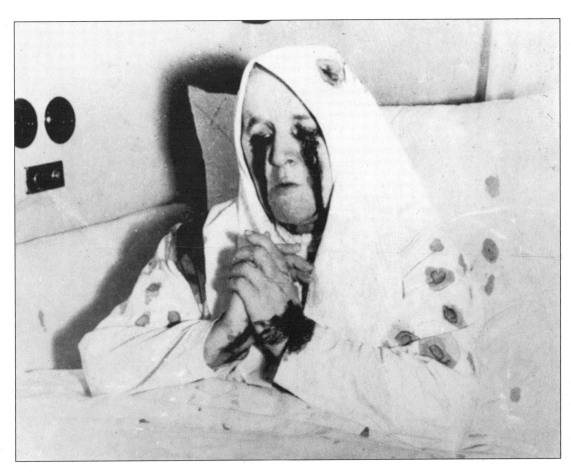

HUMAN COMBUSTION

*"*A*ttribute it to whom you will, or say it might have been prevented how you will, it is the same death eternally ... Spontaneous Combustion"*

Charles Dickens

IN 1951 THE REMAINS of Mary Reeser of St. Petersburg, Florida, were found in her apartment. The chair on which lay what little remained of Mrs. Reeser was burned down to its springs, but apart from a small circle of charred carpeting around the body, the apartment was virtually undamaged – a pile of papers near the remains was not even scorched.

Dr. Wilton Krogman, a forensic scientist from the University of Pennsylvania investigated this inexplicable death. Although no doubt used to gruesome scenes, he was astonished; particularly by the fact that the deceased woman's skull had shrunk to not much more than the size of an orange. Dr. Wilton wrote:

"... the apartment and everything in it should have been consumed. Never have I seen a human skull shrunk by intense heat. The opposite has always been true .... I regard it as the most amazing thing I have ever seen ... the short hairs on my neck bristle with vague fear. Were I living in the Middle Ages, I'd mutter something about black magic."

Mary Reeser
The remains of Mary Reeser (below), a 67-year-old Florida widow who was mysteriously consumed by fire on the night of July 1, 1951. Although heat had shrunk her skull to grapefruit-size, nearby papers were undamaged. The amount of heat necessary to cause such damage to her body should have destroyed the rest of the building – instead, the fire went out.

"CORRUPTED HUMOURS"

One famous case of literary spontaneous human combustion is found in Charles Dicken's *Bleak House*. A drunkard named Krook's alcohol soaked body burst spontaneously into fire – nothing was left behind but greasy soot (above). Although there was a popular nineteenth-century theory that if anyone was to spontaneously combust, it would be a person who was saturated with drink, many readers and critics thought the whole episode quite ludicrous and openly said so. Yet Dickens defended himself vigorously against such allegations, referring to a number of what seemed to be well-attested incidents of spontaneous human combustion. To, for example, the curious case of the Countess Bandi whose remains, in 1731 were found near her unsinged bed as:

"a heap of ashes ... two legs untouch'd stockings on, between which lay the head ... among which [the ashes] were found three fingers blacken'd. All the rest were ashes which ... left in the hand a greasy and stinking moisture."

Dickens seemed to imply that spontaneous combustion was the direct result of evil turning on itself; he describes Krook's death as being "inborn, inbred, engendered in the corrupted humours of the vicious body itself ... and none other of all the deaths that can be died."

Many other nineteenth-century authors also wrote about the strange phenomenon, spontaneous human combustion, including de Quincey and Zola.

Irving Bentley
The bottom portion of his left leg was all that remained of the body of John Irving Bentley, a 93-year-old retired Pennsylvania medical practitioner, when it was found on the morning of December 5, 1966 (below). The fire had been of such intensity that a large hole had been burned in the floor – but the rest of the apartment was virtually undamaged. Science, and the sceptic, has yet to satisfactorily explain spotaneous human combustion.

Dr. Krogman's own theory seemed quite as unlikely as the idea that black magic was involved; he suggested that Mrs. Reeser had been kidnapped, then murdered by someone with access to a crematorium in which he had subjected her body to enormous heat, and then returned it to the armchair in her apartment.

It is, in fact, very difficult to burn a human body to the point of calcination – even in the high temperatures employed in modern crematoria it is often the case that sufficiently large bones still survive that have to be ground into powder by mechanical means.

Scientists deny the possibility of spontaneous human combustion, yet it is extremely difficult to explain a substantial number of deaths by fire on any other hypothesis. Clearly such deaths deserve more serious investigation than has so far been given.

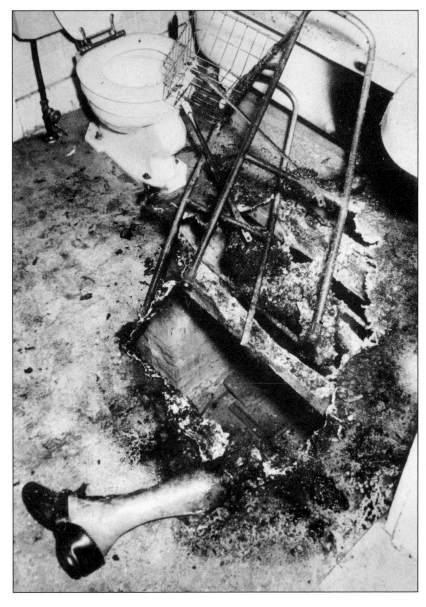

SUPERNORMAL POWERS

*"I teach you the superman.
Man is something to be surpassed"*

Friedrich Nietzsche

EXHIBITIONS OF SEEMINGLY supernormal powers have often been observed and reported by people who are bitterly hostile to the religious beliefs of the persons who have displayed them, and are therefore the least likely "believers".

Such observers have had a strong predisposition to denounce such exhibitions as fraudulent but have often been forced, by the evidence of their own senses, to accept the probability of them being genuine – and to argue the possibility of diabolical intervention in order to bolster up "false religion". So, for example, Jesuits who witnessed the supernormal feats of strength performed by Jansenist enthusiasts in early eighteenth century Paris, attributed them to the work of Satan.

Yet it is not only religious devotees of one faith or another who have displayed seemingly supernormal abilities; some people seem to have been born with "wild talents", the sceptic might say an innate ability to deceive others,

Magnetic Man

The picture (right) shows a Soviet man who is supposedly possessed of a natural bodily magnetism. This magnetism is of sufficient strength to attract large ferrous objects to his skin where, so it is claimed, they are retained so strongly that a considerable physical effort is required in order to detach them from his body. Many suggestions have been made as to how the effect could be fraudulently produced, many of them even more improbable than the idea that the man is genuinely magnetic. It has been suggested, for example, that the man has lodged extremely powerful magnets in his gullet, stomach, and bowels.

Hindu Devotee
The woman shown here (left) has had pins placed through her skin, probably at a wedding ceremony, yet she seems totally impervious to any pain. A Hindu ascetic, such as this female devotee, may be a pure mystic – a seeker after union with the divine whose mind is quite free of any desire for supernatural powers. On the other hand, some ascetics are primarily concerned with a quest for supernormal powers of the type supposedly demonstrated by the Hindu holy man in the 1950s and '60s. These included the materialization of solid objects, for example, statuettes, "holy ash" for administration to the sick, and gold coins.

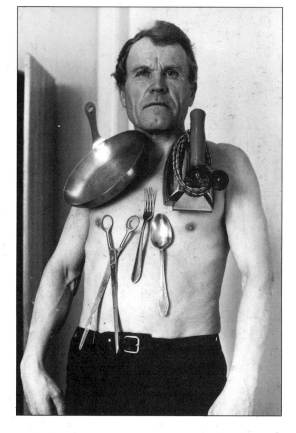

HARRY HOUDINI
The greatest of all escape artists, Harry Houdini, was believed by many to possess supernatural powers. He, himself, admitted to receiving instructions from a voice in his head that reassured him of the eventual success of his dangerous feats. He studied the methods of the yogi of India claiming to have mastered their arts of controlled breathing to the extent that he could survive without air for an incredibly long period of time, making his escapes seem all the more extraordinary. He was an obsessive psychical investigator, who used his knowledge of magic and the occult to expose a number of fraudulent mediums.

which enable them to perform extraordinary and inexplicable feats. They appear to handle red-hot objects without suffering burns, to "see" through their skin, to move objects without handling them, and so on.

↦ NINA KULAGINA ↤

A woman who appeared to have powers of this sort was Nina Kulagina of Leningrad, investigated by several western psychical researchers in the 1970s. Benson Herbert, an English psychical researcher, was greatly impressed by her and reported some odd personal experiences. On one occasion, for example, she held his arm above the wrist for a few minutes. He felt a sensation that was new to him, resembling both an electric shock and the application of heat. Then he collapsed – when he recovered, his arm was red, as if burned, and the mark was distinguishable for over a week.

James Randi, the American illusionist, and a lifelong sceptic, was less impressed by Nina, arguing that she was a clever fraud. Such sceptics tended to explain the favourable reports of Benson Herbert and other researchers as being the consequence of gullibility, self delusion, and a strong will to believe in the authenticity of supernormal phenomena. It was pointed out, for instance, that Herbert had investigated the possibility that some devotees of modern witchcraft had paranormal abilities – this was supposed to be evidence of his credulity.

Walking on Fire
A Buddhist monk (left) walking over red-hot coals without feeling any pain. This is taking place at the annual Buddhist fire-walking ceremony celebrated at the foot of Mount Taiko, Japan, and dedicated to universal peace. Bystanders rub ailing limbs with sticks and throw them on the fire in the hope of being cured.

Another Fine Mess
Harry Houdini (below) in a typically sticky situation.

THE ASTRAL WORLD

*"The heaventree of stars
thung with humid nightblue fruit"*

James Joyce

HELENA PETROVNA BLAVATSKY was a key figure in the history of modern western esotericism. Through her books, *Isis Unveiled* and *The Secret Doctrine*, she conveyed the nature of ancient occult teachings – albeit, perhaps, in a slightly distorted form – to a host of readers previously unacquainted with them.

Since their first publication in the late nineteenth century, these books have been almost continuously in print. Their popularity may be explained by the sources upon which they were based. According to Colonel Olcott, one of Blavatsky's closest friends and disciples, *Isis Unveiled* was written by its author:

"... pen ... flying over the page... she would suddenly stop, look into space with the vacant eye of the clairvoyant seer, shorten her vision so as to look at something held invisibly in the air before her, and begin copying on the paper what she saw. The quotation finished, her eyes would resume their natural expression ...."

Olcott was suggesting that Madame Blavatsky was consulting long lost books and manuscripts that had been preserved in the astral or "akashic" records. These records, many esotericists have affirmed, are the imprints of

Astral Body
An artist's impression of an astral body leaving a physical body (right). Some psychics have reported clairvoyantly perceiving something very similar – an image of the physical body hovering above the material form. Some believe that the astral body and the soul are the same thing. The "chord" that binds the astral body to the physical is cut at death in order to liberate the spirit.

Free Spirit
A William Blake illustration (below) for The Grave, *the imagery of which was drawn from a wide variety of literary and pictorial sources. From, for example, the astral theories of the renaissance occultist, Paracelsus, from the engravings that illustrated the works of Boehme, and from the writings of Swedenborg.*

everything that has happened and everything that has existed on the material plane, upon the subtle astral world, which supposedly underlies dense matter and energy. They state that imprints of Lincoln making the Gettysburg Address, and Shakespeare's original manuscript of *Hamlet* are contained in the astral records and can be heard or read in the mind's eye and ear, by the gifted clairvoyant or psychic.

→ ASTRAL PROJECTIONS ←

A modified form of occult theory concerning the existence of astral records is adhered to by some esotericists influenced by Jungian depth psychology. They identify the astral world with the Collective Unconscious defined by Jung, and assert that astral records are not without us, but within the depths of our minds.

Most of those who believe in the existence of the world (or worlds) of astral consciousness accept that it is possible for the psychic component of the human totality to journey into the astral planes – to "astrally project" – and that most spontaneous out-of-the-body experiences are involuntary astral projections. Western esotericists employ techniques similar

Astral Forces

The image (right) illustrates an attempt to give a two dimensional representation of astral forces. Such attempts have been made since the beginning of the nineteenth century by artists with occult leanings, or those who are painting under the instruction of ritual magicians, and clairvoyants who claim to have discerned such forces in action. However, such attempts can never, by definition, be completely successful; for the artists in question have attempted an impossible task, the delineation, in terms of spatial relationships, of forces that exist outside of space as we understand it.

Muldoon

An illustration of the projection of the astral body as described by Sylvan Muldoon and Hereward Carrington in their seminal study The projection of the Astral Body *(bottom right). They describe numerous methods of achieving projection. All the procedures outlined involve the use of imagination or "creative visualization" while lying on one's back. For instance, imagining going up in an elevator as one is about to fall asleep.*

to autohypnosis in order to "project themselves into the astral world" or, as those influenced by Jungian ideas might put it, to "enter the inner space of the Collective Unconscious".

All of these techniques involve concentrating vision and consciousness upon some simple and intrinisically uninteresting object or shape – for example, a candle flame or a pool of black liquid. The objective is to induce a state of bored concentration in which the psyche, to relieve itself of insufferable tedium, journeys elsewhere – to "the astral world" or "the plane of archetypal consciousness".

The problem with this technique, however, is that it produces uncontrolled visions, which may be meaningless or excessively diffuse. Still worse, they can be of an unpleasant nature – "astral projection" or "veridical day-dream" is transformed into a nightmare far worse than anything experienced during normal sleep. To avoid this uncertainty, many western esotericists

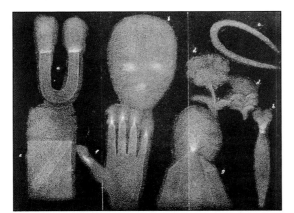

use geometric symbols as objects of concentration that are intended to induce first, autohypnosis, and then astral projection. The symbols provide the key to different areas of the astral world, or alternatively, segments of the Collective Unconscious.

The symbols generally used are those that were employed by the esoteric order of the Golden Dawn (p.76): a red equilateral triangle, a yellow square, a sky blue circle, an indigo ovoid, a silver crescent, and twenty dual combinations of these – for example, a silver crescent on a yellow square.

→ TRY FOR YOURSELF ←

Today these symbols are used in many different ways. One technique is simply to shut your eyes and visualize a symbol as if it were drawn upon a curtain. After sustaining the visualization for a period of 5 to 15 minutes, you may find that the curtain seems to swing aside of its own volition and, in the mind's eye, a landscape appears. You then enter a state that has been termed "controlled veridical day-dreaming" in which you visualize a journey through the landscape, observing, and even conversing with, the entities encountered. The nature of these entities supposedly depends upon the symbol that you choose to visualize on the curtain.

In practice this technique is a great deal more difficult to execute than it sounds – people find it hard to concentrate on a simple symbol for more than a minute or two without the mind wandering. Nevertheless, persistence with this method has often paid off.

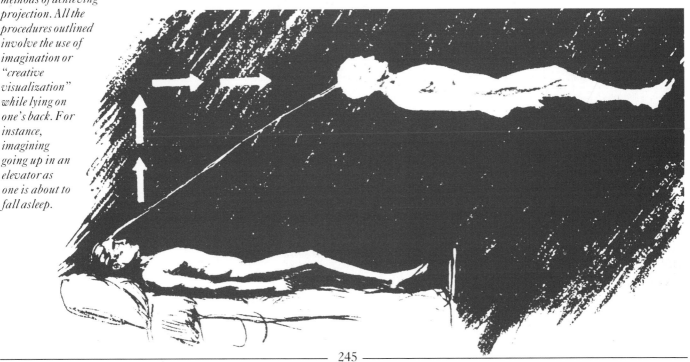

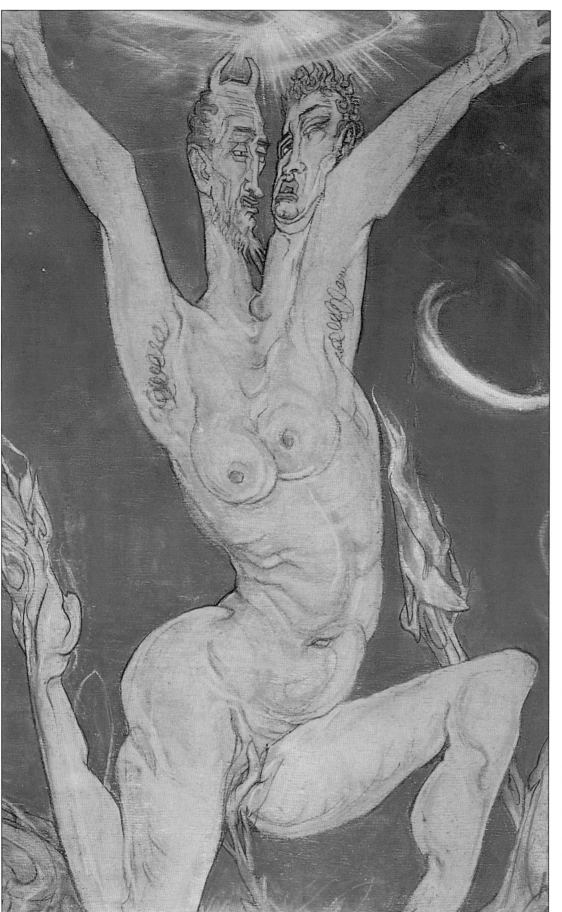

Spare Painting
No artist of modern times has been more concerned with supposed astral realities than A.O. Spare, an eccentric genius whose Astral Realms *(left)* typifies one of the styles in which he drew and painted. Spare claimed to have been given secret "astral teachings" by an elderly witch, a Mrs. Paterson. For a time he was a member of an occult society, the Silver Star, which was headed by the notorious magician, Aleister Crowley.

Auric Egg
The astral body and its colours as discerned by clairvoyants have been described in detail by a number of twentieth-century occultists. Prominent amongst them have been several members of the Theosophical Society, notably the late C.W. Leadbeater, a Church of England clergyman who became an occultist and headed the still active Liberal Catholic Church. The auric "egg" *(above)* is a delineation of the astral aura of a depressive, showing that person's colours. The colours would change as the person's mood changed.

To read certain descriptions of the astral worlds is to induce an immediate scepticism. There are, for instance, descriptions of astral "heavens" populated by departed spirits who smoke astral cigars, drink astral brandy, and even play astral golf. It all sounds like self delusion or even deliberate parody. Yet, interestingly enough, a number of occult students have claimed that the very vulgarity and silliness of such descriptions is evidence of their genuineness.

Such occultists do not, needless to say, affirm that spiritual, or even astral, reality is in accordance with such descriptions, and that we can all look forward to a post mortem state in which we will spend eternity in a prosperous suburb; what they assert is that the "stuff" of astral existence is, as it were, plastic in nature and is moulded into whichever forms the astral entities choose to shape it into.

↠ GOLF, CIGARS, AND BRANDY ↞

The astral plane, they argue, is the realm of feelings and emotions and its forms reflect the deeply held beliefs of every human being who has ever lived. On it, built by human belief, so it is argued, are the hells and heavens of Christian, Buddhist, and Muslim popular cosmology; the mythical animals, such as dragons and unicorns, of alchemical symbolism; all the saints, heroes and villains of legend; and the heavens of those whose conception of bliss has not risen above perpetual rounds of golf followed by cigars and brandy.

To the occultist, the question of whether the astral plane enjoys an objective existence or whether, as Jung would suggest, it is no more than a psychic construct, is of great importance. He or she affirms that while the Collective Unconscious posited by Jung may well exist, it is only a reflection of an astral reality – and a distorted reflection at that. In the unconscious mind, says the occultist, is present a "magical mirror" that contains images of astral and spiritual reality. But that mirror is tarnished, streaked, and malformed; the image it provides is, at best, blurred and out of focus. The person who perceives the astral world through the Unconscious sees it under the guise of symbol, it is claimed; thus, for instance, the astral forces looked upon as the subtle energies underlying human sexuality might manifest themselves symbolically as a white eagle and a red lion.

The records of supposed adventures on the astral plane often feature the appearance of such unlikely creatures. Men and women have told how they have wandered in astral form, through strange landscapes quite as alien as

HAMZEH CARR

those described in the novels of C.S. Lewis or J.R.R. Tolkien. They have described their encounters with phoenixes and dragons, have given dramatic accounts of their battles with red giants and black dwarfs, and recorded the teachings they have been given by astral entities. There is no doubt that most of those who claim to have experienced such strange dimensions of consciousness have wholly believed in the genuineness of their experiences.

They do not feel that they have been having nothing more than day dreams, or even that they have encountered images rising from their own, or a collective, unconscious. They feel that they have been in touch with forces that are greater than themselves.

↠ GENUINE EXPERIENCE ↞

However, precisely the same conviction that a genuine experience has been undergone has characterised those who have "visited the astral plane" and found it populated by cigar smoking, brandy swilling, golfers.

Perhaps all experimenters with such techniques as that outlined on page 245 should keep in mind the teachings of many western occultists; that astral realities are usually veiled in illusion, and that what is discerned should be interpreted in the light of reason.

Light of Asia
The Light of Asia *(above) depicts the full glory of the Buddha, who, having escaped from the cycle of birth and rebirth through his enlightenment, becomes "the ruler of space and time". An enlightened being is said to be free to choose whether or not he or she will have a mortal life, whereas others are compelled to be reborn. The mother of Winston Churchill was, like many of her contemporaries, totally ignorant of Buddhism and referred to a Burmese Buddhist monk as "chanting the Koran". Today things are very different, and many westerners regard Gautama Buddha, whom some think to have been an avatar of Krishna, as the "Light", not just of Asia, but of the whole world, East and West.*

FURTHER READING

This reading list is not a comprehensive bibliography. However, it is intended to give the reader the opportunity to read around some of the many subjects covered in this book. Indeed, some of the books listed go into considerable depth about a particular subject. All the books listed are available either from bookshops or public libraries.

Adams, Evangeline,
Astrology for Everyone, New York 1960 reprint
Agrippa, Cornelius,
Fourth Book of Occult Philosophy, London 1977 (a photographic reproduction of the London edition of 1655)
Arundale, George S.,
Kundalini: An Occult Experience, Adyar 1962

Baird, A.T.,
One Hundred Cases for Survival After Death, London 1943
Bell, E.T.
The Magic of Numbers, New York 1946
Blofeld, John,
The I Ching, London 1965
The Way of Power, London 1970

Case, Paul Foster,
The Tarot, Richmond New York 1947
Cavendish, Richard (editor),
Encyclopedia of the Unexplained, London 1972
Man, Myth and Magic, (7 vols.), London 1972
Cavendish, Richard,
The Magical Arts, London 1984
The Tarot, London 1986
Cheasley, C.W.,
Numerology, London 1926
Clodd, Edward,
Magic in Names, New York 1921

David-Neel, Alexandra,
Initiations and Initiates in Tibet, London 1932
Deacon, Richard,
The Book of Fate, London 1976
Douglas, Alfred,
The Tarot, London 1972
Douglas, N., and White, M.,
The Black Hat Lamas of Tibet, London 1975

Eliade, Mircea,
Shamanism: Archaic Techniques of Ecstasy, London 1964
Evans-Wentz, W.Y.,
The Tibetan Book of the Dead, Oxford 1928
The Tibetan Book of the Great Liberation, Oxford 1954
Tibet's Great Yogi Milarepa, Oxford 1956
Tibetan Yoga and Secret Doctrines, Oxford 1935

Fitzherbert, Andrew,
Hand Psychology, New South Wales 1986
Fortune, Dion,
The Mystical Qabalah, London 1935
Applied Magic, London 1962 reprint
Aspects of Occultism, New Jersey 1962
The Cosmic Doctrine, New Jersey 1966

Gaddis, V. and M.,
The Curious World of Twins, New York 1972
Garrison, Omar V.,
Tantra, the Yoga of Sex, New York 1964
Gettings, Fred,
Palmistry Made Easy, Hollywood 1973
The Book of the Hand, London 1965
Gilbert, R.A. (editor),
The Sorcerer and His Apprentice, Wellingborough 1983
Ginsburg, C.D.,
The Kabbalah, New York 1970 reprint
Goldsmith, J.,
The Art of Spiritual Healing, New York 1959
Güenther, Herbert V.,
The Life and Teachings of Naropa, Oxford 1963

Hall, Angus, and King, Francis X.,
Mysteries of Prediction, London 1978
Hall, C.S.,
The Meaning of Dreams, New York 1959
Hall, Manly Palmer,
The Philosophy of Astrology, Los Angeles 1943
Harrison, Michael,
Fire From Heaven, London 1977
Hartley, C.,
The Western Mystery Tradition, London 1968
Hartmann, Franz,
Principles of Astrological Geomancy, London 1913
Head, J., and Cranston, S.L.,
Reincarnation: An East – West Anthology, New York 1961
Hill, Douglas,
Magic and Superstition, London 1968
Fortune Telling, London 1972
Hirst, Desiree,
Hidden Riches, London 1963
Hone, Margaret,
Modern Textbook of Astrology, London 1975

Huson, Paul,
The Devil's Picture Book, London 1972
Huxley, Aldous,
The Doors of Perception, London 1954

James, E.O.,
The Cult of the Mother Goddess, London 1959
Jung, Carl G.,
Archetypes and the Collective Unconscious, London 1959
The Interpretation of Nature and the Psyche, London 1959
Memories, Dreams, Reflections, London 1968
Mysterium Coniunctionis, London 1963
Synchronicity, London 1972

King, Francis X.,
Rudolf Steiner and Holistic Medicine, London 1987
Witchcraft and Demonology, London 1987
Palmistry, London 1979
Tantra for Westerners, Wellingborough 1987
King, Francis X., and Kingston, Jeremy,
Mysterious Knowledge, London 1978
Krippner, Stanley and Rubin, David,
The Kirlian Aura, New York 1974

Lau, Theodora,
Handbook of Chinese Horoscopes, London 1987
Laver, J.,
Nostradamus, or the Future Foretold, Harmondsworth 1952

Mathers, S.L. MacGregor,
Astral Projection, Ritual Magic and Alchemy, 1987
The Tarot, London 1888
McIntosh, Christopher,
Eliphas Levi and the French Occult Revival, London 1972

O'Flaherty, Wendy,
Asceticism and Eroticism in the Mythology of Shiva, Oxford 1973

Parker, Derek and Julia,
The New Compleat Astrologer, London 1984
Payne, Ernest A.,
The Saktas, Calcutta 1933

Raphael (i.e. Smith, Robert Cross),
The Philosophical Merlin, (most easily found in Skinner's *Oracle of Geomancy*, in which it was reprinted as an Appendix)
Rawson, Philip,
Tantra: The Indian Cult of Ecstasy, London 1974
The Art of Tantra, London, 1974

Regardie, Francis Israel,
The Art of True Healing, Toddington 1964
The Middle Pillar, St. Paul 1971
The Golden Dawn (originally 4 vols., currently available as 4 vols in 1) Minnesota 1970
Reid, Howard and Croucher,
The Way of the Warrior, London 1983

Sharpe, Elizabeth,
Secrets of the Kaula Circle, London 1936
Skinner, Stephen,
Oracle of Geomancy, Bridport, UK 1986
Terrestrial Astrology, London 1978
Suster, Gerald,
The Truth About the Tarot, London 1990

Thouless, R.H.,
Experimental Psychical Research, London 1963
Thurston, Herbert,
The Physical Phenomena of Mysticism, London 1952
Tilley, Roger,
Playing Cards, London 1973

Veith, Ilsa
The Yellow Emperor's Classic of Internal Medicine, USA 1966

Waite, A.E.,
The Pictorial Key to the Tarot (numerous reprints since first published London 1910)
The Holy Kabbalah, University Books, New York
Walker, Benjamin,
Body Magic, London 1979
Man and Beasts Within, New York 1977
Sex and the Supernatural, London 1970
Tantrism, Wellingborough 1982
Wambach, Helen,
Life Before Life, New York 1979
Watts, Alan W. (editor),
The Two Hands of God – The Myths of Polarity, New York 1963
White, John (editor),
Kundalini: Evolution and Enlightenment, New York 1979
Wilhelm, Richard,
I Ching, London 1951

Yeats, W.B.,
Autobiographies, London 1926

Zain, C.C.,
Predicting Events, Los Angeles 1934

INDEX

ACKNOWLEDGMENTS

Author's acknowledgments
I would like to offer my thanks to the ever informative and constructive staff of the Library service of the London Borough of Richmond – and particularly to those of its Teddington branch. I would also like to thank those who have generously helped or advised with one aspect or another of this book. In particular, I would like to thank Richard Cavendish for his timely assistance, Benjamin Walker, my patient and helpful editors, Susie Behar, Sean Moore, and Damien Moore, and the art editor, Nigel Partridge.

Dorling Kindersley would like to thank the following: Jane Rollason and Gillian Prince for their invaluable editorial help; Vanessa Card for artwork (except p. 28 by Hardlines); Anthony Duke for the border artworks; Rupert Thomas, Patricia Wright, and Jacquie Burgess for their assistance with picture research; Hilary Bird for compiling the index; Emma Matthews for keying in text; Graham Powell; Virginia Fitzgerald; Mrs. Mary Wright; William Miller; Edward Gribben; Michael Tambini; and Stephen Skinner.

Dorling Kindersley would also like to thank the following for supplying props: The Acumedic Centre, Camden High Street, London; Artistic Treasures, Richmond, London; Japan Centre, Brewer Street, London; The Natural History Museum, London; New World Aurora, Neal's Yard, London; Ainsworth's Homeopathists, London; Lion Antiques, Richmond, London; Brian Tull Ltd, Richmond, London; Mysteries, London; Chelsea Garden Physic, London; and The Operating Theatre Museum, London.

Dorling Kindersley would like to thank the following for their permission to reproduce material:

(Abbreviations: t = top; b = bottom; c =centre; r =right; l =left)

Aerofilms: 144 bl
Allsport / Rick Stewart: 154 bl
Aquarius Picture Library: 52 t, 53 bl, 53 tr, 60 b, 17 br, 237 tl
Ardea: 32 bl

Barnaby's Picture Library: 141 br, 197 b; / Rudy Lewis: 199 tl; / Marie Mattson: 194 tr
Art Library: 24 b; / Museo Galerie Nazionali Di Capodimonte: 27 br; / Chateau de Versailles: 47 tl; / Magritte, The Restless Sleeper. © The Tate Gallery, A.D.A.G.P., Paris and DACS, London, 1991: 50 tl; / Musee des Augustins, Toulouse: 51 b; / Max Ernst, The Entire City. © Zurich Kunsthaus, A.D.A.G.P., Paris and DACS, 1991: 55 t; /

Private Collection: 62 t; / Hofkirche, Innsbruck: 73 1; / Casino Pallavicini-Rospigliosi, Rome: 82 b; / British Library, London: 126 tr; / Carlos Schwabe. © Collection Robert Walker, Paris and DACS, 1991: 127 l; / Musee Conde Chantilly: 183 t; / Victoria and Albert Museum, London: 200 bl
British School of Osteopathy: 225 t

Camera Press: 176 tr, 177 tr, 178 cr; / Karsh of Ottowa: 48 bl, 176 bl / Van Parys: 179 tr
Jonathan Cape / Jerry Bauer: 32 br
J. Allan Cash: 27 tr, 219 t, 224 tr

The Dickens House: 241 tl
Douglas Dickins' Picture Library: 198 bl, 206 tl
C. M. Dixon: 193 br, 202 b, 203 tr

Robert Estall Photographs: 23 t, 26 t, 26 br; / Malcolm Aird: 30 bl
Mary Evans Picture Library: Back Cover top, 16 bl, 36 b, 37 br, 44 b, 49 tr, 54 t, 57 tc, 67 tl, 69 tr, 75 b, 76 tr, 76 bl, 81 tc, 81 br, 83 tl, 83 br, 85 bl, 89 b, 92 tl, 92 bl, 94 t, 102 t, 104 b, 107 br, 114 t, 114 bl, 119 tl, 122 tr, 135 b, 141 tl, 144 t, 147 tr, 158 tr, 161 tr, 164 bl, 168 b, 169 tr, 199 b, 221 t, 234 tr, 234 bl, 235 tr, 238 t, 238 bl, 239 br, 244 tr, 244 bl, 245 b, 246 cr; / The Hutchinson Library: 166 tr / Guy Lyon Playfair: 58 bl, 231 br; / Jeffrey Morgan: 105 c; / Psychic News 117 tl, 122 c, 122 b, 124 t; / Harry Price Collection, University of London: 136 b

Joel Finler: 47 br; / 56 b, 57 tl, 139 t
Fortean Picture Library: 15 tr, 96 tr, 120 tl, 137 b, 205 tl, 234 br, 240 b, 241 br; / Dr. Elmar R. Gruber: 43 bl, 43 tl, 138 t, 231 tl, 239 cl; / B. Larry, E. Arnold: 241 br; / Dr. B.E. Schwarz: 117 bl; / Ken Webster: 119 bl

Raymond Galbraith: 113 b

Sonia Halliday photographs: 29 br
Robert Harding Picture Library: 196 bl
John Hillelson Agency: 14 t, 15 bl
Michael Holford: 150 bl, 192 b, 201 t
Geoff Howard: 146 tl
Hsinhua News Agency: 192 tl
The Hutchison Library: 190 br, 211 t, 214 tr; / J.G. Fuller: 207 bl; / Felix Greene: 191 t; / C. Maurice Harvey: 200 tr; / Christine Pemberton: 205 tr, 243 tl

Images Colour Library: Front Cover l, 50 br, 68 b, 72 tr, 72 b, 75 tc, 90 tr, 96 bl, 103 tr, 103 bl, 106 c, 107 t, 125 tr, 75 tc, 90 tr, 96 bl, 103 tr,, 103 bl, 106 c, 107 t, 125 tr, 126 bl, 128 b, 129 tl, 129 br, 130 b, 131 c, 140 b, 158 bl, 164 t, 165 tl, 166 bl, 186 tr, 195 t, 195 bl, 203 l, 212 bl, 228 tl, 245 cl, 246 l, 247 tr; / Pierette Colomb: 190 t

Al Johnson: 40 t

Kandinsky, All Saint's Day. © A.D.A.G.P., Paris and DACS, London, 1991: 97 b
Francis X. King: 100 bl
The Kobal Collection: 208 bl, 209 b, 236 b; /

Miloslav Mirvald: 237 br
Tony Morrison South American Pictures: 12 tr, 13
The Mansell Collection: 80 l, 80 br, 85 t, 88 tr, 133 bl, 232 bl, 233 t

Peter Newark's Western Americana: 14 br

Miranda Payne : 147 tl
Popperfoto: 160 tl

Rex Features: 42 bl; / Dezo Hoffman: 46 b

Salisbury and South Wiltshire Museum: 25 t
Science Photo Library: / Dr. Thelma Moss: 59 tl; / NASA: 63 br
Mick Sharp: 29 tl
John Sims: 54 bl
Colin Smythe: 116 tr
Frank Spooner Pictures/ Kaku Kurita: 242 bl
Sport and General Press Agency: 95 br
The Swiss Gnostic Catholic Church: 84 tr
Syndication International Library: 17 t, 37 t, 11 tr, 118 bl, 119 br, 121 b, 134 bl, 135 t, 145 br, 161 b, 167 tr, 180, 181 tl, 220 bl, / Bibliotheque Nationale: 68 tl; / City of Birmingham Museum and Art Gallery: 66 b; / British Museum: 90 bl, 157 r, 218 b; / Collections of Library of Congress: 133 t; / Garnstone Press: 30 tr; / Lang/Rune Hassner: 113 t; Keystone, Tokyo: 168 tr; / Lang Publ. Co.: 230 bl; / Mrs. M. Lethbridge: 20 bl; / Josef Muench: 218 bl; National Monument Record: 132 tr

Tass: / V. Askochensy: 240 tr; / A. Avduyevsky: 220 t
Topham Picture Library: 322 tr, 243 b; / Associated Press: 187 b

Werner Forman Archive: 112 l
Whitworth Art Gallery: 38 br
Woodmansterne: 28 cr

University of Durham, Oriental Museum: 196 r

Every effort has been made to trace the copyright holders and we apologise in advance for any omissions. We would be pleased to insert the appropriate acknowledgment in any subsequent edition of this publication.